Naval Warfare

Naval Warfare

A Global History since 1860

Jeremy Black

ROWMAN & LITTLEFIELD
Lanham • Boulder • New York • London

Published by Rowman & Littlefield
A wholly owned subsidiary of
The Rowman & Littlefield Publishing Group, Inc.
4501 Forbes Boulevard, Suite 200, Lanham, Maryland 20706
https://rowman.com

Unit A, Whitacre Mews, 26-34 Stannary Street, London SE11 4AB,
United Kingdom

British Library Cataloguing in Publication Information Available

Library of Congress Cataloging-in-Publication Data
Names: Black, Jeremy, 1955– author.
Title: Naval warfare : a global history since 1860 / Jeremy Black.
Description: Lanham, MD : Rowman & Littlefield, [2017] | Includes bibliographical
    references and index.
Identifiers: LCCN 2016034077 (print) | LCCN 2016034393 (ebook) | ISBN
    9781442270411 (hardcover : alk. paper) | ISBN 9781442276314 (pbk. : alk. paper) |
    ISBN 9781442270428 (electronic)
Subjects: LCSH: Naval history, Modern. | Naval strategy—History—20th century. | Sea-
    power—History—20th century.
Classification: LCC D436 .B55 2017 (print) | LCC D436 (ebook) | DDC 359/.030904—
    dc23
LC record available at https://lccn.loc.gov/2016034077

Printed in the United States of America

For Roger Morriss
Colleague and Naval Historian

Contents

Preface

The modern age of naval warfare began with the combination of steam power, iron warships, and modern artillery in the mid-nineteenth century, to be rapidly joined by advanced mines, torpedoes, and submersible war craft. This combination launched a new period of acute naval competition. Moreover, this period was of marked international and geopolitical significance. This was because of the central roles of oceanic trade and transoceanic possessions in economic development and imperial expansion. The growing global importance of the United States and Japan from the late nineteenth century was also crucial to this focus on naval power. The period saw a marked improvement in the capability of surface warfare. At the same time, innovators were fast developing subsurface threats to the new form of (ironclad) capital ships, namely combined defenses in the form of forts, obstructions, and minefields backed by shallow-draft ironclad monitors, rams, and torpedo boats. The use of mine-laying and torpedo weaponry became marked during the First World War when most vessels sunk were due to mines or torpedoes. At the same time, another form of asymmetric warfare began with aerial threats to warships.

This book provides an accessible account of naval warfare, one beginning in the 1860s and going into the future. The last British wooden sailship of the line, the *Ganges*, launched in 1821, served as an important unit until 1865. The book focuses on the interplay of technological development, geopolitics, and resource issues in order to provide a dynamic account of strategy and warfare. The emphasis will be global so as to cover not only the leading powers but also the others involved in naval conflict. Alongside due attention to the leading naval powers, there is a global, comparative perspective rather than national narratives about individual countries and navies. The coverage is according to chronological divisions, in each of which there is a focus on the elements mentioned above, as well as on conflict itself.

I have benefited greatly from the opportunity to teach military history for more than three decades, at the universities of Durham and Exeter and more generally. For this book, I profited particularly from opportunities to speak at the Armourers and Braziers Company, the College of William and Mary, the Devonport Maritime Centre, and the New York Historical Society and to visit China, Cuba, France, Germany, Italy, Japan, Panama, Spain, and the United States. The sites of naval warfare offer varied resonances. To consider the naval dimension of the 1898 Spanish-American war from the memorial-ization in Cuba (at Santiago), Spain (the Naval Museum in Madrid), and the United States (a number of sites) is instructive.

The anonymous reviewer who commented on the proposal greatly im-proved it. So did the comments of John Beeler, Christopher Bell, Pete Brown, Mike Duffy, Howard Fuller, Richard Harding, Heiko Henning, Da-vid Morgan-Owen, Roger Morriss, Ryan Patterson, John Reeve, Matthew Seligmann, Mark Stevens, and Jon Sumida on earlier drafts or parts of earlier drafts. I much appreciate their efforts, but I alone am responsible for any errors that remain. I have benefited from discussion with or advice on specif-ic points from Michael Axworthy, Harry Bennett, Troy Bickham, Mike Cailes, Robert Citino, Olavi Falt, James Goldrick, Greg Kennedy, John Maurer, Malyn Newitt, Kaushik Roy, José Sardica, Stephen Schuker, Ian Speller, Mark Stanhope, Tassapo Umavijani, Dukhee Yun, and Carlos Alfaro Zaforteza.

The collaborative nature of the project is further exemplified by the im-portant role of my editor, Susan McEachern. She has provided the necessary mix of enthusiasm, skill, and wisdom that makes for a great editor. This book is dedicated to Roger Morriss, friend, colleague, and distinguished naval historian.

Abbreviations

REFERENCE ABBREVIATIONS

Add.	Additional Manuscripts
AWM	Canberra, Australian War Memorial
BL	London, British Library, Department of Manuscripts
CAB	Cabinet papers
FO	Foreign Office
JMH	*Journal of Military History*
KV	Records of the Security Service
LH	Liddell Hart Archive, King's College London
NA	London, National Archives
NAA	Canberra, National Archives of Australia
NWCR	*Naval War College Review*
PREM	Prime Minister's Office Records
WO	War Office

ABBREVIATIONS

ASDIC	sonar
A2/AD	anti-access/area-denial
BMD	ballistic-missile defense

EU	European Union
HMS	His/Her Majesty's Ship
LCS	littoral combat ship
NATO	North Atlantic Treaty Organization
PLA	People's Liberation Army
RAF	Royal Air Force
RFC	Royal Flying Corps
RNAS	Royal Naval Air Service
SAM	surface-to-air missile
SS	steamship
USAF	U.S. Air Force
VLR	very long range
V/STOL	vertical/short takeoff and landing

Chapter One

The Age of the Ironclad, 1860–80

> The passages of Cuba will not be closed and opened by the fluctuations of
> wind and weather, they will be patrolled and governed by the navy which
> possesses a general ascendancy. The accidents and vicissitudes of local war at
> sea are superseded by the steady predominance of steam. [1]

In arguing, in 1857, that steam power, by defying both storms and currents,
had transformed the maritime strategic value of Cuba, Frederick, Lord Napier, the British envoy in Washington, captured a general sense of newfound
potential.

The mid-nineteenth century is the appropriate starting point for a study of
modern naval warfare. That age witnessed a major technological transformation in warships and weaponry. As far as the former was concerned, maritime
architecture, both warship and commercial vessels, was rapidly changing,
notably hull construction and propulsion systems. Navies needed, and, as
significantly, they believed that they needed, to adapt and, indeed, to transform themselves in the face of these new technologies. Not to do so was to
court defeat in battle, or at least to appear obsolescent and to suggest a more
general obsolescence for the power in question. These new technologies
created new uncertainties for naval and political leaders. The questions and
problems posed today by the dramatic changes taking place in technology,
and the great uncertainty about what might happen in future naval conflict,
can be viewed in the mirror of history, specifically of the nineteenth century.
Each episode is distinctive, but there are valuable similarities, and the disruption of the mid-nineteenth century was greater than that of the present despite
the rhetoric surrounding the latter.

This chapter focuses on these changes, on the American Civil War
(1861–65), and on the possibility of British intervention in it. An assessment
of the role of naval power in this situation will be continued by an assessment

of the subsequent decade and a half, to include the Austro-Italian conflict in 1866, the very limited role of naval power in the Franco-Prussian War of 1870–71, its more significant place in the 1878 international crisis focused on confrontation between Britain and Russia, and the situation in Latin America.

NEW TECHNOLOGY

A range of technologies were totally transformed over the nineteenth century, notably those of propulsion, firepower, and armor, but also a number of others, including, with electricity, the means of power within a ship and the related ability to light up the dark. In many respects, and linked to this transformation, there was also much continuity in the Western naval situation, and certainly so when contrasted with the situation for East Asian powers. In the West, there was a continuing commitment to specialized warships; the stress was on permanent naval forces, navies depended on a sophisticated infrastructure of bases and supply systems; and, for the major powers, this infrastructure, and the linked commitments, were wide ranging.

While technologies improved the power of warships, they also drove new attempts to curb this power. Indeed, new technologies increasingly favored coastal defense. These included heavy guns that were always better mounted in shore batteries than afloat, electrically fired minefields (protected by forts), iron-backed obstructions, torpedo boats with locomotive torpedoes, and monitor ironclads and ironclad rams. The ironclads and rams offered the most concentrated form of armor and heavy-caliber armament, as well as shallow draft, at the direct expense of long-range "sea-keeping" naval characteristics.

Warships were the product of an advanced military-industrial system. Technological advances became operative in this context and were therefore dependent on economic and political parameters. Given its role in the Industrial Revolution, this situation contributed greatly to British naval superiority, a superiority that was apparent to most observers, albeit one that the British worried about. Indeed, much of Britain's early ironclad program was dominated by defensive considerations: how to win the next battle of Trafalgar, as well as to prevent invasion and protect trade.[2]

British naval superiority faced limitations, but it was readily apparent when contrasted with other powers. Much of this superiority was due to strategic context, political culture, and the weight of history. There was also a range of specific skills, for example in the charting of the oceans. Turning to the industrial background, Britain had both the largest and most successful navy in the world and the leading industrial economy, more particularly (as China was also a major economy) the leading economy that took part in large-scale foreign trade. These factors were all linked. The greater effectiveness of the Royal Navy (the British navy) was largely due to its capacity to build and maintain ships, and different types of ship, as well as its long-standing extensive and effective administrative infrastructure, the global network of its bases and thus the strength of its power-projection capability, the strength of British public finances, and good naval leadership. These were all factors that interacted and built up a more general positive synergy. A reason Britain's navy was the largest was because the British Empire was the most maritime and the most spread out across the globe. Established in war with France and its allies in 1793–1815, British naval mastery endured into the new era because Britain was the first country to industrialize, while its global network of bases retained and even increased its value with the need for coaling (taking on coal) to support steam-powered warships. Indeed, the introduction of iron and steam warships had enormous hidden costs as the shore infrastructure had to be almost totally replaced.

The empire required constant local naval protection with long-term reliefs standing by, which explained the need for well-maintained dockyards. The number of warships was based on the shifting likelihood of having to fight a local power, especially France in European waters and perhaps Russia, or a combination of the two. Thus, Parliament rarely sanctioned more force on paper than was really needed for what to the British were defensive purposes. With a range of shipbuilding facilities, Britain could build ships more quickly and cheaply than its rivals, and had important technological leads in metallurgy and hydrodynamics. The Royal Navy, moreover, benefited greatly from the quality and size of Britain's merchant marine and the number of shipbuilding firms. As a consequence of these factors, it was not surprising that Britain was best placed to take advantage of technological developments.

STEAM POWER

The most significant development was the harnessing to shipping of an already-established, but still rapidly improving, technology, the steam engine. Steam power eventually replaced dependence on wind. This made journey times by sea far more reliable, predictable, and short, as they were no longer dependent on the seasonal effect of the weather, and this was the case for both warships and merchantmen. The transformation, however, took time, not least because early steamships suffered from poor reliability, boiler explosions, slow speed, a high rate of coal consumption, the difficulties posed by side and paddle wheels, problems in building and maintaining reliable engines, and the space taken by engines, paddles, and the mechanism. Side and paddle wheels were also vulnerable to enemy fire; indeed, similarly so to the rigging of sail ships. The high rate of coal consumption meant that much coal had to be carried and that coaling stations had to be made available.

Steam power in practice involved a series of innovations. A key one was the stern-mounted screw propeller which, in the 1840s, became a feasible alternative to the paddle wheel. The propeller made the propulsion relatively safe. As a result, it was now possible to carry a full broadside armament. Screw-driven ships of the line were launched from 1850, with the initial French lead in this technology rapidly eroded by the British, who proved able to adopt and adapt quickly and effectively.[3] This was an instance of the degree to which both the Americans and the French drove some of the major technological changes in this period as a way of responding to the potential threat of British naval intervention. For the Americans, this process began with the War of 1812.

Thanks to steam, warships were able to maneuver in calms and make headway against contrary winds, even though winter weather continued to be a consideration, as for the British when considering action against the Union (Northern) side in the American Civil War in late 1861. As a consequence of steam, the independence of individual warships in a fleet action was considerably extended, which greatly increased tactical opportunities and the range for command skills. Moreover, the increased maneuverability of ships, notably their capacity to act in the face of adverse winds, made it easier to operate inshore and in hazardous waters, to attack opposing fleets in harbor, to mount landings, and to remain on a blockade station over an extended time.[4] The ability of steamships to work with confidence close inshore affected the tactical, operational, and strategic potential of naval power. At the same time, steam proved significant to the defense. The Russians mobilized a large number of steam-powered gunboats with heavy pivot guns to defend their naval base of Cronstadt off St. Petersburg against possible British attack in 1855–56 during the Crimean War.

All of these possibilities, however, increased the need for coal. There were tactical, operational, and strategic implications. For example, the time to "fire up" a "cold" steam boiler was great. Given the hunger of steam engines, a naval siege of a harbor with modern ships became impractical: whereas earlier bases could obtain food and wood at local foreign markets, coal was not that easily available.

So also with the ability of ships to operate in rivers: steam proved very important for the penetration of continental river systems and for inland navigation into the twentieth century. Gunboats played a major role in the American Civil War, for example iron-armored Union boats on the Cumberland and Tennessee Rivers in the critical campaign in central Tennessee in February 1862, as well as on the Mississippi in the crucial 1863 campaign. The Russians used steam-driven launches for their crossing of the Danube in 1877 in the face of Turkish opposition.

Steamships devoured coal, which made the ability to carry sufficient coal, and its availability, key operational and geopolitical factors that were very much discussed as crucial. In late 1861, as war with the Union apparently neared, Britain sent coal to the West Indies to support a larger naval presence there. Earlier that year, the British government was concerned that France might try to establish a coaling station in the Cape Verde Islands.[5] The lack of coal and iron in the Netherlands affected the Dutch ability to develop a significant modern navy. However, a lack of funding was also important, as was a reliance for trade security on British naval dominance.

As the ability to use sail reduced the need to rely on coal supplies, most steamships retained their sailing rigs. At this stage in the development of steam engines, the need for a secondary propulsion system was great. Moreover, sails helped prevent ships from rolling too heavily. It was not surprising that the dual propulsion system of sail and steam remained, albeit only on small warships, until the 1890s. This was significant for navies with global maritime interests, especially Britain and France. Similarly, Spain commissioned the *Numancia* from a French shipyard and then sent it to South American waters.

But more local powers were developing new types of steam-powered, shallow-draft "ship-killing" ironclads, like monitors and rams, which gave them a tactical advantage. As a result, the launch by Britain in 1871 of *Devastation* was significant. This mastless turret ship could cross the Atlantic without refueling and was the first true "capital ship" of the modern age. Even then, seagoing turret ships were vulnerable to monitors of equal displacement, as the latter were more potent in gun size and thickness of armor plating. Moreover, underwater threats in the form of torpedoes became more reliable in the 1870s. The last British armored warships (excluding sloops) with a full-masted rig were laid down in 1881, although the rigs were removed straight after their trials. The last fully rigged French cruisers were laid down in 1885. It was no longer necessary to rely on the range of sailing ships. Nevertheless, prior to that, steam had already brought many advantages, most notably when speedy movements were required.

Steam capability changed the geopolitics of naval power as well as its strategy and operational and tactical geography. These changes led to new senses of opportunity and vulnerability, senses that were reflected in intelligence reports and public discussion.[6] For example, a fear of invasion across the English Channel by French steamships, notably from the base at Cherbourg, led to the construction in the 1860s of major coastal-defense works on the south coast of England in order to protect the naval bases, especially Portsmouth, from amphibious as well as naval attack. The steam/iron revolution also affected strategic concerns with particular areas. Interest in the Baltic, the classic source of naval stores in the age of sail and wood, declined, which eventually helped lead to improvements in British ties with Russia.

Steam power was not the only technological change transforming naval capability. Indeed, the interlinked nature of change is such that the isolation of individual factors for analysis is problematic. For example, alongside steam increasing the maneuverability of warships along coasts, long-range artillery and the defensive strength of armor plate were both significant, as they made warships more effective against coastal forts. The British bombardment of Alexandria in 1882 deployed far more power than that on Algiers in 1816. However, aside from that, Alexandria's defenses were shoddy from poor management. The British naval bombardment drove terrified, half-trained gunners from their posts but did not do enormous damage to the works. The British turret guns were lucky to discharge once every eight to ten minutes. It was landing parties that did the real work in the attack.

In turn, long-range artillery was put in coastal forts in Britain and elsewhere in order better to resist attacks. Forts built in southern England to protect the naval bases were strongly built and mounted the latest guns. Such defenses were very strong, particularly if combined with obstructions, mines, and coastal-defense warships. However, given the advantage of transporting large guns on a ship, especially its mobility, there was a huge disadvantage for land-based artillery. The transport of large-caliber guns was often only possible with a rail-based transport system. Even eight-inch guns could only be transported by rail. During the First World War, the American army fitted former fourteen-inch guns from coastal-defense installations onto railway carriages in order to give them at least limited mobility.

The development from the 1820s of more effective shell guns ensured the availability of cannon able to fire large projectiles and gave them a high enough initial speed to pierce the side of a big ship and explode inside. Whereas it had been difficult to sink a ship of the line with solid shot in the Nelsonian era, the threat shell guns posed to wooden ships was demonstrated by the total destruction of a Turkish squadron by a Russian fleet off Sinope in the Black Sea on November 3, 1853. Moreover, the weight and strength of modern guns made the old "armed merchant ship," which had a military value, no longer practical. Cargo ships were no longer able to outrun or outgun (smaller) warships.

Creating a new vulnerability, shells helped lead, in response, to armored warships. The first British iron warship, the *Warrior*, an armored frigate, was laid down in 1859 and completed in 1861. It is still afloat in Portsmouth where it can readily be visited. The 9,140-ton *Warrior* was an iron-framed, iron-hulled ship with bulkheads. The casemate area was additionally plated with 4.5 inches of iron, backed by 18 inches of teak. Wood penetrated by shot was easier to plug than iron, but the *Warrior* had to be made of iron because her length was too great for contemporary wooden-ship technology. In contrast, the 5,630-ton French *La Gloire*, laid down in 1858, to which the

Warrior was a response, was a smaller wooden frigate fitted with 4.5-inch-thick metal plates.

Developments reflected the nature of the respective economies. The French had the infrastructure to build a few big iron ships, but not a new fleet, while the British had been building large iron ships for some time. They had the experience of the merchant marine, of skilled shipbuilding, and of ambitious and innovative ship designers, such as Isambard Kingdom Brunel, on which to draw. Brunel's *Great Britain*, which had innovatory iron and screw features and was the first large vessel in which the screw propeller was used, made her first transatlantic voyage in 1845. It was to be followed by the massive *Great Eastern*, which was laid down in 1853 and launched in 1858. This situation underlined the extent to which naval power rested on a more general shipbuilding and industrial capacity, as well as on a maritime culture that produced sailors. Political support and fiscal strength were also key elements. The *Warrior* cost £377,000 to build, then a formidable sum. [7]

There was a clear purpose. The *Gloire* was a natural extension of defensive thinking that recognized the power of exploding shell fire, while armoring a frigate was to give capital ships longer life in any high-seas engagement. The *Warrior* was then built as a response to the *Gloire*. The British government was worried that its naval lead was being eroded, and was concerned that Napoleon III might attempt to coerce Britain into accepting French hegemony and expansionism on the Continent. [8] Radical Liberals in Britain opposed expensive ironclads and pressed for cheaper gunboats, but their argument lacked political traction. With its watertight compartments below, the *Warrior* set the pattern for the first British armored frigates, which on average were 60 percent larger than their French counterparts.

However, as a reminder of the need to consider a range of factors in the evaluation of capability and effectiveness, the French enjoyed an advantage laying down more modest warships. In contrast, the *Warrior* and her sister ships nearly broke the private-contracting shipbuilding industry in Britain, which was unprepared for constructing such huge vessels requiring a large quantity of armor plate, and in a hurry. As a consequence, most of these yards had to improve their facilities first, a process that reflected the value of the availability of investment capital in Britain. The royal dockyards had to do the same before vessels like the *Achilles* could be built at Chatham. These large vessels also took longer to complete than smaller ironclads.

Iron ships were structurally stronger than wooden ones. As a consequence, the ability to salvage or repair ships was affected by the introduction of iron ships. However, because they were built of wood, which floats, it was harder to sink wooden ships, unless they burned to the waterline or blew up, than iron ones. Moreover, the ability to repair damaged iron ships with onboard tools was limited, although the heroic rescue of the USS *Houston* in 1944 showed that, even with onboard tools, a modern ship could be saved.

The shift to iron reflected not simply the vulnerability of wooden ships to shell fire but also success in overcoming the problems that had delayed the use of iron. These included its effect on magnetic compasses, the fact that iron hulls fouled very much worse than wooden ones that were copper bottomed, and the difficulties of securing sufficient consistency and quality in the iron. The ability to overcome these problems was a product of the strength of the British economy in the acquisition, creative potential, and application of relevant knowledge, but it also indicated the difficulties posed by competition with France. It was swiftly clear that a new weapons platform, carrying thicker armor and heavier guns, was required. Steam engines used in steel production allowed the production of modern, more robust armor plates.

Shipbuilding capacity and maritime expertise could be enhanced in part by buying ships and hiring sailors from abroad. However, this could prove less effective and more costly than using domestic resources. Nevertheless, by whatever method, states rapidly borrowed each other's best practice in an effort to reduce the threat posed by others. For example, Russia invested in steam-propelled gunboats in the mid-1850s and, from 1861, in ironclads. Spain and the Netherlands improved their navies. Poorer states, such as Portugal—which had an empire, mostly in southern Africa, that stretched to Macao in China—clung to sail and wood longer.

Alongside the combination of the screw propeller and armor, there were also improvements in armament. John Ericsson and Cowper Phipps Coles simultaneously invented turrets that were similar in concept but quite different in design. Neither led directly to the modern gun turret, but Coles incorporated the roller patch, which was a key element in modern big-gun mountings. Ericsson's turret system was powered by steam, not rotated laboriously by hand, which made them, in his own words, more semiautomated "machines" than traditional men-of-war. This language looked toward modern talk of "drone warships." The revolving turret began with the American *Monitor* in 1862, and the practice of mounting heavy guns in an armored casemate with the Confederate (Southern) *Virginia* in 1862, although she was not seagoing, and then with the British *Research* in 1864. This was followed in 1866 by the larger *Bellerophon*, a battleship protected by six inches of armor plating. This was a more compact warship than some of the earlier ironclads, but one that contained much armor and mounted heavy guns.

These were not the limits of innovation in the mid-century years. The American Civil War saw important innovative work on submarines, especially with the Confederate *Hunley*, which sank the Union corvette *Housatonic* off Charleston in 1864. The *Hunley*, which was hand-crank powered, was itself most likely destroyed by the force of the explosion. The remains of the *Hunley* have been retrieved and can be visited in Charleston. In addition, there were Davids, steam-driven Confederate semisubmersibles with a conning tower and stack above water that made them a surface craft. They were designed to do battle with Goliath: the Union navy. Later, in 1864, in Albemarle Sound, North Carolina, the first successful torpedo-boat attack occurred when the Union sank the *Albemarle*, a Confederate armored vessel, with a spar torpedo fitted to a launch.

The modern self-propelled torpedo, a kind of underwater cruise missile very different from the fixed spar torpedo, originated with the development by Robert Whitehead in 1864 of the Austrian idea of a submerged torpedo driven by compressed air with an explosive charge at the head. When adopted by the Austrian navy in 1868, it was capable of a modest speed of sixteen kilometers an hour, about eight knots, the speed of most ironclads in combat environments of the period, if not slower. Britain and most other European maritime powers bought the license to manufacture it. The first successful attack with a Whitehead torpedo occurred in January 1878 when the Russians sank the Turkish harbor guardship at Batumi (modern Georgia) with two torpedoes fired from launches. Torpedoes were eventually equipped with gyroscopes to provide an automatic means of steering. As with improvements in guns, this improvement enabled naval combatants to stand off more effectively. Thus, although the essentials of naval power, such as the relationship between economic strength and naval capabilities, were not changing, the means of maritime force were being transformed.

In 1860, naval strength helped Britain curtail France's designs on Italy, although other factors also played a role, including the mobilization of British naval resources at the end of the Crimean War and the raising in 1859–60 of a large volunteer army in Britain. Furthermore, British strength was in part potential, as the two powers were nearly equal in the number of screw-propeller warships, while the British were still working on their first ironclads and on the Portsmouth forts.[9] Britain and France took part in a major ironclad naval race in 1859–65 that was won by Britain with its greater resources and commitment. Yet, as a reminder of the extent to which capability gaps were eroded, by 1865 modern coastal defense was a major obstacle to any direct application of "offensive" naval power by Britain (or any other power), while steam-powered commerce raiders, such as the Confederate *Alabama*, had shown the potential of a lethal new era of *guerre de course*: attacks on commerce.

AMERICAN CIVIL WAR, 1861–65

Naval power played a key role in the American Civil War, even though all the major battles in it were fought on land. Indeed, this contrast looked toward the situation during the Cold War and subsequently. It underlined the extent to which the frequency of naval battles, both prior to 1815 and in the two world wars, did not establish a general model for our entire period. Moreover, battles at sea were generally rarer than those on land, and decisive ones even rarer. Indeed, blockade had been the major strategic weapon of the Royal Navy in the age of sail.

The Civil War began on April 12, 1861, as a consequence of the Union attempt to maintain Fort Sumter, a position that sat defiantly off the city of Charleston, the leading Atlantic port of the Confederacy. Confederate coastal batteries prevented relief and reduced the fort to surrender on April 13 after setting fire to the wooden buildings in the fort.

Ultimately, the navy of the Union became what was then the second strongest in the world, with (figures vary) 650–675 warships, including 49 ironclads. The Royal Navy, in contrast, predominantly invested in blue-water, not brown-water, units. They were good for command of the sea but problematic in American waters. During the war, the capability of American ironclads increased, as the Union developed an impressive coastal protection force. Whereas the *Monitor*, a ship that symbolized the power of the machine, had two guns in one steam-powered revolving turret, the Union laid down *Onondaga*, its first monitor with two turrets, in 1862. The Union also laid down the four dual-turreted river monitors of the *Milwaukee* class and the four *Miantonomoh*-class oceangoing monitors armed with four fifteen-inch guns.

Difficulties were encountered by both the Union and the Confederacy in building up naval strength and capability. Particular problems focused on developing the capacity to roll the necessary iron plating and in building iron ships using the traditional methods of shipbuilding with wood. Nevertheless, the Union's navy was a key strategic asset. This was especially so in economic warfare and in power projection by means of amphibious capability. The blockade of the Confederacy was to be permeable by small, fast steamships until late in the conflict and only really ended with the fall of Wilmington. In short, a land solution, not a naval one, was crucial to the issue of blockade-runners. However, ably organized by the Blockade Board established in 1861, the Union demonstrated the potency of economic warfare. A total of 295 Confederate steamers and 1,189 sailing ships were destroyed or seized, and the blockade greatly affected the economy of the Confederacy, as well as its morale. Indeed, blockade was the key Union naval policy and means.

In turn, the Confederacy issued letters of marque to a number of privateers in 1861, which posed a major challenge.[10] The Confederate effort failed because of the difficulty, even early on in the war, of bringing a prize home safely through the Union blockade to a Confederate port. As a result, Confederate maritime entrepreneurs turned almost exclusively to blockade-running to make their fortunes. Effective disruption of Union trade came at the hands of raiders that were commissioned in the Confederate navy, such as the *Alabama*, *Florida*, and *Shenandoah*, rather than by privateers. In 1865, the *Shenandoah*, the first composite-hulled (iron and wood) cruising warship, wrecked much of the New England whaling fleet in the northern Pacific. It was never defeated.[11] The possibilities of using steam warships to destroy enemy commerce were grasped by Stephen Mallory, the Confederate secretary of the navy, and he ordered speedy raiders built in Britain and France. Instead, some were impounded, and most of these ships ended up in their navies, as well as in those of Denmark, Prussia, and Japan.

The blockade of the Confederacy drew on American experience against Mexico in the successful war of 1846–48. The Union blockade was the last major one before, successively, torpedo boats, submarines, and air power transformed the parameters for blockade, especially for close blockade, and indeed for sea denial in general. The Union blockade also helped limit Confederate efforts to build up their own fleet. Even before the blockade became effective, the Confederacy had made insufficient efforts to import rolled iron and machinery. This was serious because the Confederacy was so short of iron that it had to pull up railway track. A largely agrarian nation, the Confederacy lacked the capability to create the infrastructure to make modern products.

There was no effective general staff for either side, and the inexperienced Abraham Lincoln initially played a cautious role. However, his secretary of the navy, Gideon Welles, was skillful. Lincoln's commitment to the navy led him to become a frequent visitor to Washington's naval yard where he took an interest in the development of naval weapons.[12]

The Union's early strategy, the Anaconda Plan, included an important amphibious dimension. This led, on May 1, 1862, to the capture of New Orleans, which was the largest city and principal port in the Confederacy. In doing so, David Farragut overcame the Confederate warships (the massive *Louisiana* could not move for want of her engines, while the *Manassas* only mounted one thirty-two-pounder) and bypassed, at night, two substantial forts, but only after the river was freed of obstacles. The fate of New Orleans affected Confederate shipbuilding capacity. Alongside the campaign for the Mississippi, bases on the coastal periphery of the Confederacy were a priority. For example, Port Royal Sound was seized in late 1861 in order to provide a base from which maritime links between Savannah and Charleston could be cut. The record of "[Union] ships versus [Confederate] forts" was mixed. If troops could be skillfully utilized, as with Grant and Foot's operations in early 1862, then forts could be compelled to surrender fairly quickly. The Union's amphibious capability tied up large numbers of Confederate troops in coastal defense.

Army-navy cooperation, however, was generally mixed for both sides. Without army support, naval attack could prove unsuccessful, as Union warships discovered at Charleston in 1863. Rear Admiral Samuel F. Du Pont commanded a powerful force of nine Union ironclads, but they were hampered by mines and exposed to fire from shore batteries. Benefiting from offshore islands, Charleston was protected by a network of defensive positions. One ironclad, the fixed-tower, thinly armored *Keokuk*, was sunk, while three of the seven monitors were damaged enough to be sent for repairs, although they were all ready for action within a month, and only one man was killed. Charleston withstood all army-navy attacks and was therefore like Sevastopol in Crimea in 1854–55: mines and obstructions playing a crucial role alongside the effective new land-based rifled artillery. [13]

Moreover, in what proved a recurrent pattern for amphibious operations, the Union found that advancing from coastal positions into the interior was less successful and effective than amphibious attacks on coastal positions. Yet both approaches were less successful than advancing overland from areas held in considerable depth. Victory indeed was won by the Union on land and by forces that had advanced overland: Charleston finally fell to General Sherman in 1865, not to amphibious assault.

Despite this, the Union's maritime and riverine campaigns were more than incidental to the war's outcome. The early coastal operations greatly contributed to the effectiveness of the blockade. And so on with later operations, as when the Union fleet successfully fought its way into Mobile Bay on August 5, 1864, despite mines which claimed one ironclad and could have claimed more had they worked better. The fortifications at the bay's entrance were the principal Confederate defensive asset in that clash. [14] The following January, an amphibious operation covered by fifty-eight Union warships, the largest fleet hitherto assembled in the war, testified to the size of the Union navy. It captured Fort Fisher and thus closed the port of Wilmington, North Carolina. However, this assault was carried out with the direct support of an army division and had to be made twice before it succeeded in overwhelming the fort. Such operations faced logistical problems but maintained the impression and reality of Union pressure. This was particularly so in late 1864 and early 1865, as Sherman maneuvered in the Confederate rear near the coast. By threatening a siege, he forced the surrender of Charleston in 1865: the port was still open, but due to the blockade, little traffic went in or out.

In addition, the "brown-water" (inland) navy repeatedly played a key role in the success of Union operations in the Mississippi basin, notably in the crucial siege of Vicksburg in 1863. These operations both severed the Confederacy and secured the Midwest for the Union. The army was committed to the building of ironclads for their operations in the West. The Union army also ably linked river and rail transport in order to establish an effective logistical system that helped maintain the momentum of the advance. [15]

Faced with an industrial backwardness and lack of resources that made competition in shipbuilding impossible, the Confederacy sought to offset

Union superiority by using mines, submarines, and commerce raiders. Large naval actions were nonexistent, in part due to the dispersed nature of the Confederate warships and the Southern interest in blockade-running and commerce raiding. Instead, most of the naval conflict involved clashes between Union warships and Confederate shore defenses, or between individual ships, most famously, and frequently illustrated, the *Monitor* and the *Merrimac* (renamed the *Virginia* by the Confederates after being salvaged) in Hampton Roads on March 9, 1862. That the first clash between ironclads occurred during the American Civil War was because the European navies that had already commissioned ironclads had not fought one another: the Anglo-French naval race had been peaceful. In this duel, cannon shot could make little impact on the armored sides of the two ships, even though they fired from within one hundred yards. This showed the limited penetration power of the cannon used.

The absence of fleet-sized naval battles left unclear the full extent to which steam power and iron ships might have changed the nature of naval warfare. This was even more the case because, despite the Union blockade, neither Britain nor France intervened against the Union, as had appeared very possible in late 1861 and 1862. In preparing for war against the Union, the British and French benefited from their naval race, although it did not make them ready for the conflict they would have faced. The likely consequences of such intervention attracted much discussion and influenced procurement and deployment thereafter during the war. As a result, the Union continued to fortify New York City and San Francisco against naval attack.[16]

Leaving aside the problems faced for Britain by the defense of Canada, whether Britain's potential for coastal assault could effectively act as a form of strategic deterrent was unclear. The prospect frightened Union leaders enough in 1861–62 to lay down a large number of coastal-defense monitors, as well as to improve coastal fortifications armed with fifteen-inch Rodman guns. This potential was enhanced by the lack of a British standing coastal assault flotilla, a problem for Britain that had also occurred during the Crimean War (1854–56). A sense of an inability to wage war against increasingly dangerous littorals increased anxiety on the part of the Admiralty and compromised the ability of the British government to risk interventionist conflict. The evidence from both Union and Confederate official reports and letters, and from postwar books, was that naval warfare was seen as enhancing the powers of coastal defense. After the war, American defense boards emphasized the value of a combination of forts armed with fifteen-inch smoothbores and rifled guns, surrounded by protecting minefields and obstructions, all supported by heavily armed and armored shallow-draft monitors and rams.

After 1862, there was still a fear on the part of the Union and Britain that the Civil War would broaden out. The Union's ironclads were in part designed to resist British warships, which had nearby bases, including Bermuda and Halifax. Largely submerged below the waterline, the monitors offered only a concentrated armor protection scheme along the exposed hull and especially the gun turrets. The Union utilized radical new technologies: the *Winnebago* (of the *Milwaukee* class) loaded its guns below deck, as well as rotating the guns and elevating them, all by steam. The testing of armor plate and cannon was an active part of the process of consideration and preparation. The likely resilience of the American defense was not the sole factor. In addition, British distrust of France helped hinder the prospect of intervention, as did the significance of transatlantic trade. More generally, long-standing Anglo-American tension over empire and trade was strong in this period, but neither power pressed issues to the point of conflict.[17]

The Civil War saw an expansion of the American naval presence in the Pacific. The Union sent an ironclad monitor, the *Camanche*, to San Francisco in order to protect California from British attack or Confederate raids. The ship was built in 1862–63, then divided into parts and shipped around Cape Horn: as yet there was no transcontinental railway. Once at San Francisco, it was reconstructed. In 1865–66, another ironclad, the double-turreted monitor *Monadnock*, steamed around Cape Horn to California. The war was followed by Pacific expansionism by America, with the purchase of Alaska and the annexation of the Midway Islands, both in 1867, and with interest in gaining Hawaii as well as rumors about American ambitions in the Galapagos Islands and Brunei.

The Civil War had a major impact on naval developments in a number of other countries. For example, Spain decided that it was necessary to focus on ironclads to protect Cuba against a possible American attack. Italy switched from building wooden warships to ironclads. The Argentine ambassador to Washington, Domingo Faustino Sarmiento, brought some of the American ideas and lessons home. He was president from 1868 to 1874 and is credited as the founder of a permanent Argentine navy in 1870. In 1872, a naval academy was established, and the coast was divided into three naval regions. A small coastal-defense fleet was built, two small turret ironclads being commissioned in 1875, alongside eight other ships.

EUROPEAN NAVAL CONFLICT IN THE 1860s

The largest naval clash in the 1860s, and indeed between Trafalgar (1805) and Tsushima (1905), occurred not off North America, as had appeared likely, but in the Adriatic. The Battle of Lissa on July 20, 1866, was an episode in the war between Italy and Austria,[18] a war that occurred as a result of the conflict between Austria and Prussia, a conflict that provided Italy with an opportunity for gains. Lissa reflected Italian ambitions because, despite talk of threatening the flank of the Italian army, the Austrian navy largely remained on the defensive. Alongside conquering Venetia from Austria, Italy was interested in seizing the regions of Istria and Dalmatia on the other side of the Adriatic, which was a key aspect of the naval race between the two powers in the 1860s. [19]

The Italians first planned to seize the island of Lissa, but its fleet was attacked by a smaller and less heavily armed Austrian fleet under Baron Wilhelm von Tegetthof, who tried to compensate for these weaknesses by ramming the Italian warships. Some commentators erroneously saw this method of attack as a key lesson of the battle. In practice, the battle, the first between fleets of ironclads (seven Austrian versus twelve Italian) became a confused melee of ship-to-ship actions in which Italian unpreparedness and lack of command skills played a role in leading to their heavier losses. The key moment was when the *Ferdinand Max* rammed and sank the *Re d'Italia*, which had been immobilized earlier when her steering gear was shot away by gunfire. In other words, it was almost impossible for moving ships to ram one another; the hope was to immobilize an opponent first and then ram it. More significantly, Austrian victories over Italy on land and sea were more than counteracted by the impact of Prussia's victory over Austria, a victory entirely won on land.

Earlier, Prussia and Austria had fought Denmark in 1864. Although this conflict was determined on land, there was a naval dimension not seen in the Austro-Prussian War of 1866. Britain decided not to intervene with its fleet on behalf of the Danes, in particular to stop the Adriatic-based Austrian fleet from entering the Baltic. The Danes did well at sea against the Austrians and the Prussians.

Similarly, although the French intervention in Mexico from 1861 demonstrated the significance of naval potential, this again was not decisive. The French capture of Mexican ports, especially Vera Cruz on the Caribbean and Acapulco on the Pacific, highlighted the contrast between input, in the shape of force projection, and outcome, in the shape of control over the interior. French naval strength enabled coastal success, as with the capture of the port of Guaymas in 1865 and the reinforcement that year of Matamoros, which thwarted an attack on that port. The French were able to operate in Mexico but could not end resistance and abandoned their commitment to their Mexican royalist protégés as a result of Prussia's total victory over Austria in 1866. Thus, there were no specific naval reasons for French failure in Mexico, although this failure served as a potent qualification of the advantages brought by power projection.

Naval strength was also exerted elsewhere. The French used naval power projection in order to send troops to protect the papal position in Rome from Italian nationalists. In 1862–63, a crisis in Greece caused by the deposing of the king led to a British naval deployment. [20]

EUROPEAN AND AMERICAN NAVAL POWER IN THE 1870s

Another potent qualification of naval power was apparent in the 1870–71 Franco-Prussian War, the first major conflict for each power after those discussed above. France had the larger and better navy, but it did not serve to counter the rapid and overwhelming Prussian success that was achieved on land. The French did not translate ideas of Baltic landings into action, while two German squadron sorties from Wilhelmshaven did not lead to conflict. A longer war might well have created opportunities for naval action (for example the blockade France sought to impose might have hit harder), but they did not arise. The actual war suggested that naval power was of limited value in conflict between contiguous states. In 1914, Germany was to pursue a similar strategy.

The French need after 1871 to focus on rebuilding their army and on fortifying a new frontier led to a lack of attention to the navy, a factor also seen in earlier conflicts as in the 1690s and 1700s. Combined with the rapid American demobilization of the Union fleet after the end of the Civil War in 1865, this situation ensured that the British were able to muddle along, reasonably secure in their naval primacy and spending relatively little on the navy in the late 1870s. Indeed, due to a lack of investment in the Royal Navy, there was a need for new boilers and new ships by the 1880s.

The increasing size and sophistication of major warships helped drive up their cost. The tension between armor and armament, weight and maneuverability, not least the mutually interacting need for more effective guns and stronger armor, led to changes in armor and hull materials. Wooden-hulled ironclads were quickly superseded in the 1860s. The wrought-iron navy was followed in the late 1870s, after experimentation with iron and wood armor, by one using compound armor plate: the iron and steel navy. There were also moves toward the first all-steel battleships in the 1870s. Two all-steel cruisers were completed for the Royal Navy in 1879. Ship designers faced the problem of juggling the three desirable, but mutually antagonistic, qualities required of a weapons platform: speed, armament, and armor. One could only be enhanced at the expense of the others because of the weight problem, although replacing iron with steel was understood as the solution pretty early on. Experimentation led to false turns, including some spectacular failures, as well as to successes. During the first three decades of iron, steam warships saw some extraordinary advances as efforts were made to probe possibilities for design and construction. Moreover, the infrastructure to construct and maintain such warships had to be created and maintained, notably the necessary facilities in naval bases. Larger warships required deeper anchorages and large dry docks.[21]

The 1877–78 Anglo-Russian crisis indicated the potential capability and range, and also limitations, of naval power. Successfully expanding at the expense of the Turks, Russia backed a larger Bulgaria in order to gain access to the Mediterranean through a Russian presence on the Aegean Sea. However, British and Austrian pressure thwarted this ambition. The defense of British India against Russian threats was linked to British concern about the Mediterranean. Russian and French naval power, from Sevastopol in the Black Sea and Toulon respectively, would, it was argued, have to be repelled there. In 1878, in the face of the Russian advance, having defeated the Turks in Bulgaria, to near Constantinople (Istanbul from 1930), the Admiralty could not guarantee the ability to force open the Dardanelles en route to Constantinople. However, in the event, in accordance with the wishes of Benjamin Disraeli, the prime minister, the fleet did pass through them and reached Constantinople. Indian army units were swiftly sent by Britain to Malta via the Suez Canal, which had been opened in 1869 and in which Britain had purchased the majority share in 1875. In addition, a British base was established in Cyprus.

Another British squadron was mobilized for the Baltic and, unlike the Mediterranean Fleet, this posed a direct threat to St. Petersburg, the Russian capital, although it would have faced formidable defenses, as would any attack in the later stages of the Crimean War. As an instance of the extent to which what is subsequently considered of significance was less important at the time, this British squadron has received less attention, as is also true for the fleet sent to the Baltic during the Crimean War (as opposed to that dispatched to the Black Sea). Yet it was not necessary to act or fight in order for a navy to have a strategic point and consequence.

In turn, the Russians in 1877–78 planned commerce raiding in the Atlantic and Indian Oceans and attacks on the ports of the British Empire, such as Sydney in Australia, which encouraged defensive preparations there. There was no war, but the possible character of the conflict influenced naval commentators and planners. The nature of British naval power was instructive. As a means of coastal assault, it was limited if opposed by effective defenses. However, "command of the sea" was a major element, both strategically and in political terms. This element included winning any "Trafalgar"-style challenge by a rival battle fleet, blockade of an enemy's ports, and sweeping the seas of enemy commerce while protecting British imperial lines of communication and supply, the latter bringing command of the situation.[22]

In America, in contrast to Britain, the economy expanded rapidly without any significant commitment to naval power after the end of the Civil War. High levels of debt from the Civil War restricted America's ability to act and also encouraged a dependence on British financial markets and a wish to see economic growth through trade with Britain.[23] Demobilization did not mean that the American navy did not develop. Instead, there were changes not only to its warships but also in its infrastructure. For example, in 1877, the navy established a coaling station and bought land on Parris Island in Port Royal

Sound in South Carolina, a useful deepwater anchorage between Charleston and Savannah for projecting power toward the Caribbean approaches. As a classic instance of the multiple links of technology, the coal was brought by rail which, in 1873, had connected Port Royal Island to the mainland. The coaling station and dry dock were not to be abandoned until 1901.

GLOBAL DIMENSIONS, 1860–80

Naval power was a key means by which states displayed, exerted, and maintained power. This was conspicuously the case with the major imperial powers. Naval power, for example, was the basis for the Franco-Spanish intervention in Vietnam, which led to the seizure of Danang in 1858 and Saigon the following year, both crucial positions vulnerable to naval attack. As a result, Cochin China and Cambodia became French protectorates in 1863. In addition, in 1862, France had acquired the port of Obok in what became French Somaliland, now Djibouti, a base en route from the Suez Canal to the Indian Ocean.

Naval power was significant for lesser powers such as Spain, which, under the interventionist Leopoldo O'Donnell, who held power from 1856 to 1863, used its navy in the 1860s to act in the Dominican Republic and Morocco, as well as against Bolivia, Chile, Mexico, and Peru. Spanish concern both about disorder in the Philippines, a Spanish colony with unsettled boundaries, and about possible imperial rivals advancing claims led to an expedition to Sulu in the southern Philippines in the 1870s. This naval and amphibious expedition served as a basis for an agreement with Britain in 1885 that settled territorial differences arising from the British presence in northern Borneo.

Meanwhile, Portugal used the small number of warships it maintained in its colony of Mozambique to help suppress the slave trade and to establish control over coastal communities. Nevertheless, the conquest of the colony was largely to be achieved by the army.

Wars between powers could also involve a significant naval dimension thanks to the importance of amphibious operations. This was true of the War of the Pacific of 1879–83 in which Chile heavily defeated Bolivia and Peru, in part thanks to such operations. In 1879, Chile gained a dominant naval position as a result of the victory of its ironclads over the Peruvian ironclad *Huáscar* off Punta Angamos. Armor-piercing Palliser shells, fired from the nine-inch (British-produced) Armstrong guns of Chilean warships, forced the badly damaged *Huáscar* to surrender, as the eight inches of wrought iron on its turret had proved no defense against the shells. The Chileans then landed at Pisagua, captured Dolores, defeated a Peruvian force, and captured Iquique, the Peruvian export port for nitrates.[24] In 1880, Chilean naval strength enabled attacks on the Peruvian coast in which railways and ports were damaged in order to underline a sense of vulnerability, but two Chilean warships blockading the port of Callao were sunk by Peruvian torpedoes. The Peruvian capital, Lima, another port, fell the following year to Chilean forces, although Chilean victory on land, at Chorillos, was crucial. The *Huáscar* can still be visited at Talcahuano in Chile. The war also saw the use of mines.

At every level, naval strength was designed to provide the same strategic advantages: a deterrent against the threat from other powers but also a proactive means to ensure respect for interests and concerns. At the same time, the major powers could act, on their own terms, to protect the interests of the weaker. Thus, in 1860, a British warship turned the leading American adventurer of the period, William Walker, over to the Hondurans, who executed him. In 1866, American pressure helped lead Spain to end hostilities with Peru and Chile. At the same time, smaller powers turned to rival ironclad systems, such as coastal vessels that could thwart the naval pretensions of ostensibly stronger powers with seagoing ironclads, as in 1866 when Chile defied the prospect of Spanish bombardment.

Alongside this emphasis on the use of warships in the very varied relations at the international level, it is important to stress their crucial role in maintaining internal order. Thus, the Italian navy was employed at the time of a rebellion in the south in 1866 and the Spanish navy during the Second Carlist War of 1873–76 (a civil war within Spain) and during the large-scale colonial rebellions in Cuba and the Philippines. The role of navies in civil wars could vary. In Chile in 1890–91, the army backed the president, and the navy, eventually victorious, the Congress. In Brazil in 1891, a naval revolt in support of the vice president helped lead to an overthrow of the president, only for the authoritarianism of the new leader to result in a fresh naval revolt in 1893, which, however, was unsuccessful in the face of army support for the government.

Outside the West, the period 1860–80 saw efforts to improve naval capability, notably in Japan where it was part of a process of self-conscious modernization and Westernization, one also seen with the army. Britain eventually proved a support to naval Westernization in Japan, although in 1864 the American government had taken care to reassure Britain that no warships would be supplied to Japan until the latter's differences with Britain were over.[25] There were also developments in China. At the Fuzhou Naval Dockyard, founded in 1866, the ships launched were obsolescent when they left the slipway, although their quality improved: steam-powered but fully rigged wooden ships were superseded by more advanced vessels. In addition, steam-powered gunboats were launched at the Jiangnan arsenal from 1868.[26] Thus, variety in the character and use of naval power in 1860–80 emerges clearly as a conclusion alongside the pressures created by technological change and the complex interactions of power politics and naval strategy.

Chapter Two

Naval Dreams and Races, 1880–1913

Naval power and warfare in the late nineteenth century are generally discussed in terms of the run-up to the First World War, a traumatic and transformative conflict that broke out in Europe in 1914 and involved most of the world, directly or indirectly. This approach is both appropriate and yet misleading. Much of the naval capability of the period 1880–1913, and notably of its last decade, was indeed to be used in that conflict, and, in particular, the naval leadership and much of the manpower of the First World War had been recruited and trained earlier. Moreover, the naval preparations of the late nineteenth century were certainly made in preparation for a major struggle and in light of what was considered to be the likely nature of conflict then.

The actual character of that conflict was not anticipated, notably the key role of submarines, although Julian Corbett, a profoundly historical thinker who understood the Royal Navy, had flagged them as an unknown factor in the next war. However, despite some changes in the character of conflict at a tactical and operational level, the outline character of the First World War at sea would have been comprehensible to an admiral of an earlier age: no dreadnoughts (modern battleships) were lost in the North Sea to a torpedo, and, as in the eighteenth century and the Napoleonic Wars, Britain relied on a slow process of economic warfare while supporting Continental allies. [1]

Although a major conflict involving the large-scale use of warships was anticipated on a number of occasions, the war did not begin until 1914. Until then, naval conflict took a different turn to the First World War, with shorter and more decisive campaigns, both in terms of individual battles and with reference to their apparent consequences. At the same time, competition was repeatedly a key theme, both naval competition and that focused on factors that might affect it. Thus, in 1912, Rear Admiral Ernest Troubridge, the chief of the War Staff of the British Admiralty, in a memorandum on the Italian occupation of certain of the Dodecanese, Turkish islands in the Aegean Sea, particularly Rhodes, noted of British policy,

> A cardinal factor has naturally been that no strong naval power should be in effective permanent occupation of any territory or harbour east of Malta, if such harbour be capable of transformation into a fortified naval base. None can foresee the developments of material in warfare, and the occupation of the apparently most useless island should be resisted equally with the occupation of the best. The geographical situation of these islands enable the sovereign power, if enjoying the possession of a navy, to exercise a control over the Levant and Black Sea trade and to threaten our position in Egypt.[2]

1880s, CHANGING TECHNOLOGIES

Radical technological developments ensured an assumption of continuing change and also that a high degree of uncertainty grew up about the likely nature of naval combat, about the strengths and weaknesses of the new ship types, and about what effect all this might have on the organization of fleets, tactics, strategy, and maritime dominance. With their options increased by technological change, states watched the naval developments of each other keenly, and accordingly worried about the best places to put their money. Costs were increased by the extent to which many technological advances made new platforms necessary. Proven reliability clashed with the adoption of technological innovation, in a context in which it appeared mistaken to rely on established systems and techniques.

Meanwhile, the size and cost of major warships increased significantly. The tension between armor and armament, weight and maneuverability, not least the dynamic character of the mutually interacting need for more effective guns and stronger armor, led to changes in armor and hull materials. In place of warships designed to fire broadsides came guns mounted in center-line turrets, which were able to fire end-on as well as to turn. Moreover, firing armor-piercing explosive shells, guns became more effective and certainly more capable of inflicting damage. Whereas in the age of sail the key element was, perforce, the destruction of personnel and the damage of rigging and masts to incapacitate the weapons system, the new industrial naval firepower aimed at the destruction of the platform. However, alongside the changing technology, crossing the T remained a favorite of naval tacticians.

These were ships clearly designed for battle. From the 1880s, it became common for them to be called battleships, ships that were defined by their function, albeit also reliant on a huge support train, one greater than that of wooden ships of the line. Although evidence on the point was limited, while ship design was developing to counter the danger, it possibly required much less effort to destroy a steel battleship with high-explosive armor-piercing shells than a wooden ship of the line with cannon. As a result, warships became more vulnerable. Guns also became more rapid firing as, increasingly from the 1870s, breechloaders replaced muzzle-loading guns, which took a long time to load with large shells. Rifled artillery, percussion detonators, and high explosives, especially cordite and melmite in the 1880s and 1890s, also affected the relationship between naval bombardment and coastal fortifications. This was important to the process of power projection and to the need for a new type of coastal fortification and a new attitude toward the attack on, and protection of, littoral regions.

Some commentators, however, publicly wondered in the 1880s if battleships had a future in the face of the new development of torpedoes, the development of which attracted numerous inventors and much testing and speculation. This race prefigured that between tanks and antitank weaponry but was more central to force structures. From 1879, the British, who were to develop effective torpedoes in the long run, pioneered steam torpedo boats,[3] only for France to respond. The innovative Swedish-American inventor and consulting engineer John Ericsson (1803–89), who had played a key role in the development of ironclad monitors, was far more interested in the 1870s and 1880s in underwater weapons and effective torpedo-carrying warships, building the *Destroyer*, an armored prototype of the latter, in about 1880.[4]

As the Royal Navy was not yet willing to abandon the practice of close blockade, it was felt necessary in the British maneuvers of 1885 to plan for the establishment of a defensible advance base so as to reduce the vulnerability of the fleet to torpedo attack. Maneuvers acted as a register of apparent norms of power and also as a way to test the consequences of operational possibilities and thus to redefine the latter.

Concern about torpedoes, which appeared to many to be the weapon of the future, reconceptualizing firepower and mobility, and as both a means and a symbol of change, was an aspect of a wider sense of uncertainty about the role of large warships and the nature of naval warfare. In fact, as this book will indicate, the critics of a reliance on battleships were correct, but also, in the event, their criticisms were very early and, therefore, highly premature. The dreadnought battleship would have a remarkably short run as a capital ship, compared with the sailing warship, which, with singularly few changes in the seventeenth, eighteenth, and early nineteenth centuries, had changed the geostrategic nature of the world. Damaging as they were, it was not underwater weapons, in the shape of mines and torpedoes, that were to doom the battleship but, in the 1940s, air attack, which also made fortified harbors vulnerable to enemy attack. In the meantime, the apparent threat from torpedo boats in the 1880s, a threat underlined by the development of flotilla tactics, helped to ensure that, except in Italy and Russia, battleship building slowed down rather drastically. No one quite knew what to do about torpedo boats, nor what they might mean for the future, and the increased effectiveness of torpedoes underlined the problem. Torpedo boats were too vulnerable because the short range of torpedoes and the need to get close to their target to fire them prolonged the exposure of the torpedo boats to the new quick-firing guns of their opponents.

In France, there was an interesting transformation in naval doctrine, one that, as so often happens with such developments, was linked to changes in weapons systems and to the presentation of their potential. While an emphasis on battleships remained strong among the naval professionals of Britain, France's leading rival at sea, the situation was very different in France. Faced, after the Franco-Prussian War of 1870–71, with political concern about the German army and the heavy costs of the French response on land, Admiral Théophile Aube, author of *La Guerre Maritime et Les Ports Françaises* (1882) and the navy minister in 1886–87, and what was termed the French *Jeune École* (Young School) provided a doctrine that for opponents of battleships amounted to an ideology. This doctrine gained at least some support in every Western navy and, with its discussion of asymmetric issues and capabilities, remains relevant today.

At the same time, it is important to note the political context: the all-too-frequent depoliticization of naval history is one of the more common faults of the subject. The failure of the French naval leadership to explain the role the navy did indeed play in the war was significant. This had a political dimension, as the naval establishment was mostly monarchist, which was a position that was unacceptable to the governments of the Third Republic. In contrast, Aube sided with the Left, which saw the *Jeune École* as a republican way of war, prefiguring the comparable situation in Russia after the Revolution (see chapter 5).

In the context of financial concerns as well as military considerations, the *Jeune École* pressed for the less expensive option of unarmored, and therefore faster, light cruisers, which would use less coal than battleships and thus be able to go further on each ton of coal. This ability would improve the operating range of the cruisers. Without armor, they would also be faster and more maneuverable than battleships and therefore, at the tactical level, be able to avoid the firepower of the latter and thereby require less armor. As a result, cruisers were presented as able to protect sea lanes, to advance imperial expansion, and to attack the commerce of opponents.

That was not all. The contemporary preference for the offensive made sense in terms of the then developing naval technology. In line with this, Aube favored the torpedo boat, claiming that it nullified the power of the British battleship and could break any British blockade. The *Jeune École* used the development of the self-propelled torpedo to argue that close blockade had become too costly. This tactical countering of the advantages of battleships over less heavily gunned and armored warships was designed to ensure, or at least justify the claim, that the latter would be able to leave harbor without interception and therefore provided these warships with operational and strategic opportunities. In doctrinal terms, the *Jeune École* believed that their cruisers would be able to launch a war on enemy trade that would be more potent because it would be a form of total war in which "everything is . . . legitimate."[5] This concern with trade reflected the extent to which it played a major role in the perception of vulnerability and thus in the discussion of strategy. In addition, French doctrine appeared to take advantage of more modern technology, as well as to offer the mobility and glamour of attacking or circumventing the anachronistic bigger and slower battleships.

The conceptual and methodological challenge posed by the French was not only a matter of a different force structure focused on cruisers, but also a mixed-arms doctrine that looked toward twentieth-century doctrine and practice, especially the attempt to combine battleship and submarine operations in both world wars and the integration of air power with naval operations in the Second World War. With cruisers, the necessary speed and range were obtainable only in big cruisers, which, while able to carry more coal than smaller ones, were also expensive. The dynamic nature of the technologies available posed a series of challenges. For example, improvements in metallurgy ensured that the side armor of the fast cruisers France built from the mid-1890s was able to resist shells fired by the six-inch guns of British cruisers, which created pressures on Britain for a new solution for trade protection.

There was scant naval warfare in the 1880s by which torpedoes and other issues could be evaluated. The lack of any large-scale naval actions in the late nineteenth century, which caused so much attention to be focused on Lissa with questionable conclusions drawn, also led to a disproportionate amount of attention being devoted to some very minor events in the wars of the period.[6] Two boats using spar torpedoes helped naval firepower to ensure a French victory over a Chinese squadron at Fuzhou in 1884: six Chinese cruisers, all built of wood, were sunk, while the shore installations were destroyed.[7] Self-propelled torpedoes were a far greater threat than the tactically more limited spar torpedoes.

The ideas of the *Jeune École* also had an impact outside France. Concern with trade as well as status had led the Germans to develop their fleet after the Franco-Prussian War of 1870–71. Helped by reparations levied on the defeated French, as well as by the strength of Germany's industrial base, the pace of German naval construction rose greatly in 1873, and by 1883 Germany had the third-largest armored fleet in the world. It had developed an extensive, technologically advanced and effective fleet from a standing start. German interest in cruisers increased in the 1880s as the German overseas empire rapidly developed from 1884 in sub-Saharan Africa and the Pacific, and there were new maritime routes to defend. In German naval thought, there was also an emphasis on commerce raiding.[8] Seeking to use cutting-edge technology in order to counter more established navies, the Germans were very interested in torpedo boats. By 1888, with the active backing of Leo, Graf von Caprivi, chief of the Admiralty from 1883 to 1888, and under the dynamic leadership of Alfred Tirpitz (later von Tirpitz), appointed director of torpedo development in 1878, Germany had commissioned seventy-two torpedo boats and developed the manufacture of good torpedoes.[9] The likely impact of this system was unclear to contemporaries, especially the British.

After 1905, Tirpitz, the state secretary of the Imperial Naval Office from 1897 to 1916, was opposed to submarines, in part because he wished to focus expenditure on battleships, as he indeed did. Nevertheless, the emphasis on torpedoes in the late nineteenth century looked toward later German interest in the submarine. A strict comparison between torpedo boats and submarines, however, faces limits because torpedo boats were too restricted to pose a comparable challenge tactically, operationally, or strategically. They were too vulnerable and also unviable as independent seagoing warships; in contrast, submarines had greater capabilities under both heads. Working submarines were first used in 1776, albeit with scant capability, and effectively from the late nineteenth century. The first steam-powered submarine, the thirty-ton *Resurgam*, was launched by George Garrett in 1879. Working with the Swedish arms manufacturer Thomas Nordenfelt, Garrett began work in 1882 on the *Nordenfelt I*, a sixty-ton submarine, the first to be armed with self-propelled torpedoes. France completed a submarine powered while submerged by an electric battery in 1888. However, it was only the development, in the early 1900s, of reliable diesel propulsion that ensured that the submarine could be a wide-ranging platform, as opposed to a submersible largely useful for harbor defense, and could therefore play a significant role in the First World War.[10]

BACK TO BATTLESHIPS

While a reaction against battleships affected many (though certainly not all) naval thinkers and planners in the 1880s, there was a major shift back to them in the 1890s. In part, this shift back reflected growing awareness of the potential of defenses against torpedoes and investment, accordingly, in these defenses. Torpedo nets and thick armor around the battleship waterline were particularly important. Electric searchlights, first fitted on a battleship with the British *Inflexible*, launched in 1881, were seen as important in detecting torpedo boats. They were an application, for enhanced capability, of electricity, which had been used on warships from the 1870s. Moreover, quick-firing medium-caliber guns could provide a secondary armament for use against torpedo boats, rather as anti-aircraft guns were later to be regarded as a protection against air attack. In addition, the advent of smokeless powder lessened the artificial "fog of war" that the *Jeune École* commentators had optimistically assumed would provide cover for their torpedo-boat attacks against larger warships. Instead, in a marked tactical variation, such cover was to be sought by submarines operating below the surface.

The mix of gun calibers on many warships was also partly a consequence of the poor accuracy that could be obtained by contemporary gunnery methods. Bradley Fiske, an American naval officer, noted in 1905 that for the "typical" pre-dreadnought, with, for example, four twelve-inch guns, eight eight-inch guns, and twelve six-inch guns, the much higher rate of fire of the smaller pieces (a six-inch gun fired eight times as many rounds as a twelve-inch) was likely to ensure far more hits than the more deadly twelve-inchers could obtain, quantity, as it were, making up for quality.

Tactics changed in response to the threat from torpedoes, as did force structures. There was the development of the, originally specialist, torpedo-boat destroyer, or all-purpose "destroyer," as it later became. Thus, in a number of respects, the threat to battleships was neutralized to a considerable extent, although, in the absence of large-scale conflict in the 1890s, it was not known how far.

Separately, there was skepticism about the actual threat from torpedoes. There were concerns about the level of seaworthiness of torpedo boats and also about the reliability of torpedoes. This reliability, indeed, remained an issue well into the Second World War. Even in Japan's decisive victory over a Russian fleet at Tsushima in 1905, the torpedoes were only used to finish off already-disabled Russian warships. The threat posed by torpedo boats never equated with seizing "command of the sea," insofar as that was in any way a helpful concept. To a degree, torpedo boats appeared to offer the prospect of sea denial in narrow waters. From the 1890s, torpedo boats influenced, but did not end, British naval interest in littoral warfare.[11] However, torpedo boats did not threaten oceanic communications nor the "command of the sea" of battleships. For several decades, the threat from torpedoes was more apparent than real. During the Spanish-American War of 1898, although both sides had torpedoes, neither used them. When the Spanish squadron sortied from Santiago, the first two ships were torpedo boats, neither of which fired any torpedoes.

Changes in warship capability were crucial to the shift back to battleships. Despite the earlier appearance of steam, iron armor, and breech-loading guns, the true oceangoing, all-steam battleship did not really emerge until the 1890s. A number of different but linkable changes were important to this development. The invention of the barbette was significant to ship design. It was a fixed armored trunk or tube protecting the gun mounting, which revolved within it and, in the original version, fired over the rim. Later, a light gunhouse was added, revolving with the mounting, to form the beginning of the modern armored gun turret, which rests on the fixed barbette.

This system was important to the development of more effective ocean-going battleships, as it allowed guns to be mounted in central locations on deck (rather than firing from the side of the ship) without compromising the stability of the ship, a stability that was important to seaworthiness and to gunnery. As a result, the low freeboard of the earlier ships was no longer necessary. With a higher freeboard, warships could more readily travel any-where in the world. A key shift was being able to mount the new heavy guns high enough out of the water to enable a ship to go to sea in more difficult waters. Raft-like, low-freeboard vessels were far steadier weapons platforms than high-freeboard vessels prone to rolling and pitching, but there was the question of how well a monitor could fight in heavy seas without the risk of flooding beyond the pumps' capacity to cope. However, very few naval engagements took place in stormy weather, not least due to the difficulty then of seeing the target and, therefore, of aiming: there was no equivalent to radar. In practice, the biggest drawback of monitors as warships was that they boasted relatively shallow hulls, which limited their coal-carrying ca-pacity and therefore their strategic range of potential operations. Ericsson attempted to solve the issue in 1862 by designing a deep-draft (twenty feet) monitor, *Dictator*, which could carry one thousand tons of coal and cross the Atlantic without refueling.

The key movers in the invention of the barbette were the French. They were often slightly ahead of the British in important aspects of technical development. However, France still did not have an industrial infrastructure to implement innovations comparable to that of Britain.

The range of developments in the 1880s and 1890s was impressive. Moreover, this range encouraged a sense of dynamism and thus competition in discussions about warships, in procurement, and in naval maneuvers, such as the annual British ones that began in 1885. The marine turbine engine was developed by Sir Charles Parsons in 1884. The eight 14,150-ton British battleships of the *Royal Sovereign* class, laid down under the Naval Defense Act of 1889, and the largest battleships yet built, were, thanks to better engines (albeit triple-expansion reciprocating rather than turbine engines), capable of eighteen knots. This speed was a response to the threat from torpedo boats.

The age of sail appeared long past. In the first act of Gilbert and Sulli-van's comic operetta *Utopia Limited*, which was first staged in 1893, the fictional Captain Sir Edward Corcoran of the Royal Navy sings,

> I'll teach you how we [the British] rule the sea . . .
> If sailor-like you'd play your cards,
> Unbend your sails and lower your yards,
> Unstep your masts—you'll never want 'em more.

> Though we're no longer hearts of oak,
> Yet we can steer and we can stoke,
> And thanks to coal, and thanks to coke,
> We never run a ship ashore!

Nickel-steel-armor was developed in the 1890s, after trials in America in 1890 had shown that carbon-treated nickel-steel was more effective in resisting gunfire than compound armor. Nickel-steel was improved in 1892, when the German Krupp works introduced a process of "gas cementing." This process gave added strength per ton of armor: additional protection without added weight. This protection was a necessary response to the development of chrome steel shells and armor-piercing shell caps, which had increased the effectiveness of major pieces of naval ordnance. This effectiveness provided a greater role for large ships able to carry such guns. Advances in machine tools, metallurgy, and the understanding of explosives ensured that more accurate guns, capable of far longer ranges and employing better explosives, could be produced. In turn, hydraulic motors enabled guns to be turned or elevated mechanically.

The ability to increase protection without added weight, and the need to do so, encouraged the construction of bigger ships. This process required a sophisticated shipbuilding industry and much greater expenditure. More generally, the net effect of technological change was a frequent retooling in order to retain competitive advantage. As a result, warships became obsolete far more rapidly than in the earlier age of wooden warships. In the latter case, *Victory*, Nelson's flagship at Trafalgar in 1805, had been laid down in 1758. The introduction of steam power, iron plating, and breech-loading artillery each represented paradigm shifts in production requirements and also in maintenance. Moreover, for each, there was a lesser tolerance of variations, let alone mistakes, in both the production process and the use of the subsequent systems. Weapons and other aspects of warships became precision machines. Advances in metallurgy, marine engine design, and torpedoes were each part of the process. Aside from their individual impact, they had a cumulative effect. The key developments that made long-range, sail-less warships practical were the introduction of the compound steam engine (culminating in the triple-expansion engine), the cylindrical high-pressure steam boiler (culminating in water-tube boilers), and the development of new lubricants to facilitate faster-running pistons, leading to fast, reliable, and economical engines.

Developments with explosives were more generally indicative of the pressure for change and the processes of change. The search for a new propellant involved a range of specifications. It was designed to provide increased velocity and range, to reduce greatly the volume of smoke, and to be safer, as well as more powerful, than gunpowder, not being as susceptible either to temperature changes or to handling dangers. Successive explosive compounds were tried. The Royal Navy turned to cordite, a powder made from a blend of nitroglycerine and gun cotton mixed with acetone. In a classic instance of technological advances requiring a number of steps, cordite was adapted to meet the ballistic requirements of the larger steel guns that the navy had deployed. Initially remade into tubes in order to produce an even burn rate, cordite was modified by adding indentations along the tubes so as to increase the combustion rate and thereby maintain gas pressure as a shell shot down the barrel, ensuring that a shell traveled at an increased rate as it cleared the bore. This resulted in a greater range.

These and other changes had a major impact on skill requirements. Sailing rig had been a complex technology. Nevertheless, the sophisticated equipment of the late nineteenth century led to a need for better, or at least differently, trained officers and sailors, and therefore to the creation of new colleges and educational methods. Professionalization, administrative efficiency, and the ability to respond to technological innovation all became necessary criteria. As it was more important to ensure continuity of service in navies, so there was a development of career conditions and structures. Although to a lesser extent, this process also affected ordinary rankings. The possibility of using "merchant" sailors directly in modern warships shrunk. At the same time, it is necessary to note the harshness of working conditions, notably in the engine room: steamships lacked reliable air conditioning.

There was also a professionalization, or rather change in professionalization, of naval construction. Developing a trend that had begun in the second half of the eighteenth century, the emphasis now was on scientific methods of design and construction that rested on careful mathematical calculations and detailed projections rather than on intuition and half-hull models. The age when one "shipbuilder master" could plan and build an entire ship was over. Instead, the distribution of tasks involved in shipbuilding became a more complex process, with the move from one shipyard to a collection of factories that produced goods that would be put together in shipyards. This development was a key aspect of modern production techniques.

Professionalization was matched by close relations between navies and large industrial concerns, relations that ensured a synergy in which the needs of the latter proved of particular significance. In turn, the interests of these concerns were politically important. Shipyards, for example those on the Clyde in Scotland, which themselves had large workforces, were linked to other heavy engineering works, notably for ships' engines, as well as to iron and steel manufacturing.

NEW DOCTRINE

In part, the shift to the battleship, alongside the continued emphasis on cruisers, was reflected by, and was a reflection of, the works of the most influential writer on naval power, Captain, later Rear Admiral, Alfred Thayer Mahan (1840–1914), an American naval officer of great talent who was lecturer in naval history and tactics at the Naval War College in Newport, Rhode Island, from 1885, becoming the president of the college from 1886 to 1889 and from 1892 to 1893. Emphasizing the importance of command of the sea, notably in his *Influence of Sea Power upon History* (1890), Mahan regarded the destruction or blockade of the opponent's battle fleet as the means to achieve this goal and treated commerce raiding as less important. In terms of force structure, the Mahanian approach led to a stress on battleships, not on cruisers, let alone torpedo boats.

The idea of command of the sea was also ventilated in Britain. This was particularly so with the book of that title published in 1894 by the influential journalist and military commentator Spenser Wilkinson. Admiral Philip Colomb's *Naval Warfare: Its Ruling Principles and Practice Historically Treated* (1891) was also important. There was a parallel between the benefits widely supposed to stem from command of the sea and those that were being allegedly gained from the scramble for overseas empire. The discussion of the topic was especially important in Britain, not only because of its history but also as a consequence of its current position. In Britain, themes of commerce protection, imperial expansion, and amphibious operations proved particularly significant aspects of the goals and means of naval dominance.

The nineteenth-century practice of validation by historical example was important to the habit of looking for continuities in naval power and of searching the past to understand the present. British commentators looked back on centuries of naval conflict. The Elizabethan War against Philip II of Spain in 1585–1604 proved an especially attractive lodestar, including for novelists and painters, while the later wars with France from 1689 to 1815 also attracted much attention, and for Mahan as well. The emphasis was on warrior roles and not on what were seen as more tedious commerce-oriented roles, notably convoy duty.

Mahan was influenced by the German historian Theodor Mommsen (1817–1903), who, in his *History of Rome*, presented Roman naval power as playing a crucial role against Carthage in the Second Punic War. Reading this in Lima in 1884, while on naval duty protecting American interests, Mahan was struck by "how different things might have been could Hannibal have invaded Italy by sea . . . instead of by the long land route; or could he, after arrival, have been in free communication [with Carthage] by land." Hannibal had invaded Italy via eastern Spain and southern France, then crossing the Alps. The easier sea passage from Carthage, which is near modern Tunis, to Italy was blocked by Roman naval strength. Mahan's focus, seen with his *The Interest of America in Sea Power, Present and Future* (1897), was on how the United States should draw on the example of Britain to use naval capability best in order to become a great power. He was particularly concerned that America have a navy to match its interests, geography, and society. Mahan argued for the relationships between geographic and social factors and sea power, for a larger American navy, and for professional naval education. The vulnerability of America and its trade to naval attack was one of his major themes. [12]

Mahan's views were widely disseminated. His *Influence of Sea Power upon History* (1890) was much read in Britain and was translated into both German and Japanese in 1896 (the year in which he retired), albeit with changes introduced. Mahan's influence on American policy owed something to his friendship with Theodore Roosevelt, with whom he served on a war strategy board during the 1898 war with Spain. Assistant naval secretary then, Roosevelt was later, as president (1901–9), a keen advocate of naval strength and power projection. He and Mahan both wrote histories of the naval aspects of the Anglo-American War of 1812, which had lasted until 1815. This conflict enabled them to discuss the naval policies of both America and Britain. Although the War of 1812 was waged with a very different technological base, it appeared highly relevant to many writers and readers less than a century later.

The notion of decisive victory leading to a command of the sea that could be employed to strategic effect was an account of how to win wars that did not require the acquiescence of the defeated (although Sir Julian Corbett, author of *Some Principles of Maritime Strategy* [1911], offered a different and, as it turned out, more realistic appraisal [13]). In short, a prospectus and potential were asserted, or (to its protagonists) grasped, a view that accorded with Mahan's strong belief in divine sovereignty and providentialism, [14] but one that was, in practice, to be more elusive for many victors of individual battles. The will to believe in victory, notably decisive victory, was important to the analysis. Combined with the creation of naval planning staffs, an emphasis on control of the sea, a more modern and nuanced notion than command of the sea, encouraged the development of strategic naval plans. Germany's first war plan against Britain, drafted in 1897, was followed in 1900 with an implausible German plan for an attack on the United States. After their entente in 1904, Britain and France were to plan jointly how to deploy their naval forces in the event of war with Germany, and notably where to focus their strength. This planning was an important factor when the First World War broke out in 1914.

The emphasis on the battleship certainly did not mean identical doctrines and plans. Indeed, there were major differences in strategic culture and tasking which affected powers that had access to similar weaponry. Thus, Britain had to protect maritime routes that provided her with food and raw materials as well as the most extensive and far-flung imperial system. In 1890–1914, Britain carried about half the world's maritime trade. In turn, challengers of Britain, especially France in the late nineteenth century, Germany in both world wars, and the Soviet Union during the Cold War, sought a doctrine, force structure, strategy, and operational practice that could contest these routes. Differences in strategic culture and tasking lent point to the discussion of sea power and, indeed, to its ideological character. Moreover, this discussion was made dynamic by new potentials and capabilities. Thus, naval capability indicated the dynamic relationship between doctrine, which was based on established practice and therefore, in part, on historical analysis and example, and, on the other hand, the real, apparent, and potential pressures for change stemming from new technology.

In the case of Britain, the Near East crisis of 1878, with its prospect of war with Russia, helped lead toward a sense of uncertainty if not insecurity and, for some, acute anxiety. Convoys and their cruiser escorts no longer appeared the best way to protect trade. This was in part because, although many merchant ships were still sailing vessels, some merchant steamers were now as fast as warships. To protect trade, a large navy, able to carry the war to the enemy by close blockade and by attacks on enemy warships in ports, was regarded as the best way to win at sea and thus for Britain to avoid, or lessen, the need for a large army or alliances.

This requirement entailed a large peacetime navy capable of fast mobilization so that the opposing fleet would be confined to port as long as it was not already mobilized or on a training sortie. At the same time, the necessary size of this navy was unclear. As a result of the Naval Defense Act of 1889, its requirement for a battleship fleet at least equal to the combined strength of the next two largest navies and the £21.5 million voted by Parliament, British naval estimates rose from £11 million in 1883 to £18.7 million in 1896, and £37 million in 1905 (out of total government spending, excluding debt service, of £121 million). Moreover, the number of British battleships rose from thirty-eight in 1883 to sixty-two in service or construction in 1897. W. H. Smith, the First Lord of the Admiralty (and the model for the ludicrous First Lord, Sir Joseph Porter, in Gilbert and Sullivan's 1878 comic operetta *HMS Pinafore*), told the House of Commons that the 1889 act was necessary because of the naval programs of the other European powers. However, the act may have been a substantial overreaction to the navy scare of 1888–89 about a Franco-Russian threat that was less serious than was alleged and, in particular, by the Beresford group within the navy. The attaché reports and other sources of intelligence were consistently dismissive of French and Russian naval capabilities (and continued to be until 1905), but, once the impetus for a big program had become irresistible, the Admiralty's threat assessments were alarmist, presumably in order to boost the funding that could be obtained from Parliament. In practice, French battleships were mostly weak, while Russia had very few battleships. [15]

The construction program that followed the act envisaged a balanced navy, with battleships to overawe or defeat opposing fleets, while cruisers, which became more powerful as specifications were raised, [16] utilized the subsequent command of the sea, ensuring a commercial dominance that provided support for the navy from financial circles in the city of London. The commitment to maintaining a two-power naval standard led to an ongoing rise in expenditure, which created serious concerns in the 1900s, leading the Treasury then to press for cuts. Imperial overstretch and public finances became an issue.

Doctrine was linked to strategic need and thus geopolitics. The development of global trade and Western colonial empires led to an emphasis on naval power. This emphasis involved not only modern warships but also the related "relays" of power, particularly naval bases and coaling depots. As a result, the speed of individual warships could be converted into planned action at the will of the center. The extension of the network of British coaling stations ensured that their steam-powered armored warships could be used in waters across the world. This was an extension advocated in 1881–82 in reports produced by the Carnarvon Commission. [17] So also for other powers. French bases included Martinique and Guadeloupe in the West Indies, Dakar (Senegal), Libreville (Gabon), Diego Suarez (Madagascar), Obok (Djibouti), Saigon (Vietnam), Kwangchowwan (China), New Caledonia in the southwest Pacific, and Tahiti in the southern Pacific. Already, in the House of Commons in 1883, W. H. Smith had warned about the problems posed for Britain by having serious naval commitments, requiring the use of ironclads, around the world, which indeed was the case.

NAVAL OPERATIONS, 1880–99

The prospect of war with Russia continued to affect British planning in the 1880s. In 1885, during the Penjdeh crisis over Afghanistan, the Royal Navy was placed on full alert, for the crisis to the British threatened the route to India. British plans for attacks included a bombardment of Kronstadt, Russia's Baltic naval base, and amphibious operations against Batumi on the Black Sea (now in Georgia), Russia's main port in the Caucasus, and against Vladivostok, Russia's Pacific naval base. The latter operation was to have been preceded by the establishment of a base in Korea. In turn, the British were concerned by the extent to which the Royal Navy could be used to help the defense of India's landward frontier from overland Russian attack via Afghanistan and to guarantee the defense of India's coasts, while the prospect of repeating naval power projection into the Black Sea was thwarted by opposition from Turkey and Germany. General Frederick Roberts, the senior commander in India, noted in 1885 that the ports there were poorly defended, adding,

> What we require is long reaching guns for our batteries, both land and floating, and swift powerful torpedo boats. In addition, and this I believe will prove the most efficient defence, our ports should be protected by one or two swift steamers with long-range guns.[18]

In the 1880s, public discussion of naval issues increased in Britain. On July 4, 1885, "Fresh Paint," a cartoon in *Punch*, the leading British satirical magazine, depicted a navy in difficulties. Britannia, presented as the figure-head of a British warship, holds only an olive branch as a carpenter (resembling the Marquess of Salisbury, the prime minister) notes that there was no time to modernize the warship before she must go to sea, while his helper (resembling Lord Randolph Churchill, the secretary of state for India) stands on a ladder and recommends a cosmetic paint to provide an appearance of power.

Naval expenditure in Britain in practice was close to the combined figure of the next two high-spending powers, France and Russia. Nevertheless, although there was no other individual navy able to pose a fundamental challenge to Britain's naval position, the creation of a Franco-Russian alliance posed what appeared to be a clear threat to Britain. The exchange of naval visits at Toulon and Kronstadt in 1891 and 1893 provided a clear demonstration of the threat latent in the treaty and military convention of 1892 and 1894. In 1894, the new prime minister, Lord Rosebery, informed the Austrian foreign minister, Count Gustav Kalnoky, that a British fleet could no longer be deployed to defend Constantinople against a Russian attack for fear of what the French navy would then do in support of Russia in the western and central Mediterranean, severing the route to the Suez Canal. Two years later, the director of naval intelligence conceded that the Darda-nelles could not be held by the Royal Navy and that therefore the Russian Black Sea fleet would be able to sortie into the eastern Mediterranean and thus threaten the Suez Canal, fears that were to recur in the twentieth century and to be inherited by the United States.[19] In practice, the effectiveness of this alliance was exaggerated in Britain, while British agreements with both Austria and Italy in 1887 in any event strengthened Britain's position.

Russian naval ambitions were seen both in shipbuilding and in expanding the network of bases. In what was clearly a major challenge to Japan, the Russians developed a major naval presence in Manchuria in northern China, building ports at Darien and Port Arthur on the Liaotung Peninsula, which was leased to them.

Confrontation between major naval powers was matched at a more modest scale. The success of Chile's blue-water navy in the War of the Pacific in 1879–83 over that of Peru led to a transformation in the Argentine navy, a transformation that was encouraged by the prosperity stemming from greater Atlantic trade. In the early 1880s, there was considerable expansion, with the launching of a central-battery ironclad, a torpedo ram, and four torpedo boats in 1880, followed by a corvette in 1884 and a cruiser in 1885. Competition with Chile led to the completion of three protected cruisers, two small coastal-defense battleships, three torpedo gunboats, and eighteen torpedo boats in the early 1890s. Later in the decade, armored cruisers were purchased from Italy, and four destroyers were added to the navy. In 1902, part of the British arbitration that settled the Argentine-Chile boundary dispute included a naval disarmament agreement. Argentina had to abandon most of its major expansion program, ending the building of two 15,000-ton battleships and the purchase of six destroyers from Italy. Two almost complete armored cruisers were sold to Japan. Meanwhile, Argentinian naval expansion had prompted a Brazilian determination to restore its naval lead.

Naval construction and international competition shared common characteristics. There was an irony of deterrence, fear, and capability, as, for example, French naval building, in response to British moves, in turn generated new British naval construction. In the Fashoda crisis of 1898 over competing interests in Sudan, the British sent the Channel fleet to Gibraltar in order to put pressure on the French position in the Mediterranean. Abandoned by Russia and conscious, not least as a result of the 1897 British Diamond Jubilee Fleet Review, of being weaker at sea, France gave way to Britain. As a key element of British maritime geopolitics, the Suez Canal was deepened by the British in 1898. It carried over twenty million tons of shipping in 1913.

In turn, the Germans built up their fleet, in part in response to British naval strength and partly as a result of German impotence in southern Africa prior to, and at the time of, the Boer War (1899–1902). German sympathy for the Boer (Afrikaner) republics of Transvaal and the Orange Free State in their conflict with Britain could not be translated into action, largely because these republics did not have a coastline, and Germany had no way to challenge the Royal Navy. Moreover, from 1897, Britain kept a naval force in Delagoa Bay (in the neutral Portuguese colony of Mozambique) larger than that of any other power. This force ensured an ability to prevent supplies from reaching Transvaal via Mozambique. The German 1898 Naval Law, and the 1900 amendment to it, were designed to build up the German fleet against the Royal Navy and were generally seen in that light in Britain.

Other powers also extended their naval reach. In 1898, in key episodes in the Spanish-American War, the Americans destroyed Spanish squadrons off Santiago in Cuba and in Manila Bay. Complete victory was obtained on July

3 over the Spanish fleet off Santiago under Admiral Pascual Cervera, with the Spanish warships, four modern cruisers and two destroyers, sunk as, and after, they left the protected anchorage, in an easy but badly commanded American victory over warships in poor condition. This victory gave vital leeway in Cuba to the inadequately trained American army and also encouraged the Spanish commander in Santiago to surrender. Moreover, the operational advantage provided by naval strength was demonstrated on July 21 when an American squadron captured Bahia de Nipe on the north coast of Cuba, destroying the Spanish warship guarding the port and providing a new sphere of operations for the army.

In Manila Bay, the six-ship American Asiatic Squadron, under the well-prepared Commodore George Dewey, destroyed seven Spanish ships, essentially colonial gunboats, and silenced the shore batteries, at the cost of eight Americans wounded, on May 1, 1898. Having had most of his ships destroyed, Rear Admiral Patricio Montojo surrendered. The absence of American bases in the region made this achievement especially impressive, as did the lack of reliable intelligence. The Spaniards had fewer large guns on their warships but benefited from the shore defenses. Dewey employed a technique he had observed when taking part in Farragut's attack on New Orleans in 1862: passing heavily fortified shore positions at night. To ensure supplies, Dewey had purchased British merchant colliers, providing floating support.

However, without troops, Dewey was unable to capture Manila and had to wait for the army's arrival. Dewey's victory made naval success appear easy, but in practice it was hard going because the gunnery was so uncertain. Only a small percentage of the American shells found their targets. This was an aspect of the problems with new technology also seen with torpedoes. Another naval aspect of the crisis was provided by the nearby presence of a larger force of German warships, which posed the threat of German territorial claims. To prevent this, the victorious Dewey established and enforced a naval blockade of Manila Bay. In practice, the exclusion of Germany owed much as well to the dispatch of a British squadron.

The American fleet played a major role in isolating Spanish forces both in the West Indies and the Philippines. Naval power was crucial in the capture of Puerto Rico from Spain, enabling successive bombardment (May), blockade, and invasion (July) in 1898.[20] The following year, with new commitments now across the Pacific, the American navy established coal depots at strategic ports around the world.

NEW GLOBAL DIMENSIONS, 1880–1905

The strong emphasis on naval strength, and on battleships as its measure, extended to the non-Western world. This represented a change from an earlier situation in which this world had essentially experienced naval power, a situation that had very much been the case from British pressure on China in the 1830s on. This element, however, continued to be significant in parts of the world into the twentieth century, and indeed was an aspect of Western imperialism, for example with the use of British warships in the Red Sea in support of operations against Mahdists in Sudan, as in 1884.

In particular, in the process that had started in the 1820s, naval power became more significant than hitherto in internal waterways. Steam enabled ships to move upstream. Iron ships were more potent than their wooden predecessors: far less vulnerable to tropical parasites, less prone to catch fire, lighter, and stronger, the last important if they ran aground. Although liable to damage and technical problems, the French used steam gunboats on the rivers of West and Equatorial Africa, including two gunboats on the Niger when they successfully advanced on Timbuktu in 1894. Gunboats linked France's riverine forts. The Dutch used gunboats in Borneo and the Portuguese on the Rivers Limpopo and Zambezi in Mozambique. The Portuguese gunboats both supported military campaigns and sought to stop gunrunning to their opponents by European freebooters. In 1898, having helped the British army's advance on the Mahdists, leading to the Battle of Omdurman, in which they played a role, five gunboats took the commander, General Kitchener, to Fashoda on the Upper Nile in order to intimidate the smaller French force that had advanced there overland from the west.

Until the 1890s, even the strongest navies employed fully rigged screw steamers to show the flag on non-European stations. Navies were faced with the dilemma of maintaining fairly distinct forces in home waters (an armored battleship-centered fleet) and on colonial/overseas stations: a hodgepodge of unarmored ships and gunboats whose fighting value was relatively far less.

What was seen, highly misleadingly, as the "white man's burden" could also be used to justify naval expenditure in support of colonial policing, for example against pirates, slavers, and smugglers. This gave delegated diplomatic authority to relatively junior officers. Much of the gunboat activity was by relatively small ships, such as the British schooners on the coast of British Columbia, which overawed Native Americans. Britain's Australian colonies acquired gunboats in 1882: the origin of British colonial navies and one very much focused on regional goals.

Operations against pirates were wide ranging. Those by the British on the Malayan coast enabled them to extend their influence way beyond their Straits Settlements—Penang, Singapore, and Malacca—and, combined with these positions, gave Britain the dominant position on the route between the

Indian Ocean and the Far East, a route currently threatened by China. The British presence in waters off north Borneo and South China owed much to such operations against pirates.

This activity is a reminder of the extent to which navies were the sharp end of aggressive foreign and imperial policies, and much of the naval action experienced by the commanders who were to lead in the First World War came from such coastal operations. Western publics saw this process in blinkered terms, which encouraged the British, in particular, in their cozy assumptions about naval power as exemplary. Yet, alongside the pirates and slavers who were pursued, came, for example, art and other treasures seized by sailors, as well as other forms of disruption stemming from the use of naval power.

In the late nineteenth century, non-Western powers looked to the West. This process had begun earlier in some cases, notably the Ottoman Empire (Turkey), but it now gathered pace. For example, Japan and Turkey were among the powers that turned to Britain for naval advice. In Japan, where a naval academy was established in 1871, admission, by the end of the century, was on merit, which was an important step toward naval professionalism. Whereas the army looked to French and, later, German models and military missions, the navy looked to Britain for warships and training. In 1871, Heihachirō Tōgō, who was to defeat the Russian fleet at Tsushima in 1905, arrived in Britain for training, while, in 1873, a Royal Navy training mission arrived in Japan. Japanese warships were also sent on training cruises to America or Europe. In 1874, Formosa (Taiwan), a Chinese territory, was unsuccessfully attacked by Japan, while Russian expansion in the Kuriles and Sakhalin, islands to the north of Japan, helped lead to pressure in Japan for a naval buildup.

So also with the Turks and the response to Russian expansionism. The Turks developed a steam navy, including ships on the Danube. When, in 1914, all foreign warships being built in British yards were sequestered, these included two large battleships being prepared for the Turkish navy. William Armstrong (1810–1900), the British armaments king, who built warships on the River Tyne, entertained foreign rulers seeking arms deals, including Nasir-ud-Din, the shah of Persia, in 1889, and Rama V, king of Siam (Thailand), in 1897. From 1881, when the Chilean *Esmeralda* was laid down, Armstrong's works at Elswick built cruisers for Argentina, Austria, Chile, China, Italy, Japan, and the United States. Persia, however, found the British reluctant to provide warships, and anyway could not afford to purchase a battleship. Britain remained the dominant naval power in the Gulf, and Persia had few, and only weak, warships into the twentieth century.[21] A similar process could be seen within the West, with the shipbuilding states dominating a system that others could only enter on their terms, albeit that competition between the major states was the crucial element. Despite rivalry with

France, Germany (which sold two small warships to Persia and two battle-ships to China), and the United States, Britain, the world's leading shipbuild-er, remained the major supplier of warships to other powers, and notably outside Europe.

Some non-Western powers failed to develop naval strength. An impres-sive regional naval power in the late sixteenth century, with technically ad-vanced ships then including early ironclads, Korea, under the Joseon dynasty from the seventeenth to the early nineteenth century, was not indifferent to its naval forces. However, chronic shortages of money and manpower continu-ously frustrated governmental efforts at a naval buildup. Because many peo-ple were reluctant to serve in the navy, they increasingly bought exemptions. As a result, the Korean navy's ability to act as a fighting force deteriorated seriously.

The clash with an armed American merchantman, the *General Sherman*, that had sought to open up Korea to trade in 1866; the French expedition to Korea that year; and the destructive American expedition of two warships to Korea in 1871 in revenge for the burning of the *General Sherman* aroused the Korean government's sense of crisis.[22] In all three of these incidents, the traditional navy performed virtually no defensive role. As a result, there were several attempts to strengthen the navy in order to provide coastal defense. These attempts included the construction and repair of traditional warships (including an ironclad "turtle" ship of the sixteenth century), as well as an increase in the size of the navy and an improvement in the treatment of sailors. In addition to constructing traditional warships, the Korean govern-ment tried to build a steamer using the remains of the *General Sherman* as a model, although this effort was unsuccessful.

However, the Korean government was short on money, mainly due to its disastrous economic policies. As a result, it could not strengthen the navy and the palace guard units simultaneously. After 1874, defense policy was mainly focused on the protection of the royal palace, which meant strength-ening the guards, a priority similar to that of some "Third World" states today. In consequence, the budget for naval development was greatly cur-tailed and the Korean government essentially left its coastal defense to the navy of China, its traditional patron and its protection against Japanese attack when last attempted in the 1590s. However, China was no longer able to protect Korea effectively. In the 1890s, the Korean government once again began to pay attention to its coastal defense. Well aware of the deficiencies of the traditional navy, the government tried to purchase several modern vessels, to establish a royal naval academy, and to invite military instructors from Britain. As a result, two Royal Navy personnel, William Callwell and James Curtis, arrived in Korea in 1894. However, political turmoil due to the internal peasant rebellion (1894) as well as the outbreak of the Sino-Japanese

War (1894–95) hindered effective military education until the contracts with the British instructors terminated in 1895.

The Korean government attempted its final effort at naval modernization when it proclaimed an empire in 1897. As a part of this effort, the government tried to purchase two modern warships from Japan: one of them turned out to be an old freight vessel which Japan purchased from Britain. This final effort was frustrated for at least two reasons. First, the emperor, his ministers, and his officers had no knowledge about a modern navy or, indeed, modern warfare. They also had no viable plan for naval development apart from the purchase of ships. Secondly, the financial footing of the government was very weak due to the lack of modern industry and to corruption. Therefore, the Korean navy remained extremely tenuous until its armed forces were disbanded by Japan in 1907 following Japan's success in the Russo-Japanese War of 1904–5, a success that led to the Japanese takeover of Korea. Naval modernization had eventually failed, partly due to a lack of funds but mostly due to geopolitics, notably Japanese dominance.

In Siam (Thailand), the navy was modernized by using American and British steamships. Rama IV (r. 1851–68) and Rama V (1868–1910) employed British and German officers to train and operate their "Westernized" navy. There was one ironclad steamship named *Pittayamronaynth*, which was built in Scotland. The other warships were wooden steamships equipped with modern breech-loading Armstrong guns. Steamship engines were imported from Britain and the ships assembled in Siam. Under Rama III (r. 1824–51), who, in an arms race with Vietnam, focused on cannon-armed sailing ships, there had been an unsuccessful attempt to build steamships locally. The navy also had torpedo boats: Rama V imported three Japanese ones in 1908. Ironclad steamships remained the minority among Siamese steamship gunboats into the twentieth century. The navy suffered a major humiliation at French hands in 1893, with several gunboats severely damaged by French warships with their superior firepower and accuracy. Thus, the "modernized" navy had failed to provide any strategic advantage even as a "fleet-in-being" deterrent. France made territorial gains as a result.

Another would-be modernizer, King Kalākaua of Hawaii commissioned and fitted out a sometime guano trader as a warship, the *Ka'imcloa*. Intended as a training vessel for the fledging Hawaiian navy, this was equipped with four brass cannon and two Gatling guns. The captain was British, and the standing regulations for the British navy were adopted for its Hawaiian counterpart, which was designed to give effect to the plan for a Pacific confederation of Hawaii, Samoa, Tonga, and the Cook Islands, intended to prevent Western annexation; to that end, the ship was sent to Samoa in 1887. Germany saw this as interference in its plans, and German warships shadowed the *Ka'imcloa*. There was no conflict. Faced by serious indiscipline among the crew, the Hawaiian vessel was recalled and mothballed.[23]

Other powers were more successful, most clearly Japan, which benefited from resources, political cohesion, governmental determination, a lack of hostile foreign interference, and the assistance of Britain, the leading naval power. This assistance was particularly valuable in the shape of training. Japan was successful at sea and on land, both against China in 1894–95 and against Russia in 1904–5. In 1894–95, the well-trained Japanese fleet won the Battle of the Yalu River (September 1894) over the less speedy and maneuverable Chinese. The Chinese squadron took refuge in the fortified harbor of Weihaiwei where, in January 1895, it was destroyed by a Japanese invasion force that was able to bombard it with artillery: anchorages were now more exposed by the greater range and power of artillery. Despite their efforts in the "Self-Strengthening" movement, the Chinese had not adequately responded to technological developments and had been affected by the high cost of warship manufacture as well as by corruption and maladministration. In the war, the Japanese also benefited from amphibious capability, as in their capture of the Pescadores Islands. However, the geopolitical context of naval (and land) power was shown by the successful pressure from Russia, Germany, and France on Japan to limit its gains.

In turn, in the more dramatic and larger-scale Russo-Japanese War, big twelve-inch guns on the Japanese warships inflicted the damage at sea. Much of the fighting was on land in Manchuria, but Japan won key battles at sea. Japanese victory on August 10, 1904, at the Battle of the Yellow Sea, with the Japanese turning back the Russian attempt to break out of the besieged fortress-port of Port Arthur, was followed at Tsushima on May 27, 1905, by an outstanding triumph: all ten Russian battleships there were sunk or taken, whereas Japan only lost three torpedo boats. The Russian fleet, which had been largely outclassed by superior (mostly larger, faster, and newer) Japanese ships, especially numerous cruisers, and by better-trained crew, was destroyed, not damaged. Just as with American naval victories over Spain in 1898, but far more spectacularly, Tsushima appeared to vindicate Mahanian ideas: a high-sea encounter would occur, it could be a decisive battle, and the result would then affect the fate of nations. Aside from the highly important consequences of the battle for Japan, Russia, Korea, and China, the Russian global threat to the British Empire was lessened while Japanese expansion in the Pacific was foreshadowed. Russia's military reputation was far higher than that of Spain, and its ambitions bolder, and therefore the international impact of the war was far greater than the defeat of Spain. So also with the impact on Germany's naval position in the Baltic (and therefore by extension elsewhere) and with the long-term position of the navy in Russian military culture.

In practical terms, however, Japanese success in the war, a success that left Japan dominant in Manchuria and able to annex Korea, was not simply due to victory at sea. Indeed, the Battle of the Yellow Sea was important because the Japanese siege of Port Arthur led to the loss of four Russian battleships and two cruisers to Japanese siege guns, while another battleship was scuttled when Port Arthur surrendered on January 2, 1905. This surrender meant that the Russian fleet had fewer options for refuge when engaged in the Battle of Tsushima.

Tsushima, and the subsequent cult of the victorious Japanese commander, Tōgō, proved misleading when it was employed to argue that a sweeping victory in battle would result in success in war. This was an attitude that helped lead the Japanese to the foolish attack on America at Pearl Harbor in 1941. In 1905, there were, in practice, other factors explaining Japanese success. These included not only the conflict on land in Manchuria, but also the fiscal pressures affecting Russia, as well as the internal opposition there that in part was stirred up by the Japanese secret service as well as the serious pressures resulting from the land war in Manchuria. As a reminder of the problems of extrapolating success from naval victory, Japan itself faced serious difficulties, both in financing the war and in the campaigning on land in Manchuria, and was unable to force the Russians to the negotiating table. At the strategic level, while Tsushima prevented Russia from mounting naval attacks on Japan and on Japanese supply routes to Korea, it could not ensure victory in the war.

Tsushima, nevertheless, helped make the Japanese navy popular, linking it with views on the national destiny as well as encouraging politicians to associate themselves with the navy, which in turn helped secure its expansion. As such, the battle gave Japan a version of the naval confidence and ethos seen in Britain and also served to act like the victories of 1898 for the United States. After the war, the idea of a ratio in the size of the Japanese fleet, vis-à-vis that of the United States, was to be advanced. This idea was to be influential until the Second World War.

The battles of the Yellow Sea and Tsushima led many commentators and planners to conclude (correctly) that, due to new advances in range finding and gun sighting, future battleship engagements would be fought at a great distance. The battleships would therefore be outside the range of torpedoes. This situation reinforced the case for the heavily armored, all-big-gun battleships, as these guns permitted hits at unprecedented distances.[24] Accuracy, however, was a different matter, and this underlined the unpredictability of the situation.

THE *DREADNOUGHT* AND THE NAVAL RACE

The case for the all-big-gun battleship was to be embodied by the British *Dreadnought*. Designed before Tsushima, but apparently validated by it and completed in 1906, the *Dreadnought* had ten twelve-inch guns paired in five turrets. The first of a new class of all-big-gun battleships, it was the first capital ship in the world to be powered by the marine turbine engine. In the design of the ship, technology was reimagined as a scientific means to ensure efficiency and economy, notably in speed and firepower.

Whereas the *Inflexible* completed in 1881 had taken seven years to build, the *Dreadnought* was completed in one year, with some judicious spin about exactly when her keel was laid and how long she took to fit out, a process helped by using guns and mountings originally ordered for other vessels. This spin was intended to produce a propaganda coup that was designed to demonstrate the futility of seeking to match Britain in a naval race. The effect was similar to the building of the American Liberty ship *Robert E. Peary* within four and a half days in the Second World War. The effect was heightened in 1906 by the secrecy of the design and of other aspects of the project. This effort reflected the belief in a "silver bullet" or technological trump card, which forced other players out by overawing or bankrupting them. The word used by Sir John Fisher, the First Sea Lord, was "plunging," which was less a belief in a single trump card than in a process of escalating one-upmanship. [25]

The public image of naval capability and proficiency, an image that helped to foster popular support, was matched by a determination to use the news in order to underline an impression of power, an impression resting on the fact that the Royal Navy was the most powerful instrument of naval force afloat. This use helped feed the increase in printed discussion of naval issues in Britain from 1904–5. The role of perception was institutionalized by the presence of naval attachés that reported on developments. The attachés were the legitimate end of information-gathering processes that became increasingly systematic. In part, this was because of the possibility that other states could alter their relative position by new developments. Naval espionage became much more important in this period, and the British kept a close eye on the number and design of major warships that Germany was building. [26]

Whatever the spin, no battleship of the size of the *Dreadnought* had ever been built so quickly. Her construction reflected the industrial and organizational efficiency of British shipbuilding. This was an efficiency linked to the well-organized responsive discipline that characterized the Royal Navy as a system of command and coordination. A range of values played a role. Fisher's support for the development of the *Dreadnought* rested in part on his determination to achieve change and his conviction of the moral as well as practical worth of efficiency. Fisher's strong Protestant faith, Liberal Unionist political commitment to a rational and mighty British Empire, and interest in electrical equipment, and technology writ large, all combined in his interest in, and understanding of, efficiency. For Fisher, warships were efficient machines for concentrated firepower and an aspect of a total reform package that included improved officer training and the scrapping of obsolete ships in order to focus on modern ones.[27] In contrast to earlier unsustainable deficit spending, the reform of the tax system by the Liberal government led to an increase in revenue that permitted greater expenditure on both warships and old-age pensions. Both also offered an economic stimulus program. Moreover, naval shipbuilding had positive economic effects. The ships required special steel and other high-technology equipment, the producers gained experience, production facilities were built, and it was possible to use the knowledge and capability on nonmilitary products.

The emphasis on the battleships interacted with that over how best to protect Britain. There was a long-standing dispute, both between army and navy and within each. Broadly speaking in the late Victorian British army, Field Marshal Frederick Roberts offered a "continental view" based on India and her army (allegedly "an English barracks in an Eastern Sea"), and, in contrast, Field Marshal Sir Garnet Wolseley offered a "maritime" strategy based on the Royal Navy and the home army.[28] In the years leading up to 1914, Roberts, then the most distinguished former commander, whose fame had risen with his success in the Boer War (1899–1902), opposed the "blue water" school's belief that the navy would protect the country from any possible German invasion and predicted that they would be able to land a large force. Roberts encouraged William Le Queux to write *The Invasion of 1910* in support of Roberts' campaign for compulsory military service. In line with his argument during the late nineteenth century that the navy would frustrate any French or Russian attempt to invade Britain, Roberts (rightly) presumed that Germany was a greater threat than France or Russia had been.

The rising cost of battleships and cruisers posed a major financial burden for Britain, a burden that was more pressing as a consequence of the great cost of the Boer War of 1899–1902. The new class both offered the possibility of a different navy and made the Royal Navy's existing numerical superiority in first-class capital ships disappear: with their pre-dreadnoughts obsolete (albeit not immediately), this superiority had to be rebuilt and, in the meanwhile, could be challenged by other powers. In theory, fewer, newer, more powerful ships would be less expensive, but both dreadnoughts and battle cruisers cost more than the ships they replaced and therefore sent the cost of the estimates spiraling. Moreover, the problem that a warship cannot be in two places at once remained. Even though a battle cruiser might be used both to patrol the seaways for trade defense and also to protect the British Isles against invasion, it could not do both at the same time. Thus, warships for both functions were required in large numbers. Compared to the dreadnoughts, there was no comparable reconceptualization and restructuring of the army.

The volatility of the situation was underlined by the significant increase in the range of naval guns. As the distance of engagement rose, accuracy became more of a problem. This provided opportunities for lightly protected ships firing with a degree of impunity but posed major issues for accurate range finding. A number of systems were on offer, for example, in Britain, those of Arthur Pollen and Frederic Dreyer, both of whose systems incorporated the single-use calculator designed by John Dumaresq. After extensive testing, the Royal Navy concluded that the Dreyer system better suited their needs. Whether they were right in a choice that affected gunnery in the First World War is a matter of controversy, but they made an informed choice.

Competitive emulation between navies set the pace in Europe, the Pacific, and elsewhere. This emulation both fitted into, and accentuated, already-potent public governmental and popular concern with naval strength. Manifestations included the development of naval leagues, as well as the extensive celebration of warship launches. These leagues were popular movements for stronger navies that were pushed by governments, special interests, and committed publicists. That in Britain was founded in 1894. The extensive celebration of warship launches was also significant. The vast crowds that attended launches, especially in Britain and Germany, but also elsewhere, were joined by those who read about them in the illustrated press or watched early newsreels. Over 2.5 million visitors thronged to the naval exhibition on the Thames embankment in London in May to October 1891. Navalism affected journalism, fiction, and writing for children.[29]

This process was significant to the creation of mass constituencies for naval power, and these were seen as important, given the need to vote substantial sums through representative bodies. Thus, naval power was reconceptualized for a new democratic, or at least populist, age. There were expectations that in any war the drama of the launch of large warships, and the dominant theme was one of scale, would be replicated in naval conflict. The status of size has a modern equivalent with the cult of the aircraft carrier. This status sits alongside, and possibly in part conditions, rational discussion of the merits of these warships.

The *Dreadnought* was faster and more heavily gunned than any other battleship then sailing and made the earlier arithmetic of relative naval capability redundant. This redundancy encouraged the Germans to respond, although their *Nassau* class, laid down from 1907 (when the Germans increased their construction rate from three to four large ships per annum), put more of a stress on protection than armaments, for what was believed would be close-range clashes, and did not use turbines. At the same time, the expense, and therefore opportunity costs, of the apparent need to respond to the British put major pressure on the Reichstag's support for naval plans.

The German navy, the fourth in number of battleships in 1905,[30] was the second-largest navy in the world in 1914; although virtually in a tie with the United States. From the 1898 German Naval Law and its subsequent implementation, although there was still concern in Britain about France and Russia, the British Admiralty was aware that Germany's naval building program might become Britain's foremost maritime threat. This was both a quantitative and a qualitative judgment. The Royal Navy was very unimpressed by Russian ships, training, and nautical bearing, but nobody doubted German engineering capabilities. The Russian navy was hit very hard by Japan in 1904–5, and relations between Britain and both France and Russia greatly improved.

In the event, Britain won the naval race with Germany,[31] as it had also beaten France in the mid-nineteenth century. In 1909, in response to governmental and press concern about German moves, Britain was able to lay down eight dreadnoughts in place of the four per year still sought by many ministers. In 1906–12, Britain launched twenty-nine capital ships and Germany seventeen. Helped by having a much higher earlier basis of naval expenditure, Britain was both willing to pay to win the new battleship race and was also prepared to invest in fast warships: four *Invincible*-class armored cruisers (only three were built) were authorized at the same time as the *Dreadnought*.

These cruisers were intended to permit a rapid reaction to crises around the world, a reaction that would be aided by improved communications. These well-armed cruisers, later reclassified as battle cruisers in 1911, were in part designed to meet the threat to trade from Germany's fast ocean liners and the danger that the latter could be armed for commerce raiding.[32] The former were faster than the warships afloat, had reinforced decks, and had crews that included many naval reservists. A broader threat environment was at issue. The rising cost and size of armored cruisers and Britain's determination to have clear superiority in this class necessitated their further development of battle cruisers to maintain control of the imperial seas, where cruisers, rather than battleships, were Britain's main enemy. These battle cruisers may have been the initial British preference for new capital ships and were, for a while, possibly intended to be the capital ships of the future. They entered service in mid-1908.[33] The capital ships were to be supplemented by the use of submarines and torpedo boats for the defense of home waters and therefore, to use modern terms, "A2/AD" (anti-access/area-denial) systems.

The rapid expansion of the German battle fleet, combined with improved relations between Britain and France from 1904 and Russia from 1907, led to a British strategic, operational, and tactical emphasis on how best to win a battleship struggle with Germany in the North Sea. The Royal Navy created a North Sea Home Fleet in 1902 and added progressively to its North Sea forces thereafter. The aggressive German rhetoric in the 1905 Moroccan crisis helped focus British concern on Germany. In contrast, competition with France in the Mediterranean was no longer crucial for Britain. Moreover, British strategic worries elsewhere were greatly eased by alliance with Japan from 1902. This greatly lessened Britain's strategic concerns, both in the Pacific and about Russia. Improved relations with the United States were also significant. In 1908, the Committee of Imperial Defence and the Foreign Office concluded that the possibility of war with the United States was remote. In 1911, during the second Moroccan crisis, British ministers feared a surprise German attack on the British fleet.

Against Germany, the British emphasis until 1912 was on a blockade, both as a vital means of economic warfare and also as a means to deny German warships access to the oceans and/or to force the German fleet to sea. It has been argued that the preferred British tactic was a major pulse of firepower which required battleships.[34] However, this interpretation has been strongly challenged.[35] As an aspect of the broadly based nature of British maritime strength, British plans for blockade and, crucially, trade protection included armed merchant cruisers.[36] Antisubmarine operations in the North Sea were part of the equation.[37]

While in Britain, naval policy was very much affected by political divisions, related social-cultural assumptions, and partisanship within the navy,[38] in Germany, the naval race was closely tied to the ambitions, interests, and ideology of its protagonist, the Anglophobe Admiral Alfred von Tirpitz, the state secretary of the Imperial Naval Office from 1897 to 1916, who sought to turn the German navy into his own empire in order to make Germany the dominant empire. Naval officers who disagreed with Tirpitz were replaced by his protégés from his time running the Torpedo Branch, the so-called Torpedo Gang.[39] Factionalism was frequently important in naval command systems. Tirpitz was supported by the Anglophobic Emperor Wilhelm II (the head of the navy), who was greatly impressed by Mahan's work. However, the policy failed to command support across the political spectrum. The Social Democratic Party, which did well in the January 1912 Reichstag elections, was particularly opposed, not least because the Tirpitz Plan challenged their interpretation of the role of the Reichstag. As far as some of the other politicians were concerned, however, Tirpitz co-opted, rather than challenged, the Reichstag.

The bigger British second-generation (super-)dreadnoughts put even greater pressure on the Reichstag's support for a naval race. The combination of this unexpected, although in practice predictable, British resolve in opposing the German naval buildup; the development of Russian military capability, including for movement of forces toward Germany's frontiers by the means of railways; and the passage of French legislation designed to strengthen the army caused momentum within the German military and political leaderships, and in the dominant parties in the Reichstag, to move back in favor of the army. This situation was reflected in the successful German Army Bill of 1913, which was, in effect, a unilateral German declaration of naval arms limitation, albeit at a very high level of annual naval construction. The army's emphasis on the needs of a two-front war on land, with France and Russia, interacted with the concern about naval costs felt by Theobald von Bethmann-Hollweg, who became chancellor in 1909; by the Foreign Office; and by successive treasury secretaries.

Moreover, Tirpitz's tactical, operational, and strategic assumptions and planning were greatly flawed, and this undercut his achievements in training and procurement. Germany also faced serious and structural strategic problems in establishing itself as a sea power. Its distance from the Atlantic posed a key problem, as did the intervening position of the British navy. Germany also had only a relatively narrow coastal position on the North Sea, while the Russian navy posed a challenge in the Baltic where its navy was concentrated.

More generally, the wisdom of German policy was highly problematic as, aside from diverting resources from the army, this policy helped cement Britain's position in the anti-German camp, a situation that otherwise would not have been obvious. Britain, indeed, had no grand strategic alternative to a commitment to naval power. As an imperial maritime power, Britain had to dominate its key strategic environment. Therefore, the German policy of challenging British security was highly provocative. On May 18, 1912, Winston Churchill, the First Lord of the Admiralty in 1911–15 and 1939–40, both offered Germany a cessation of capital ship construction and warned that, if Germany added more capital ships to its existing program, Britain, in its program, would double each additional German ship. Germany rejected the proposal, which Churchill twice repeated in public in 1913. [40]

Tirpitz and Wilhelm II were determined opponents of Britain. Indeed, both wanted more money for the navy and more warships. However, the German commitment to battleships was based on a serious failure to understand the respective strength of the naval powers and the potential of the German navy. The British focus on Germany in turn had implications elsewhere, notably in the development of Dominion navies within the British Empire. Canada decided to create its own navy in 1910, seeing it as an expression of sovereignty. Established in 1911, the Royal Australian Navy gained *Australia*, a British-built battle cruiser, two years later. These navies represented an attempt to influence imperial policy, notably against Japan, as well as a potent testimony to the role of navalism in feelings of sovereignty. [41]

GLOBAL DEVELOPMENTS, 1906–13

While Britain and Germany competed, the rest of the world scarcely stood still. Indeed, part of the significance of the Anglo-German naval race rested on its wider resonance, which included not only the example of naval strength and development, but also the production of warships for friendly powers, which provided a way to share costs, test technology, and gain influence. There was actually little warfare involving military actions by warships, certainly compared to the activity in 1898–1905. The most important conflict was the First Balkan War of 1912–13. In this, the Greek navy, which had been developed from the 1880s with French expertise, loans, and warships, cut Turkish communications in the Aegean Sea and covered amphibious attacks there that resulted in the capture of islands including Lemnos, Chios, and Samos. Less spectacularly, the Bulgarian navy cut Turkish communications in the Black Sea, which increased the pressure on the Turks in the Balkans. As part of the crisis of Turkish power, the Italian navy supported the invasion of Libya, a Turkish colony, in 1911 and also attacks on Turkish islands in the Aegean, notably Rhodes. Tripoli was isolated and bombarded, Turkey blockaded, and the Italian navy also operated off Lebanon, in the Red Sea, and in the Adriatic.

Other powers that had larger fleets did not take part in naval warfare in this period. France, by 1914, had dropped from second to fifth among the world's navies, in part as a result of the major expansion of new German and American naval power. However, in the wake of the launch of the *Dreadnought*, the French shifted to battleships from enthusiasm for the ships advocated by the *Jeune École*, under whose influence French experience in building, crewing, and operating battleships had fallen. These battleships now appeared necessary because, with Britain confronting Germany in the North Sea, France needed to be able to resist any moves by Germany's allies, Austria and Italy, both of which had increased their navies. The Mediterranean theater led to the construction of a specific kind of ship that lacked the range to operate outside of that sea. Founded in 1904, the Austrian Navy League was instrumental in the increase of the Austrian naval budget and in a program of dreadnought construction that touched off a naval race with Italy and affected France. In addition, France's colonial competition with Italy in North Africa was a factor, as was the need to protect the key Algiers–Marseilles route. This route would be needed in the event of war in order to move troops from North Africa, where Algeria was France's leading colony, to France.[42] Meanwhile, Russia sought to rebuild its fleet after its defeats at the hands of Japan.[43]

THE UNITED STATES

The Spanish-American War of 1898 had been followed with great attention by an often stridently nationalistic American public. The culture of print rushed to inform. For example, the "Strategic Map of Our War with Spain" provided distances and listed principal American and Spanish vessels, as well as pins and discs so that these vessels could be located and moved. The war encouraged the already strong development of American navalism.[44]

The buildup of American naval power from the 1880s and, even more, 1890s with the "New American Navy" owed much to East Coast industrial interests, especially Pennsylvania shipyards and steelworks, linked to politicians and commentators keen not only to present America as a great power, but also as able to take a central role in global power politics. Presidents Benjamin Harrison (1889–93) and Theodore Roosevelt (1901–9) were strong supporters of the naval buildup. The latter was responsible for the establishment of the Charleston Navy Yard in 1902, a base that supported power projection into the Caribbean.[45] These developments were the culmination of a period of evolution in ship types and strategy from the mid-1870s.

The Spanish-American War was followed by increased investment in the navy, which became the world's third largest. From the late 1880s, the navy developed a concept of offensive sea control by a battleship fleet and pressed successfully for the launching and maintenance of an offensive battle fleet in peacetime. It also developed a military-industrial complex and a chain of protected bases from the Atlantic to the Pacific via Panama in order to be able to support a large fleet in the Pacific. The Panama Canal became a key project for American naval power, with some valuable economic side effects. The fleet of a potential enemy could be restricted to one ocean while the American fleet could move between them.[46]

The dispatch of a fleet, the "Great White Fleet," to show the flag by sailing around the world in 1907–9 was significant as an affirmation and means of power, and the fleet had a major impact along its route, for example in Australia.[47] The Americans laid down their first dreadnought in 1906, the Japanese following with two in 1909. Concern about an apparent threat from Japan to America's new Pacific interests provided a justification for the new American investment. Moreover, the resulting geopolitics of energy supplies affected the nature of American warships, and not only them. By 1909, American battleships were being designed with larger coal bunkers allowing a steaming radius of ten thousand nautical miles,[48] which was a major increase on the range of the 1890s. However, the testing of engines by the American navy from 1898 led, in 1913, to the adoption of a policy of only building ships with oil-firing steam engines.

Although the United States produced large quantities of coal in West Virginia and Kentucky, America lacked the necessary colliers, while the network of bunkering coal merchants around the world, and also many of the colliers, were under the control of Britain which, from 1902, was an ally of Japan. As the circumnavigation of the world in 1907–9 revealed, the American fleet could not cross the Pacific without British coal. The "Great White Fleet" was not the sole instance of the American navy gaining experience in mass long-distance movements: in the decade before 1914, the navy was also regularly holding maneuvers in the Azores and Caribbean. The Russian fleet sunk at Tsushima in 1905 had sailed from the Baltic, being recoaled on its long voyage by sixty German colliers from the Hamburg-Amerika Line, generally on the high sea since the Russians had no permission to enter neutral harbors. This proved that a large fleet of capital ships could be supported without a friendly harbor, a lesson the American navy took forward.

The American navy helped greatly in imposing control in the Philippines in the early 1900s. It also enabled the United States to project its power in Latin America, while also encouraging American interest in the development of the Panama Canal, which was taken over from France and finally finished in 1914. In 1894, a strong naval demonstration had a powerful impact on the civil war in Brazil, which was a blow to British influence there.[49] American naval power also played a major role in the Venezuelan crisis. Warships carried a marine expeditionary force to ensure a peaceful (albeit coerced) election in the Panama Canal Zone in 1908, represented the United States at the inauguration of the new Cuban president in 1909, and landed marines in Cuba in 1912. In 1913, a policy of keeping three or four battleships in Mexican waters was followed as a means of supporting American interests in Mexico. The navy supported the landing of marines at Veracruz in Mexico in 1914 and also the occupation of the Dominican Republic in 1916. Guantanamo Bay in Cuba was retained as a sovereign base after the Spanish-American War, as it remains.

Meanwhile, although there were serious deficiencies, notably in hydrographic knowledge[50] and base improvement, American naval effectiveness was improving. As inspector of gunnery training from 1902 to 1907, William Sims greatly reduced firing times and improved accuracy. His belief in gunnery was encouraged by his reporting as an observer of the Russo-Japanese War of 1904–5, a conflict that was very important to contemporary views of naval potential, as well as encouraging widespread concern about Japan. Like other navies, the American one had to respond to a rapidly changing technological context, for example the introduction of torpedoes with a range of ten thousand yards, a development that challenged rigid command-and-control practices as well as forcing a need for accurate gunnery at ever-longer ranges. In responding, there was not yet the administrative centralization and doctrinal formation that ensured a greater consistency in tactics later in the century. Instead, the response was more contested and contingent.[51]

NEW TECHNOLOGY

The 1900s and early 1910s saw major changes as a result of experimentation or were linked to it. Propulsion systems were a key instance. Like the Americans, the Royal Navy followed a course toward oil-firing engines, in the British case because of the enormous technical advantages of using oil.

Whereas the United States had plenty of oil of its own, British interest encouraged intervention in the Persian Gulf to secure supplies and enhanced existing British strategic interest in the eastern Mediterranean as protection of the Suez Canal. Moreover, by 1912, the Royal Navy had begun to install geared turbines in its destroyers.

Other changes were to be even more significant, notably the introduction of naval aviation and radio. In the United States, the Jamestown Exposition of 1907 saw attempts by pilots and engineers to demonstrate the usefulness of aircraft to the American navy. The first aircraft takeoff from a ship occurred there in November 1910, and the first landing on a ship the following January. The potential for armament was rapidly pursued in America, with Glenn Curtiss playing the key role. Dummy bombs used on target ships in June 1910 were soon followed by live ones, and the trials, moreover, saw the employment of primitive bomb-aiming sights. Curtis also developed seaplanes. Strategic implications were rapidly suggested. In 1910, a reflective American admiral, Bradley Fiske, felt able to propose that the defense of the distant and recently conquered Philippines should be left to air power. He sought to develop torpedo-carrying aircraft.[52]

Naval requirements were to the fore for Britain in the adoption of new weaponry and in devising plans and methods to benefit from, but also to counter, it.[53] In Bernard Partridge's cartoon "Neptune's Ally," published in the British magazine *Punch* on May 25, 1914, Winston Churchill, the ever-active First Lord of the Admiralty, was depicted as blowing aircraft and airships forward to aid Neptune and the Royal Navy in protecting Britain from invasion. The first British airship in 1911 was followed in 1912 by the first launch of a British seaplane. Churchill played a central role in the formation of the Royal Naval Air Service (RNAS), devoting considerable attention to the details and displaying a conspicuous personal interest that was shown in his flying over the fleet in 1914. In 1913, Churchill pressed for the fitting of radios in seaplanes.[54] In a pattern that was to be all too typical of air power, his interest was competitive, with a clear argument that naval air power was more significant than the land equivalent. On February 10, 1914, Churchill wrote,

> The objectives of land aeroplanes can never be so definite or important as the objectives of seaplanes, which, when they carry torpedoes, may prove capable of playing a decisive part in operations against capital ships. The facilities of reconnaissance at sea, where hostile vessels can be sighted at enormous distances while the seaplane remains out of possible range, offer a far wider prospect even in the domain of information to seaplanes than to land aeroplanes, which would be continually brought under rifle and artillery fire.[55]

This was highly perceptive given the critical importance of intelligence in naval warfare, as such warfare is less about maneuver than about finding and striking within a vast oceanic environment. In 1912, the Royal Navy carried out trials to discover if submarines could be detected and attacked from the air. Given the capacity to carry bombs and the size of the aircraft, the job of submarine hunting in the close vicinity of a land base was possible, but further range was limited.

Integration with other services and goals was a significant theme. By 1914, with the active support of Churchill, the Eastchurch naval air station had created a defensive system in which British aircraft fitted with radios cooperated with ground observers. At the start of the war, the Royal Naval Air Service numbered thirty-nine aircraft, fifty-two seaplanes, seven airships, and about 120 pilots. The French had the first warship able to transport seaplanes: the *Foudre*, modified in December 1911, entered active service in August 1912 and transported four seaplanes in 1914.

Naval powers also responded to the transforming potential offered by radio, which developed swiftly in the 1890s and, more especially, once Guglielmo Marconi sent radio signals over three thousand miles across the Atlantic in 1901. Already in 1899, the British Admiralty had made extensive experiments during the summer maneuvers. These led the Admiralty to decide to provide warships with radios. Britain was not alone. In 1912–14, Germany developed a highly sophisticated radio network that permitted communications with its vessels over the entire world, with the exception of a dark spot on the western side of the Americas. This system offered an alternative to the use of telegraph cables laid on the floor of the ocean, cables that could readily be cut, as was to be the case by the British in 1914. Radio, the origin of modern network-centric warfare, proved a crucial tool in command and control (at least up to a point) and launched the process of increasing the amount of information that commanders had to handle and rapidly.[56]

CONCLUSION

The navies that entered the First World War therefore did so as rapidly changing bodies. This was certainly the case technologically, although the extent of tactical and operational change was as yet smaller. The buildup to 1914 was focused by an arms race of oceangoing capital ships to win the next "Trafalgar." The war that resulted was characterized, however, not so much by the major Anglo-German battle at Jutland in 1916 as by the pervasive fear of risking capital ships in mine- and submarine-infested waters; by blockade, the most cost-effective and fairly safe form of naval offensive; and then by the German submarine campaigns themselves.

The war was to expose the difficulty of predicting developments, and thus the limitations of much prewar planning and speculation. In particular, the notion of the dreadnoughts as constituting a revolution in naval warfare, an idea then applied to describe alleged earlier revolutions, was deeply problematic, as indeed was the supposed revolutionary character of these earlier revolutions.[57] It is also possible to draw links across time between weapons systems—for example, from battle cruisers to aircraft carriers and from torpedo boats to submarines—but these need to be handled with care.

Large navies were important national symbols. It was less clear, however, how far, in the event of war, it would be possible for any of them to realize command of the seas, or at least a sea, and what this would amount to. It was also unclear how far the earlier limitations of strong navies both in preventing commerce raiding and in ensuring amphibious capability had been overcome. Furthermore, the impact of naval strength and amphibious capability on conflict on land was less direct than was sometimes suggested. Compared to the period covered in chapter 1, there had been a development in doctrine and in operational planning, but the likely consequences were uncertain.

Chapter Three

The First World War, 1914–18

Germany's failure to knock France rapidly out of the war in 1914 made the First World War a conflict in which naval power was crucial even if there were no decisive naval battles in the sense of overwhelming victories. As in 1870, when France's navy had been larger than that of Germany, the German military leadership in 1914 sought a campaign and a victory on land before the equations of naval power could kick in. The territorial gains pursued by Germany were largely in Europe, although there was interest in a larger African empire. This attempt to direct the strategy of the war assumed that British entry on the side of France and Russia would not matter, as Britain would be isolated by French and Russian defeat. In the event, the German failure to knock France out in 1914 helped to ensure that the war in part became that of continental versus oceanic power. Much else was involved, but this dynamic was significant throughout and was important both to the basic strategic situation and to the outcome of the war.

1914

Thanks to the strength of the Royal Navy, which remained the largest and most powerful navy in the world throughout the conflict and the leading member of the foremost naval alliance, the British retained essential control of their home waters. They were able to avoid blockade and serious attack, although German warships bombarded English east coast towns, notably Hartlepool, Scarborough, and Whitby on December 16, 1914, causing great popular outrage by doing so. Scarborough was a seaside resort town and Whitby a fishing village. The only significant target was Hartlepool, where guns fired back and hit two of the attacking ships.

These were only raids. In contrast, Britain was able to maintain the flow of men and munitions to the army in France unmolested, to retain trade links that permitted the mobilization of British and imperial resources, and to use stop and search to impede the flow of contraband to Germany. The last was the crucial aspect of economic warfare.

On November 3, 1914, Britain declared that the North Sea would be a military area with shipping subject to Admiralty control. Germany, however, continued to receive imports at the beginning of the war through neutral ports, notably the leading Dutch port, Rotterdam. This access to trade was gradually reduced as the Allies steadily increased pressure on neutral powers to stop the lucrative practice of reexporting their imports to Germany, with particular pressure on the Dutch not to reexport food to neighboring Germany. British actions breached the Paris (1856) and London (1909) agreements on wartime trade, but they appeared necessary if economic warfare with Germany was to work. This indicated the fragility of attempts to restrain the operations of international powers. British actions were justified, on a legal basis, as reprisals for Germany's equally unlawful submarine campaign, although the British never intended to abide by the London agreement.

Economic warfare was supported by a system of preemptive purchasing, for example of Norwegian fish and pyrites, that was important to the international control of raw materials, as well as greatly influencing neutral economies. In particular, cutting off trade with Germany lessened American economic and financial interest in its success. Intelligence about shipping and commercial movements was also crucial to the blockade.[1] Economic warfare made it difficult for planners in Berlin to realize schemes for increased production. It contributed greatly to the sense of frustration and anger that increasingly affected German strategy and that, along with German failure to win on land, led to unrestricted submarine warfare. In turn, economic warfare only really became effective once the United States, hitherto the leading neutral, entered the war.

Alongside resources, geography was a key factor, with the Germans bottled up in the North Sea by Britain's location athwart their routes to the oceans. To contemporaries, this helped underline the significance of geopolitics and geostrategy. There was periodical German interest in sending cruisers out into the Atlantic, and further afield, in order to harry British trade. However, aside from the issue of coaling such ships once they were at sea (problems that could be overcome), the location of British bases was a key problem. The German route to the Atlantic was threatened by the major base of Scapa Flow in the Orkneys, which anchored the British naval position. Moreover, in 1909, a new base forward of Scapa Flow, at Rosyth on the Firth of Forth, in east Scotland, had been begun in order to help the British Grand Fleet contest the North Sea.

Ironically, Tirpitz had once believed that geography helped Germany as he anticipated a British attack on the German navy in German waters. As it was also at one stage assumed that the Royal Navy would mount a close blockade of Germany, so it was assumed that Britain would enable Germany to fight defensively, and thus employ torpedo boats against British battle-ships to deadly effect. This was regarded as a means to ensure a decisive battle. Thus, the purpose of defeating a close blockade was to wear down the Royal Navy to the point that the Germans could attack with some prospect of success. This would have been a viable strategy for the Germans, which was why the Royal Navy abandoned the close blockade. As often, there was wishful thinking that the opposing side would do what was more convenient for the commentator. The Germans did the same in their strategy toward France in 1914.[2] The Germans, anyway, failed adequately to appreciate the nature of the strategic situation, in particular the fact that Britain was part of a global maritime system, one with considerable resilience. Defeating a British close blockade could only achieve so much in that context.

While economic warfare threatened the German productive system and affected German military options, Britain's supply system was that of a country that could not feed itself; nearly two-thirds of British food consumption was imported. Britain also had an imperial economy that relied on global trade, and a military system that required troop movements within the vast empire. For example, during the war, 1.3 million men were sent to serve outside India, while 332,000 Australian troops served overseas. Canada's ability to contribute was very important to the British war effort in France. The sea constituted Britain's interior lines.

All this, and the capacity for ready responsiveness it indicated, was challenged by German warships. However, those outside Europe were hunted down by Britain and its allies in the early stages of the war. The East Asia squadron under Vice Admiral Maximilian Graf von Spee was the leading German naval force outside Europe at the outset of the war. It sailed to Chile where, off Coronel on November 1, a weaker and heavily outgunned British force under Rear Admiral Sir Christopher Cradock was defeated with the loss of two cruisers. Spee then sailed on to attack the Falkland Islands, a British colony in the South Atlantic which had, at Port Stanley, a naval base, including crucial coaling facilities. Fisher had already sent two battle cruisers and six light cruisers there to hunt Spee down. Spee, surprised, was defeated off the Falklands on December 8, with all but one of his ships sunk, although only after a prolonged chase that practically exhausted the magazines of the British battle cruisers.

Thereafter, outside Europe, the Germans only had individual warships, including armed merchant cruisers, at large, and these were eventually hunted down. As a result, the threat to the Allies from German surface raiders was essentially restricted to the opening months of the war. Indeed,

Allied success in blockading the North Sea, the English Channel, and the Adriatic (where Germany's ally Austria had a coastline in modern Croatia and Slovenia), and in capturing Germany's overseas colonies, ensured that, after the initial stages of the war, and despite the use of submarines and new surface raiders, the range of effective German naval operations was smaller than those of American and French warships when attacking British interests between 1775 and 1815. Germany would need to change its maritime geography for the situation to be different, as occurred in 1940 with the conquests of Norway and France.

Allied sea power was crucial in supporting operations against German colonies and, in particular, wireless stations and ports, with the Japanese capturing undefended German possessions in the northwest Pacific, as well as Germany's base of Tsingtao on the coast of China. Allied forces conquered German colonies in the southwest Pacific such as Samoa and German New Guinea. The British and French conquered Germany's colonies in Africa, although the British encountered great difficulties in German East Africa (modern Tanzania).[3] In 1915, exploiting their control of the Persian Gulf, British forces were landed in southern Iraq and Iran in order to oppose Turkish moves.

On August 6, 1914, Britain and France signed a naval convention under which the French navy was responsible for much of the Mediterranean and the British for the remainder of the world. As a result, there were no French warships in the North Sea, the key area of conflict between the British and German surface fleets. Aside from providing the bulk of Allied troops on the Western Front, the French role was more than might appear as it helped provide the Royal Navy with a sufficient margin of power over the Germans to survive losses. With British as well as French warships present, German and Austrian naval power was outnumbered and outclassed in the Mediterranean, which enabled France to move troops from North Africa safely and also greatly affected the military and political options for Italy.[4]

The small German squadron in the Mediterranean, the battle cruiser *Goeben* and the light cruiser *Breslau*, shelled the ports of Philippeville and Bone in the French colony of Algeria on August 4, 1914; evaded British attempts to intercept them; and took shelter with the Turks later in August. The ships entered Turkish service, and their actions against the Russians in the Black Sea helped bring Turkey into the war against the Allies at the end of October.

In the North Sea, there were surface actions in 1914, but no battle between battleships and nothing to match the struggle on land. The British had decided to rely on a distant, not a close, blockade, and this strategy denied the Germans the major struggle they sought, although the British were also determined to limit German operations in the North Sea. In the Battle of Heligoland Bight on August 28, British battle cruisers played the decisive role in an engagement that started as a clash between British and German squadrons of light cruisers and destroyers. The Germans lost three light cruisers and one destroyer. In contrast, although one British light cruiser and two destroyers were badly damaged, the fact that none was lost helped ensure that the battle was presented to the Allied public as a striking victory. In practice, it was not so much a coherent, highly structured battle but rather a series of individual ship engagements conducted in the poor visibility caused by dense fog. The British were hindered by the general lack of coordination in the Admiralty; the force composition for the raid; the limitations of, and constraints on, gunnery and torpedo skills (which ensured that the heavy use of ammunition and torpedoes brought few successes); and the quality of the British shells: many failed to explode. British torpedoes also faced problems.

Given these and other deficiencies, it is unsurprising that the British did not inflict heavier losses on the Germans in this battle. Nevertheless, all the latter's warships were outgunned by their British counterparts, while the German torpedo boats were outclassed. The Germans were also affected by serious tactical problems, and communications were an issue. In addition, there was a poor command response to the British raid and, in particular, a lack of coordination, and an inaccurate assessment of likely and actual developments. Most significantly, the battle reflected, and strengthened, a sense of psychological inferiority on the German part. This confirmed their cautious use of the fleet. The belief that the British would not send heavy units into the Bight had proved misplaced, while the Germans were both properly, and yet overly, anxious about risking their better ships, which greatly affected their response to the raid. Wilhelm II felt justified in his instructions that battle was to be sought only under the most favorable circumstances. These restrictions were now underlined.[5]

In 1914, the loss of ships to German submarines and mines cost the British more men and major ships than the Germans lost in battle, but the impact of these British losses was less dramatic in terms of the perhaps crucial sense of relative advantage. Indeed, submarines and mines appeared to be a means only to snipe at the British naval advantage rather than be an effective counter to it. Moreover, Wilhelm's restrictions helped ensure that the surface war at sea would probably be lost by Germany through limited contest. Wilhelm's tight rein was no way to challenge the British blockade, although the fleet-in-being remained a threat to Britain. The British naval war effort had suffered from an inadequate war staff, but it proved able to adapt to the strategic circumstances of 1914. By the end of 1914, foreshadowing events in the Second World War, the Allies, working in unusual concert, had cracked the three German naval codes. While the Germans appeared oblivious to this, the Royal Navy repeatedly, through slovenliness or mistrust, arguably failed to exploit this advantage to its full potential.[6]

The aircraft of the British Royal Naval Air Service conducted effective raids from Antwerp in September and October 1914. Twenty-pound bombs were dropped on Zeppelin sheds at Düsseldorf on October 8, destroying one airship. The Zeppelin base at Friedrichshafen on Lake Constance was attacked on November 21. As a result of this success, the British Admiralty developed an interest in strategic bombing.

1915

In 1915, although the Germans attacked at sea, their bold plan, to fall upon part of the British Grand Fleet with their entire High Seas Fleet, and thus achieve a superiority that would enable them to inflict serious casualties that affected the overall situation at sea, was not pursued. Instead, on January 23, a German force of four battle cruisers and four light cruisers under Admiral Franz von Hipper put to sea in order to lay mines in the Firth of Forth, threatening the British base at Rosyth, and also to attack the British fishing boats on Dogger Bank in the North Sea, boats which were correctly seen as an intelligence asset. The interception of a German naval signal led to a loss of surprise, but the British missed the opportunity to deploy their navy so as to cut off the German force and instead relied on battle cruisers, which were not inherently designed for this role. Nevertheless, the scale of the battle was bigger than that of Heligoland Bight.

On the morning of January 24, in the Battle of Dogger Bank, five British battle cruisers under Vice Admiral David Beatty engaged the Germans. However, in a stern chase, it proved inherently time consuming to close, and this problem enabled the German ships to concentrate on his leading ship, the flagship *Lion*, which took serious damage. By contrast, confused signaling by Beatty, the fear of submarine attack, and a lack of initiative by subordinate commanders, each a factor on a number of occasions during the century, ensured that the British force focused on the *Blücher*, an armored cruiser with medium guns. This was sunk, but the other German ships were able to escape and the Germans had learned valuable lessons in the deficiencies of their own ships and in how to fight the British. The British were affected by the contrast between the long range at which shells could be fired and their limited number of hits, while heavy smoke affected the optical range finding crucial to gunnery.[7] Yet, alongside these disadvantages, the British Grand Fleet was becoming both absolutely and relatively stronger, with five newly operational dreadnoughts added to it in the winter of 1914–15. At the same time, there was to be no battleship confrontation until Jutland in 1916.

There was no other battle in the North Sea in 1915 and even less surface naval warfare elsewhere. Italy's decision to abandon Germany and Austria, with which it had agreed to a naval convention in 1913, and instead to join Britain and France in May 1915 ensured that the Mediterranean was controlled by this alliance. A French squadron at Corfu off northwest Greece and most of the Italian fleet at Taranto supported by British, including Australian, warships confined Austrian surface ships to the Adriatic and sought to stop submarines from getting into the Mediterranean. In the Black Sea, the Russians had more warships than the Turks and were able to blockade the Bosporus, but no decisive blows were struck.[8]

In the Baltic, the Russian fleet was weaker than the forces the Germans could deploy if they moved in some of their High Seas Fleet units from the North Sea via the Kiel Canal. This indicated what the Americans could do at a far greater scale with the Panama Canal. Although there were battles off Riga in 1915 and 1917, this German capability encouraged Russian caution, which was also in keeping with a stress on the Russian army, with long-established Russian naval doctrine, and with the Russian emphasis in the Baltic on local naval operations. Defeat by the Japanese navy at Tsushima in 1905 was scarcely an encouragement for bolder operations. The Russians laid extensive minefields to protect the Gulf of Finland and staged raids into the southern Baltic in order to mine German shipping routes, while the Germans, in turn, also laid mines.

Although the British, prior to the war, had considered sending a fleet into the Baltic in order to help Russia, threaten an attack on northern Germany, force battle on the Germans, and cut German trade with Scandinavia, no such expedition was mounted, although planning continued, and some of the ships later used in the Dardanelles were designed and built for a prospective Baltic operation. However, the latter was both risky in itself and a diversionary challenge to the numbers necessary for British naval superiority in the North Sea. The Germans had sufficient mines and submarines to make Fisher's Baltic plans so unrealistic that more prudent Admiralty and War Department planners ignored or blocked the schemes, encouraging the emphasis on the blockade. There was also little mileage in the idea that naval power could make a material difference to operations in Flanders, an idea pushed by Churchill as First Lord of the Admiralty. Aside from the serious naval problem of operating inshore against a protected coast, there was also the difficulty posed by the strength of German forces with the mobility offered them by the railway. Fisher and Churchill did not order monitors with anti-torpedo bulges until after the war had begun, and these monitors were too late to help the British Expeditionary Force's race to the sea in 1914 or at the Dardanelles in 1915. Nor had the German navy invested much in coastal assault vessels like monitors. Once the British heavy monitors appeared off the Belgian coast, they discovered that the Germans had erected ever-heavier shore batteries that could outrange them and had the advantage in terms of ship versus shore accuracy. More generally, naval operations in the Adriatic, Baltic, and Black Seas made little difference to the course of the First World War on adjoining landmasses.

An Anglo-French fleet was given a major role in 1915. It was sent to force open the Dardanelles en route to threatening Constantinople, the Turkish capital, itself. However, this poorly planned attempt was stopped by minefields, shore batteries, and an unwillingness, in the face of the loss of ships, to accept the risk of further naval operations. There had been a misplaced belief that naval power alone could force a passage through the Dardanelles because of a serious underestimation of the Turkish minefields and the mobile shore batteries protecting them, and of the Turkish ability and willingness to resist attack. Corbett advised against operating without a combination of army and naval forces. Moreover, the viability of any strategy of knocking Turkey out of the war by this means, and thus helping Russia and affecting Balkan developments, was dubious. As an instance of new vulnerabilities, a British officer recorded a German aircraft flying low and machine-gunning a sailor on a destroyer.[9]

At the same time, the scheme, which owed much to Winston Churchill, the First Lord of the Admiralty, showed the extent of British naval power as the naval force sent, mostly older capital ships, did not endanger the situation in the North Sea.[10] In place of the unsuccessful naval attempt, the Allies switched to an attempt to take control of the western side of the Dardanelles, but the amphibious capability revealed was not matched by success on the part of the forces once landed. However, Allied naval power was such that it was possible to supply these forces and, eventually, to withdraw them successfully.

SUBMARINE WARFARE

The Atlantic trading system on which the British economy rested, and which was a core component of its maritime position and power, was the prime target for German naval warfare by 1915. Trade played the key role in accumulating and mobilizing the capital and securing the matériel on which Allied war making depended. Neither Britain nor France had an industrial system to match that of Germany, which by 1914 had forged ahead of Britain in iron and steel production. As a result, the Allies were dependent on America for machine tools, mass-production plants, and much else, including the parts of shells. American industrial output was equivalent to that of the whole of Europe by 1914, and the British ability to keep Atlantic sea lanes open ensured that America made a vital contribution to the Allied war effort before its formal entry into the war in 1917, although the financial cost to Britain of this contribution was heavy. Transoceanic trade and naval dominance also allowed Britain and France to draw on the resources of their far-flung colonial empires. Canadian help proved especially significant.[11]

Submarines had not featured prominently in naval operations over the previous decade, and their potential had been greatly underestimated by most commentators. Britain, which had only launched its first submarine in 1901, had the largest number—eighty-nine—at the outbreak of the war, many intended for harbor defense, but had not found answers to the problems of the defense of warships and merchantmen against submarines.

Once war had begun, the Germans stepped up the production of submarines, but relatively few were ordered and most were delivered late. In part, this was because of problems with organizing and supplying construction. Germany, as in 1939, also started war at what turned out to be the wrong time for the navy. A lack of commitment from within the German navy to submarine warfare was very important. Instead, its preference was for surface warships, which required more maintenance in wartime. Crucially in Germany, alongside the dominance of strategy by the army, a dominance Wilhelm II did not challenge, there was a long-standing concentration of industrial resources on the army, a pattern that was to be repeated in the Second World War. As a result, although submarines swiftly affected the conduct of operations, the Germans did not have the numbers to match their aspirations. In early 1915, only twenty-nine German submarines were available, and by the end of the year, only fifty-nine.

Aside from using scarce resources, the submarine also faced serious deficiencies as a weapons system. To move submerged, submarines were dependent on battery motors that had to be recharged on the surface where the submarines were highly vulnerable to attack. In addition, submarines were slow, and this lessened their chance of maintaining contact and of hitting a warship moving under full steam. The low silhouette of a submarine provided an advantage as it made it harder to locate, but also, without radar, it limited the area a submarine could oversee. Even with radar, the problem of low height limited the range of any line-of-sight instrument. Using a highly placed radar, a destroyer could survey a much greater area than a submarine could with its much lower-placed radar.

Submarines, however, benefited over time from an increase in their range, seaworthiness, speed, and comfort; from improvements in the accuracy, range, and speed of torpedoes (which, by 1914, could travel seven thousand yards at forty-five knots); and from the limited effectiveness of antisubmarine weaponry. These improvements reflected the possibilities for war making of a modern industrial society, with its ability to plan, design, manufacture, and introduce better specifications for instruments and processes.

In time, submarines came to play a significant role in naval planning, both tactically and operationally, in terms of trying to deny bodies of water to opponents and sinking warships. In practice, however, merchant shipping, not warships, proved the most important target for German submarines and ensured that they were given a role in strategic planning. Indeed, by attacking merchantmen, the Germans were demonstrating that the sea, far from being a source of protection for Britain, could in fact be a serious barrier to safe resupply.

Operating commerce raiding by the well-established prize rules was restricted submarine warfare, and without regard to these rules, unrestricted. The prize rules were essentially to stop suspected vessels, search them for contraband, and, if contraband was found, take them into port where the ship could be condemned by a court as a prize. If it was impossible to get the vessel into port, the prize rules stipulated that the ship was to be scuttled after provision had been made for the crew and passengers by allowing them into the lifeboats or by holding them on board the submarine. This approach entailed the submarine coming to the surface to stop the vessel and subsequently sinking it, usually by gunfire; submarines carried a deck artillery piece as well as torpedoes, and the former used less bulky ordnance and was more accurate. Moreover, U-boats carried very few torpedoes. For example, the U-31s to U-41s of 1915 carried six torpedoes, so U-boat commanders preferred to use their gun whenever possible. In one cruise in 1916, the submarine ace Arnaud de la Perière sank fifty-four ships in a U-boat armed with only six torpedoes. Even the boats of 1917–18 carried only twelve to sixteen torpedoes, so that if they were to sink enough merchant shipping to win the war, they still needed to use their guns on the surface. However, coming to the surface entailed the risks of being detected and sunk, not least by "Q" ships, converted merchant ships designed to look vulnerable but equipped with hidden guns. The effect of the Q ships was less in the actual number of submarines sunk than in the possible threat of sinking, which forced a change in the behavior of the submarines.

In 1915, Germany increased the threat and tempo of their assault on Allied shipping by declaring, on February 4, unrestricted submarine warfare, which began on February 18. This policy entailed attacking all shipping, Allied and neutral, and without warning, within the designated zone. The *Lusitania*, the largest liner on the transatlantic run as well as a British ship, was sunk off Ireland by *U-20* on May 7. Among the 1,192 passengers and crew lost, there were 128 Americans, and there was savage criticism in America. In response, Germany offered concessions over the unrestricted warfare. It was finally canceled on September 18 in order to avoid provoking American intervention. Aside from the impact on neutrals, Germany was unprepared for such a war, as it lacked sufficient submarines, trained crew, or bases to mount an effective blockade of Britain. The Germans sank 748,000 tons of British shipping in 1915, only for Britain to launch 1.3 million tons. Moreover, although a heavy burden, the British could afford to take the loss of trained crew.

1916

In 1916, the Germans sought again to implement their plan to fall upon part of the British Grand Fleet with their entire High Seas Fleet. Having been attempted in three sorties earlier in 1916 that did not result in a battle, the plan, tried again, led to the Battle of Jutland of May 31 to June 1. With a reasonable grasp of the operational as well as strategic situation, the British did not fall for the German plan. Nevertheless, despite having the larger fleet at Jutland, they failed to achieve the sweeping victory hoped for by naval planners and the public, whether their reference was to Trafalgar (1805) or Tsushima (1905).[12]

Instead, in the battle, the British suffered seriously from problems with fire control; inadequate armor protection, especially on the battle cruisers; the unsafe handling of powder in dangerous magazine practices that were an effort to compensate for the poor gunnery of the battle cruisers; poor signaling; and inadequate training, for example in destroyer torpedo attacks and in night fighting. For the Royal Navy, there was a general problem of underperformance. German gunnery at Jutland was superior (more accurate) to that of the Royal Navy, partly because of better optics and better fusing of the shells, and partly because of the advantages of position, notably the direction of light. The Germans were far less visible to opposing fire, and their range firing was therefore easier.

Command decisions were important. Jellicoe's caution, not least about night action, possibly denied the British the victory they might have obtained had the bolder Vice Admiral Sir David Beatty, commander of the battle-cruiser squadron, been in overall command, but Beatty's rash performance at Jutland also suggests that, had he been in overall command, there might have been more serious losses. As an aspect of the manner in which the politics of command, personality, and faction affected current, as well as subsequent, assessments, the view that he might have delivered victory was encouraged by Beatty when he was First Sea Lord from 1919 to 1927. However, as Churchill was to point out, Jellicoe, who enjoyed the support of Corbett, only needed to avoid losing. Moreover, from before the war, Jellicoe was concerned about how best to protect the fleet from German torpedoes, and at Jutland he used the tactic of turning away from destroyers and torpedo boats that had been considered prewar. Indeed, the German torpedo attack had little impact. Jellicoe's tactic, however, lessened the options for sustained British battleship fire.

As with American commanders at Midway (1942) and Leyte Gulf (1944), Jellicoe was also faced by the problems of managing and winning a naval encounter of unprecedented scale and complexity. Jellicoe confronted an incomplete picture of the battle, not only of the Germans but also of the British fleet, because subordinates failed to report expeditiously. The technological possibilities of radio communications were not matched by operational practice and tactical implementation. The latter was also true with spotting for naval bombardments in amphibious operations, notably that of the British at the Dardanelles in 1915.[13]

In the equations of loss and casualties, the British lost more ships and men at Jutland than the Germans: fourteen ships, including three battle cruisers, and 6,097 men, compared with eleven ships, including one battle cruiser, and 2,551 men. The British ship tonnage lost was about twice that of the Germans. In addition, there was much damage to ships and many wounded, including, on *Warspite*, Walter Yeo, who was the first to receive plastic surgery.

Wilhelm II announced at the North Sea naval base of Wilhelmshaven on June 5, "The English were beaten. The spell of Trafalgar has been broken." Nevertheless, the German fleet had been badly damaged in the big-gun exchange. Its confidence had been seriously affected by the experience of the power of the Grand Fleet, which had superior gunnery. Moreover, the strategic situation prior to the battle still pertained. Thereafter in the war, the High Seas Fleet sailed beyond the defensive minefields of the Heligoland Bight on only three occasions, the first on August 18, 1916. On each occasion, it took care to avoid conflict with the Grand Fleet.

In turn, the High Seas Fleet and the fact that it was not confined to port posed a major threat as a fleet-in-being, and this threat acted as a restraint on British naval operations by containing the Grand Fleet's activities. Their losses at Jutland made both Jellicoe and the Admiralty more cautious. British plans for bold large-scale operations, especially for sorties into the Baltic to help Russia, were not brought to fruition.

Yet the British employed their fleet by deterring the Germans from acting and thus challenging the British blockade or use of the sea. This deterrence thwarted the optimistic German plan of combining surface sorties with submarine ambushes in order to reduce the British advantage in warship numbers, a plan for attrition that was difficult to implement. This advantage was supplemented by British superiority in the intelligence war, especially the use of signals intelligence. The location of German warships was generally known by the British.

Jutland, indeed, was decisive in that it demonstrated to the Germans that a gradual degradation of the Grand Fleet was unlikely to be possible. While, therefore, the High Seas Fleet always posed a threat and was active on occasion, it left Germany without a clear fleet strategy. On July 4, 1916, recognizing that Jutland had left the British still dominant in the North Sea, the German commander there, Vice Admiral Reinhard Scheer, the commander of the High Seas Fleet, suggested to Wilhelm II that Germany could only win at sea by means of using submarines. In practice, though, there was still a surface threat. In particular, German cruisers and destroyers were to inflict serious damage on two Scandinavian convoys in October and December 1917.

Further afield, German surface raiders were no longer a major problem, although the potential for damage was revealed by *Moewe*, an armed merchant cruiser that sank many ships in 1916–17; *Seeadler*, which sank American cargo ships in the Pacific in 1917 before being shipwrecked near Tahiti; and *Wolf*, an armed freighter, dispatched from Kiel in November 1916. In an epic journey, it returned home in February 1917 having sunk or mined twenty-nine Allied ships off South Africa, India, Sri Lanka, Australia, and New Zealand, having thus created widespread alarm. [14]

In October 1916, Jellicoe, who was to become First Sea Lord in December, observed that the greater size and range of submarines and their increased use of the torpedo, so that they did not need to come to the surface to sink their target by gunfire, meant that the submarine menace was getting worse. Indeed, during the war, most vessels sunk were due to mines or torpedoes. [15] The following month, Arthur J. Balfour, who lost office as First Lord of the Admiralty in December, wrote, "The submarine has already profoundly modified naval tactics . . . it was a very evil day for this country [Britain] when this engine of naval warfare was discovered." [16]

The greater emphasis on submarines altered the nature of the war at sea, as submarine warfare did not offer the prospect of a decisive victory in a climactic engagement. Instead, the submarine conflict helped to ensure that the attritional dimension of naval warfare became more pronounced. This had been an inherent conflict within Mahan's views, which emphasized battle but stressed the slow working of sea power, but, in contrast, the attritional, trade-centered approach was consistent with Corbett's ideas. Combined with the British blockade of Germany, the submarine conflict ensured that the war was more clearly one between societies, with an attempt to break the resolve of peoples by challenging not only their economic strength but also their social stability and, indeed, demographic health. The role of food shortages in weakening resistance to disease was well understood. As such, this means of war led to a sense that extreme means were already at play.

1917

In 1917, having failed, in 1916, to drive France from the war at the Battle of Verdun (on land), and the British at Jutland, and having, in turn, experienced the lengthy and damaging British attack in the Somme offensive (on land), the Germans sought to force Britain from the war by resuming attempts to destroy its supply system. There was a parallel with the invasion of France via Belgium in 1914, in that the strong risk that a major power would enter the war as a result, Britain in 1914 and America in 1917, was disregarded on the grounds that success could be obtained as a result of the German attack and the resulting broadening out of the war. In 1917, however, the Germans, unlike in 1914, had had plentiful warnings as a result of their earlier use of unrestricted submarine warfare in 1915. There was also a serious failure of planning, as the anticipated outcomes from the submarine assault did not arise, and the timetables of projected success totally miscarried. This situation reflected a confusion about submarine capabilities and mirrored German strategic overconfidence in 1914, as well as reflecting an overconfidence in technology-based solutions to problems.

As so often with naval history, this account, however, both underplays differences within the U-boat lobby and assumes a rationalist balance of risks and opportunities. The latter ignores the extent to which the decision to turn to unrestricted submarine warfare reflected an ideology of total war, as well as a powerful Anglophobia based on nationalist right-wing circles, for example the Pan-German League, which saw British liberalism and capitalism as a threat to German culture and failed to appreciate the positive aspects of British socioeconomic structures. These ideas were given political bite by the argument that the German government, especially the chancellor, Bethmann-Hollweg, was defeatist and interested in a compromise peace, and instead that support for unrestricted submarine warfare was a sign of, and security for, nationalist commitment. Indeed, Tirpitz, who had links to such circles, was allowed to resign in March 1916 because his support for unrestricted submarine warfare had led him to quarrel with the chancellor and to challenge the position of Wilhelm II. The following month, an American protest resulted in Wilhelm ordering the suspension of the permission given that February for the sinking without warning of armed freighters, but not of passenger ships.

On January 31, 1917, however, Germany announced, and on February 2 resumed, unconditional submarine warfare. This resumption led to America breaking diplomatic links the next day and declaring war on Germany on April 6. Congress had approved the decision, although six senators and fifty congressmen opposed it. The German military leadership, increasingly politically influential, was unsympathetic to American moralizing. Moreover, as in 1941, there was also the view that America was already, in practice, helping the British and French war effort as much as it could commercially. The economic capability of American industry was not understood.

In addition, there was a conviction that Britain could be driven out of the war rapidly by the heavy sinkings of merchantmen. This reflected a belief that the submarines could achieve much, and that this achievement would have an obvious consequence. It was claimed that Britain would sue for peace on August 1, 1917. This represented an aspect of the total war also seen with the air assault on London in 1917 and the bombing of civilian targets. Furthermore, many German submarine enthusiasts assumed that their force would be able to impede the movement of American troops to Europe very seriously, which was an aspect of a more general failure to appreciate American strength. On January 31, 1917, Eduard von Capelle, the German secretary of state for the navy, unwisely told the budget committee of the Reichstag that, from a military point of view, America was as nothing. Aside from overestimating German and underestimating Anglo-American capabilities, notably the military consequences of economic power, there was a failure to understand the ability of Britain and America to respond and adapt.

In 1914, there was active hostility in America to the idea of participation in the European war, a war that was presented as a struggle of the "old world," in large part for base motives. However, the unrestricted submarine warfare that sank American ships ensured that many, if not most, Americans became persuaded of the dangerous consequences of German strength and ambitions, and did so in a highly moralized form that encouraged large-scale commitment. Thus, America constructed national interest in terms of the freedom of international trade from unrestricted submarine warfare. The alternative of limiting trade with the Allies was not pursued. [17]

Ironically, America's entry into the war increased the importance of submarines to German capability as it further shaped the balance of surface warships against Germany. This prefigured the situation in 1941, when the United States entered the Second World War against Germany, although then the German surface fleet was weaker in relative terms. In 1917, America had the third-largest navy in the world after Britain and Germany, and the Navy Act of 1916 had increased the shipbuilding program, although it had not yet come to fruition. Moreover, in part due to the dominance of the army's needs, and certainly compared to the grip of the British Admiralty over wartime procurement, the Germans added fewer battleships and battle cruisers during the war than the British (four and three compared to fourteen and five). For example, the battleship *Valiant*, which fought at Jutland, had been completed earlier that year on the Clyde. This contrast ensured that the pronounced British numerical superiority of 1914 was greatly expanded. Victory in the prewar naval race was followed by victory in a wartime naval race that attracted, and has continued to attract, less attention, which is not surprising given that prewar building rates prefigured the outcome. Thus, the Germans did not have the margin of success in a large-scale shipbuilding program on which to fall back.

Nor, more seriously, did the Germans have the prospect of support from the warships of new allies that the Allies gained with the alliance of Italy (1915) and, even more, America (1917). Italy was the European neutral with the largest fleet. Portugal, which also joined the Allies, had a modest fleet. Brazil, which also suffered from the unrestricted German submarine warfare, followed America by declaring war in October 1917, but the small squadron it eventually dispatched did not see active service. Furthermore, in late 1916, in accordance with a British request, four Japanese warships were sent to the Mediterranean. Based in Malta, they added to the escort capacity, as well as strengthening the Allied position in the equation of naval power. These additions more than nullified the success of German submarines in sinking Allied warships. Moreover, in 1917, the British lost only one pre-dreadnought battleship and one armored cruiser this way. The Allies lost the support of Russia in 1917, but of no Atlantic naval power, unlike in 1940.

These factors affecting surface warship strength accentuated the importance of the submarine war on British trade. Indeed, the initial rate of Allied shipping losses was sufficiently high to threaten defeat. Serious losses were inflicted on Allied, especially British, commerce, in large part due to British inexperience in confronting submarine attacks. The limited effectiveness of antisubmarine weaponry was also an issue, as depth charges, another new technology, were effective only if they exploded close to the hull of the submarine. This was also a period when effective artillery techniques on land were having to be worked out. It took time to establish and disseminate such techniques. From February to April 1917, 1,945,240 tons of British shipping were sunk, with only nine German submarines lost.

In the event, as later in the Second World War, Britain survived the onslaught, and, as in the later conflict, thanks to both outfighting the submarines and to success on the home front. The introduction, from May 10, 1917, of a system of escorted convoys cut shipping losses dramatically and helped lead to an increase in the sinking of submarines. Convoys, which were introduced first in February 1917 to protect ships carrying coal to France, in response to calls from the French government, and then, in April, for the Scandinavian trade, might appear such an obvious solution that it is surprising they were not adopted earlier and that they were introduced in a piecemeal fashion. However, there were counterarguments to convoys. These included the number of escorts required, the delays that would be forced on shipping, congestion in harbors as a result of convoys, the lack of a dedicated bureaucracy, and the possibility that convoys would simply offer a bigger and slower target to submarines. Convoys were also resisted by certain naval circles as not sufficiently in touch with the bold "Nelson touch," which they believed necessary and appropriate. To look after convoys did not appear the role of warriors. Nineteenth-century Royal Navy culture had obfuscated the success of convoys in the French Revolutionary and Napoleonic Wars from 1793 to 1815.[18]

However, against a background of resource superiority and a degree of naval control that enabled them to choose options, the Admiralty eventually took the necessary steps. The Naval Staff had already created a dedicated antisubmarine section, and it became better organized in 1917. Convoying proved effective: only 393 of the 95,000 ships that were to be convoyed across the Atlantic were sunk. Convoys facilitated the transport of over two million American troops to Europe aboard thousands of ships and thus provided a vital new force for the Allies on the Western Front. Only three transports, one of which managed to limp to the French Atlantic port of Brest after being torpedoed, were lost, and only sixty-eight soldiers drowned. Another two million troops were ready to sail to France when the war ended.

This convoying was the priority for the American navy, and convoying owed much to American support. Although they lacked experience in antisubmarine warfare, the Americans deployed their fleet to help protect communication routes across the Atlantic. From May 1917, American warships took part in antisubmarine patrols in European waters, initially with six destroyers based in Queenstown in southern Ireland where Admiral Sir Lewis Bayley, the British commander, was a key figure in fostering Anglo-American cooperation. The resourceful Vice Admiral William Sims, commander of American naval forces in European waters, was important in encouraging convoying. To assist convoying in the Mediterranean, American warships were based in Gibraltar. American escort vessels rapidly contributed to the effectiveness of convoying, the key help being in destroyers. They were fast enough to track submarines and to keep them submerged, which reduced their effectiveness.

More generally, convoying was an aspect of the direction on a global scale by the Allies of most of the world's shipping, trade, and troop flows. The Allied Maritime Transport Council oversaw an impressive system of international cooperation at sea, allocating shipping resources so that they could be employed most efficiently. This was important as an aspect of economic warfare and also in lessening targets for German submarines. British merchant shipping provided close to half of France's imports, which was a key aspect of the British maritime contribution to the war effort.[19] British control of the shipping of neutral Norway, which was unable to protect its shipping, increased greatly as a result of the new German policy, and Norway's ships were transferred to the British flag.[20]

Convoys not only reduced the targets for submarines but ensured that, when they found the convoys, the submarines could be attacked by escorts and by escorts with appropriate goals and weaponry. In providing sufficient numbers of the latter, the British were helped by their wartime shipbuilding program, which included fifty-six destroyers and fifty antisubmarine motor launches. Having had an average loss of 630,000 tons of merchant shipping in the first four months of unrestricted attacks, the tonnage lost fell below half a million in August 1917.

Convoys also benefited from the "shoal" factor: submarines, when they found one, only had time to sink a limited number of ships. In coastal waters, convoys were supported by aircraft and airships. Viewing submerged objects is far easier from above than from sea level. This support forced the submarines to remain submerged, where they were much slower.

Aside from convoying, there was a major effort to employ intelligence, especially the use of radio and the possibilities it offered, in defeating the submarines. Command and control was a key area of naval operations that benefited greatly from technological improvement. Developments with radio made it easier to retain detailed operational control. Directional wireless equipment aided location and navigation and was employed to hunt German submarines by triangulation, while radio transmissions changed from a spark method to a continuous wave system. Submarines had an inherent operational disadvantage in that it was not necessary to sink the submarine but only to have shipping come safely home. This was a weakness appreciated during the next war when air cover forced U-boats to submerge and allowed convoys to outrun them. Nevertheless, it was also important to weaken the submarine force by sinking boats, killing crew, and weakening morale. Thanks to the tracking of submarine movements, the British acquired an edge. However, there was not yet any equivalent to the sonar used in the Second World War in order to provide a local tactical advantage, and this absence affected the level of submarine losses.

Mine laying, generally an underrated activity and one treated as unheroic, was very significant in the war with U-boats, indicating the degree to which antisubmarine warfare displayed the complex relationships between technological advance, industrial capacity, organizational capability, operational experience, and tactics. Although convoys definitely limited the potency of German attack, mines sank more submarines than other weapons, while mine barrages limited their options. Intelligence information was important in the planning of mine laying. The Allies laid massive barrages across the English Channel at Dover in late 1916, which limited the movement of German submarines into the Channel, and across the Straits of Otranto at the entrance to the Adriatic. The largest, containing seventy-five thousand mines, was across the far-greater distance of the North Sea between the Orkneys and Norway, from March 1918, with the Americans playing a major role. Drawing in part on German mines, there were also important improvements in mine technology during the war; magnetic mines were developed and were laid by the British. There were also improvements in navigational skills, such that it was possible to cross one's own minefields more successfully. The British also made valuable advances in firing depth charges.

Yet, alongside incremental improvement, there were limitations. Aircraft were not yet able to make a fundamental contribution to antisubmarine operations because key specifications they had by the Second World War were lacking during the Great War. Moreover, the antisubmarine weapons dropped by aircraft were fairly unsophisticated compared to those of the Second.

The strategic limitations of submarine warfare were underlined by the success of the British government, helped by better weather, in improving cereal/grain production. In part, this improvement came from converting land from the production of meat and milk. In addition, coal and food were rationed in Britain from 1917, which both controlled and directed demand. Thus, submarine warfare helped greatly in moving Britain toward a total war mobilization of the resources of society and the capabilities of government.

1918

By 1918, the rate of Allied tonnage sunk per German submarine lost had fallen. Nevertheless, the Germans continued to inflict considerable damage, with at least 268,000 tons of British shipping sunk each month from January to August, and heavy concentrations of losses in the Western Approaches and the Irish Sea. By the end of 1917, it was believed that the Dover Patrol had failed to prevent submarine movements. The hard work of convoying under continual threat of submarine attack continued until the end of the war, and the threat from submarines led to a bold and partly successful attack on April 22–23 on the Zeebrugge entrance to the canal to Bruges, from which German submarines based in Belgium sortied. A similar attack on Ostend followed on May 9, 1918. Falling German effectiveness ensured that only 288,000 tons of British shipping were sunk in September and October 1918 combined.

German surface ships made far less of an impact other than in diverting Allied resources. However, in January 1918, the *Goeben* and *Breslau* sortied from the Black Sea into the Aegean, sinking Allied shipping until the *Breslau* hit a mine and the *Goeben* returned to the Black Sea. British aircraft and submarines had failed to sink it.

The arrival in France of American troops and matériel made the strategic irrelevance of the German navy in 1918 abundantly clear, although it always remained a fleet-in-being fixing the Grand Fleet. Moreover, American entry into the war made any idea of a decisive German naval sortie less credible and thus paralleled the buildup of American troops in France, which also helped limit German options. Five American dreadnoughts, the Sixth Battle Squadron, a formidable force, joined the British Grand Fleet in December 1917, four of them sailing with it on April 24, 1918, when it failed to intercept an ultimately unsuccessful German sortie into the North Sea aimed at a Scandinavian convoy.[21]

In the face of the clear Allied superiority, a decisive German naval sortie was less credible. The German surface fleet languished, while its men became seriously discontented, leading to their mutiny at the end of the war. This matched the breakdown in the Russian and Austrian fleets in 1917 and 1918, respectively. The mutiny of the sailors in the German High Seas Fleet on October 27, 1918, proved a key precipitant for rebellion across the country, as well as thwarting the German naval command's plan for a final sortie that was designed to justify postwar political support for the navy. The fleet had also been sent to sea in 1917 to campaign in the eastern Baltic against Russia, in part in order to quell unrest among the sailors. In 1918, the idea of a glorious last sortie proved unpopular.[22]

In the event, the fleet sailed forth only to surrender, nine battleships and five battle cruisers entering the Firth of Forth to do so on November 21, 1918, escorted by the Grand Fleet in an impressive display of British naval power. In addition, 176 German submarines were handed over after the war. German naval power had been totally destroyed.

NAVAL AIR POWER

The impression of naval potency had been amplified during the war. The battleship remained the key currency of naval power and its most potent demonstration. However, aside from submarines, naval air power suggested another future. Air power developed at sea in a number of directions. Airships were much used for reconnaissance, Jellicoe warning, "The German airships will be of the greatest possible advantage to their fleet as scouts."[23] Although their range was shorter than that of airships, aircraft proved less exposed to the weather. Prior to the conflict, Britain and France had converted ships to provide seaplane tenders. Seaplanes, generally operated from naval bases, but also able to perform sea takeoffs and landings and to be catapulted from ships, as well as aircraft operated from coastal air stations, were more important at sea during the war than airships. Britain took a lead in the use of aircraft for reconnaissance, spotting naval gunfire (in order to improve accuracy), patrols against submarines, and attacks on shipping, although the French also played a role. On December 5, 1914, a French squadron of seaplanes was deployed at Port Said, with French pilots and British observers, in order to protect the Suez Canal and to observe Turkish naval and land moves. In April 1916, the squadron was moved to Greece.[24] In 1915, British seaplanes employed torpedoes against Turkish supply ships. In August 1918, British seaplanes eliminated an entire naval force: six German coastal motorboats.

Visibility was a key element. In 1916, both the British and German fleets failed at Jutland in the North Sea, in poor visibility, to use their air reconnaissance adequately when they clashed in the largest naval battle of the war. The *Campania*, a British seaplane carrier with a flush deck, was left behind in Scapa Flow. The *Engadine*, a seaplane carrier, was with the Grand Fleet but was used to little effect. However, airships and aircraft offered an advantage in dealing with submarines, as viewing submerged objects is far easier from above than from sea level. With the limited submerged endurance of the submarine, aircraft were most effective in searching large areas for surfaced submarines, and then in possibly attacking them as they dived. However, the French aircraft operating from North Africa from January 1916 to November 1918 against German submarines in the Mediterranean only sank one.[25]

In July 1918, Britain conducted the first raid by aircraft flown off an improvised aircraft carrier, a technique not used by any other power. In September 1918, *Argus*, an aircraft carrier capable of carrying twenty aircraft, with a flush deck unobstructed by superstructure and funnels—in short the first clear-deck carrier—was commissioned by the British, although she did not undergo sea trials until October 1918. At the end of the war, the British were planning an air attack, with Sopwith Cuckoo torpedo bombers designed for the purpose, on the German High Seas Fleet in harbor at Wilhelmshaven on the North Sea, an attack that had been postponed to 1919. The plans look toward the successful British attack on the Italian fleet at Taranto in 1940.

Naval air power was also introduced elsewhere. For example, the antecedents of Australian naval air power began during the war, with seaplanes flown off the major ships of the Royal Australian Navy and with Australian personnel in the British Royal Naval Air Service. There was also a short-lived Royal Canadian Naval Air Service, which served from Nova Scotia hunting for German submarines.[26] America did not take any aircraft to sea.

CONCLUSION

Naval power played a key role in the conflict, and with far fewer casualties than in the war on land. However, many of the bolder hopes of such power on the attacking side were not fulfilled. This was not only the case with the absence of a decisive battle. The navalist emphasis on ship-to-ship engagement overshadowed amphibious operations, but these also proved a disappointment. Winning dominance of the sea had to come before its use for force projection, but this led to a neglect of planning for the latter. This relative neglect was accentuated by the greater prominence of commerce raiding and protection that arose from the development of the submarine, and from the relative unimportance of amphibious operations in the 1890s and in the first four decades of the twentieth century. The course of the First World War did not really bear out the claim in Charles Callwell's *Military Operations and Maritime Preponderance: Their Relations and Interdependence* (1905) that there was a close connection between command of the sea and control of the shore. Already, prior to the war, the British had concluded that amphibious operations against Germany were not practical. Plans in 1914–15 for an attack on Schleswig, the part of Germany south of Denmark, a part exposed to British naval power in the North Sea, were not pursued. More-

over, in 1915, the attempt to use naval power to force a way to Constantinople failed. Plans for coordinated operations in Flanders were vitiated by the
strength of the German resistance. There were fewer amphibious operations
than in the Second World War.

In both May 1915 and December 1916, the British Admiralty leadership
changed as a consequence of perceptions of failures. Yet much was achieved,
and British naval leadership has been positively reassessed.[27] Naval dominance had been achieved and had ensured that the Allied war effort could be
mobilized, applied, and sustained. The hopes that commerce could continue
in war had been fulfilled.

As far as the First World War was concerned, the submarine appeared
much more relevant than aircraft. The submarine was future potential turned
into present reality. The submarine created a very distinctive and troubling
image of naval conflict, one that answered to a different analysis of modernization and potential to that of the battleship.[28] A fictional echo was provided
in 1917 when Arthur Conan Doyle, the British author, in *The Last Bow*,
published "The Bruce-Partington Plans," a short story set in 1895. In this,
Mycroft Holmes, the intellectual panjandrum of the British government, told
his brother Sherlock about

> the plans of the Bruce-Partington submarine. . . . Its importance can hardly be
> exaggerated. It has been the most jealously guarded of all government secrets.
> You may take it from me that naval warfare becomes impossible within the
> radius of a Bruce-Partington operation.

The global dimensions of the struggle deserve attention. The war very
much indicated the value of maritime links. For example, the British effort to
resist the German and Turkish presence in Iran was mounted by sea, whereas
German and Turkish forces moved overland. The Russian presence in northern Iran was supported by ships operating across the Caspian Sea.

These global dimensions related not only to the major states, but also to
others. Some gained experience in coalition warfare that looked toward a
later pattern of multilateral global naval operations. Expertise was spread.
Argentina sent a naval mission to the United States in 1917 to obtain training
in naval aviation and submarines, training at Pensacola and Newport, respectively. The Argentinian navy pilots then flew combat missions in Europe
during the First World War, while the submarine officers remained in the
United States as instructors at the submarine school. These officers went
back to Argentina and were promoters of the Naval Air Arm and the submarine force.

At one level, the war had served primarily to show that battle fleets were
of defensive value, with Britain and France successfully defending their control of the oceans,[29] rather than being a successful offensive tool that had the

capability to deliver victory. At the same time, this defensive value, which had been vindicated by Corbett, was a key aspect of the durability of an alliance that was able to mobilize and deploy its forces for victory. The railway gave Germany and its allies valuable interior lines in Europe, facilitating the application of the resources of a continent, but the sea did so for those of the world.

Chapter Four

Aftermath, 1919–31

In many senses, the naval situation was in the 1920s similar to that in the modern world. After a period (the First World War for then, the Cold War for now) that had defined naval superiority, there was no large-scale conflict to chart subsequent shifts in capability nor the impact of technology. The First World War defined naval superiority in terms of Allied, especially British, predominance, although with the Americans now also taking a key role. However, the issue of submarine versus battleship was partly unresolved, while the role of naval air forces remained completely undefined.

In the interwar period (1919–38), shifts in capability and the impact of technology were both important, as was the key role of political concerns in shaping strategic tasking and plans. From the outset, the growth of Japanese naval power proved a threatening and unpredictable challenge for Britain and the United States, rather as that of China has been for the United States over the last decade, although China today lacks the aggressive military culture and potent naval commitment Japan had in the interwar years, or, rather, does not have it to the same extent. China is a continental power able to enter the maritime environment because it is currently not threatened on the landward frontier by Russia.

NAVAL LIMITATIONS

The war was followed by the removal of the naval strength of the defeated, by a degree of demobilization among the victors, and by an attempt to prevent any future naval races. There was to be no return to the situation in 1914. Germany, the world's number-two naval power in 1914, lost its strength and its potential. The Germans scuttled their interned ships at Scapa Flow on June 21, 1919, providing plentiful entertainment for modern deep-sea divers, while also greatly increasing the relative size of the Royal Navy. The Peace of Versailles of that year denied Germany permission to build a replacement fleet, limiting both the number and type of warships it might have. As German air forces were prohibited, there was also no fleet air arm and therefore no buildup of the relevant talent. Moreover, as part of the 1919 peace settlement, the merchant ships seized from Germany were allocated to the victors in proportion to their wartime maritime losses. The German capacity for naval rearmament was also affected by reparations and the occupation of key economic areas.

Austria (really Austria-Hungary) had had the world's eighth-largest navy in 1914. This disappeared with the collapse of the Habsburg monarchy and the loss of an Adriatic coastline, now divided between Italy and, to a larger degree, Yugoslavia.

Russia had a different fate as a result of the Bolshevik Revolution in 1917, in which the sailors in the Baltic Fleet played a particularly revolutionary role,[1] and of the subsequent large-scale civil war and foreign intervention. Its navy and shipbuilding capacity were badly affected by both. The Bolsheviks also focused on the army. In 1926, the navy was reduced to a section of the army, and it did not regain an independent status until December 1937. Concern about possible mutiny might have been a factor. Even then, there was no return to prewar Russian priorities. For example, no attempt was made to rebuild a Far East fleet. Instead, war plans with Japan were to center on long-range bombers and on the army.

Naval power politics were transformed after the First World War. The naval challenge to Britain now came from the increased naval power of two of her wartime allies: the United States and Japan. This competition was to be played out after the war in the diplomacy of naval limitation that, in accordance with the disarmament provisions of the Treaty of Versailles, led to the Washington Naval Conference of 1921–22 and the Washington Naval Treaty of 1922. The scholarly emphasis can be on suspicions and rivalries, and this is understandable in light of Japan's attack on the United States and Britain in 1941. However, in the 1920s, wartime alliances followed by these negotiations ensured that naval competition ceased to be the key theme that it had been prior to the outbreak of the First World War with the Anglo-German naval race.

Britain's wartime alliance, indeed, led to postwar interest in cooperation, notably with the United States, as in the suggestion by the influential British geopolitician Halford Mackinder, in his book *Democratic Ideals and Reality: A Study in the Politics of Reconstruction* (1919). He suggested joint Anglo-American trusteeship over the key naval positions of Singapore, Aden, Suez, Malta, Gibraltar, and Panama in order to assure the "peace of the ocean." Such notions were fanciful. Nevertheless, they looked toward later cooperation, while Britain, in the Washington Naval Treaty, accepted naval parity with United States, voluntarily relinquishing its traditional superiority at sea while maintaining sufficient naval strength nonetheless to protect its vital interests.[2]

This was a marked departure from the two-power naval standard, a navy equal in size to the next two naval powers—which, having been developed against France and Spain in the eighteenth century, had been pursued by Britain in the late nineteenth century—and the "one plus 60 percent" standard pursued before the First World War. This development, however, did not represent a straightforward case of decline. In each case, the British maintained a standard that best provided security against the potential threats it faced, and a one-power standard against the United States meant a roughly two-power standard against Japan and France.

The world order, nevertheless, had changed. America was the leading industrial and financial power, while Britain was under pressure from economic problems, from harsh fiscal circumstances, from demands for social welfare, and from extensive postwar military commitments, especially in India, Iraq, Ireland, and Russia. In addition, the British were in the shadow of the buildup of the American navy ordered in 1916, which, had it happened postwar, Britain could not have matched. In the event, Congress did not vote the money for what was proclaimed as the "Navy Second to None" until 1940, when the situation was very different.

The Washington Naval Treaty fixed the ratios for the major naval powers, and did so with a focus on battleships, reflecting the lessons learned from the First World War about what was seen as the decisive arm. However, war gaming at the American Naval War College in 1921 led to a measure of skepticism about the value of battleships. There was interest in their vulnerability to air attack. Nevertheless, the battleship remained key. A 5:5:3 ratio in capital ship tonnage for Britain, the United States, and Japan was agreed in the Washington Naval Treaty, with 525,000 the total battleship tonnage for each of the first two. The meaning of the one-power naval standard was adjusted to take account of Japan and the problem of projecting British naval power into the Far East.[3] The quotas for France and Italy were 35 percent of the capital ship tonnage of Britain. The French had unsuccessfully hoped for parity with Japan, but Japan's quota was 60 percent of British or American tonnage. Equality in capital ships for France and Italy meant, because of France's global commitments, de facto Italian predominance in the Mediterranean at a time when France counted on North Africa to supply close to one-third of its troops. As a consequence, the French, who refused to reduce their battleships to naval parity with Italy, tried to get the British to sign a Mediterranean naval agreement at the 1930 conference, only to be turned down.

Russia was left out of the Washington Naval Treaty. It was still ostracized as a consequence of the Russian Revolution, but it also lacked a strong oceangoing navy and had been unable to counter British, French, Japanese,

and American naval power during the Russian Civil War. As a result, the
major powers were able to decide on preferable levels of naval strength
without worrying about any Soviet naval threat.

Limitations as well as ratios were a key element. The treaty involved an
agreement to scrap many battleships, in service or under construction, and to
stop most new construction for ten years; the three major navies were allowed to complete two new battleships each, and America and Japan were
permitted to complete two incomplete ships as carriers. The latter provision
was extended by the London Naval Treaty of 1930, an agreement designed to
last until 1936.[4] By fixing ratios, the Washington Naval Treaty appeared to
end the prospect of expensive and destabilizing naval races between the
major powers and to fix the character of battleship size and technology. The
treaty limited warships other than battleships and carriers to ten thousand
tons and eight-inch guns but placed no treaty limits on the number of warships displacing fewer than ten thousand tons. As a result, the great naval
powers could build and maintain as many cruisers and destroyers as they
wanted to afford. A competition started in the so-called treaty cruisers, heavy
cruisers displacing ten thousand tons and carrying eight-inch guns, rather
than in the battleships built prior to 1914. Although *Nelson* and *Rodney*, two
battleships (with sixteen-inch guns) were completed in 1927, Britain did not
lay down any battleships between January 1923 and December 1936. While
on paper the Americans had parity with Britain, and a comfortable superiority over Japan in the number of battleships, it had, in practice, a decided
superiority, as American battleships on average had more heavy guns.[5]

The limitations on battleships under the treaty, and the consequences of
postwar downsizing and fiscal retrenchment, helped ensure in the 1920s that
carriers, as yet largely untested, could be more rapidly produced by converting existing warships than by building new ones. As a result, and in a largely
unexpected fashion, the cost of investing in new technology, in the shape of
carriers, was cut. The conversion of battle cruisers (which were less armored
and faster than battleships) helped to ensure that carriers were faster than the
standard battle fleet, centered as it was on the battleship. This basis was to be
important to a key characteristic of carrier warfare, the relatively high speed
of the carriers, which reduced the consequences of their vulnerability to
surface fire and to interception.

Despite British efforts in 1922 and 1930, there were no limitations on
submarines, although the Peace of Versailles had banned Germany from
using them. The French were keen to prevent limits on submarine warfare
and built the most in the 1920s, in part in response to the limitations on their
fleet under the Washington Naval Treaty and in part in response to an emphasis on a defensive fleet: some of the submarines were for coastal defense.
In particular, this was a French response to Italian naval expansion. France
went on to build the cruiser-submarine hybrid *Surcouf*, which was an inter-

esting design but, given its cost and the resources involved, a huge risk for the French navy. The 1930 London Conference's decision that submarines should sink noncombatant ships only after giving fair warning did not represent a practical limitation on what submarines might do in the future and, indeed, was not to be heeded, being already redundant before the Second World War, as the warlike conduct of Italian submarines during the Spanish Civil War (1936–39) showed.

The role of Japan in the treaty clauses reflected its improved relative position as a result of the First World War, having been an active member of the Allies. Moreover, Japan's postwar position as one of the leading states to intervene in the Russian Civil War further affirmed both its significance and the importance of its cooperation with America and Britain. Japanese naval power in the Pacific was recognized in the Washington ratios, while the 1922 treaty also included a clause stopping the military development of American colonies in the western Pacific, the British base of Hong Kong, and also many of Japan's island possessions in the region.

This clause greatly affected the American ability to exercise sea power against Japan, as it meant that naval bases in the western Pacific, notably Guam, could not be improved. However, America's relative position was enhanced because the Anglo-Japanese Alliance of 1902, which was up for renewal, was replaced instead by a Four-Power (Britain, United States, Japan, and France) Treaty, committing the powers to respect each other's Pacific possessions and to consult in the event of conflict. As a result, there was no specific agreement between Britain and Japan, which lessened American vulnerability in the western Pacific.

NAVAL ACTION

This period was not one of significant conflict between navies, but they were used extensively to support imperial and national interests, and in both "hard" and "soft" power roles and means. This was particularly so for Western states seeking to expand, sustain, and defend their empires, which was a major activity of the period, but there was also activity by lesser powers. Britain, France, the United States, Italy, and Japan were especially prominent in defense of their imperial interests. For example, the French navy was used in support of imperial control, notably in North Africa and Syria, and the Italian navy similarly in Libya and the Adriatic. In 1920, Italian naval bombardment led the Albanian irregulars that had entered the port of Valona to withdraw.

The use of the Royal Navy was most extensive, and it underpinned British imperial operations, notably from Southwest Asia to Russia. In 1919, aircraft were sent from Egypt to British Somaliland on the carrier *Ark Royal* in order to attack Sayyid Mohammed Abdille Hassan (to them the "Mad Mullah"), an operation crowned with success. The navy played a major role in the Russian Civil War, notably in the Baltic and Black Seas.

The American navy played a key role in fostering America's informal empire in the Caribbean and Central America. This was especially so in the Dominican Republic, Haiti, and Nicaragua. In December 1929, for example, 350 marines were sent on the cruiser *Galveston* from the American base at Guantanamo Bay in Cuba in order to support American operations in Haiti. In April 1931, the Sandinista siege of an American-held position near the Caribbean coast of Nicaragua led to the dispatch of marines from the American-governed Panama Canal Zone on the *Asheville*, while a light cruiser was sent from Guantanamo Bay.

Lesser powers also turned to naval power. In 1921, the Spaniards responded to defeat in Morocco by dispatching several warships to Moroccan waters, and in 1922 a blockade of the coast was announced. In 1925, with French naval support, Spain launched a successful amphibious assault in the Bay of Alhucemas, a key move in its eventually successful campaign in Morocco.

In the Caribbean, naval power proved very valuable as a means of informal empire. So also, but to a much lesser extent, in China. Eight foreign warships were deployed off Guangzhou (Canton) in 1925 at a time of anti-foreigner demonstrations, as a warning and a refuge. However, in the coastal waters and, even more, rivers that were the crucial spheres for operations there, it was Chinese interests, and their shallow-draft boats, that played the key roles. In December 1920, Sun Yat-sen, the leader of the Guomindang (Nationalists), established his position in Guangzhou, his arrival backed by the navy's First Fleet. Five years later, Guomindang gunboats bombarded mercenary positions in fighting outside Guangzhou. In March 1926, three warlord gunboats attacked the Dagu forts, while other warships escorted transports landing five thousand troops nearby. The politics of naval power was significant. In the spring of 1927, the defection to Jiang Jieshi (Chiang Kai-shek) of the Fujian Naval Fleet gave him control of the Yangzi River, and he reached Nanjing on one of his new warships.

The British, American, Japanese, and French commanders considered responding to Guomindang actions against foreign interests by sending warships up the Yangzi River, sinking the Guomindang fleet, destroying their arsenals at Hankou and Guangzhou, and possibly preventing Guomindang forces from crossing the Yangzi on their Northern Expedition. In the event, these steps were not taken. Instead, although the international concession at Shanghai was protected by a deployment, British interests in Hankou were abandoned. However, the divisions between the Chinese warlords, and their consequences in terms of civil war and a related lack of coherence in naval forces, had greatly affected the possibility of creating an effective Chinese national navy.

FORCE STRUCTURES

Alongside the commitment to battleships, the combined impact of submarines and air power in the First World War, and their likely future role, suggested to some a fundamental change, both in naval capability and in the tactical, operational, and strategic aspects of naval power. As a consequence, many commentators argued, naval methods and goals had to be rapidly rethought.

At the same time, the specific strengths and character of weapons' systems had to be understood. For example, for submarines, there was a contrast in roles between the emphasis on stealth, which enabled a submarine to mount surprise attacks and thus to counter the greater firepower advantage of warships, and, on the other side, the need, if action was to be more effective, to come close to, or to, the surface, in the former case to periscope depth and in the latter to make more speed. However, in doing so, submarines compromised stealth as, even if not on the surface, periscope and torpedo wakes could be tracked. Moreover, close to the surface, submarines were visible to, and detectable by, aircraft and vulnerable to air attack. This use of aircraft had developed from the latter stages of the First World War.

Submarine warfare emphasized a major difference between naval and land capability. The resources to build and maintain naval units was restricted to relatively few powers, and thus the options to be considered by contemporaries in terms of strategic goals and doctrine were relatively limited. Echoing earlier fears of torpedo boats, Admiral Lord Jellicoe, the former British First Sea Lord, argued that submarines destroyed the feasibility of close blockades of opposing harbors so as to prevent hostile warships from sailing out and instead led to a reliance for trade protection on convoys protected by cruisers, which required a large number of the latter. Jellicoe was worried that Britain had insufficient cruisers both to do this and to work with the battle fleet in a future war.

Cruisers were regarded as a protection of imperial maritime routes, but, between *Enterprise* in 1918 and *Berwick* in 1924, the British laid down no new cruiser. Nor did any other European state. Only the Americans and the Japanese laid down new cruisers. British Admiralty concern about the impact of naval limitations on the size and number of ships was also expressed by Admiral Sir Charles Madden, the First Sea Lord, in a meeting of the Cabinet Committee preparing for the 1930 London Naval Conference. He "explained that it was not possible to build a battleship of less than 25,000 tons with the necessary quantities of armament, speed and protection, which would include an armored deck of 5" [thick armor] and 6", to keep out bombs and plunging shell, and have sufficient protection under water against mines, torpedoes and bombs. . . . The Admiralty required a sufficient number of cruisers to give security to the overseas trade of the Empire against raiding forces of the enemy and a battle fleet to give cover to the trade-protecting cruisers."[6]

This dual need reflected a long-standing pattern that was not dependent on the technological parameters that affected its particular manifestations. Thus, this contrast had been noted with the Royal Navy in the eighteenth century. The contrast had clear implications as far as doctrine was concerned and with regard to strategy, operations, and tactics. The variety in warships ensured an asymmetrical quality to naval conflict itself, even while this quality frequently inherently arose from fundamental asymmetries in goals and related capabilities.

In the 1920s and 1930s, the problem with negotiating arms control agreements, whether or not in the shape of parity of percentages, was that every naval power had different force requirements to meet its strategic needs. For example, with less long-range trade to protect, the Americans needed far fewer cruisers than the British, and the Americans also sought to limit the number of British cruisers so that Britain would find it harder in wartime to blockade neutral commerce, which had been a key point of tension in Anglo-American relations since American independence in 1783. This difference led to a serious Anglo-American dispute over cruiser numbers at, and after, the Geneva Naval Conference of 1927. The Americans wanted bigger cruisers with longer cruising ranges because they lacked Britain's first-rate network of bases at which their ships could refuel. Since disarmament agreements worked on the basis of total tonnage, the Americans preferred fewer (but bigger) cruisers, and the British, in contrast, preferred more (but smaller) cruisers. However, again as a reminder of the complex factors affecting force structures, for the Royal Navy, if American-style bigger cruisers were built by Japan, then the smaller British cruisers would be outgunned. Therefore, the British Admiralty wanted qualitative arms limitations rather than quantitative. The 1927 crisis failed to reach an agreement, while the British side was divided anyway over whether to defend their position on belligerent rights to blockade in the face of American objections.

At the 1930 London Naval Conference, quantitative limits (overall tonnage restrictions on each class of warship) were placed on the great naval powers in addition to the 1922 restrictions. The British government agreed to a limit of fifty cruisers, as opposed to the seventy the Admiralty sought. In practice, the financial cuts enforced in the late 1920s ensured that the British cruiser program was not sustainable anyway.

In many respects, the type of cruiser was an easy topic to debate, for in contrast, as had been the case prior to the First World War, efforts to develop naval strength and weaponry were complicated by acute controversy over the potential of different weapons systems in any future naval war. The respective merits of air power (both from aircraft carriers and shore based), surface gunnery (especially from battleships), and submarines were all extensively discussed, as well as their likely tactical and operational combinations and strategic consequences. These debates were part of a more long-standing process of naval development seen in the rapid and almost continual adoption of new types of warship, naval armament, and naval tactics in the period from the 1830s in response to fundamental changes in ship power and design. This situation owed much to an industrial culture in which it was easier than hitherto to embrace the positive response to technological innovation and then implement it.

Some theorists argued that battleships were now obsolete in the face of air power and submarines. There was, for example, a revival in France of the *Jeune École* ideas of obsolescence associated with the battleship, ideas that were especially relevant given both the naval race with Italy and the Washington provisions. Nevertheless, big surface warships had a continued appeal, and not simply for the European powers. Indeed, there was considerable opposition to making carriers the key capital ship. Instead, in the 1930s, the Americans, British, and Japanese put a major emphasis on battle-fleet tactics based on battleships. Given the serious weakness of naval aviation, this emphasis was not simply a sign of conservatism, as was to be suggested at the time and, even more, subsequently. For example, as commander-in-chief of Britain's Mediterranean Fleet from 1930 to 1932, Admiral Alfred Chatfield, later First Sea Lord from 1933 to 1938, sought to introduce an effective tactical doctrine for the use of aircraft in naval battle, albeit with limited success. Conservatism, indeed, played an important role in support for battleships, but the British, who, with the largest fleet, had the greatest interest in maintaining existing systems, also displayed adaptability in their tactics. The Germans, French, Soviets, and Italians were also greatly interested in developing an effective battleship capability.

It was argued that, thanks to antiaircraft guns on them and on supporting warships, battleships could be protected against air attack. Moreover, carriers (correctly) appeared vulnerable to gunnery and could not operate at night or in poor weather, and the First World War had shown that submarine campaigns could be beaten. Carriers lacked artillery and carried fragile biplanes. Indeed, to many contemporaries, they were more like civilian ships than true warrior ships. Carrier decks were a large and vulnerable target. Moreover, once badly damaged, the carrier became useless. The individual aircraft could carry the equivalent of one battleship shell; indeed, at Pearl Harbor, Japanese bombers used modified fifteen-inch shells. As a result, with all aircraft active, they could only deliver a few minutes of fire. Carriers, therefore, had serious weaknesses. Pre-1939 navies, the Japanese providing an especially good example, conceived of carriers and submarines as a subordinate part of fleets that emphasized battleships—indeed in part as anti-battle-ship aids to their own battleships—only to find in the Second World War that, while battleships were important, carriers proved more useful in many circumstances.

Gunnery experts were particularly keen on battleships, and these experts were important in senior ranks. There was no comparable lobby for carriers or submarines. The continuing role of battleships was enhanced by the absence of a major change in battleship design comparable to those in the late nineteenth century and the 1900s. Indeed, with the arrival of the dread-noughts, battleship architecture had reached a new period of relative stability in which existing battleships remained effective. For example, the USS *New York* of 1914, *Texas* of 1914, and *Nevada* (BB-36) of 1916 participated in the D-day bombardment of 1944. The ten fourteen-inch guns of the *Texas* (which can be visited near Galveston) could fire one and a half rounds per minute, each armor-piercing shell weighing 1,500 pounds. There was still great interest in such weaponry, both for ship destruction, of comparable as well as of different ships, and for shore bombardment, including the destruc-tion of harbors and the covering of amphibious attacks. No other system, including bombers, could provide such firepower. Given the problems posed by defensive gunfire, entrenchments, and concrete fortifications, battleships, despite the low trajectory of their main guns limiting their value against modern coastal defenses, appeared to be the best means available to engage with coastal positions and to maintain an amphibious capability.

Moreover, as prior to 1914 with the threat from torpedo boats, there were considerable efforts to strengthen battleships, as well as other ships, in order to increase their resistance to air attack. Brigadier General Billy Mitchell, the top American combat air commander and assistant chief of the American Air Service in 1919–25, argued that aircraft could sink any ship afloat. The latter assertion, which resulted in the test sinking of a seized German battleship, the *Ostfriesland*, in twenty-one and a half minutes of bombing in 1921, led Mitchell into furious rows with the American navy. The value of the test sinking was compromised because the battleship was stationary and unable to fight back. Moreover, Mitchell violated the rules of the test in numerous ways. For example, he claimed he could hit ships from high altitude, but, during the test, the bombers came in at almost mast height and would have been highly vulnerable even to the primitive antiaircraft capability of the day. The bombs were so heavy that the aircraft could hardly get off the ground and would have been vulnerable to fighters providing protective cover for the ship. Mitchell was eventually court-martialed for insubordination.

The success of Mitchell's tests led to prominent calls, especially in the *New York Herald*, to convert incomplete capital ships into carriers and re-sulted in the navy creating a Bureau of Aeronautics and improving the air defenses of its warships. Mitchell, however, was critical of carriers, as he feared they would make it harder to wage a unified air war under a single air command. He preferred shore-based aircraft.[7] The carrier aircraft of the time were not very rugged and lacked range. Also, the communication between aircraft and carriers was unreliable.

On battleships, armor was enhanced to resist bombs; outer hulls were added to protect against torpedo attack from aircraft, submarines, or surface ships; and antiaircraft guns and tactics were developed, not least with improved fire control. Furthermore, as prior to the First World War, more accurate fire with the main battleship guns was achieved through the addition of primitive computer-like calculators to integrate course and speed calculations into fire-control systems. Air spotting for naval gunfire also developed in the 1920s and 1930s with better communications between aircraft and battleships. This improvement in battleship capability is a reminder of the danger of assuming that a weapons system is necessarily static, which is a conclusion too often drawn when discussing battleships. As an armored, mobile, big-gun platform, the battleship had much to offer, both on its own and in combined operations, and battleships were readily understood in that light.

Indeed, in the Second World War, although there were spectacular losses, notably the *Prince of Wales* to Japanese torpedo bombers in December 1941, many battleships took considerable punishment before being sunk by air attack. At Pearl Harbor, only two battleships were a total loss, while two others damaged were back in service as early as March 1942. Battleships were not supposed to operate by themselves but in tandem with auxiliary ships that could serve to enhance antiaircraft capabilities, as in the successful American (and British) response to Japanese kamikaze air attacks in 1944–45. During the war, air attack was less effective than some had expected, in part due to very effective anti-air coordination, which included air cover. Surface ships also provided the prime means of fighting at night. In addition, battleships were still necessary while other powers maintained them because they provided the required offensive armament and defensive armor with which to fight, and thus deter and control, other battleships.

There was no experience, from the First World War or subsequently, with conflict between carriers, but there was considerable confidence in their potential, as also later in the event of NATO–Warsaw Pact conflict. In 1919, the year in which an American Coast Guard NC-4 flying boat became the first aircraft to cross the Atlantic (a feat the British claimed for a bomber),[8] Jellicoe, who was very concerned about the strategic relationship with Australia and New Zealand, pressed for a British Far East Fleet, to include four carriers as well as eight battleships, in order to deter Japan,[9] while, in 1920, Rear-Admiral Sir Reginald Hall MP argued in the *Times* that, thanks to aircraft and submarines, the days of the battleship were over. The British Admiralty remained convinced of the value of battleships but was not opposed to carriers. Interwar British planning called for a carrier to every two or three capital ships. The key to British attitudes was that aircraft had to be integral to the fleet, whereas in the American and Japanese navies, although that doctrine was present, there was a greater willingness for carriers to operate separately. In America, the National Defense Act had placed air power under the Army Air Service (rather than creating an equivalent to the RAF [Royal Air Force]), but naval aviation was kept separate. [10]

A determination to employ the new capability offered by naval aviation was rapidly apparent. Carriers were used when Britain intervened against the communists in the Russian Civil War, an intervention that was important in keeping Estonia and Latvia out of communist hands. In addition, the carrier *Argus* was stationed near the Dardanelles during the Chanak crisis between Britain and Turkey in 1922, when Britain sought to deter the Turks from attacking British forces in the region. There was also a carrier on the China Station in the late 1920s, first *Hermes* and then *Argus*. *Argus* landed six aircraft at Shanghai in 1927,[11] strengthening the Western position in the International Settlement in the face of the conflict between Chinese forces. Another carrier, *Furious*, took part in the major naval exercises in the late 1920s.[12] *Eagle*, commissioned in 1923, was the first British flush-deck carrier, while the Fleet Air Arm of the RAF was formed the following year. The number of aircraft in the Fleet Air Arm rose, but, due to the RAF's clear focus on land-based power, only to 144 by the end of the 1920s.

Eagle was a converted dreadnought battleship, while *Argus* was built on a hull intended for a passenger liner, and *Furious*, *Glorious*, and *Courageous* were converted from the battle cruisers of those names. Prior to the *Illustrious* class, only *Hermes* (commissioned 1924), of Britain's original six carriers, was built keel-up as a carrier. *Furious*, when first converted, had separate fore and aft decks, separated by the ship's original centerline battle-cruiser superstructure, and therefore did not become a flush-deck carrier until a subsequent more radical reconstruction.

Showing considerable flexibility, the Americans and Japanese made major advances with naval aviation and aircraft carriers, in part because they would be key powers in any struggle for control of the Pacific. They also built carriers on the hulls for battle cruisers and battleships canceled as a result of the 1921–22 Washington Naval Conference.[13] The *Langley*, a converted collier, was, in 1922, the first American carrier to be commissioned, followed, in 1927, by two ships originally laid down as battle cruisers, the *Lexington* and the *Saratoga*. This basis helped to ensure that American carriers were very fast: thirty-three knots against a twenty-one-knot battle fleet, which forced the carriers to operate separately and made it difficult for the American navy to develop an integrated naval system of battleships and carriers. The *Lexington* and *Saratoga* were each designed to carry sixty-three aircraft.[14]

The Japanese commissioned six carriers between 1922 and 1939, some converted but others purpose-built as carriers. The *Akagi*, a converted battle cruiser, commissioned in 1927, was designed to carry ninety-one aircraft, the *Kaga*, with ninety aircraft, following in 1928. There were many similarities with the American and British navies. Indeed, a British civilian mission under William Forbes-Sempill, an RAF veteran, that was in Japan in 1920–23 trained Japanese aviators, including in torpedo bombing. Sempill brought plans of British carriers and passed on sensitive information, and in 1925 a prosecution of him under the Official Secrets Act was seriously considered.[15] In 1927, as part of his graduation exercises at the Japanese Naval War College, Lieutenant Commander Tagaki Sokichi planned an attack by two Japanese carriers on the American Pacific base at Pearl Harbor, although, in the evaluation, he was held to have suffered heavy losses. In 1929, the *Saratoga* launched eighty-three aircraft in a simulated raid on the Panama Canal.[16] The defenses built there reflected American sensitivity about the canal. At sea, however, whatever their apparent potential, air power was restricted in the 1910s and 1920s by the difficulty of operating aircraft in bad weather and the dark, by their limited load capacity and range, and by mechanical unreliability.

PLANNING FOR THE PACIFIC

Speculation about the likely role of carriers, and of carriers as opposed to battleships, focused on the Pacific. It was there that Japan, the United States, and Britain competed. Indeed, in 1919, an Admiralty memorandum warned that the British navy was likely to be weaker than that of Japan in the Far East. It suggested that using Hong Kong as a base would expose the British fleet to overwhelming attack from Japan, a reasonable view about the vulnerability of forward bases, notably, but not only, to surprise attack. Instead, the memorandum recommended that Singapore be developed, as it was sufficiently far from Japan to permit reinforcement without peril.[17] The Treasury proved reluctant to share the Admiralty's concern, which was a tension familiar to all powers, but the creation of a Singapore base and the development of the so-called Singapore Strategy were critically important to the Royal Navy in the 1920s.

Japan represented a different threat to the British Empire than that earlier posed by Russia. The British response to Russia had been military and diplomatic policies focused on the Asian landmass, crucially to protect the land approaches to India, with the Royal Navy playing only a supporting role. Now there was the prospect of a naval challenge to Britain in Far Eastern or even Indian waters, one that could not be countered by British strength in home waters and that required a regional capability.[18] In his *Rulers of the*

Indian Ocean (1927), George Ballard, a retired British admiral, argued that the rise in Japanese and American naval power meant that it was no longer sufficient for Britain to prevail over European rivals in order to win global naval dominance. This was a challenge that was more direct for Britain than for other European naval powers. The rise of a potentially hostile Japanese navy changed the traditional Royal Navy strategic landscape. Earlier, if all naval rivals could be locked up in Europe or chased when they evaded blockade, then Britain had global command. However, fiscal issues, combined with the Japanese navy, created a situation in which Britain had a two-ocean empire, threatened at each end, and a one-ocean navy to defend it.

The Americans were also concerned about Japanese intentions and naval strength, indeed increasingly concerned. A collision of American and Japanese interests in the Pacific region had been building since Japan's stunning victory in the 1904–5 Russo-Japanese War eliminated her sole naval threat in the region.[19] That same year, America strengthened its fleet in the Philippines as a buffer in the event of war with Japan. Both countries now recognized each other as a potential threat to their respective interests and ambitions. Japanese naval commanders, fearing Japan would lose in a sustained war, hoped that quick decisive naval battles would enable it to establish a defensive perimeter against the American navy, as Japan had done against Russia in 1905. In 1921, America regarded Japan as the most probable enemy.[20] The tonnage limitations of the Washington Treaty assumed that America, Britain, and Japan could each only dominate its own geographic sphere in the Pacific. There were, however, specific American interests in the western Pacific, including the territories of the Philippines, Guam, and Samoa; trade; and a strong commitment to the independence of China and to an "open door" allowing other powers that did not have territorial bases there, notably the United States, to share in Chinese trade. This concern led to American planning for war with Japan, which was correctly seen as menacing all these interests. More than any other navy, the American one got the war it expected in the 1940s. Naval exercises that were a bridge from the naval thought of the pre-1914 Mahanian period to the American strategy pursued in the Second World War were conducted. War Plan Orange of 1924 called for the "through ticket." This was a rapid advance directly from Pearl Harbor, the American base in Hawaii, to Manila, the capital of the Philippines, followed by a decisive naval battle with Japan and then starving Japan by blockade. For both sides, war games prepared options, while Hector Bywater's *The Great Pacific War* (1925) was a very good guess about a future naval war between Japan and the United States.[21]

Moreover, the American navy continued to gain experience in large-scale movements and maneuvers. The Atlantic Fleet would regularly join the Pacific Fleet in the Caribbean or the eastern Pacific for maneuvers. For example, in 1925, the Pacific Fleet engaged in maneuvers with the Atlantic Fleet off Panama; then both fleets went up the West Coast of the United States for "fleet week" events, after which they engaged in maneuvers from California to Hawaii, and then, while the Atlantic Fleet went home, the Pacific Fleet went to Australia and New Zealand. By 1940, no other fleet had as much experience in such large-scale movements.

LATIN AMERICA

Some lesser powers also developed their navies. Latin American tensions over prestige and border disputes, several of which looked back to earlier conflicts, such as the War of the Pacific in 1879–83, led to naval races. Regional powers lacked their own capacity to build complex warships but benefited from the overcapacity in the shipyards of European states and the United States to build up their naval strength. The United States built four submarines for Peru, which were commissioned in 1926–28. In turn, the Chileans regarded their existing destroyers as inadequate in countering these boats, which indeed would make the battle group centered on the British-built dreadnought battleship *Almirante Latorre*, a surface-action group, vulnerable to attack. The Peruvians, in turn, had no surface vessels to challenge the *Almirante Latorre*. Strengthened by new British-built destroyers from 1929, its battle group was then seen as able to counter the Peruvian submarines. As a related point, the perceived naval threat to Chile from Argentina increased from the mid-1920s when the government of the latter authorized the expenditure of seventy-five million gold pesos on a ten-year naval building program, buying two heavy cruisers, a light cruiser, twelve destroyers, and three submarines, mainly from Britain and Italy. The key role of naval power appeared readily apparent to these and other second-rank powers.

Warships were easy to deploy if a logistical support system was in place. They had particular value for states that had only a limited air force. Moreover, there was an availability of naval power in the 1920s. This owed much to the buildup of naval strength over the previous decade, to the willingness of some states to decide that they had surplus warships and to pass them on, and also to the need for naval shipbuilders to find foreign markets. This situation was greatly exacerbated by the naval limitation regime of the 1920s and early 1930s. The economic recovery and growth of the 1920s was also significant.

Latin America was particularly important for the position outside Europe, the United States, and Japan, as it contained many of the independent states that had both coastlines and a tradition of naval power. Very few other states with these characteristics became independent in this period, and many already independent states remained weak at sea, for example Persia, China, and Thailand. So also with newly independent or formed states, such as Iraq and Saudi Arabia. In Africa, only Ethiopia and Liberia were independent, and they lacked naval power.

CONCLUSIONS

The 1920s do not tend to attract attention in naval history other than with respect to the naval limitation treaties. The decade was not one of conspicuous naval conflict, and the doctrinal and technological developments and issues appeared less significant than those in the 1930s when new warships were being built and active preparations made for a new large-scale war. Moreover, the Spanish Civil War (1936–39) and the outbreak of the Sino-Japanese war in 1937 ensured a strong pulse in naval confrontation and usage from 1936 for which there was no comparison in the 1920s. Indeed, of the postwar years, 1919 was more significant for the use of naval power, especially in staging Western intervention in the Russian Civil War, than any of the individual years in the 1920s. In addition, postwar retrenchment affected naval preparedness, and not only for the major powers. Visiting Australia in 1919, Jellicoe was made aware of Australian reluctance to spend more on the navy. So also with Canada.

Nevertheless, naval power was widely used in the decade, and the use then, as in the 1930s, has much to offer modern commentators, as there is more in common between the situation then and now than with the total war scenarios of the two world wars. However, the naval history of the 1920s and 1930s does not engage the imagination of the modern public. Nor does the maritime dimension of the 1920s and 1930s, although the consequences of merchant shipping provision then were to be very important to the Second World War. For example, during the 1920s the increase in the volume of goods to be traded globally did not keep pace with the rise in the number of ships available to transport them; British shipping was hit hard by this global overcapacity of shipping, but it was to be significant to the subsequent conflict and notably to the struggle then with submarines. As with the German submarine assault in the First World War, there was a distinction between the ability to sink many ships and the capacity to stop overseas trade. The 1920s therefore looked toward the Second World War in a variety of significant ways.

Chapter Five

Preparing for War, 1932–39

In 1931, Japan sought to intimidate China during its occupation in Manchuria by holding naval exercises in the Yangzi River and sending ships up the Whangpoo River, both means of bringing pressure to bear on Shanghai, China's leading port. This intimidation was a small-scale Japanese commitment compared with what was to come later, but the conquest of Manchuria helped increase international tension, and such tension encouraged planning for war, especially in the United States, Britain, and Japan. More generally, the aggressive spirit and quest for national greatness that would increasingly fuel expansionist powers during the 1930s sealed the collapse of the old order after the First World War, while giving full play to military authoritarianism in Japan, Stalinist communism in the Soviet Union, and Fascism in Italy and Germany.

CONTESTING THE PACIFIC

The likely character of a major future war in the Pacific led to a new geography of commitment and concern that was reflected in the development of naval bases or the consideration of alternatives. The Mobile Naval Base Organisation was designed to allow the forward commitment of the Royal Navy against Japan at a time when new naval facilities were not being pursued. However, the strategy came to be focused on a major base at Singapore, which, in 1932, the British Cabinet decided to complete.[1] The United States focused on Pearl Harbor. Moreover, the switchover from coal to oil as the power source of major warships helped ensure that the previous system of coaling bases was obsolete. In addition, the expansion in the size of battleships from the deployment of the dreadnoughts in the mid-1900s had made the existing imperial harbors at Hong Kong, Singapore, and Trincomalee inadequate. The British chiefs of staff urged that Singapore should be not only a modern naval base but also the location of an army able to act as a strategic reserve forward of India,[2] a measure aimed at Japan and to protect India, Malaya, and Australasia.

In turn, the strategic value of Pearl Harbor for controlling the eastern Pacific and advancing across the western Pacific was clear to the American Joint Army and Navy Planning Committee in 1919. Pearl Harbor would be crucial for the planning that superseded the "through ticket" outlined in the American Plan Orange of 1924, planning in which there was now greater interest in a slower, three-year process of seizing the Japanese islands in the Pacific—the Marshalls, Carolines, and Marianas—which they had gained from Germany as mandates in the Versailles peace settlement. The capture of these islands would provide the Americans with forward bases en route to the Philippines and deny them to the Japanese. Without control of this area, it was argued, a naval advance to the Philippines would be unsuccessful. The logistical challenge of projecting power into the western Pacific was formidable. It included an erosion of efficiency as warships responded to fouled hulls and reduced speeds. The more cautious voices had prevailed over the "through-ticket advocates" by the mid-1930s.[3] The evolution of American strategy reflected the sophistication of American planning, notably the War Plans Division within the Office of the Chief of Naval Operations.

Options were tested in fleet exercises and in war games.[4] In an American 1933 war game, Captain Ernest King chose a northern attack route on Japan, via Hawaii, Midway, Wake, and the Marianas, while the president of the Naval War College, Rear Admiral Laning, preferred a southern route, beginning with Micronesia, and criticized King's plans as the worst possible. A decade later, King put his plan into action, while Douglas MacArthur put Laning's plan into action, but they each took far longer than expected. Moreover, practicalities such as fuel and ammunition were underplayed in the planning and exercises. When operating at peak performance, carriers need to refuel very often.

The need to plan for conflict across very large bodies of water encouraged an emphasis on a greater range for ships and aircraft and led both Japan and the United States both to convert ships to carriers and to commission purpose-built carriers. Thus, the Japanese commissioned six carriers between 1922 and 1939. American naval leaders and planners responded to the lack of adequate bases in the western Pacific by favoring technological, operational, and force-structure solutions, including underway replenishment and carriers.[5]

There was also a focus on increasing the range, size, and speed of submarines. The American S class of 1918–21, with a range of five to eight thousand miles at a surface speed of ten knots, was replaced by the B class (twelve thousand miles at eleven knots), and then by the P-boats of 1933–36, which were the first American submarines with a totally diesel-electric propulsion. These were followed by the *Gato* class introduced in 1940: double-hulled, all-welded-hull submarines with a range of 11,800 miles and a surface speed of twenty to twenty-five knots. By the time of the Japanese attack on Pearl Harbor, the American navy had 111 submarines in commission, although their cautious use in the first year of the war reflected deficiencies in interwar doctrine.[6] Poor torpedoes were also a major issue.

In turn, the Japanese had sixty-three oceangoing submarines. Their *Sento-ku*-type I-400 submarines had a range of 37,500 nautical miles, a surface speed of 18.7 knots, a submerged speed of 6.5 knots, and carried two seaplanes and supplies for sixty days. In the event of war with the United States, the Japanese planned to use their submarines to sink American warships steaming from Hawaii into the western Pacific. They therefore intended to employ the long range of their submarines as a major preliminary component in subsequent fleet action. In the event, Japanese submarines repeatedly failed to fulfill expectations, which was unsurprising as prewar exercises had indicated significant deficiencies as well as focusing on submarines as a support "part" of the normal fleet.

The need to plan for conflict with Japan accentuated the problems for Britain and the United States, powers with major commitments in both the Atlantic and Pacific, for they had to think about how best to distribute naval forces and how vulnerabilities would affect policy. There was a de facto division of spheres of activity, with the United States dominant in the Pacific but having no role in the Indian Ocean, which was very much a British sphere. The British were more prominent than the Americans in the South Atlantic and in East Asian waters, although the Americans had a small Asiatic Fleet to defend the Philippines and their interests in China. As Admiral Montgomery Taylor, the Asiatic Fleet commander from 1929 to 1933, pointed out, this force was too small to thwart Japanese moves, and any intervention would probably prove counterproductive.[7]

With the exception of carriers and cruisers, the American surface navy was smaller in 1938 than it had been in 1925, while the marines were a small and inadequately equipped force.[8] Nevertheless, although the size of the navy was limited as a result of the treaty holiday in shipbuilding, and this compromised Plan Orange, the American navy was being expanded rapidly by the late 1930s, notably with the building of the *North Carolina* and *South Dakota* classes of fast battleships, with their sixteen-inch guns, authorized in July 1937. In addition, the navy's tactical doctrine had become reasonably sophisticated. It focused on all-arms coordination, tactical flexibility, and a decentralized command structure.[9] As a result of the earlier freeze on battleship construction, the Americans had devoted appropriate attention to carriers and submarines, while the lack of base fortifications in the islands of the northwest Pacific ensured that the navy had had to focus on warships of greater range, build floating dry docks, and invest in logistical capability. [10]

The British failed to agree among themselves, or with the Americans, on how best to contain the Japanese threat. In response to Treasury opposition in 1934 to sending a fleet to the Far East and, instead, concern about Germany and support for a British focus on air power, it was argued by both the Admiralty and the Dominions Office that this was an unacceptable stance due to the impact on Australia and New Zealand of leaving them without support. [11] More generally, whereas the Royal Navy sought to focus on Japan, the politicians, the Treasury, and the RAF wanted to concentrate on Germany. The British government was developing serious doubts at the highest level about its ability to project power effectively into the Pacific. The navy developed plans to achieve this end, only for the politicians consistently to deny it the resources to do what it thought necessary. The Admiralty was ready to consider a forward policy of projecting a battle fleet into Far Eastern waters (thus protecting Hong Kong) to provide support against Japan, but that policy required an American willingness to move naval units to East Asian waters as an aspect of a coordination that did not yet exist. Fearing that this would leave Hawaii vulnerable, the American Naval Department, which anyway included Anglophobes, was unwilling to support such a scheme.

A forward policy of sending much of the fleet to Singapore in the event of crisis with Japan was developed in the early 1920s and then went through several significant shifts in timing and force structure, notably in 1937–41 as Britain grappled with the problems of fighting a three-front war and facing substantial risks in European waters. By April 1939, the Admiralty was no longer willing to specify how soon and what size of a force would be deployed to Asian waters in the event of an Anglo-Japanese war arising. In 1941, Churchill decided to send the *Prince of Wales*, a modern battleship, and the battle cruiser *Repulse* to Singapore in order to deter the Japanese and impress the Americans. However, this decision rested on a misreading of the strategic situation in the Far East, as the Japanese could not be deterred. Moreover, the availability of warships for Singapore depended on commitments against Germany and Italy in home, Atlantic, and Mediterranean waters and on the fate of the British fleet in any conflict that might arise with these powers. After the sinking of the *Prince of Wales*, Churchill told a secret session of the House of Commons on April 23, 1942, "While we are at war with Germany and Italy we do not possess the naval resources necessary to maintain the command of the Indian Ocean against any heavy detachment from the main Japanese fleet." [12]

In 1935–36, at the Second London Naval Conference, Japan demanded equality of tonnage with Britain and the United States, which would have meant Japanese naval superiority in the Pacific and Far East. British attempts at negotiating compromise failed, and the Japanese left the talks in January

1936. Already in December 1934, Japan had provided the necessary two years' notice under the treaty regime to end their commitments.

Japan, therefore, launched the Marusan Program of shipbuilding, which was designed to prepare for victory over American and British fleets. The buildup of their navy included the largest capital ships in the world, the "super-battleships" *Yamato* and *Musashi*, ordered in 1937, each displacing seventy-two thousand tons and carrying nine 18.1-inch guns. Their size and gunnery were designed to compensate for Japan being heavily outnumbered by American battleships, but they were to be sunk by the Americans in 1944 and 1945, air power, or rather the lack of their own air power, proving the nemesis of this class.

The militaristic nature of Japanese naval policy and culture calls into question claims, generally made with reference to America and Britain, that navies have usually been associated with liberal commercial values. The Japanese focused on the force structure of a large navy based on battleships and on the goal of victory stemming from a decisive battle. This was the lesson the Japanese had taken from their victory at Tsushima in 1905.

Seeking international power through naval strength, and naval strength through international power, many Japanese naval commanders and planners opposed the naval limitation treaties because they believed that the Japanese navy should be closer in size to the American navy, an idea first expressed in 1907 when a ratio of 70 percent or more had been advanced. As a consequence, the 1922 Washington Naval Treaty ratio of 60 percent was regarded as unreasonable, a humiliation, and a threat both to national defense and to the ability of the navy to act as a deterrent force. Indeed, in November 1930, the prime minister was assassinated after he signed the London Naval Treaty. The militarist/nationalist resentment against the ratio system ignored the fact that, in an all-out arms race with the United States, Japan had no chance of achieving either a 60 or 70 percent ratio. Therefore, arms control actually worked to their advantage.

Throughout the interwar period, the Americans, who had enforced Japan's entry into modernity in the 1850s, were seen as the likely enemy by Japanese naval planners. Moreover, those who opposed this stance lost their position in the navy as the Fleet Faction consolidated its dominance. A purge in 1934 led to the promotion of aggressive officers, and, as a result, Japanese naval preparations focused on war with America. This, moreover, gave the navy a central role in military affairs, which contrasted with the army's determination to prepare for war with China or the Soviet Union. The Japanese focus was very much on opposing the United States, as Britain did not appear a comparable threat.

Both the Japanese and the American naval leadership focused on a decisive battle centered on battleships, with air and submarine attacks being preliminary blows, while mundane items like support ships and salvage training were ignored by the Japanese. The Japanese also put an emphasis on preliminary damage from nighttime cruiser and destroyer torpedo strikes and produced an effective surface-launched torpedo, the oxygen-fueled Type 93 or "Long Lance." Moreover, as an instance of the relationship between tactics and equipment, the Japanese increased their capability for nighttime attack by developing impressive light-gathering optical devices, as well as high-explosive propellants that were nearly flashless. The Americans lacked a comparable torpedo (and comparable propellants), and the contrast in tactics affected conflict in the Guadalcanal campaign in the Solomon Sea in 1942. As far as warships were concerned, the Japanese added armor, upgraded engines, and increased the gun elevation of their warships in an attempt to outclass the Americans at extreme range and thus be able to damage them prior to conflict at closer range. At the same time, Japanese naval tactics have been seen as overly dogmatic.[13] In response, the Americans did the same in an effort to secure an initial advantage.

NAVAL AIR POWER

Improvements in naval air effectiveness in the interwar years (1919–38) were particularly the case in the 1930s. New arrester gears were fitted that helped to slow aircraft down when landing on carriers, and, in addition, the equipment could be reset automatically, which was useful when more than one aircraft were landing. Hydraulically reset traverse arrester gear was in use by the British navy by 1933. Improvements in carriers and aircraft helped to ensure that carriers, rather than seaplanes, which were indeed significant, or airships, were seen as the way to apply air power at sea and made it easier to envisage using carriers for operational and strategic ends. Naval air doctrine and tactics also advanced. The value of attacking first was understood as what would hinder the chance of an opponent's carrier responding, notably as it was difficult for defenders to stop an air attack. Defending fighters and their control system lacked this capacity, while antiaircraft guns at the time were of only limited value, not least in protecting such a big target as a carrier.

There were some distinctly Japanese approaches to naval aviation. In particular, the Japanese navy focused not only on carriers but also on land-based bombers as an offensive force. These long-range bombers were capable of bombing and torpedoing ships, which was not the case with the American and British navies. This was partly because the Japanese navy thought it convenient to utilize the Pacific colonies it controlled, notably the Marianas, to provide forward air bases from which to intercept the advancing American fleet. Moreover, the Japanese navy enjoyed relative organizational autonomy in developing naval aviation as far as its army counterpart was concerned. While there was notoriously severe interservice rivalry between the army and the navy over budget, personnel, and resources, the Japanese navy was less restricted in terms of developing naval aviation and less threatened by proponents of an independent air force than the British and American navies. This was linked to the extent to which the Japanese Naval Air Force was larger in size and better in equipment than the Japanese Army Air Force, a contrast with the situation in the United States. In 1938, the Japanese concentrated all maritime and shore-based air power into a combined naval air wing.

However, Japanese naval aviators were mostly noncommissioned officers: officers comprised fewer than 15 percent of its aviators. The Japanese navy initially tried to have an all-officer pilot corps, but it gave this up for fear of destabilizing the existing personnel hierarchy because a lot of aviators were needed. Instead, the navy introduced the Yokaren system, recruiting civilians between fifteen and seventeen in order to train sufficient noncommissioned officers to fill the lower ranks. This practice led to less organizational and political representation of aviators within the navy, which hampered the necessary transformation from a battleship-oriented navy to an air-centered one. Although that was not the sole reason hampering this transformation, it was an important one, and it is always appropriate to note the role of institutional and political factors.

Britain and the United States had carrier fleets that were intended to compete with that of Japan. In contrast, Germany, Italy, and the Soviet Union did not build carriers in the interwar period, and France only had one, the *Béarn*, a converted battleship that was insufficiently fast to be considered an important asset. The Soviet emphasis not on carriers but on shore-based aircraft reflected the extent to which it was assumed by the Soviets that their naval operations would take place in the Gulf of Finland or otherwise close to Soviet-controlled coastlines and the air cover they offered.

Britain's carrier construction gave an important added dimension to her naval superiority over other European powers. In addition to the carriers in commission in the 1920s, four 23,000-ton carriers, the *Illustrious* class, each able to make over thirty knots and having a three-inch armored flight deck, were laid down in 1937, following the 22,000-ton *Ark Royal* laid down in 1935 and completed in November 1938. The 23,450-ton *Implacable* was laid down in February 1939, although it was not commissioned until August 1944. The British carriers, however, lacked modern aircraft at the beginning of the war. Unlike the Americans, the British never developed an effective dedicated (carrier-capable) fighter.

British and American carrier and aircraft design diverged because of differing conceptions of future naval war. In the Second World War, the British armored deck carriers proved less susceptible to bombs and Japanese kamikaze aircraft than the American wooden-deckers as they tended not to penetrate the former. Japanese carriers also had wooden decks. The lighter-weight wooden decks were linked to the larger fuel capacity necessary for Pacific operations. Moreover, the wooden-deck carriers had capacity for more aircraft. In contrast, the British navy's most important task was protecting national waters and the major imperial trade route through the Mediterranean. Both tasks were well within the existing and forecast zones vulnerable to attack from land-based aircraft, notably from Italy. In the 1920s and 1930s, it was held that such aircraft would hold a major advantage over the slower and longer turning circle of carriers and the problems posed by headwinds for aircraft taking off and landing. However, that was not the key reason for armored decks. Instead, the British navy sought a line of carriers sailing in parallel with, but further away from, the battleships, which would be the primary ships to engage the enemy. The original carrier specifications called for the armor to stretch over both sides of the ship as protection against naval gunfire. Cost was the reason the side armor was dropped. Armor ensured that there was less space below the deck for the repair and storage of aircraft, and British carriers carried fewer aircraft per tonnage than their American and Japanese counterparts.

Despite pressure from the Royal Navy, naval air power in Britain lacked a separate institutional framework. The RNAS merged with the RFC (Royal Flying Corps) into the RAF in 1918. The RAF was primarily concerned with land-based aircraft and had little time for their naval counterparts, and indeed for maritime operations; RAF Coastal Command was short of aircraft in the war. In 1931, the RAF had pressed for major cuts in naval aviation. The decision to separate embarked (onboard) aviation and its necessary shore support, but not land-based maritime air or aircraft procurement, from the RAF and return it to the navy was announced by the Inskip Award of 1937 and came into effect in May 1939.[14]

In France, the Air Ministry, established in 1928, gained nearly all naval air assets, and this helped ensure that plans for more carriers were not pursued there until 1938. In 1936, the French navy had regained control of naval aviation. In Germany, the *Luftwaffe* took control over all military aviation, angering the navy, which had earlier developed an air capacity even though that was forbidden under the 1919 Versailles peace settlement. In the United States, there was a very different situation thanks to the Bureau of Aeronautics of the American navy created in 1921. The bureau stimulated the development of effective air-sea doctrine, operational policies, and tactics. American air-sea doctrine emphasized attacking capital ships. The number of aircraft in the American Naval Air Arm rose from 1,081 in 1925 to 2,050 in 1938, a larger figure than in the Army Air Corps. The United States had a third air arm in the Marine Corps. In the Netherlands, the navy was able to resist political pressure and maintain a separate Naval Air Service.

Aside from the construction and enhancement of carriers, there were also marked improvements in naval aircraft, notably as air frames became larger and more powerful in the 1930s, although carriers could not accommodate twin-engine bombers in this period. The Americans and British developed dive-bombing tactics in the 1920s and, subsequently, dive-bombers. However, they did not replace torpedo bombers, aircraft capable of launching torpedoes. Torpedo bombers were vulnerable to defensive firepower but were best able to sink armored ships.[15] Improved torpedoes were deployed. In 1931, the Japanese introduced the Type 91 Mod 1 antiship torpedo.

The emphasis on carrier attack should not crowd out other uses for naval air power. Many aircraft were employed at sea to help battleships spot the fall of their shells. They were launched from catapults on the top of the turrets. Aerial reconnaissance, notably by seaplanes, which had a much better range than the smaller carrier or cruiser aircraft, was also crucial in the location of shipping.[16] A clear future for air power at sea was suggested by the British fleet reconstruction program of 1937, which aimed, by the late 1940s, to have twenty new battleships and twenty new carriers at the core of the battle fleet. In America, the emphasis was also on carrier support for battleships. From hindsight, the battleship appears redundant, but that was not how it seemed to contemporaries. Instead, it was believed that battleships could be protected against air attack, while carriers appeared vulnerable to gunnery, and thus to require protection, as well as being essentially only fair-weather and daytime warships. This need for carrier protection was enhanced by the limited range of aircraft, which meant that carriers had to approach their targets, thus making them vulnerable.[17]

EUROPEAN CHALLENGES

It was not only in the Pacific that a revisionist power threatened the existing international order. The same was true of Europe, with Italy and Germany. Benito Mussolini, the Italian Fascist dictator from 1922, greatly expanded the Italian navy in rivalry with France and in order to challenge the British position in the Mediterranean. This was the crucial axis of the British Empire as the shortest route to India, Australasia, and the Far East via the Suez Canal. It was an axis that was dependent on naval power and related bases at Gibraltar, Malta, and Alexandria (in Egypt), with Cyprus also a British colony.

However, like Hitler, Mussolini was less interested in naval affairs than in the situation on land, and he lacked both relevant knowledge and an understanding of the strategic situation. It was possible to talk of unlocking the gates of the Mediterranean at Gibraltar and Suez, but, as the ambitious Italian Naval Staff noted, there was really only hope of Italy controlling the central

Mediterranean. A lack of carrier air cover, and a battle fleet that could not match those of Britain and France, rendered other schemes futile. Despite some new warships, including battleships, cruisers, and submarines, the Italian navy also had tactical, resource, and weaponry deficiencies, especially weaknesses in gunnery training and shell manufacture, a shortage of oil, and the fact that some of its numerous submarines were outdated.

Britain and Italy came close to conflict as a result of the Italian invasion of Ethiopia in 1935–36, a step condemned by the League of Nations. In October 1933, the Chiefs of Staff Sub-Committee of the British Committee of Imperial Defence had warned that "our defensive arrangements in the Mediterranean are in many respects obsolete and have not been adjusted to the development of the French and Italian navies, and the increasing range and strength of French and Italian military aircraft."[18] However, in 1935–36, the Royal Navy, despite weaknesses, including a lack of sailors, reserves, and antiaircraft ammunition, and concerns about Italian submarines based at Leros in the Dodecanese Islands (an Italian colony in the Aegean), was confident of success. It had bases at Gibraltar, Malta, and Alexandria, although the Mediterranean Fleet was withdrawn from Malta to Alexandria due to fear of Italian air attack. The significance of naval bases was such that the priority thereafter was to improve Malta's defenses against air attack rather than against bombardment or invasion. Matching their confidence that antiaircraft guns could protect warships, the Royal Navy was certain that such improvement could be made, whereas senior airmen were convinced that sustained and heavy air attack could prevent safe use of the island and its naval base.

As a might-have-been war, the confrontation in 1935–36 was significant in the establishment of relative capability and in the development of plans. During the confrontation, the British planned a carrier attack on the Italian fleet in harbor at Taranto. One, indeed, was to be successfully launched in November 1940.

In the event, in 1935–36, the British government considered oil sanctions as well as the closing of the Suez Canal. However, the government did not wish to provoke war with Italy, not least as it hoped to keep Mussolini and Hitler apart, and did not intend to antagonize the Americans by stopping their oil tankers. The British failure to intimidate Italy was more a consequence of an absence of political will than a lack of naval capability. A failure to secure a promise of French naval cooperation was also significant. Mussolini pushed forward naval construction from 1936, improving Italy's battleship and submarine fleet. By the outbreak of war for Italy in 1940, the fleet included six battleships (two of them new), nineteen cruisers, and 113 submarines, but no aircraft carriers. In Eritrea, Italy had a colony on the Red Sea, with a port at Massawa, where destroyers were based, and, in Somalia, a colony on the Indian Ocean, with a port at Mogadishu. Yet, with the British in control of Egypt, the Italians were in no shape to aid these colonies.

Germany had a greater industrial capacity but was more restricted by treaty in the 1920s and early 1930s. Under the Weimar Republic, which was the government system between the First World War and the Nazi takeover of power in 1933, the Germans enhanced their naval strength through responding to the Versailles (1919) constraints on the maximum tonnage of German battleships by designing the *Deutschland* class. The *Deutschland* was classified by Germans as a *panzerschiff* or armored ship, and by others as a pocket battleship. Exploiting the discrepancy between the Versailles Treaty, which bound them, and the Washington Treaty, which bound everyone else (eleven-inch guns against eight-inch), the firepower of this class was superior to the cruisers of other navies. The *Deutschland* had six eleven-inch guns. Moreover, their new diesel propulsion gave them a speed of twenty-eight knots, which was faster than most other battleships, offering a mobility designed to allow the *Deutschland*-class ships the prospect of engaging with a target of opportunity, but to escape if the situation proved hazardous. Laid down in 1928, the *Deutschland* was commissioned two months after Hitler came to power in 1933. Over the following years, the specifications of the class improved. In practice, the ships did not equal their promise, as they were badly overloaded and their engines extremely unreliable. Also, the design itself, with only two turrets for the main guns, made the ships vulnerable in battle.

The development of this class was an instance of German strategic culture. The stress was on using technology to permit a major change in the international system. Surface warships and submarines provided key instances, whereas, in Britain, technological developments, such as changes in battleships, were pursued according to a more defensive strategic culture.

Britain sought to use naval issues as a means to stabilize Nazi Germany's position in the international system. The Anglo-German Naval Treaty of June 18, 1935, was a British attempt to provide an acceptable response to German demands for rearmament. Under this, the Germans were to have a quota equivalent to that of France or Italy under the 1922 Washington Treaty, with a surface fleet up to 35 percent the size of that of Britain and a submarine fleet of 45 percent, later 100 percent. Hitler, however, (characteristically) ignored these restrictions in his naval buildup.

Like Stalin, Hitler was fascinated by battleships, ordering the 42,000-ton *Bismarck* and *Tirpitz* (not the 35,000-ton figure provided to the British),[19] and he then planned another six battleships. In March 1939, Hitler arrived in the *Deutschland* at Memel (modern Klapeida) to take control of his new acquisition from Lithuania, thus displaying power as well as avoiding the need to cross Poland. In April, Hitler renounced the 1935 Anglo-German Naval Treaty. When he successfully attacked Poland that September, the latter's navy was heavily outnumbered and rapidly succumbed.

This German focus on battleships was to the detriment of smaller, frequently more effective warships. Indeed, at the outset of the Second World War, Germany had only fifty-seven submarines, of which twenty-three were seagoing, and all of obsolete design. The navy's commander, Admiral Erich Raeder, was also committed to battleships, arguing that antisubmarine warfare by Germany's rivals, notably the development of ASDIC (sonar), would counter the German submarines. Indeed, in the last stage of the Second World War, after he had been dismissed by Hitler, Raeder was to try to write the history of the Imperial German Navy prior to 1914. Raeder planned a balanced fleet. The buildup of the navy was designed for conflict with France and the Soviet Union, and, after relations deteriorated, Britain from 1938, but, in accordance with an assurance to Raeder from Hitler, it did not assume war until the mid-1940s. By then a far larger German navy was planned, one able to compete with the Royal Navy in battleships and also to contain carriers. Plan Z, approved by Hitler in January 1939, planned to have 13 battleships, 12 battle cruisers, eight carriers, and 249 submarines eventually, and 13, 3, 2, and 194 respectively by 1944. Ironically, the conquest of France in 1940 affected German planning for warship design, which had been predicated in part on conflict with French warships.[20]

The German emphasis on battleships, which made far more of a show for morale purposes, did not mean that submarines were ignored. Banned under the Versailles Treaty, they were built in the 1930s. Karl Dönitz, a First World War submarine commander who was appointed chief of the submarine force in 1935, sought to create a capability, aimed at the British, that was more effective than that seen in the First World War. He developed wolf-pack tactics in which a group of submarines, coordinated by radio, was to attack convoys on the surface at night, overwhelming the escorts. Dönitz planned an autonomous role for submarines focused on attacks on trade, and he wanted as many submarines as possible, whereas Raeder saw submarines both in this role and as performing those of fleet support and screening, for which he sought a small number of large, fast, and long-range submarines. However, the Germans did not carry out adequate cost-benefit analyses of naval power, whether surface or submarine, and did not properly think through their strategic weaknesses in this respect.

THE BRITISH EMPIRE

Within the British Empire, there was a tendency to rely on Britain, and, under financial pressure, the Dominions were reluctant to spend. Nevertheless, by 1938, Australia, which had partly modernized its navy in response to the Japanese challenge, had six cruisers and five destroyers. Canada, however, had only six destroyers and five minesweepers, New Zealand two light cruisers, and India only eight small coastal ships. Britain very much kept the Indian focus on the army. Cooperation with Britain was eased by the extensive use of British equipment and tactics.

The Royal Navy had also been hit by cuts. Although equality of size had been conceded to the Americans at the Washington Conference in 1922, the Royal Navy remained the world leader in prestige and reputation, while also having an unrivaled chain of fleet bases, which, in effect, were battleship bases. As a sign of their standing, British warships occupied pride of position on the *Bund* at Shanghai, the prime anchoring position in China. Nevertheless, as a consequence, in part, of the economic difficulties, social policy, and disarmament priorities of the Labour government of 1929–31, British naval expenditure had been cut seriously in 1929–34. For example, cuts in fuel and ammunition in 1931 hit training, while the substantial pay cuts for ordinary seamen announced by the national government in 1931 led to sailors refusing to muster and a reduction of the pay cuts from 25 to 10 percent. Between *Achilles* in 1931 and *Ajax* in 1933, no new cruiser was laid down, and the same was true for destroyers. By 1936, there was a degree of obsolescence in parts of the navy.

However, the British then responded to the buildup of German strength.[21] British naval planning correctly anticipated that war with Germany would result in a determined air-sea offensive against the British maritime system, with a naval dimension proving central to a lengthy struggle of industrial attrition.

From 1936, helped by an increase in the navy estimates, the Admiralty was free to pursue ambitious policies. Many carriers, battleships, cruisers, and destroyers were laid down: the battleships those of the *King George V* class, which had ten fourteen-inch guns. The first two of them, the *King George V* and the *Prince of Wales*, were laid down on January 1, 1937, the first date permitted under the naval limitation regime. In 1937, the first *Dido*-class cruiser, a dedicated antiaircraft cruiser, was laid down, offering a new cruiser design, although it suffered from inadequate armor and firepower. The Fleet Air Arm was greatly expanded. Radar sets were installed in British (and German) warships from 1938. There were weaknesses in 1939, notably a lack of mines and torpedoes, as well as a failure to appreciate that convoy protection was best ensured by escorts and not by hunting groups at sea.[22] There was only limited equipment for, and experience in, amphibious operations.[23] British naval bases, for example Alexandria, Malta, and Hong Kong, lacked adequate defenses against air attack. The Royal Navy was in a much better state than it had been in 1931, but it faced major commitments around the world. For example, Admiral Sir Geoffrey Layton noted in his war diary that, in early 1942, in the face of Japanese advance, "the problem of retaining control of the coastal waters of Burma was quite beyond our powers in the absence of either air superiority or fast patrol craft with good AA [antiaircraft] armament so numerous that we could afford substantial losses."[24] The British lacked an adequate land-based air force in India.

FRANCE

Just to the west of Germany, France, like the Soviet Union to Germany's east, could be classified as having a medium-sized navy relative to the world's leading fleets. It played a supportive role to the army and operated within defined waters. France's focus was on its army and fortifications. Nevertheless, there was also concern with naval strength and on protecting links with the colonies. Having competed with Italy in the 1920s and responded in particular to the Italian-Spanish alignment, including with preparations for coastal defense, the French were challenged by the laying down of the *Deutschland* in 1928. This led the French to lay down new battle cruisers in the early 1930s, the *Dunkerque* and the *Strasbourg*. The name of the latter, an affirmation of France's commitment to the territory regained from Germany in 1918–19, was, as so often, an indication of the symbolism of naval power. Designed to pursue the *panzerschiff*, these battleships were fast. In turn, these ships were followed by the 35,000-ton *Richelieu*-class battleships, such that in 1939 France had the fourth-largest navy in the world. In response to the German naval buildup, the French navy refocused its attention from the Italians and the Mediterranean and established a battleship-based *Force de Raid* at Brest, France's major Atlantic base. This force was designed to protect French trade routes. From 1938, in part as a result of Italian naval expansion, an ambitious three-year shipbuilding program was pursued. As a result, the French fleet had effective ships that were to be important to the power politics of 1940–42, notably in the Mediterranean. France also had the *Béarn*, a dreadnought converted into a carrier, and laid down a second carrier, the *Joffre*, in 1938. However, more effective land-based aircraft in the 1930s threatened carrier operations in European waters, especially from the Italians in the Mediterranean, and this lessened French interest in carriers. France's strategic situation posed major problems. It was dependent on transporting troops from North Africa and also drew most of its oil supplies from the Caribbean and was thus dependent on Britain for control of the North Atlantic sea lanes.

The navy frequently sought to bring its strategic requirements to the attention of the army through the *Conseil Supérieur de la Defense Nationale*, but it did not prove successful. This was a long-standing issue in the strategic culture of France and one that affected the French navy whatever the technological and geopolitical situation. This priority reflected not just concern about European neighbors and the weight of the past, but also the use of the army as the ultimate guarantor of political stability and governmental concern, as, for example, in 1968. The navy could not fulfill this function and was anyway considered too independent minded.

THE SOVIET UNION

Given its importance as a naval power prior to the First World War, and again during the Cold War from the 1960s, it is instructive to consider the development of the Soviet navy in the 1920s and 1930s. It underlined a point that is more generally true but that tends to get underplayed for other navies, that is, the role of political considerations in strategy and doctrine, rather than the centrality of weapons capabilities.

There was significant continuity from the tsarist period into the Soviet era that began in 1917, not least continuity in terms of doctrine and leadership. The emphasis, under what was later called the "Old School," was for a defensive posture in both the Gulf of Finland (to the west of St. Petersburg/Petrograd/Leningrad) and the Black Sea. Submarines and torpedo boats were to weaken attacking fleets, most probably the Royal Navy, which had played a major role against the communists in the Russian Civil War, prior to a battle in which the Soviet navy would use its full power in a decisive engagement. This strategy accorded with the state and size of the Soviet navy, which did not benefit from new construction in this period and which was very much overshadowed by the army.[25] Unlike in the 1890s and 1900s, there was no strong naval concern with the Far East.

The drive for something more than a defensive strategy combined with ideological, political, and generational contrasts to lead the "Young School" (based on the French *Jeune École* of the 1880s) to challenge these ideas from the late 1920s. The Young School were communists and also sought a strategy that conformed more to the attacking plans of the Red Army. Arguing for the role of submarines and aircraft, the Young School questioned the idea of command of the sea as well as the belief in a superior navy with the attendant stress on powerful surface ships, which the Soviet Union did not have. In contrast to the Old School, and the more general international adherence to Mahanian ideas, the Young School claimed that a decisive battle was a mistaken goal and, instead, that the submarines, torpedo boats, and aircraft of the Soviet navy could nullify the impact of the opposing fleet so as to enable the Soviet navy to assist the army.

This approach pleased Josef Stalin, the Soviet dictator, who in 1930 purged the navy and promoted the Young School. As a result, in the early and mid-1930s, their ideas shaped doctrine, training, and procurement. The Second Five-Year Plan (1933–37) pressed for submarine production, while the annual maneuvers of the Baltic Fleet, the main Soviet fleet, focused on amphibious attacks in support of the army. Such attacks could be launched against the Baltic republics, Poland, and Germany. Stalin considered a new naval response following Hitler's rise to power in 1933.

In 1937–38, there was another transformation in leadership and a related reversal in doctrine. Imposing total control, Stalin purged the navy in 1937 at the same time as he brutally purged the army and air force.[26] The Young School was destroyed, while political commissars were given the task of jointly signing orders with commanding officers. This purge reinforced and reflected Stalin's commitment to big ships. Stalin had come to focus on them in part in response to the commitment to such ships by Germany, Japan, and Britain. In particular, the development of the German fleet challenged the Soviet position in the Baltic and was interpreted in that light by Stalin. Stalin saw the battleship as the foundation of naval power. He was thwarted in his plans to order the world's largest battleship from an American yard, but by 1939 there were three 59,000-ton battleships under construction in the Soviet Union, as well as two 35,000-ton battle cruisers, which were designed to be faster.[27]

None, however, was ever completed. In part, there was no time to create a fleet of big ships before the Soviet Union was plunged into war with Germany in 1941, but the purges were also a factor. They affected the shipyards and greatly exacerbated the problems created by Stalin's unrealistic assumptions. This situation led to a serious decline in quality. Much of the armor of Soviet warships was inadequate, and complex gun mountings posed a particular problem. Due to such problems, much of the investment of resources was wasted. There were some parallels, but also scant comparison, with the Chinese buildup in the early twenty-first century, as the latter rested on a stronger and more broadly based economy and focused on a range of military systems.

In addition, Stalin's purges, which were continued into the 1940s by fresh killings, helped ensure a serious shortage of experienced officers, and of noncommissioned officers, as the latter were promoted to fill the gaps. Training regimes were seriously affected, the frequency of accidents rose, and there was less emphasis on annual maneuvers. As a result, the effectiveness of the navy at combined-arms operations, notably coordination with aircraft, declined.

The range of naval capabilities that had to be established and maintained at an effective pitch was indicated by the significant deficiencies in the Soviet naval forces at the close of the 1930s. These included the absence of dive-bombers, advanced torpedoes, and sonar equipment, and the fact that only one ship was equipped with radar. Although there was a large submarine force, it was poorly trained, and, in the event, its wartime effectiveness proved limited. In part, this was because submarine aiming and firing techniques were poor, while Soviet doctrine emphasized remaining in fixed positions and waiting for enemy vessels to appear. The situation underlined the more general difficulty of developing capability and the requirement for more than resources.

The Soviet Union could have been exposed to naval warfare, but the clashes with Japan in 1938 and 1939 were both limited and restricted to land combat in border regions. Thereafter, after an agreement in 1941, the two powers did not fight until 1945. Moreover, alliance with Germany in 1939–41 ensured that the Soviet Union was not exposed to attack by the larger German navy until such time as the latter was heavily engaged by Britain, which had not gone to war with the Soviet Union when it was allied with Germany.

NAVAL CONFLICT IN THE 1930s

Warships played a role in many of the conflicts of the 1930s. Navies remained significant in both civil conflicts and in those between states. The scale, intensity, and duration of such fighting varied greatly. For example, in 1931, a navy mutiny in Chile was suppressed. About twenty aircraft failed to make any direct hits when bombing the warships and only caused three casualties, but the air attack, combined with government firmness, combined to hit the mutineers' morale and the mutiny ended. In Spain, the navy played a role in suppressing a coal miners' uprising in the Asturias region in northwest Spain, the cruiser *Libertad* shelling the town of Gijon.

Most of the Spanish navy supported the government against the Nationalist uprising that led to the Spanish Civil War (1936–39). The navy potentially played a key role at the outset, blockading Spanish Morocco where the Nationalists had many troops. However, the blockade was circumvented by means of air transport. Supplied by Italy and Germany, Nationalist aircraft proved a major threat to Republican warships. So also did Italian submarines, which in 1937, in response to a Nationalist request, and despite the reluctance of the naval leadership,[28] launched unrestricted submarine warfare in order to stop Soviet supplies to the Republicans and, more generally, to harm the latter. Moreover, Italy sold four submarines and four destroyers to the Nationalists. The strength of the Republican navy did not sway the struggle. Indeed, from bases in the Balearic Islands, Nationalist, German, and Italian warships and aircraft sank many ships making for Republican ports.[29] Britain had doubts about the coordinated anti-Italian Mediterranean naval strategy France proposed, but the Royal Navy provided destroyers to patrol for submarines and to deter attacks on trade, and the show of force proved effective.[30]

In China, Japan made much use of its navy in the war that broke out in 1937. That year, naval gunfire played a major role in stemming the initial Chinese attack on the Japanese positions in Shanghai. Having taken Shanghai, Japanese aircraft sank an American gunboat on the Yangzi, but isolated ships in confined waters were especially vulnerable to air attack. The following year, Japanese warships sailed up the Yangzi and directly engaged Chinese positions. The Japanese employed only a portion of their navy in China and, notably, few of their aircraft carriers, but they had fleets on the Yangzi and off China.

The Japanese made much use of amphibious attacks. An amphibious landing that threatened to cut off the Chinese forces there was crucial to the capture of Shanghai in 1937, the ports of Xiamen (Amoy) and Guangzhou (Canton) in 1938, and the island of Hainan in 1939. Largely as a result of initiatives by the army, Japan made the most progress among the powers, both in developing types of landing craft and in building a reasonable number of ships. Their *Dai-Hatsu* had a ramp in its bows and was to become the key type of landing craft. The navy built up its amphibious capability by developing units that specialized as *rikusentai* (landing parties). They were given infantry training, and by the late 1930s, the navy had permanent landing units that were based ashore and armed with heavy weaponry including artillery. This represented a type of jointness in that amphibious capability was enhanced, but it also represented the extent to which the army and navy fought separate wars.

With far more expertise than other powers, the Japanese developed an amphibious doctrine and practice. They put the emphasis on attacking at night or at dawn and on landing at several points simultaneously and then concentrating on land. Their experience was to stand them in good stead in 1941–42, especially in their rapid conquest of Malaya, the Philippines, and the Dutch East Indies. This was a key bridge between the interwar period and the Second World War.

A more benign imperial use of naval power was seen in the Persian Gulf where in 1932 Britain deployed warships in order to gain landing rights for aircraft en route to India. In 1937, a warship dispatched to Dubai served to underline British views on freeing slaves. [31]

CONCLUSION

Doctrine, planning, and procurement all reflected tasking. For example, the need for deep-sea British air capability in any war with Germany appeared lessened by the vulnerability of German naval power to land-based air attacks. The lesson of the First World War appeared to be that the Germans could be bottled up in the North Sea. In 1940, however, they were to transform the situation by seizing Norway and France. More generally, the British, American, Japanese, and German navies failed to realize fully the contribution that air power could make to the conduct of war at sea.

The navies built up in the 1930s were to be those that fought the Second World War. At the same time, the war involved the destruction of all or most of these navies. In doing so, the war increased the need to construct new warships. This proved a test for strategic prioritization, resource allocation, and industrial capacity. In particular, America was to build a bigger and better fleet (as well as merchant fleet), and one that incorporated both prewar lessons and those of the early section of the war. [32]

At the same time, it is important, yet again, to note the range of naval trajectories. For example, the weakness of Iran's navy, not least in the face of piracy and smuggling in the Persian Gulf, led to the buildup of a navy in the 1930s, with warships built in Italy and officers trained there. This was an instance of the more widespread situation in which naval strength, or at least presence, was seen as important for sovereignty and national prestige.

Chapter Six

Naval Armageddon, 1939–45

The Second World War saw the largest-scale naval warfare in history, most notably so from December 1941 when the Japanese attack on the American naval base of Pearl Harbor and the subsequent German declaration of war on the United States increased the number of participants and greatly widened the geographical range of conflict. The "world ocean" became a unified theater of naval warfare. Already, however, the naval warfare had involved the European powers, notably Britain, Germany, and France, all from 1939, and Italy from 1940, and, from June 1941, the Soviet Union, and had ranged across much of the world. In that warfare, as well as in that from December 1941, there was a full variety of types of naval conflict, including battles between surface warships, amphibious operations, submarine warfare, carrier-based missions, and blockades.

Any narrative of the naval dimension of the war poses issues of explicit or, far more commonly, implicit emphasis. Much derives from differing national perspectives. There are contrasts in American and British views. In part, issues of emphasis relate to one aspect of naval warfare as opposed to another. However, there is also the question of the significance of cooperation of naval forces with others, both in combined operations and otherwise. Separately, there is the issue of the relative importance of naval power as opposed to other forms of power. These factors should be considered as implicit within the narrative and will be discussed in an explicit fashion both at the close of this chapter and in the conclusions to the book.

In many respects, the war represented *the* crisis for the prime naval power, Britain, and, as a linked but separate matter, its empire. Yet France, the Soviet Union, Italy, Germany, and Japan suffered far more serious blows to their navies, and these require due attention while also shedding light on the resilience of the Royal Navy, which was responsible for most of the damage to the German and Italian navies. The war also saw the triumph of American naval power and a significant rise in that of Canada. In each case, fighting quality, leadership, strategic roles, and organizational sophistication were linked to impressive feats of shipbuilding.[1] It was suggested by one of the readers that the length of this chapter meant that it should be divided: into chapters on the war with Germany and that with Japan. However, to do so risks taking attention away from the range and severity of the issues confronting Britain and America and the scale of their responses.

It is also important to note the importance of the war at sea for states not generally noted as naval powers, such as Thailand, Sweden, and Finland. For example, Vichy French warships defeated the Thais in January 1941 at the Battle of Koh-Chang when Thailand attacked French Indochina. The Vichy navy launched an incursion in response to the Thai attack on land. Five Vichy ships, including a light cruiser, used their overwhelming firepower against three Thai warships (two of them torpedo boats), causing heavy casualties. The Thais suffered from not using their four newly acquired Japanese-built submarines to patrol their waters, as these submarines could have destroyed the Vichy warships. As a reminder of the need to contextualize naval achievement, the success of Thai forces on land and, even more, the geopolitical situation, with Japan supportive of Thailand and Vichy France, in contrast, isolated, were such that peace was obtained at the price of French territorial cessions to Thailand in Indochina.

Sweden remained neutral during the war, but its navy, 47 vessels strong in 1939 and 126 in 1945, escorted convoys bound for Germany so as to protect them against Soviet submarines, being helped by the limitations of the latter. This naval strength, which included six destroyers commissioned during the war, was very important to the continued movement of iron to supply Germany's steel industry and thus its munitions production. Similarly, in the First World War, neutral Sweden had protected ships bound for Germany from British and Russian submarines. For such states, war repeatedly indicated the importance of the maritime dimension and of naval power.[2]

Neutrals faced differing vulnerabilities and threats in part due to power politics but also to the extent to which they had a coastline and could therefore be more readily invaded. The significance of their territories for maritime routes, for example of the Azores, a Portuguese possession, for air cover over a large part of the mid-Atlantic, was also notable.

THE WAR BEGINS

In 1939, Britain, despite its strengths, lacked a navy capable of fighting Germany, Italy, and Japan simultaneously. That was the product of the stop on capital ship construction under the Washington Naval Treaty, as well as the lack of sufficient British industrial capability and fiscal strength. At the same time, the buildup of the strength of these three powers was a key element. The political context was significant. To expect the arithmetic of naval power to provide for conflict at once with all three states was to anticipate a margin of superiority that was unreasonable given the state of Britain and the fact that its potential enemies were well apart, but also one that diplomacy sought to avoid the need for. British naval strategists planned that, if necessary, operations against threats arising simultaneously would be conducted sequentially in separate theaters. This strategy assumed that operational flexibility could help lessen the constraints posed by tough fiscal limits.

In addition, war was likely to bring Britain the support of allies. France was seen as a key help against Italy if the latter entered the war, which it did not do until June 1940.[3] The loss of French naval support in the aftermath of German conquest in May–June 1940 was unexpected. However, the Japanese entry into the war in 1941 led to a crucial alliance with the United States. The naval history of the war thus demonstrated the importance and unpredictability of the political dimension of warfare. The idea of a navy capable of holding off Germany, Italy, and Japan at once would have been out of line with nineteenth-century assumptions.

Naval warfare played a key role from the outbreak of the Second World War. It was crucial to the Allied plans to weaken Germany by means of containment, blockade, and cutting it off from the non-European world, and thus lessening its appeal to potential allies and leading Hitler to negotiate or be overthrown. This approach, the so-called long-war policy, represented a reading from the role of naval blockade in Germany's defeat in 1918, as well as a reflection of where Britain had its greatest power.[4] However, the German-Soviet alliance enabled Germany to obtain supplies from the Soviet Union, including food and oil, and thus to evade blockade. In February 1940, Germany sold the incomplete cruiser *Lütow* to the Soviet Union.

Thanks to naval dominance, Britain and France were able to move their forces, with the British Expeditionary Force transported to France in 1939, as were French forces from North Africa. Britain and France, however, were unable to provide naval assistance to Poland, whose small fleet was rapidly overwhelmed by the Germans, although the best Polish warships (two recently built large destroyers) and some others escaped to Britain. In order to cut off Swedish iron-ore supplies to Germany, Churchill advocated the dispatch of a fleet to the Baltic specially prepared to resist air attack. This rash idea, a new version of that considered prior to the First World War, would have exposed the fleet to air attack in confined waters and without local bases, but it was thwarted by his naval advisors. Naval power was important to amphibious capability, and there were plans for such Allied attacks in a number of places.

NORWAY, 1940

Amphibious capability came to the fore with the Norway campaign in April–May 1940. Anxious to preempt the danger of British moves against German imports of Swedish iron ore by sea through Norwegian waters, and keen to establish submarine bases from which to attack British shipping,[5] the Germans invaded Norway, conquering Denmark in addition in order to ease this invasion. In Norway, the Germans largely relied on amphibious landings. The capital, Oslo, however, was captured by airborne troops, although only after the loss to coastal-based torpedo fire of the *Blücher*, a heavy cruiser escorting an attempted German amphibious landing that was thereby blocked.

The German ability to mount landings represented a success as well as a failure for naval power, notably a failure for the poorly directed Royal Navy to prevent the initial landings or, subsequently on April 9, to disrupt them. It was part of a more general failure of intelligence and naval management, with the British initially wrongly convinced that the Germans were planning to sail into the Atlantic.[6] A *Luftwaffe* (German air force) attack ended moves by the British surface fleet on invasion day, although British submarines had a valuable impact. Moreover, the possibility of naval action was shown on April 10 and 13 when British warships sailed into Ofotfjord to wreck the German squadron that had attacked and occupied the town of Narvik in northern Norway, destroying ten German destroyers. These destroyer losses effectively scuppered naval support for any cross-Channel invasion: thereafter, the Germans did not have enough to ward off any British destroyer attack. More generally, German losses of warships in the campaign had a long-term strategic consequence by weakening the German surface fleet.[7]

Thanks, however, to German air power, the British forces in Norway were totally defeated. General Auchinleck, who commanded the Anglo-French expeditionary force to Narvik, attributed the German victory primarily to air power, commenting, "The enemy's supremacy in the air made the use inshore of naval vessels of the type co-operating with this force highly dangerous."[8] The Royal Navy had also been shown to be unable to cope effectively with German air power, and a doctrine of reliance on antiaircraft fire had been revealed as inadequate. There was a lack of enough rapid-firing antiaircraft guns. Admiral Sir Dudley Pound, the First Sea Lord, remarked to one of the senior admirals, "The one lesson we have learnt here is that it is essential to have fighter protection over the Fleet whenever they are within reach of the enemy bombers."[9]

The Royal Navy also took hard knocks from German surface warships, especially when covering the forces withdrawing from Narvik. The vulnerability of carriers to surface ships was shown, on June 7, when the *Glorious* was sunk by the battle cruiser *Scharnhorst*, although this was to be the sole British carrier sunk by surface ships during the entire war. The British failure in Norway was to be serious for the subsequent course of the naval war as it increased the possibilities for German access to the Atlantic and also provided bases for submarines (U-boats), surface ships, and aircraft that threatened the maritime route to northern Russia as well as the British Isles. In the shorter term, this failure had an influence on neutral opinion, including that of the United States. In strategic terms, the significance of Norway was to increase as a result of the subsequent Battle of the Atlantic with German submarines. This significance led both to British plans for attacks on Norway and to British concern with its security in the postwar Cold War with the Soviet Union.[10]

FRANCE, 1940

Naval conflict played only a minor role in the rapid German conquest of France, the Netherlands, and Belgium in 1940, thus repeating the situation with the Franco-Prussian War in 1870–71. However, naval power was significant in permitting the evacuation of much of the British army from France. This was a pivotal military event of the Second World War, allowing Churchill to push the case for Britain fighting on. From May 27 to June 4, 338,000 troops, including 123,000 French troops, were evacuated from Dunkirk. Although private boats and French warships also took off an important number, the Royal Navy evacuated most of the troops, an evacuation that was crucial to the subsequent strength of Britain in the event of invasion. The navy took serious punishment from German aircraft in the process.

Additional Allied units were evacuated by sea from the ports of St. Valéry-en-Caux, Le Havre, Cherbourg, St. Malo, Brest, and St. Nazaire, although others were captured. There was not a comparable movement of troops to North Africa because, although it is frequently argued that France could have done so and fought on, the capacity of the French North African ports was only sufficient to land thirty thousand soldiers a week, and it would have taken seven months to transport one million men. As the Germans advanced, 170,000 tonnes of French warship in construction, including the carrier *Joffre* and the battleship *Clemenceau*, their names resonant of the French war effort in the First World War, were sabotaged so that the Germans should not seize them.

France surrendered on June 22, 1940. Much was occupied by Germany, including all of the Channel and Atlantic coastlines. However, a new French government based in Vichy was left in control of south and part of central France, as well as of France's empire and fleet, which was largely located in Toulon in southern France and in French North Africa. Warships en route to take refuge in Britain were recalled by Vichy. The Vichy government ignored the call from the London-based Free French for continued resistance.

THE THREAT TO BRITAIN

Britain's security was now greatly at risk. German air power and submarines threatened Britain's vital sea lines of communication and supply with the outside world. Moreover, Operation *Seelöwe* (Sealion), an invasion of southern England, was planned, and preparations for the invasion were made. The *Luftwaffe* (German air force) was instructed to prepare the way, especially by driving British warships from the English Channel. Despite the failure to prevent their success on the occasion, the Norway campaign had indicated the potential vulnerability of German amphibious operations to British naval power as well as causing the German navy heavy losses, notably in destroyers. Moreover, although Italy's entry into the war in June 1940, in alliance with Germany, had increased pressure on the Royal Navy in the Mediterranean, sufficient warships remained in British home waters to challenge any German naval attack. Although successful against Norway earlier in 1940, the Germans lacked adequate experience or understanding of amphibious operations, as well as specialized landing craft. The towed Rhine barges they proposed to rely on could only manage a speed of three knots and would have failed to land a significant number of troops had any of them managed to reach England's south coast. Even had the Germans landed troops, they would not have been able to sustain and reinforce them. In practice, the invaders would probably have been killed at sea given the willingness of the Royal Navy to lose ships as required to defeat an existential threat.[11]

The failure of the *Luftwaffe* in the Battle of Britain in August–September 1940 to overcome the Royal Air Force in a struggle for air superiority over southern England helped ensure the failure of Operation Sealion, which was never launched. However, the Royal Navy was probably strong enough to thwart invasion even had the *Luftwaffe* been more powerful, not least because of the limited nighttime effectiveness of air power. The navy's vulnerability to German dive-bombers was an important factor, but these bombers were themselves vulnerable to British fighters and to antiaircraft guns. Moreover, the Germans lacked the torpedo-bomber capability that the British and Japanese were effectively to display in 1940 and 1941, respectively. The Royal Navy and the RAF contributed greatly to the abandonment of Sealion by raids on the invasion ports and the barges they contained.

WAR IN THE MEDITERRANEAN

In the Mediterranean, June 1940 introduced a period of grave danger for Britain, both with Italy's entry into the war and with the fall, soon after, of France. The sympathy of Spain's Fascist regime for Germany was also an issue. The French navy was unable to inflict serious damage on Italy. Anxiety about Vichy, and the possibility that the Germans would be able to take over the French fleet, led to the contentious British attack on the Vichy fleet at Mers el Kébir near Oran in Algeria on July 3, 1940, in which one battleship was sunk and two were damaged. [12] They also led to a subsequent poorly coordinated, mishandled, and unsuccessful British attack on September 23–25 on Dakar, the main Vichy base in West Africa, an attack in which surprise had been lost. On November 9, 1940, before Libreville in Gabon, a French colony in West Africa, a Free French warship fired on a Vichy one. Count Ciano, Italy's foreign minister, was impressed by the attack on Mers el Kébir: "It proves that the fighting spirit of His British Majesty's fleet is quite alive, and still has the aggressive ruthlessness of the captains and pirates of the seventeenth century." [13]

Whereas Germany was a Continental power with added naval interests and strength, Italy was a far-flung empire, with colonies in North Africa (Libya) and East Africa (Eritrea, Ethiopia, and most of modern Somalia). As such, Italy was dependent on maritime links and thus exposed to British naval power while, in turn, challenging the Mediterranean axis of the British Empire from Gibraltar via Malta to the Suez Canal. Admiral Domenico Cavagnari, the cautious chief of the Italian Naval Staff, had planned a fleet able to seize control of both ends of the Mediterranean so that it could operate on the oceans, but, aware of the true capability of the Italian air force and navy, he adopted a far more cautious stance once war broke out. Despite the success of individual units, especially their "human torpedoes" that fixed mines crippling two British battleships in Alexandria in December 1941, the Italians, notably their large submarine force, were unable to make a major impact on British naval strength. The Italians were short of oil and confidence. It was difficult for Italy, with its limited industrial base and shortage of raw materials, to replace losses. The Italians also lacked an effective naval air arm, and their radar was far weaker than that of Britain.

Instead, the British repeatedly took the initiative. This was true at the strategic level. Britain was able to move the forces that recaptured British Somaliland and that carried out the conquest of Italian East Africa. Part of the advance was overland, but distance, communications, and the coastal location of key Italian positions (Massawa and Mogadishu) made naval capability and amphibious operations especially significant. Moreover, in the invasion of the Italian colony of Libya in December 1940, a British naval inshore squadron played a role. The Italian colonies were unable to provide mutual support. [14]

The British seizure of the initiative was also true at the operational and tactical levels. The successful night attack by twenty-one torpedo bombers on Italian battleships moored, without radar support, in Taranto on November 11, 1940, badly damaged four of them and encouraged the Japanese attack on Pearl Harbor just over a year later. This was also so at the tactical level, with the technique of shallow-running the torpedo. Unlike with the Americans at Pearl Harbor, the Italians did not have carriers at sea elsewhere and, in addition, lacked the shipbuilding capacity to create a replacement navy. Indeed, in terms of the damage inflicted, and the number of attacking aircraft, this raid was more effective than the Japanese raid on Pearl Harbor. The long-term effect on the Italian navy was different from that on the U.S. Navy. In response to the raid, the Italians withdrew units from Taranto northward and thus lessened the vulnerability of British maritime routes and naval forces in the Mediterranean, notably by increasing the problems of concentrating Italian naval forces and maintaining secrecy. In addition to the senior commanders understanding the limitations of their ships and industrial base, Italian admirals were also averse to taking risks because they believed the war would be won or lost by Germany and that in a postwar world the navy would be Italy's most important military asset. For Britain, Taranto served as a crucial boost to public and government morale at a time of isolation and being under assault.

On March 27–28, 1941, off Cape Matapan, thanks to torpedo bombers from the carrier *Formidable*, battleship firepower, and ships' radar, the British, who had broken the Italian codes, sank three of the best Italian cruisers, *Fiume*, *Pola*, and *Zara*, and damaged the modern battleship *Vitorio Vento*. The Italian cruisers were wrecked by the fifteen-inch guns of the British battleships. This defeat ended meaningful Italian fleet operations. The Royal Navy benefited from knowing that Sealion had been canceled, which enabled them to focus their forces in the Atlantic and Mediterranean. The British had superiority in battleships and carriers in the Mediterranean.

In response to Italian defeats, and to the need to put pressure on Britain, which he wanted to drive to negotiate, Hitler sent German aircraft to Sicily from January 1941. *Fliegerkorps* X, specialists in maritime strike, challenged the British position in the central Mediterranean. This was a form of indirect attack on Britain, but the emphasis was on air power and not, as in British doctrine, on sea power. In January 1941, German dive-bombers sank the cruiser *Southampton* and crippled the carrier *Illustrious*, underlining the vulnerability of carriers. [15] The damage to *Illustrious* was significant in that it was intended to accompany the warships sent to Singapore, and the inability to send the ship deprived them of air cover.

The German presence increased in April–May 1941 with the conquest of Yugoslavia and Greece. Much of the Yugoslav navy was captured by the invading Axis forces, while many Greek warships were destroyed by German bombers. British intervention in Greece was unsuccessful. Maintaining their momentum, the Germans invaded the Greek island of Crete by parachute and glider troops, an invasion accompanied by successful resupply by air. Two German convoys en route for Crete in order to support the invasion were successfully intercepted, but the British attempt to reinforce, supply, and eventually evacuate Crete by sea led to heavy British losses, including three cruisers and six destroyers sunk. Naval operations within the range of land were now clearly vulnerable to attack unless air superiority could be gained. The British navy off Crete lacked air cover and adequate air defense in its ships. Such vulnerability affected the rationale of naval operations, because the risk of a rapid and serious loss of ships was now far greater. Moreover, such a loss would mean a failure of relative naval capability, because there would be no accompanying loss of opposing naval forces. Air power thereby threatened to limit the attritional possibilities of naval operations.

Admiral Andrew Cunningham, the able British naval commander in the Mediterranean, feared that the Germans might press on to invade the island of Cyprus, a British colony, and to deploy forces in Vichy-run Syria, threatening the British position in the Middle East.[16] In the event, there was no such exploitation, and instead the Crete invasion was a distraction for the Germans from the more important target of Malta, a British island colony, which threatened maritime and air links between Italy and North Africa. The Royal Navy helped in the British conquest of Syria in 1941, defeating a Vichy flotilla.

German submarines also made a major difference in the Mediterranean, attacking warships and merchantmen, although the British took pains to limit news of this. John Turner, a newsreel cameraman, took striking film of the torpedoing of the battleship *Barham* in 1941, in which 869 lives were lost, only to find that the film was censored.[17] *Barham*'s name referred back to the triumphs of the Napoleonic Wars.

The value of air cover was such that operations on land were regarded as crucial to naval operations, as they offered the possibility of moving airfields forward. In August 1941, General Thomas Blamey, the commander of the Australian forces in the Middle East, reported about eastern Libya, "Cyrenaica is regarded as most urgent problem of Middle East as control to Benghazi [the major city in eastern Libya] would give fleet freedom of movement as far as Malta and advance air bases to allow cover of sea operations."[18] German and Italian air attacks on Malta's harbor and airfields, and highly damaging air and submarine attacks on British convoys supplying Malta in 1941–42, especially on the convoy code-named Pedestal in 1942, were central to a sustained, but unsuccessful, attempt to starve the British-held island into surrender. Spitfires (fighters) that were delivered by carrier from March and, more successfully, May 1942 ensured that the air war over the island was won by the British that year. However, the Italians were able to keep the rate of loss on the Libyan convoy route low, which, instead of battle, was their key naval goal.[19]

Hypotheticals or counterfactuals, the "what-ifs" of history, come into play, as the fate of Malta leads to the question of whether air and sea operations against an island were inadequate unless supported by an invasion. As far as the Second World War itself was concerned, this is a question that also arises with the German threat to Britain itself, with American "island hopping" in the Pacific, and with the "endgame" for Japan. Similar questions can be raised about areas that were not islands, notably Italy in 1943–45. In short, had a combination of naval pressure and air attack made the actual presence of invading troops less necessary or even redundant? This is an issue that is still relevant today, for example with Chinese pressure on Taiwan or, in the longer term, possibly Japan.

These hypotheticals are of value because many of them played a role in strategic debate. In the specific case of Britain in 1940–43 and Malta in 1941–42, the naval pressure was far less direct than in the case of the War in the Pacific. The Germans and Italians enjoyed a surface presence in the Atlantic and Mediterranean but in each case were outnumbered by the British. Air power and submarine attacks could try to counter this, but they did not succeed in doing so to the extent of closing the sea to British shipping. Submarines provided the capacity for a blockade, but not one that was complete, and certainly not one to match the American blockade of Japan in 1945.

As a consequence, the alternatives were invasion or enforced surrender. The latter was to be the case with Japan as a result of the use of atom bombs. However, in the absence of such a strategic means, and the aerial resources of Germany did not provide one, it was necessary to invade. To launch such an invasion of Malta would have been a major diversion of German and Italian resources. Possibly it should have been the goal instead of Crete, and it was a planning option, but German forces to attack Crete were present in nearby mainland Greece. In 1941, the German focus was to be on the Soviet Union. Therefore, only a distant blockade of Malta combined with an air assault was to be attempted.

THE STRUGGLE FOR THE ATLANTIC

The Royal Navy was under wide-ranging pressure by the summer of 1941. The German conquest of Norway (April–May 1940) and France (May–June

1940) ensured that the naval situation was totally different from that in the First World War, with a German presence now all the way to Atlantic ports in France, especially Brest. It was now far harder for the British to enforce a blockade than in the earlier war. Instead of using their surface fleet as a unit and providing the British with a concentrated target, the Germans relied on raids by small squadrons or individual ships. These were designed to attack Allied shipping, but the ships were hunted down. Thus, in December 1939, the "pocket battleship" *Graf Spee*, which had attacked shipping in the Atlantic, was damaged off South America by less-heavily gunned British warships in the Battle of the River Plate. Taking refuge in Uruguay rather than fighting its way into the open Atlantic, the ship was scuttled before the arrival of British reinforcements.

The most spectacular of these raids was that by the 42,000-ton battleship *Bismarck* in May 1941. The threat posed by the *Bismarck*, the leading surface ship in the German navy, a well-armored ship with eight fifteen-inch guns capable of going at more than twenty-nine knots, helped drive American preparations. This encouraged a determination to expand the American navy and also to take defensive steps around Norfolk, Virginia, the main American naval base on the Atlantic. These preparations included the deployment of land-based sixteen-inch guns with a maximum range of 45,100 yards, capable of outfiring the *Bismarck* with its gun range of 39,900 yards, in the event of the latter trying to approach the Chesapeake to attack Norfolk. Roosevelt took great interest in the eventual defeat by the Royal Navy in 1941 of the *Bismarck*'s sortie into the Atlantic.

The *Bismarck*'s raid was designed to show that surface warships could make a major impact on North Atlantic shipping. It was strong enough to defeat convoy escorts. Well aware of the threat, the British mounted a considerable effort to keep tabs on German warships and to respond to any moves. The *Bismarck* was sent on a three-month cruise to devastate British shipping. British bombers failed to find the *Bismarck* in Norwegian waters, but on May 23 she was spotted by patrolling British warships in the Denmark Strait between Iceland and Greenland. The following day, the *Bismarck* and the cruiser *Prinz Eugen* encountered a British squadron sent to intercept them southwest of Iceland, with the British helped by radar in shadowing the Germans. In the subsequent gunnery exchange, which lasted for only twenty minutes, the *Bismarck* sank the elderly battle cruiser *Hood*, with all bar three of the crew killed, and seriously damaged the battleship *Prince of Wales*. Three shells from the latter, however, had hit the *Bismarck*, causing a dangerous oil leak that led the commander to set course for France and repairs.[20]

As a testimony to British naval strength, and the capability for a "deep response," the *Bismarck* swiftly faced a massive deployment, including battleships *King George V* and *Rodney*, two carriers, two battle cruisers, and thirteen other cruisers. The *Bismarck* was eventually crippled by a hit on the rudder by an aircraft-launched torpedo (May 26), a further demonstration of the vulnerability of surface ships to air power. Heavily damaged by fire from the battleships, the *Bismarck* fell victim next day to a cruiser-launched torpedo. Hitler then ordered the other surface raiders to be concentrated in Norwegian waters.

THE SUBMARINE ATTACK

Submarines were less vulnerable than surface ships to blockade, detection, and destruction. Moreover, they could be manufactured more rapidly and in large quantities. However, the Germans did not focus their entire naval construction effort on them until the spring of 1943. In addition, too many of their U-boats (submarines) had only a restricted range and could not therefore operate in the Atlantic. Nevertheless, submarines were more sophisticated than in the First World War; the Germans also had the effective Type 7c, operational from 1940; and they now had bases from which it was easier to threaten British shipping. As a result, the amount of shipping sunk by U-boats rose from the summer of 1940, at a time when British warships were focused on home waters to cover the evacuation of forces from France and to retain control of the Channel. There were also severe losses in the winter of 1940–41, as the U-boats attacked Atlantic convoys and developed wolf-pack tactics against their slowly moving targets. The German U-boats were supported by thirty-two Italian submarines that operated out of Bordeaux, from July 1940, but with only limited success. They tend to be forgotten, which underlines the role of recovered memory in the perception of the war. It is certainly necessary to underline the difficulties both sides faced in operations, notably the small size of the ships and submarines and the roughness of the weather in the vast Atlantic.

The situation improved for the Allies in the summer of 1941 as a result of an increased number of escort ships and aircraft, in part thanks to the lend-lease agreement with the United States. The British also cut the number of ships sailing independently. They had experimented with letting more fast ships sail outside convoys, an idea Churchill championed but gave up when Admiralty statistics made it clear that this was a bad idea. The American willingness to play a major role in the defense of shipping in the western Atlantic from September 1941 was important. In effect, there was a state of war between America and Germany in the Atlantic prior to Pearl Harbor. The British also benefited from a hard-won ability to decipher German naval codes.

The Germans had insufficient submarines to achieve their objectives, and those they had lacked air support. In 1940, the Germans lost U-boats more speedily than new ones were being brought into service. Changing goals were also significant. For example, U-boat pressure in the Atlantic was reduced in late 1941 as submarines were moved to Norwegian and Mediterranean waters in order to attack Allied convoys to the Soviet Union and deny the Mediterranean to Allied shipping. These movements reflected the range of strategic options the Germans had, but also the inability to focus that was to be seen during the invasion of the Soviet Union in 1941.

Submarines were responsible for about 70 percent of the Allied shipping destroyed by the Germans during the war. Aircraft, especially the long-range, four-engine FW-200 *Kondor*, were also significant, benefiting from bases in France and Norway. However, the *Luftwaffe* was not committed to the war against trade. Navy and army complaints about the *Luftwaffe* reflected the unreliability of its megalomaniac leader, Hermann Göring. In contrast, the army was not disappointed by the navy as it appreciated its weakness. Moreover, the navy was still in the hands of its professional officers. The Germans, however, suffered from a lack of a unified command structure and joint staff. To counter German aircraft, the Royal Navy put Hurricane fighters on merchantmen before deploying escort carriers, which were in essence tanker ships equipped with a landing deck and some aircraft service facilities. Mines and surface raiders were also significant in the destruction of shipping.

Alongside the use of intelligence, air power played a key role in resisting the German submarine assault. Most U-boat "kills" of shipping were made by attack on the surface, which rendered Allied ASDIC (sonar) less effective. In contrast, aircraft forced U-boats to submerge, where their speed was much slower and it was harder to maintain visual contact with targets. On the surface, submarines operated using diesel engines that could drive the vessel three to four times faster than underwater cruising, which was powered, by necessity, by battery-powered electric motors. This factor affected cruising range and the number of days that could be spent at sea. Long-range air power was the vital element that reduced the killing power of the German submarine fleet to the point that its effectiveness, measured by Allied tonnage lost, decreased steadily.

Nevertheless, as a reminder of the significance of tasking and goals, neither the RAF, which was interested in strategic bombing and theater fighters, nor the Royal Navy, which was primarily concerned with hostile surface warships and was content to rely on convoys, hunter groups, and ASDIC, of which there were very few sets, to limit submarine attempts, had devoted sufficient preparation to air cover against submarines. In addition, land-based aircraft operating against U-boats faced an "Air Gap" across much of the mid-Atlantic, although Iceland's availability as an Allied base from April 1941 increased the range of such air cover. Again, as a reminder of choices, the British had used carrier-based aircraft against U-boats at the start of the war; but the sinking by a U-boat of the carrier *Courageous* ended the practice, and the remaining fleet carriers were deployed against Axis surface warships. Moreover, the demands of the bomber offensive against Germany on available long-range aircraft restricted the numbers available for convoy escort, while it took time to build escort aircraft carriers: the first entered service in late 1941. It was destroyed not long afterward, although it fully demonstrated the value of this class of ship during its short operational life. The next escort carriers (all American built) did not begin to enter service until late 1942, but so great was the need for naval aviation in a variety of roles that they were not initially used for trade protection. They were not used to cover the "Air Gap" until April 1943.[21]

NAVAL POWER POLITICS

The German naval leadership had wide-ranging interests, with the Naval Staff committed to Germany becoming a power with a global reach provided by a strong surface navy, a policy seen as the way to secure resources and to gain Hitler's favor. There was interest in acquiring bases in the Atlantic, notably the Azores from Portugal and the Canaries from Spain. From these, it would be possible to threaten British convoy routes, increase German influence in South America, and challenge American power. There was also naval pressure for an increased German effort in the Mediterranean. Hitler focused instead on creating a new Europe by attacking the Soviet Union in June 1941, launching Operation Barbarossa. However, concern about German naval intentions affected American planners and played a role in the public debate within the United States over policy.

Concern about German plans and capabilities, as well as anxiety about the strength of the response, encouraged America to expand its Atlantic presence. On September 3, 1940, the United States agreed to provide fifty surplus and elderly destroyers (seven of them to the Canadian navy, the remainder to Britain), in return for ninety-nine-year leases on British bases in Antigua, the Bahamas, Bermuda, British Guiana, Jamaica, Newfoundland, St. Lucia, and Trinidad, bases that enabled President Roosevelt to claim to be supporting the defense of the Western Hemisphere. In practice, the deal was of limited military value as the largely obsolete ships took time to prepare. However, aside from the considerable psychological value at a time when Britain was vulnerable, no other power was in a position to provide such help.[22] More generally, the critical importance of American supplies was exaggerated by the British for political reasons, so as to make Britain appear stronger. In 1941, the United States went on to establish bases in Greenland and Iceland.

THE EASTERN FRONT

Launched on June 22, 1941, the German assault on the Soviet Union had a naval dimension, even though the planning largely left the navy aside. Rapidly gaining superiority in the air, the *Luftwaffe* was able to destroy ships of the Soviet Baltic Fleet. German, Finnish, and Romanian conquests also lessened the ports and areas where Soviet warships could operate in the Baltic and Black Seas. For example, in mid-October 1941, the Soviets evacuated their besieged and outnumbered garrison from the port of Odessa, an evacuation that reflected the strength of the Black Sea Fleet and the neutrality of Turkey. In the Baltic, where, although the Soviets had a larger fleet, the Germans had the naval forces and air dominance they lacked in the Black Sea, the Soviets were bottled up in St. Petersburg by late 1941, in part as a result of German mine laying. Thus, *Aurora*, the cruiser that had launched the October Revolution in 1917, was used as an antiaircraft battery, eventually being bombed and sunk by the Germans.

The Germans were less successful in the Black Sea than in the Baltic, and the Soviets were able to make major landings on the Kerch Peninsula in December 1941, which were important instances of short-range amphibious warfare. This warfare attracts less attention than its Anglo-American counterparts. In early 1942, the Axis naval flotilla, mostly of E-boats, that had been built up in the Black Sea, played a role in harassing Soviet naval links with besieged Sevastopol in Crimea, which contributed to its lack of supplies and fall to the Germans.[23] Both sides lost warships to air attack, and this led Stalin in late 1943 to ban the employment of the larger Soviet warships in the area.

The Caspian Sea Flotilla, operating from Baku, assisted in the Soviet invasion of Iran in 1941. This was a fleet of gunboats, torpedo boats, patrol craft, and floating antiaircraft platforms. In part due to defending coastal artillery, the flotilla had less effect than air attacks and land operations. The more experienced Royal Navy was more successful in its simultaneous operations against southern Iran. The sloop *Shoreham* played a key role at Abadan, badly damaging the Iranian warship *Palang* and providing machine-gun fire to help overcome resistance on land. So also at the ports of Khorramshahr and Bandar Shapur. Relatively weak warships could have a decisive impact if decisively led and if the resistance was inadequate. Prewar Italian aid to the Iranian navy proved of no value.

JAPAN ATTACKS

The passage of the Two-Ocean Naval Expansion Act on July 19, 1940, was designed to produce a fleet that would enable the United States to wage naval war against both Germany and Japan. It provided for the building, at a cost of $4 billion, of a truly massive additional complement that was designed to increase the authorized total tonnage of American warships by 70 percent, including 18 fleet carriers, 11 battleships, 6 battle cruisers, 27 cruisers, 115 destroyers, and 43 submarines. Most of these ships, however, were not due for completion until 1946–48, a similar timetable for the planned German navy. Keels were laid down for four 45,000-ton *Iowa*-class battleships in 1941, and seven were projected at over sixty thousand tons each. The act served notice on the Japanese that the Americans were going to be in a position to back up their hostility to Japanese expansionism, more particularly in Southeast Asia. The *Iowa*-class battleships were well armored and also, at thirty-three knots, very fast. American planning increasingly presumed a focus first on defeating Germany because it was feared that, otherwise, Germany might be able to knock Britain out, putting America in a much more difficult position.

Under American pressure over Southeast Asia, specifically Vietnam, the Japanese response was to press on. The army and navy agreed on June 25, 1941, that they would obtain their goals in Southeast Asia so as to be able to respond subsequently to the apparently imminent collapse of the Soviet Union. By then, Japanese naval planning had altered. In place of separating vulnerable carriers, there was a conviction of the value of massed air power at sea, and thus of a carrier group. There was a serious division of opinion as to whether to fight America or focus on other goals, and also, in the event of war with America, as to the targets to attack. Admiral Isoroku Yamamoto, the commander of the Combined Fleet, pressed for a surprise attack on the base of the American Pacific Fleet at Pearl Harbor. Other naval commanders were opposed, but Yamamoto's insistence that such an attack was a necessary prelude for covering operations against Malaya, the Philippines, and the Dutch East Indies, with their crucial oil fields, won the day. The plan was approved on November 3.

PEARL HARBOR

On December 7 (December 8 on the other side of the international date line), Japan attacked Pearl Harbor on the Hawaiian island of Oahu, without any prior declaration of war. It achieved a degree of surprise that indicated considerable deficiency in American intelligence gathering and assessment, and which has led to a morass of conspiracy theories. The Americans had considered the prospect of a Japanese preemptive strike but thought the more vulnerable Philippines the most probable target, while the Pacific Command in Hawaii focused on the threat from the nearest Japanese territory, the Marshall Islands, not from the north, the direction from which the Japanese came.

The defenses on Oahu were manned for sabotage, not air attack, which helped the Japanese greatly.

The attack on Pearl Harbor was a dramatic assault that was tactically successful but that indicated the problems with achieving strategic results. It was a classic case of an operational-tactical success, but a strategic and grand strategic failure. A total of 353 aircraft from six Japanese carriers completely destroyed two American battleships and damaged five more, while, in an attack on the naval air station at Kaneohe Bay, nearly three hundred American aircraft were destroyed or damaged on the ground.

The attack, however, revealed grave deficiencies in Japanese (and American) planning, as well as in the Japanese war machine. Only 45 percent of naval air requirements had been met by the start of the war, and the last torpedoes employed in the attack were delivered only two days before the fleet sailed. The Japanese used Type 91 Mod 2 torpedoes, which, with their heavier charge, thinner air vessel, and antiroll stabilizers, were first delivered in April 1941. Modifications of aircraft to carry both torpedoes and heavy bombs were last minute, and there was a lack of practice. Moreover, the Japanese target-prioritization scheme was poor, attack routes conflicted, and the torpedo attack lacked simultaneity. The damage to America's battleships (some of which were to be salvaged and used anew) forced an important shift in American naval planning toward an emphasis on their carriers, the *Lexington*, the *Yorktown*, and the *Enterprise*, which, despite Japanese expectations, were not in Pearl Harbor when it was attacked.[24] No attack on this scale was to be launched on any other fleet during the war.

Because of the focus on destroying warships rather than strategic assets, there was no third-wave attack on the fuel and other harbor installations. Had the oil farms (stores) been destroyed, the Pacific Fleet would probably have had to fall back to its California base at San Diego, gravely hindering American operations in the Pacific. Had the Japanese invaded Oahu, the Americans would have had to do so, but the logistical task facing the Japanese in supporting such an invasion would have been formidable.

Furthermore, the course of the war was to reveal that the strategic concepts that underlay the Japanese plan had been gravely flawed. Aside from underrating American economic strength and the resolve of its people, the Japanese had embarked on an attack that was not essential. Their fleet was larger than the American Pacific and Asiatic Fleets, especially in carriers, battleships, and cruisers, and the American fleets, as a result, were not in a position to have prevented the Japanese from overrunning British and Dutch colonies, which was their major expansionist goal. From the point of view of the Pacific naval balance, the Americans had too many warships in the Atlantic. Possible controversy over the lack of necessary American preparedness at Pearl Harbor was largely put aside in response to the shock of the Japanese surprise attack, and the devastating nature of this surprise attack encouraged a rallying around the American government.

THE JAPANESE ADVANCE, 1941–42

Naval strength was crucial to the Japanese conquest of Southeast Asia, although it was the army which had the key experience, equipment, doctrine, and responsibility for amphibious operations. Fear of Japanese air power and concern about the relative ratio of naval power led the American navy, mindful of the wider strategic position, to fail to provide the support for the Philippines requested by the commander of U.S. forces in the Far East, General Douglas MacArthur, who had failed to take the necessary precautions. A convoy of reinforcements turned back, the navy refused to fly in aircraft, and the submarines were evacuated. This left the defenders in a hopeless position. Superiority in the air (over the poorly prepared American local air force component) and at sea enabled the Japanese to land where they pleased. The main force landed in Lingayen Gulf in northwest Luzon, with supporting units landing in south Luzon at Legaspi and Lamon Bay, threatening Manila with a pincer attack.

Further east, American islands in the western Pacific were captured. Guam fell on December 10, 1941, to an expedition from the Mariana Islands and was placed under the administration of the Japanese navy. Wake Island was attacked on December 12, but the marine garrison drove off the attack, sinking two destroyers. An American failure to relieve the island ensured, however, that on December 23 a second attack, supported by carriers from the Pearl Harbor operation, was successful, although only after heavy casualties.

The successful Japanese attack on Hong Kong benefited from air support in order to block interference from British motor torpedo boats there. The Japanese invasion of Malaya was an amphibious assault. A powerful (by prewar standards) British squadron was sent to threaten Japanese landings on the coast of Malaya, but on December 10, 1941, eighty-five land-based naval bombers sank the battleship *Prince of Wales* and the battle cruiser *Repulse*. Based at Saigon in French Indochina, these bombers showed that, in a sense, when France fell, Malaya fell. When sunk, the *Prince of Wales* had the best radar suite of any operational warship in the world, including close-in radar for her antiaircraft guns as well as radar for her main guns. A modern ship, she had good compartmentalization.[25] The sinking reflected the extent to which, although the success of high-level bombers was mixed, torpedo bombers could be deadly. Japanese tactics were impressive. On the British side, there was inadequate antiaircraft armament and gunnery, but a lack of land-based air cover to compensate for the absence of a carrier was crucial.

This arose primarily from the mistakes of the force commander, Admiral Sir Tom Phillips. His poorly conceived and executed plan reflected both a serious personal misreading of the situation but also wider problems: a lack of strategic foresight about what the ships could achieve and operational weaknesses, including the problems of air-sea coordination. Churchill had mistakenly thought that Japan could be deterred, and there was no proper contingency plan for the British force. In addition, the hope that the British would benefit from the strength of the American fleet in the western Pacific proved seriously mistaken.[26] Subsequently, the Japanese advance south in Malaya, and their consequent successful invasion of Singapore, were supported by naval action. The British hope that Singapore could hold out until it was relieved by the navy was wrong on both counts: it did not hold out, and there was no relief.

The Japanese pressed on to attack the Dutch East Indies, now Indonesia, beginning on January 11, 1942, with a landing at Tarakan, and that month saw amphibious forces leapfrogging forward through the Strait of Makassar and the Molucca Passage, to the west and east of Sulawesi, capturing ports there and in Borneo. Another force captured Ambon in the Moluccas, and another advanced from Sarawak to leapfrog down the western coast of Borneo. These gains provided bases, notably air forces, from which Japanese attacks on Java (the most important island), Bali, and Timor could be prepared.

Allied naval forces tried to protect Java, unsuccessfully attacking a Japanese invasion fleet in the Battle of the Java Sea on February 27, which was the first fleet action of the Pacific War. The two fleets were relatively balanced, with five cruisers and ten destroyers in the Allied fleet, and four and thirteen in that of the Japanese. However, the latter was well coordinated, enjoyed superior air support, and benefited from good air reconnaissance and better torpedoes. In contrast, the American, Australian, British, and Dutch warships lacked an able commander or unified command structure, experience fighting together, air reconnaissance, and air cover. Heavy Allied losses, then and subsequently, including all of the cruisers, left the Japanese in a dominant position, and on the night of February 28–March 1, they landed in Java, which surrendered soon after.

Naval support was valuable for the Japanese conquest of Burma (Myanmar) from January to May 1942, although far less so than for that of the Dutch East Indies, as island seizing was not involved. Japanese strength in the region was displayed in April when a force of five carriers sailed into the Indian Ocean and mounted destructive air raids on ports in eastern India and Sri Lanka, as well as sinking two British heavy cruisers and a carrier that were inadequately protected from dive-bombers. After the sinking of these warships, the British withdrew their Indian Ocean Fleet to East Africa or Mumbai. Admiral Somerville, the commander, was now having to think about the need to protect the Arabian Sea (the waters west of India) and thus tanker sailings from the Persian Gulf, as well as the route from both the Gulf and the Red Sea down the coast of East Africa to the Cape of Good Hope.

The crisis ended in April 1942, with most of the Japanese warships being withdrawn to be deployed for an attack on Port Moresby in New Guinea. The crisis led, however, to acute concern about the security of the Indian Ocean, which indeed greatly worried the British, with their commitment to an imperial network and strategy,[27] and interested Axis naval commanders. This led the British to invade the island of Madagascar, which was held by Vichy forces. The British fleet successfully covered this invasion in May, deploying aircraft from two carriers to support the attack on Diego Suarez, the main port. In response, Japanese midget submarines torpedoed a British battleship there, which encouraged the British, urged by South Africa to capture the other ports, to press on to conquer the rest of the island.[28]

Japanese pressure in the Indian Ocean is one of the great naval counterfactuals (what-ifs) of the war. The Allied position there had serious weaknesses, especially in conjunction with Axis advances in North Africa. Britain had the resources of India and the Persian Gulf to assist it, but the British Empire was more vulnerable to Japanese attack than the United States was in the far larger Pacific. This vulnerability reflected a number of factors, ranging from the role of Vichy already seen in Indochina. There was no equivalent to Madagascar in Latin America to threaten American interests. Moreover, the entire British position in South Asia would have been challenged had either the Soviet Union or China succumbed to Axis attack. The Royal Navy had been weakened by its heavy losses in the Mediterranean and by a huge wearing down of matériel and personnel. However, instead of pursuing their advantage against the British in the Indian Ocean, where opposition to British rule in India was growing, the Japanese sent their carriers into the Pacific theater against the United States. This reflected the navy's certainty that the United States was the major challenge. While true, this approach failed to devote sufficient attention to the possibilities offered by weakening the British Empire. William Joyce, "Lord Haw-Haw," a Nazi propagandist broadcasting from Germany to Britain, declared on December 28, 1941, that "the demands on the Royal Navy were such that every single warship had to do the work of at least half a dozen."[29] While an exaggeration and not credible evidence, this comment captured an important element of strain.

WAR IN THE PACIFIC, 1942

Having brought French Indochina into their orbit and conquered the Philippines and the Dutch East Indies, the Japanese planned to press on to fix and strengthen the defensive shield with which they wished to hold the western

Pacific against American attacks. However, initial successes led to interest in a more extensive perimeter, which proved a serious mistake in terms of the eventual loss of units. The Naval General Staff considered an attack on Australia or operations against India and Sri Lanka, but the army was unprepared to commit the troops required and instead favored a more modest attempt to isolate Australia. In January 1942, Yamamoto's staff had considered invading Australia, only to decide against it.

Having captured Rabaul on the island of New Britain on January 23, 1942, the Japanese decided to seize Port Moresby in southeastern New Guinea, as well as New Caledonia, Fiji, and Samoa in order to isolate Australia. Their plan, however, was thwarted as a result of the Battle of the Coral Sea on May 7–8. This, the first battle entirely between carrier groups in which the ships did not make visual contact, indicated the failure of the Pearl Harbor attack to wreck American naval power. The Americans had intercepted and decoded Japanese messages and, in a major forward deployment of American naval power that demonstrated the threat it posed to Japan, were waiting in the Coral Sea for the Japanese. In the battle, the Americans suffered serious losses, especially the carrier *Lexington*, but the Japanese, who had failed to achieve the necessary concentration of strength and had an overly rigid plan,[30] also suffered, not least with the loss of aircraft and pilots. Crucially, the Japanese, whose naval commanders were divided over strategy, failed to persist with the operation, while American pilots acquired experience in attacking Japanese carriers. It was necessary to develop carrier warfare techniques, a formidable task, including cooperation with other surface warships.

Rather than focusing on Australia and the southwest Pacific, Yamamoto preferred a decisive naval battle aimed at destroying American carriers. The decision was made in February, but the Doolittle Raid, a symbolic American air attack on Tokyo on April 18, 1942, launched from the carrier *Hornet* (which was therefore not available for joint action with the other carriers), both raised American morale and, by demonstrating Japanese vulnerability, further encouraged the Japanese to act. Yamamoto proposed to seize Midway and other islands that could serve as support bases for an invasion of Hawaii, which he thought would lead to such a battle. Yamamoto hoped to lure the American carriers to destruction under the guns of his battleships in what would be a decisive battle.

The continued capacity of the American navy, however, was shown clearly, on June 4, with the American victory in the Battle of Midway, a naval-air battle of unprecedented scale. This battle also reflected the superiority of American repair efforts and intelligence, as well as the effectiveness of the combination of fighter support with carriers (in defense) and of fighters and bombers (in attack). The Americans encountered serious problems in the battle, and contingency and chance played a major role in the fighting, but at

Midway and increasingly more generally, the Americans handled the uncertainty of war far better than the Japanese. The Japanese navy, which had doctored its war games for Midway, was affected by the tension between two goals: those of decisive naval battle and of the capture of Midway. This ensured that the Japanese had to decide whether to prepare their aircraft for land or ship targets, an issue that caused crucial delay during the battle.

While the American ability to learn hard-won lessons from Coral Sea was highly significant, the dependence of operations on tactical adroitness and chance played a major role in a battle in which the ability to locate the target was crucial. The American strike from the *Hornet* failed, with the fighters and dive-bombers unable to locate the Japanese carriers. Lacking any, or adequate, fighter support, the torpedo-bomber attacks suffered very heavy losses. However, the result of these attacks was that the Japanese fighters were unable to respond, not least because they were at a low altitude, to the arrival of the American dive-bombers, a fortuitous instance of coordination. In only a few minutes, in a triumph of dive-bombing, three carriers were wrecked, a fourth following later; once wrecked, they sank.

These minutes shifted the arithmetic of carrier power in the Pacific. Although their aircrews mostly survived, the loss of 110 pilots was especially serious as the Japanese had stressed the value of training and had produced an elite force of aviators. The Japanese looked upon a carrier and its combat aircraft as an inseparable unit, with the aircraft as the ship's armaments, much like guns on fighting surface craft. Once lost, the pilots proved difficult to replace, not least because of a shortage of fuel for training. More seriously, the loss of four carriers' maintenance crews could not be made up.[31]

The Americans won decisively in the carrier battle, the Japanese losing all four of their heavy carriers present, as well as many aircraft. There was no opportunity for the Japanese to use their battleships, as the American carriers prudently retired before their approach, while the American battleships had already been sent to the West Coast. This was one of the respects in which Midway was no Tsushima. Yamamoto's inflexible conviction of the value of battleships in any battle with the Americans had served him ill. This poor judgment ensured that the Japanese had lost their large-scale offensive capacity at sea, at least as far as carriers were concerned. Conversely, the American admirals may have acted differently had they had battleships at their disposal. American carrier strategy was in part a lack-of-battleship strategy.[32] The battle ensured that the congressional elections on November 3, 1942, took place against a more benign background than had existed earlier in the year.

The introduction in the late 1930s and early 1940s of carrier-capable aircraft that had substantial range had improved carrier capability. Before that, it was not unusual for carrier aircraft to be limited to an operational range of only about one hundred miles, which made the carriers very vulnerable to surface attack. Indeed, during the American "fleet problems" or planning exercises, carriers were quite often "sunk" or at least threatened by battleships.

The Battle of Midway demonstrated the power of carriers, but also their serious vulnerability, not least if, like the Japanese, they had poor damage-control practices. Carriers were essentially a first-strike weapon, and their vulnerability to gunfire and air attack led to a continued stress on battleships and cruisers, both of which were also very important for shore bombardment in support of amphibious operations. Air power in the Pacific was seen as a preliminary to these operations rather than as a war-winning tool in its own right. Surface ships remained crucial for conflict with other surface ships, not least because, although there were spectacular losses, many battleships took considerable punishment before being sunk by air attack. In addition, battleships were still necessary while other powers maintained the type. Furthermore, until reliable all-weather day-and-night reconnaissance and strike aircraft were available (which was really in the 1950s), surface ships provided the means of fighting at night. Surface ships, moreover, provided a powerful antiaircraft screen for the carriers, while the Americans also had dedicated antiaircraft cruisers in the Pacific.

GUADALCANAL, 1942–43

Midway did not mark the end of Japanese advances as they sought to strengthen their perimeter. The advance on Port Moresby in New Guinea was now mounted overland, but, on July 7, 1942, the Japanese landed at Guadalcanal in the Solomon Islands in the southwest Pacific. The island, then a British colony, had strategic importance, being seen as a key forward base to cut off the American reinforcement and supply route to Australia and New Zealand, but the American attempt to regain it launched a month later took on a significance to contemporaries that exceeded both this and the size of the Japanese garrison. It was important to the Americans to demonstrate that the Japanese could be beaten not only in carrier actions, but also in the difficult fighting environment of the Pacific islands. It was also necessary to show that air and sea support could be provided to amphibious forces, both when landing and subsequently. In addition, Coral Sea and Midway had been defensive successes, but at Guadalcanal, the attack was clearly taken to the Japanese in what was the first American offensive operation in the southwest Pacific.

Eventual American naval success in the naval battles off Guadalcanal compromised the ability of the poorly commanded Japanese to support their force on the island. The naval campaign indicated the key role of warships other than carriers. Aside from their heavy losses at Midway, carriers could play little role in nighttime surface actions. Destroyer torpedo attacks could be highly successful, as when used by the Japanese, with their effective Long Lance torpedoes, off Guadalcanal on November 13 and 30, the last, the Battle of Tassafaronga, leading to the sinking of one American cruiser and severely damaging three more. The Japanese maintained a capability in naval night fighting. Moreover, Japanese submarines were responsible for important American losses, sinking the carrier *Wasp* and badly damaging the carrier *Saratoga* and the battleship *North Carolina*, whereas the poorly managed American submarine role was inadequate. [33]

In mid-November 1942, in what was to be a turning point in the war, success was won by the Americans in a three-day sea action focused on surface warships fighting by night. For example, on November 14, the radar-controlled fire of the battleships *Washington* and *South Dakota* hit hard the battleship *Kirishima*. It capsized on November 15. Japanese battleships lacked radar-controlled fire. This battle was crucial to the American success on the island in January 1943. In the campaign, the Americans developed a degree of cooperation between land, sea, and air forces that was to serve them well in subsequent operations. The naval battles around Guadalcanal involved more uncertainties than during the Battle of Midway. The latter was a classic battle, within a limited timetable and with a clear order of battle. Guadalcanal involved a much longer period. Moreover, as with the Leyte Gulf theater in 1944, there were many small islands and other underwater obstacles, and these made the battle much more challenging than the open ocean of the Battle of Midway. The Americans also inflicted important losses on the Japanese in the Guadalcanal campaign in what was attritional fighting. There was an equal loss of warships, but the buildup of American naval resources ensured that they were better able to take such losses.

WAR IN THE PACIFIC, 1943

In July 1942, the Australian War Cabinet cabled Churchill: "Superior seapower and airpower are vital to wrest the initiative from Japan and are essential to assure the defensive position in the southwest Pacific Area." [34] Due to their superior industrial capability, the Americans were able to build up their naval strength far more successfully in late 1942, and this success proved crucial both in 1943 and to the key 1944 campaign. Ten cruisers were completed or commissioned in June 1942, the production of *Fletcher*-class destroyers began in June 1942, and the first escort carriers that summer.

Moreover, the Americans developed important organizational advantages. These spanned from shipbuilding to the use of resources. The American advance across the Pacific would have been impossible without the ability to ship large quantities of supplies and to develop the associated infrastructure, such as harbors and oil-storage facilities, and the ships of the support train. In many respects, this was a war of engineers, and the American aptitude for creating effective infrastructure was applied to great effect in the Pacific.

Naval and air superiority were crucial to the American advance. They permitted the identification of key targets and the bypassing of many of the islands the Japanese continued to hold, a sensible decision given the time taken to capture Guadalcanal. Thanks to a growingly apparent American superiority at sea and in the air, the Japanese would be less able to mount ripostes, and any bypassed bases would be isolated. Thus, the Pacific War was to become one that was far from linear. Bypassing at the strategic level was not matched at the tactical level, where the navy and marines attacked island defenses frontally, frequently taking heavy casualties.

The process of island hopping in the Solomon Islands began in June 1943 with an attack on New Georgia. Carriers played a major role in the American campaign in the Solomons, but so also did other surface warships. Covering the landing on the island of Bougainville in the Solomons on November 1, 1943, a force of American cruisers and destroyers beat off an attack that night by a smaller Japanese squadron, with losses to the latter in the first battle fought entirely by radar. The Solomons advance culminated with the capture of Admiralty Island at the end of February 1944.[35]

In the central Pacific, the Americans opened up a new axis of advance, capturing key atolls in the Gilbert Islands in November 1943 in hard-fought amphibious attacks. This success helped prepare the way for operations against the Marshall Islands in early 1944. This route revived the prewar Plan Orange and represented the shortest route for an advance on the Philippines. The army wanted a southern drive, the navy a central Pacific drive, but the real story was that the Americans had enough resources to do both. The choice of strategy was important alongside the availability of resources, because, however outresourced, there were a large number of Japanese bases, and it was important not to lose too much time or manpower.

Resources were far from the only element. For example, the Americans gained cumulative experience in amphibious operations, in their coordination with naval and air support, and in naval logistical support. Superior American interwar leadership development, based at the war colleges and focused on the solving of complex higher operational and strategic problems, contributed to wartime successes.

SUBMARINES IN THE PACIFIC

The tendency is to put the submarine war in the Atlantic first. It was, indeed, crucial to the war against Germany and to the war as far as Britain was concerned, but this emphasis can lead to a stress on the failure of submarines, as in the German case in the Atlantic and that of the Italians in the Mediterranean. The American story in the Pacific reveals a very different outcome. The submarine war in the Pacific had major strategic implications. Although they had large, long-range submarines, which indeed were used to maintain links with Germany, the Japanese did not launch a submarine war against America's lines of communication in the eastern Pacific. Nor did Japan mass submarines for use in offensives elsewhere. The prestige of their submarines had suffered from their failure to make a major impact in the Pearl Harbor operation. This affected subsequent Japanese consideration of submarines as a strategic and operational tool. Instead, with a cleaving to prewar doctrine, Japanese submarines were more commonly employed as part of the battle fleet, stalking American warships, sometimes successfully but without decisive results.[36]

This Japanese failure to attack American communication links made it easier for the Americans to deploy resources against Japan and to plan for attack. As a result, there was a clear contrast with the war with Germany. An Allied invasion of France, which was not mounted until June 1944, was not feasible until after the Allies had won the Battle of the Atlantic, a victory which permitted the safe buildup and supplying of Allied forces in Britain; but there were no such constraints affecting the forward movement of forces in the Pacific by the Americans.

The Americans used submarines to greater strategic effect, notably to lessen the economic value Japan derived from its conquests.[37] Japanese industry was dependent on the import of raw materials, especially oil, rubber, and tin, from the Japanese Empire, while rice imports were also significant. The United States increasingly employed submarines to attack Japanese trade, and this stymied Japanese plans to raise munitions production. The Americans faced serious problems with their Mark XIV torpedo and Mark VI exploder torpedoes until mid-1943, problems that, for example, affected operations off the Philippines in the winter of 1941–42. Early German torpedoes also faced problems.

However, effective long-range American submarines made major inroads on Japanese trade, especially from late 1943, establishing one of the most successful blockades in naval history. Unrestricted submarine warfare, for which the Americans had no experience, had been ordered without hesitation immediately after Pearl Harbor, with the naval leadership playing the key role in this decision.[38] The Americans benefited from the quality of their submarines, including good surface speed and range; from their ability to decipher Japanese signals; and from a clear determination to attack. The Japanese did not inflict enough casualties to cause a deterioration in American submarine leadership or in the quality and motivation of the crew. Indeed, the United States became the most successful practitioner of submarine warfare in history. This provided a core basis of skill and confidence from which to use hunter/killer submarines to confront Soviet submarines in the Cold War.

The Japanese in the Pacific proved less effective than the Allies in the Atlantic at convoy protection and antisubmarine warfare, and devoted far fewer resources to these objectives, notably by not providing adequate air support for convoys. In 1942–44, successful American submarine attacks forced the Japanese to abandon many of their convoy routes. Lacking a large enough merchant fleet at the start of the war, notably of tankers, the Japanese failed to build sufficient ships to match their losses, their trade was dramatically cut, and the Japanese imperial economy was shattered. By the end of the war, American submarines had sunk 5.32 million tons of Japanese merchant shipping (and Japan had a lower tonnage than the British Empire), and there was no area of Japanese overseas and coastal trade that was free from attack. This greatly increased the uncertainty that sapped the predictability on which industrial integration depended. Japanese losses made it difficult to move raw materials or, indeed, troops rapidly. Thus, the flexibility seen in the initial Japanese conquests had been lost. Expedients, such as postponing the maintenance of shipping and leaving garrisons to fend for themselves (an equivalent in its impact to Allied island hopping), proved deleterious for overall effectiveness.

The American submarine assault was supplemented by the dropping of mines by naval aircraft, as well as by air attacks on Japanese shipping, both of which proved deadly. These means became more significant in 1945 as American air bases were established closer to Japan and as carriers also operated closer in.

THE SURFACE NAVAL WAR WITH GERMANY

Surface warships played a far greater role in the naval war with Japan than with Germany. In part, this was a result of the German focus on commerce raiding rather than battle; of the sinking of the *Bismarck* in 1941; and of the withdrawal, on February 12, 1942, of major warships from Brest, the leading Atlantic base in German hands. This withdrawal, which owed much to the vulnerability of the warships there to British bombers, as well as to concern about a possible British invasion of Norway, was a success as the British attempt to intercept them in the Channel totally failed due largely to the jamming of British radar and to effective and well-coordinated German air defenses. At the same time, the withdrawal was a strategic mistake, as it lessened the threat posed by these warships to the Allied position in the Atlantic and thus their danger as a fleet-in-being. The following month, the British launched an attack that wrecked the dry dock at St. Nazaire, the only dry dock on the French Atlantic coast big enough to accommodate the 42,000-ton battleship *Tirpitz*. Thus, the very requirements of the warship lessened its usefulness, although Hitler's insistence that she only go to sea when free from real risk was also a key restriction. This insistence was a telling mark of Hitler's ignorance in naval warfare. He saw warships as jewels to be hoarded away for their propaganda and potential value, rather than as military units with strategic purposes involving risk.

Norway was an important base for operations against British convoys sent from August 21, 1941, to take supplies to the Soviet Union. These convoys were a key source of supply that provided 4.43 million tons of matériel. One-sixth of the heavy tanks the Soviets used in the Battle of Moscow in late 1941 had come from Britain. Initially, confident of victory over the Soviet Union, the Germans largely ignored the convoys, but, from December 1941, they increased the warships and aircraft available in northern Norway to attack them. From March 1942, convoy losses mounted, notably for convoys PQ-16 and PQ-17 in May and July 1942, respectively. As such, the focus of German naval strength could be regarded as being in synergy with the German strategic concentration on the Soviet Union, rather than being extraneous to it. Overall, 7 percent of the matériel sent was lost to German attack. The supply route from Alaska to Siberia lacked this danger but did not provide supplies so close to the zone of operations. The Arctic ice forced ships closer to Norway than they would have preferred. The convoys were escorted by warships (mostly British but also American), including, from late 1942, escort carriers, and were protected, where possible, by Allied air and submarine patrols, although the range of air cover was insufficient.

The serious inroads of German aircraft and, in particular, submarines on these convoys, however, were not matched by surface ships. On December 31, 1942, in the Battle of the Barents Sea, German surface ships failed to destroy a British convoy which was ably defended by its destroyer escorts, much to the fury of Hitler. In the Battle of North Cape on December 26, 1943, the battle cruiser *Scharnhost* was slowed by a British destroyer torpedo attack and then sunk by fire from a fleet escorting a convoy. The *Tirpitz*, which had sailed to Trondheim in Norway in January 1942 and had sortied out in early March 1942 in an unsuccessful attempt to intercept a convoy, was first damaged by British midget submarines and then sunk by British aircraft on November 12, 1944, after two 12,000-pound (5,430 kg) Tallboy bombs developed for the purpose hit the ship. These heavier bombs also ensured that the RAF was able to inflict damage on the concrete submarine "pens" in Bergen in Norway.

BATTLE OF THE ATLANTIC

In 1942, the German U-boats inflicted heavy losses on Allied shipping, creating a serious situation, while U-boat losses were less than new launchings. For the first time, there were enough U-boats to organize comprehensive patrol lines across North Atlantic convoy routes. For the Germans, the naval opportunities presented by American entry into the war came not from cooperation with Japan, but from the poorly defended nature of American waters, although nothing better encapsulated Hitler's lack of grasp of maritime strategy and its relationship to international policies than the declaration of war on the United States. Due in part to an American reluctance to learn from earlier experience, and to a focus on hunting U-boats, it took time for convoys to be introduced in American waters, and there were very heavy losses to U-boat attacks in early 1942, their so-called happy time. These attacks proved the most serious assaults on American coastal control since the Civil War or, excluding that as a special case, the War of 1812. In the Caribbean, in Operation Neuland, there was a failure to focus on the particular strategic vulnerability offered by these targets (or to shell oil refineries), or to make the submarines suitable for tropical operations by fitting air conditioning. [39]

In May 1942, when U-boat attacks also led Mexico into the war, the situation improved as effective convoying was introduced. As a result, the U-boats, from July, focused anew on the mid-Atlantic. After the summer of 1942, the effectiveness of individual submarine patrols, in terms of the tonnage sunk, fell. This fall reflected the increase of convoying, introduced from Halifax to Boston in March 1942, and the greater strength of convoy escorts. The majority of merchantmen sunk that year were sailing independently.

Air power was a clear response for both the United States and Britain. The Americans built new air bases in Cuba, the Dominican Republic, Haiti, Panama, and Brazil in order to patrol against the U-boats. A debate raged in London. It is too simple to see this as the Admiralty demanding more air cover from the RAF, with the use of long-range aircraft for antisubmarine patrols opposed by Arthur Harris, the aggressive head of Bomber Command, who pressed, in contrast, for a concentration on bombing Germany. To a degree, this preference indeed reflected the doctrine and institutional culture of the RAF, which was disinclined to support antishipping operations in European waters or to build more long-range seaplanes. Instead, in this case, there was a preference for bombing the submarine bases and building yards in Europe, such as Brest and Bergen. The value of these attacks was limited by the heavy fortification of the concrete-covered U-boat "pens" and bases and by a lack of concrete-penetrating weapons. However, in addition, attacking submarines at sea proved difficult: the RAF's capacity to navigate accurately over water was poor (too many missions ending as "Convoy Not Found"), while the RAF had equipped itself with a totally inadequate series of antisubmarine weapons. In practice, there were plenty of Liberators in RAF Coastal Command, but it was not initially appreciated that they could be converted to VLR (very long range) capability. In part, this was a doctrinal failure by the RAF (including the leaders of Coastal Command), who were never enthused about operating in the mid-Atlantic, who expected the Royal Navy to develop escort carriers for this purpose, and who preferred to focus on transit routes closer to home. The Admiralty, which had its own fixation with the Biscay offensive, did not appreciate that the Liberators in service could be converted.

More seriously, the RAF did not realize the need to address the issue of commerce protection seriously, not least in order to ensure the supplies of aluminum and aviation fuel upon which its bomber offensive depended. This was an extremely dangerous attitude as the German submarines were sinking large numbers of ships, reaching a wartime peak of tonnage sunk in November 1942. The navy referred to the RAF as the "Really Absent Force" or the "Royal Advertising Force."

Churchill, minister of defense as well as prime minister, remarked that the large tonnage of shipping sunk by submarines was the most worrying aspect of the whole war, but he was at fault for the priority enjoyed by Bomber Command and the overall shortage of aircraft for Coastal Command. However, he was largely blameless for the "Air Gap," as nobody asked him for VLR aircraft until November 1942, and he immediately supported the idea. The difficulties of assessment, however, are shown by Churchill's decision to establish the Anti-U-Boat Warfare Committee in November 1942. This was an example of Churchill providing effective direction, but it might also be argued that it should have been done sooner. Churchill's strategy relied on Britain visibly striking Germany so as to resist international and domestic pressure for the swift opening of a hazardous second front in France. This strategy made the bomber offensive more politically appealing than RAF maritime operations.

New emphasis was given to the submarine war from January 1943 because, as a result of Hitler's anger with the failure in the Battle of the Barents Sea, Admiral Karl Dönitz, the head of the U-boat service, replaced Grand Admiral Raeder as the naval commander-in-chief. In 1943, however, the Allies successfully responded to the U-boats with improved resources, tactics, and strategy. They introduced more powerful depth charges, better sonar detection equipment, and increased use of shipborne radar. Enhanced antisubmarine weaponry, especially effective ahead-throwing depth-charge launchers, was important to the Allied success. So was signals intelligence, the ability to intercept and decipher German naval codes and to use the resulting material to operational and tactical effect. After serious problems for most of 1942, the Allies' intelligence on U-boats improved from December 1942.[40] Effective antisubmarine tactics by both convoy escorts and aircraft were also important. Accumulated experience increased Allied operational effectiveness. In addition, minefields were responsible for many U-boat losses.

In 1943, antisubmarine air resources became more plentiful, equipment more impressive, and tactics more effective. There was an increasing number of VLR aircraft for the "Air Gap" and the first use of escort carriers in the mid-Atlantic. With convoy escorts, there were incremental steps not only in numbers, detection equipment, and weaponry—for example, improved fuses for depth charges and better searchlights—but also in the experience of operating together, thanks to the development of effective formations and tactics. From late 1940, ASV Mk II radar, combined with the Leigh light, proved highly effective at detecting and targeting surfaced submarines. However, the radar lost its potency when the Germans were able to introduce listening receivers on U-boats. In turn, in March 1943, the Mk III radar, which could not be detected by these receivers, proved a crucial addition. Radar sets small enough to be carried by aircraft, and yet capable of picking up submarine periscopes at five miles, were a key tool. Increased resources in the struggle with submarines owed much to the growing Canadian commitment.[41]

The building of far more merchant shipping from 1942, especially by the Americans, was also very important to Allied victory, as was the availability of more escort vessels and their improved armaments. In early 1943, U-boat losses rose. In May 1943, forty-three U-boats were sunk, and on May 24, Dönitz ordered a halt to attacks on convoys in the North Atlantic and the withdrawal of submarines to areas where there was less Allied air power. To believe that tonnage sunk, no matter where, was the critical factor was a strategic error. That year, the ratio of ships sunk to U-boats destroyed was 2:1, a rate of German success well down from the 14:1 of 1940–42. Moreover, the percentage of Allied ships sunk fell considerably.

Germany throughout was at a clear disadvantage in the Battle of the Atlantic, both in warship numbers and as a result of Allied shipbuilding. Moreover, the needs of the Eastern Front from June 1941 and of countering Allied bombing attacks on Germany exacerbated the failure to provide adequate air support for the antishipping campaign. Yet, aside from these highly important elements, a range of factors helped the Allies win, including effective antisubmarine tactics, by both convoy escorts and aircraft, and intelligence. As a consequence, the number of submarines sunk per year was much greater than in the First World War, while the percentage of Allied shipping lost was lower. The strategic issue posed for the Germans by Allied shipbuilding interacted with the tactical and operational challenges imposed by improved Allied proficiency in antisubmarine warfare, and German submarine construction methods were not significantly accelerated until 1944.[42]

May 1943 was not the end of the Battle of the Atlantic and should only be seen as a turning point for the Allies if the need to continue to overcome the submarine challenge is also stressed. Indeed, in the battle of technological innovation, the Germans made important moves. When they introduced the T-5 acoustic homing torpedo in the late summer of 1943, they were at once able to sink three escorts and to launch a renewed attack on Allied shipping. This, however, was successfully counteracted by Allied air power, the application of which benefited from intercepted signals information. The determined German attempt to regain the initiative failed, and they suffered heavy losses, including thirty-seven boats in July. The German failure confirmed and underlined their defeat that May. The success of stronger convoy defenses had been apparent from late 1941 and was now combined in a more effective overall antisubmarine strategy. Moreover, the Germans proved less adept in adapting to changing tactics and technology than the Allies.

In the event, air power in the shape of long-range aircraft was important to the Allied victory in the Atlantic. Already based in Britain, Iceland, and Canada, land-based American VLR four-engine Liberators flying from the Azores were the key to closing the mid-Atlantic "Air Gap" in October 1943 and thus to denying submarines their safest hunting ground, which was to the west of the Azores. Air bases were established on the islands of Terceira and Santa Maria. They were subsequently to prove important American bases during the Cold War. Of the wartime airfields near where I live in southwest England, Dunkeswell, built in 1941–42 for the RAF, was used by the U.S. Navy from 1943 for long-range antisubmarine patrols and flew PB4Ys, a maritime version of the B-24.

Mass was a key element and demonstrated anew the ability of American industry to produce large quantities of all sorts of weapons. The production of escort destroyers began in June 1943, and the United States built over three hundred of these warships. The number of aircraft deployed against submarines in the Atlantic rose from 595 in late 1942 to 1,300 a year later, and the number of escort carriers increased.[43] The availability of more aircraft meant that submarines could not safely sail from their French bases across the Bay of Biscay on the surface, and thus they used up some of their supply of electricity, as the recharging of batteries had to be done on the surface, which made submarines increasingly vulnerable to air attack. There was also an important shift in the relative quality of personnel. German U-boat losses cost the Germans the crew and therefore the experience they offered, while the Allies built up a bank of experience.

In early 1944, the Germans fitted snorkel devices to their U-boats. These allowed them to charge their batteries while submerged, as well as enabling the underwater starting and running of diesel engines, thus reducing their vulnerability to Allied air power. The U-boats were becoming true submarines, as opposed to just submersibles. However, submarines were visible when they were below the surface if they were at insufficient depth. The snorkel did not permit running the diesels at sufficient depth to avoid detection from the air. A submarine just below the surface was visible from the air, so submarines operating in waters within the range of aerial antisubmarine patrols had to be either on the surface and maintaining aircraft watches continuously, or far enough below the surface to prevent detection from the air. The gun on the Type 7c submarine was replaced by antiaircraft guns.

The change in the specifications of U-boats did not increase significantly their attack capability vis-à-vis escorts. The improvement in Allied escort capability outweighed U-boat advances, and, demonstrating that the war in the Atlantic had been largely won, the Germans sank relatively few Allied ships in 1944–45. Furthermore, the production of a new type of submarine, the high-speed Type 21 "Electro," was badly affected by Allied bombing. The strategic failure of the U-boat offensive was clarified by Allied, especially American, shipbuilding.

Allied success in the Battle of the Atlantic was crucial to the provision of imports to feed and fuel Britain, as well as to the buildup of military resources there. Only three Allied merchantmen convoyed across the Atlantic in the first three months of 1944 were sunk. This was the background to the second front sought by the Allies, and it underlined the strategic quandary faced by the Germans, with an intractable conflict on the Eastern Front likely to be joined by fresh commitments in France. The U-boats were proven to have had only an operational capability.

PACIFIC WAR, 1944

The vast extent of the Pacific created unprecedented problems of war making and infrastructure. Substantial fleets had to operate over great distances and required mobile support and maintenance. The scale of planning was large in resources, space, and time. The American problem-solving, can-do approach to logistics permitted a rapid advance. The fleet train that provided logistical support was greatly expanded, while processes for transferring fuel and ammunition and other supplies from ship to ship at sea were developed.[44] In addition, the use, from 1944, of shipping as floating depots for artillery, ammunition, and other matériel increased the speed of army resupply, as it was no longer necessary to use distant Australia as a staging area for American operations. The vast extent also created opportunities: it was easier to isolate island targets in the Pacific than in the Mediterranean, and there was less naval exposure to Axis air attack. As a result, the American navy could concentrate force more effectively.

The Japanese continued building warships, but their numbers were insufficient and their navy lacked the capacity to resist the effective American assault. It also suffered from poor doctrine, including a lack of understanding of naval air war[45] and an inadequate understanding of respective strategic

options. Indeed, the deficiencies in Japanese planning indicated serious sys-
temic failings, including an inability to understand American policy and to
respond to earlier deficiencies in Japanese strategy and operational planning.
The Japanese military tended to lack the mental flexibility to choose an
option that would be against their moral compass. Defensive strategies were
unwelcome.

The American ability to deploy carriers both in the southwest and the
central Pacific reflected the extent to which superior American resources,
and their effective use, permitted the simultaneous pursuit of more than one
offensive strategy, with a likelihood both of success and an ability to overcome the defense and resist counteroffensives without having to call on
reserves from other "fronts." Air power could be applied from the sea as
never before, and as part of an effective and well-supported modern combined-arms force. There were now sufficient aircraft both for a carrier battle
and for protecting an amphibious assault, and the fast-carrier task forces,
combined with surface escorts, constituted a major operational-level weapon
with the necessary tactical cohesion.[46]

The Japanese aimed to destroy the spearhead of the advancing American
fleet by concentrating their air power against it. There was the hope, even
conviction, that the decisive success of the Japanese fleet over the Russians
at Tsushima in 1905 could be repeated. This reflected a more general conviction, also seen in the Midway operation in 1942, that a decisive victory could
be obtained on one front, which could overcome the more general role and
impact of Allied resources. Similar goals were pursued in 1944 at the expense of Britain (on the China-Myanmar border) and of China (in southern
China). Japanese assumptions arose from the sway of historical examples
that supposedly represented national greatness and, even more, from the role
of factors of will in Axis thinking. There was a conviction that victory would
sap the inherently weaker will of opponents and thus give the Axis the
success to which they were entitled.

Aside from the lack of political understanding underlying this policy, it
was anachronistic militarily. Defeat in 1944 on one front would have delayed
the Americans, but nothing more; and, by concentrating a target for the
Americans, Japanese strategy made it more likely that the American attack
would succeed in causing heavy casualties. The Americans had a better and
more mobile fleet, a far greater ability to replace losses, and far more capable
leadership than the Japanese.

The campaigning in 1944 saw the collapse of the Japanese Empire in the
Pacific. Without air superiority, Japanese units and logistics were highly
vulnerable, which ensured a lack of tactical, operational, and strategic capability. In addition, the Japanese were fooled by American strategy and deception. Having two simultaneous American drives created serious problems for
the Japanese navy, which itself had less influence than in 1941–42 as the

army became more powerful. The two services fought over resources, command, and priorities.

In January–February 1944, the Americans successfully attacked the Marshall Islands, which made it easier to strike at the Mariana Islands—Saipan, Tinian, and Guam—in June. This led to the Battle of the Philippine Sea, the major battle the Japanese had sought. American Task Force 58, with fifteen carriers and over nine hundred planes, was attacked by the nine carriers and four hundred planes of the Japanese First Mobile Fleet. However, located by American radar and benefiting from radio interception, Japanese air attacks, launched on June 19, were shot down by American fighters and by antiaircraft fire from supporting warships, with no damage to the American carriers. The following day, a long-range American air attack in the failing light sank the carrier *Hiyo* and damaged three others. The Japanese carriers were protected by a screen of Zero fighters, but, as a clear sign of growing Japanese weakness in the air, this was too weak to resist the fighters escorting the American bombers. Although the Japanese still had a sizeable carrier fleet, once again the loss of pilots and carrier-based maintenance crew was a crippling blow. American submarines sank two large carriers, *Shokaku* and *Taiho*. This victory enabled the Americans to overrun the Marianas, a decisive advance into the western Pacific. The islands provided not only sites for airfields, but also an important forward logistical base for the navy and for amphibious operations.

The Americans used their naval and air superiority, already strong and rapidly growing, to mount a reconquest of the Philippines from October. That operation helped ensure a naval battle, that of Leyte Gulf of October 23–26, 1944, the largest naval battle of the war and one (or rather a series of engagements) that secured American maritime superiority in the western Pacific. The availability of oil helped determine Japanese naval dispositions, and, with carrier formations based in home waters and the battle force based just south of Singapore, any American movement against the intervening Philippines presented a very serious problem for Japan. There was growing pessimism in Japan, and losing honorably became a goal for at least some Japanese naval leaders. The head of the Naval Operations Section asked on October 18, 1944, that the fleet be afforded "a fitting place to die" and "the chance to bloom as flowers of death." In Operation Sho-Go (Operation Victory), the Japanese sought to intervene by luring the American carrier fleet away, employing their own carriers as bait, and then using two naval striking forces, under Vice Admirals Kurita and Kiyohide respectively, to attack the vulnerable American landing fleet. This overly complex scheme posed serious problems for the ability of American admirals to read the battle and control the tempo of the fighting, and, as at Midway, for their Japanese counterparts in following the plan. In a crisis for the American operation, one of the strike forces was able to approach the landing area and was superior to

the American warships. However, instead of persisting, the strike force retired, its exhausted commander, Kurita, lacking knowledge of the local situation, not least due to the difficulties of identifying enemy surface ships. The
net effect of the battle was the loss of four Japanese carriers, three battleships
including the *Musashi*, ten cruisers, other warships, and many aircraft.[47]

AMPHIBIOUS OPERATIONS IN EUROPE, 1943–44

Naval strength proved a crucial element in a series of Allied invasions, with
the American and British navies playing the key role. Operation Torch, the
invasion of Morocco and Algeria in November 1942, was followed by the
invasion of Sicily in July 1943 (which involved 3,600 ships), and of mainland Italy in September. The direction of Allied success in North Africa and
Italy reflected the transformation of the situation in the Mediterranean and
developed it. Naval superiority made any sortie by Vichy or Italian capital
ships unlikely to succeed and prevented a Dunkirk-style Axis retreat from
Tunisia. Most of the Vichy navy, 250,000 tonnes of warships, had been
scuttled by the French on November 27, 1942, when, having occupied Vichy
France, German forces attacked the great naval dockyard at Toulon. Similarly, the Danish fleet was to scuttle in 1943 to avoid German takeover.

Moreover, the Italian armistice in September 1943 was followed by the
surrender of much of the Italian navy to the Allies, with the fleet sailing from
the port of La Spezia to Malta, although it was damaged by German glider
bombs. This transformation enabled the British to withdraw warships from
the Mediterranean, both to support the invasion of France and for operations
against Japan.

At the same time, Allied naval forces remained in the Mediterranean
where they supported Allied operations in Italy and the invasion of southern
France. The Torch landings had revealed a lack of appropriate equipment,
doctrine, and experience. Many of the faults had been rectified by the time of
Sicily, not least through proper reconnaissance for, and organization of, the
process of landing. Anglo-American naval bombardment was important to
the landings at Salerno in September 1943, Anzio in February 1944, and
southern France in August 1944, the last of which was particularly impressive. Carriers also played an important role: five were present for the Salerno
landings. The scale of the Allied naval support for the landings in August
1944 was impressive, with 887 warships, including 9 carriers, 5 battleships,
and 21 cruisers, supporting the 1,370 landing craft.[48]

Naval dominance provided the background for consideration of an invasion of southeast Europe. However, this idea, although supported by Churchill, was largely blocked by American opposition. The exception was a British
amphibious campaign in the Aegean in late 1943, a campaign defeated by

German land-based air power. As a result, British warships tended to keep to the dark. Despite this, six destroyers were lost.

Control of much of the Mediterranean made a major contribution to the flexibility of Allied supply links, greatly shortening the route from the North Atlantic to the Middle East. It was no longer necessary to face the choice of risking Axis interception in the Mediterranean or of sailing around South Africa.[49]

Allied naval power was employed on a greater scale and more decisively in British "home waters" in 1944. In the invasion of Normandy, launched with Operation Neptune on "D-day," June 6, the Allies suffered from significant doctrinal and planning misjudgments, notably in the attempt to destroy German shore defenses,[50] but benefited from well-organized and effective naval support, as well as from absolute air superiority. Maritime considerations were important. The Germans concentrated more of their defenses and army units in France in the Calais region, which offered a shorter sea crossing and a shorter route to Germany. Normandy, in contrast, was easier to reach from the invasion ports on the south coast of England, especially Plymouth, Portland, and Portsmouth. While the largely British naval armada provided heavy supporting fire, which, in general, was more effective than the bombers, the steel-reinforced concrete of the German casements and bunkers proved very resistant to high explosives.

The naval armada also prevented disruption by German warships. There was no equivalent to the challenge posed by the Japanese fleet to the American landings in the Philippines later that year, but attacks by destroyers, torpedo boats, and submarines based in French Atlantic ports were a threat to the landing fleet and to subsequent supply shipping that had to be guarded against, and this was done successfully.

The unsuccessful Dieppe raid on August 19, 1942, had shown that attacking a defended port in northern France was both extremely difficult and would most likely destroy the harbor infrastructure. In 1944, the Germans still, mistakenly, anticipated that the Allies would focus on seizing ports such as Cherbourg and Le Havre. Instead, despite problems, including a shortage of landing ship tanks (LSTs), the invasion marked a major advance in large-scale amphibious operations. The British military commentator and former general J. F. C. Fuller wrote in the *Sunday Pictorial* of October 1, 1944,

> Had our sea power remained what it had been, solely a weapon to command the sea, the garrison Germany established in France almost certainly would have proved sufficient. It was a change in the conception of naval power which sealed the doom of that great fortress. Hitherto in all overseas invasions the invading forces had been fitted to ships. Now ships were fitted to the invading forces . . . how to land the invading forces in battle order . . . this difficulty has been overcome by building various types of special landing boats and prefabricated landing stages.

Naval power included bringing across the Channel two prefabricated harbors composed of floating piers, the Mulberry harbors. The laying of oil pipelines under the Channel was also an impressive engineering achievement that contributed to the infrastructure of the invasion.[51] In late 1944, against far weaker German opposition, Soviet amphibious operations cleared the islands in the Gulf of Riga.

THE LAST STAGES OF THE WAR AT SEA WITH GERMANY

The buildup and supply in, and from, Britain of the massive American and Canadian forces that landed in Normandy, and subsequently, were a reflection of the failure of German submarines to achieve strategic results. After the Allied breakout from Normandy, the Germans evacuated their submarines from their bases in west France and concentrated their force in Norway. From there, however, the U-boats were able to inflict scant damage on the Arctic convoys and focused, instead, on British waters where their inshore campaign proved deadly, although they were no longer able to sink large numbers of merchantmen. Instead, the U-boats suffered serious losses, in part as a result of air attacks, notably on their bases, as well as at sea, although the sinkings at sea were due more to convoy escorts and their use of forward-firing weaponry.

Nevertheless, the submarine threat remained potent, as construction maintained the overall numbers of U-boats. This obliged the Allies to continue to devote considerable naval resources to escort duty and antisubmarine warfare, including coastal convoy routes in British waters. Given Allied, especially American, shipbuilding capability and the resulting size of the Allied navies, this task did not, however, limit or prevent other uses of Allied naval power, particularly the movement of British warships to the Indian Ocean and the Pacific. At the close of the war in Europe, there were still large numbers of U-boats, but they were unable to inflict serious losses on Allied shipping. Had new types become operational, they would have posed a more serious challenge, but, thanks to bombing, the construction of a new, faster class of submarine—the Type 21, which had a much greater battery capacity and mechanically reloaded torpedo tubes—was delayed so that it did not become operational until April 1945. This was too late to challenge Allied command of the sea; although, even had it become operational earlier, it would not have been in sufficient numbers to change the outcome of the struggles. Indeed, the trajectory of German air power, first with rockets (V-1s and V-2s) and then with jet aircraft, neither of which brought significant improvements, suggests that the possibilities from improved submarines should not be pushed too hard.

Nevertheless, in a continued determination to fight on and divide and defeat the Allies, Hitler's regime placed much reliance not only on a stronger will but also on wonder weapons, including the development of new submarine types.[52] There was Allied concern that the top underwater speed of the Type 21, 17.2 knots, would improve its capacity for evasion tactics and make it harder to destroy, but the Allies were also developing new tactics and technology, including electromechanically controlled ahead-thrown ordnance.[53]

The German surface navy was concentrated in the Baltic in order to cover the retreat of German units and civilians in the face of Soviet advances, and also to supply German bridgeheads, notably in Courland (western Latvia). In the face of a weak and poorly managed Soviet navy, and despite a shortage of oil, both of these goals were successfully executed, and about 2.5 million people were evacuated, albeit with the loss of fifteen thousand, mostly as a result of Soviet submarine attack.

THE COLLAPSE OF JAPAN, 1945

In the closing months of the war, as American operations neared the Japanese Home Islands, the Japanese increasingly turned to kamikaze (suicide) attacks in order to counter overwhelming American naval superiority: aircraft were flown into ships, making them manned missiles, although they had little or no penetrative power against large warships. Such attacks were a product not only of a fanatical self-sacrifice, but also of the limitations, by then, of the Japanese naval air arm. First mounted on October 25, 1944, these attacks led in 1944–45 to the sinking of forty-nine ships, with another three hundred damaged, and were designed to sap American will. Initially, the percentage of hits and near misses was over a quarter, but the success rate fell the following spring as the Japanese increasingly relied on inexperienced pilots, while American air defenses improved, with more antiaircraft guns and also fighter patrols, notably Hellcats, which were dispatched miles from the fleet in order to shoot down outclassed Zeros. The Americans benefited from the large number of fighters carried by their numerous carriers and from the radar-based system of fighter control. Bomber attacks on Japanese air bases also helped. The Japanese lost about five thousand men in the kamikaze attacks.

From April 1945, the Japanese also used Ohka (cherry blossom) flying bombs powered by three solid-fuel rocket motors and launched from aircraft twenty-three miles from their intended targets. They had pilots but no propeller or landing gear, thus serving even more as manned missiles. About 750 were used, mostly in response to the American conquest of the island of

Okinawa in April–June 1945, but only three American ships were sunk or damaged beyond repair as a result.

The Americans invaded the island of Okinawa on April 1, 1945. The Japanese sent their last major naval force, led by the battleship *Yamato*, on a kamikaze mission, with only enough oil to steam to Okinawa. However, it was intercepted by 380 American carrier-based aircraft, and the *Yamato*, a cruiser, and four of the eight accompanying destroyers were sunk on April 7. The vulnerability of surface warships without air cover was amply demonstrated. The battleships on which the Japanese had spent so much had become an operational and strategic irrelevance.

Japan's position in 1945 indicated the great value of Allied naval power, most of which, in these operations, was American. Although the Japanese still occupied large areas in East and Southeast Asia, for example much of China, Malaya, Sumatra, and Java, these forces were isolated. American submarines operated with few difficulties in the Yellow and East China Seas and the Sea of Japan. Carrier-borne aircraft attacked Japan, dominated its airspace, and mined its waters, while warships bombarded coastal positions as they had earlier done at Iwo Jima and Okinawa. American and amphibious operations and planning benefited from their mastery of logistics, not least in ensuring the availability of sufficient oil. The Americans could plan where they wanted to mount an invasion. Just as the Battle of the Atlantic had ended in Allied triumph, so the naval war in the Pacific had been decisively won. Despite logistical limitations, the British Pacific Fleet played a successful role. Nevertheless, the attack on Japan was very much an American triumph, and this looked toward postwar American naval dominance.

Allied fleets elsewhere hit the Japanese Empire. In their reconquest of Myanmar in early 1945, the British benefited from amphibious operations, notably in the capture of the city of Rangoon on May 3. The Royal Navy also launched attacks, especially with aircraft and submarines, on Japanese positions and shipping, for example oil refineries in Sumatra. Naval support was also significant to Australasian amphibious attacks on the island of Borneo.

The Soviet Union entered the war on August 8, 1945. Most of its attack was a land invasion of Manchuria. However, the invasion of northern Korea was supported by amphibious operations from the Sea of Japan, as was that of southern Sakhalin. The Kurile Islands were also successfully invaded. Whereas earlier in the war, the Soviets had suffered from a lack of preparation in their amphibious operations, the 1945 operations were ably conducted and supported by much naval infantry.

CONCLUSIONS

The war we have to wage against Japan is of an entirely new type. It is no mere clash of opposing fleets. Allied naval forces must be so strong in themselves, and so fully equipped to carry with them land and air forces, that they can overcome not only Japanese naval forces but also Japanese garrisons supported by shore-based air forces. . . . The bigger the Allied fleet free to seek out the enemy, the better the chances of destroying the Japanese fleet. [54]

General Ismay, in effect Churchill's chief of staff, thus emphasized scale in his stress on the naval dimension in 1944. Scale was, indeed, readily apparent. Between Pearl Harbor and the end of the war, the Americans commissioned more warships into their navy than any other combatant. More generally, most of the forty-two million tons of shipping built by the Allies during the war was constructed by the Americans. The British shipbuilding industry was affected by German bombing, as well as by serious problems of resource supply and allocation, and the capacity for expansion was limited. The Soviet industry was badly affected by German occupation. Canadian production increased, but it was the Americans who were responsible not only for much of the new shipping, but also for the rapid response to needs and for the expansion in types. Many of the new American vessels were Liberty ships, built often in as little as ten days, using prefabricated components on production lines. This was an aspect of the rapid design and production methods that characterized American procurement. All-welded ships replaced riveting, speeding up production. Despite losing oil tankers with a total tonnage of 1,421,000, mostly to German submarines, which inflicted particular damage to American inshore shipping on the Atlantic coast in the early months of 1942, the tonnage of the American oil-tanker fleet rose from 4,268,000 tons in 1942 to 12,875,000 tons in 1945. The flexibility of American society helped directly and conspicuously: by late 1944, over 15 percent of the workers in shipbuilding were women. In some yards, notably on the West Coast, the percentage was far higher. [55]

In contrast, Japanese shipbuilding faced major resource and organization problems, including a lack of steel, poor plant, scant use of welding, and an absence of standardization. This situation was crucial to the long haul after Midway, as the Japanese navy had to be beaten repeatedly in battle by the Americans, as well as weakened by repeated attacks on an already flawed war economy.

Differences in resources and shipbuilding were linked to the major buildup in the Allied navies. For example, Canada on the eve of war had six destroyers and fewer than two thousand personnel, but by 1945, resting on a massive expansion in shipbuilding, there were also two light fleet carriers, two light cruisers, a very large antisubmarine force, and 110,000 serving personnel. There were administrative problems in this expansion, but the buildup was both achieved and effective. [56]

The war at sea also led to an emphasis on the ability to articulate and integrate different arms. A long-established aspect of effectiveness, such integration became more important with the greater range of available technology. The integration of air and sea forces, both for attack and also in defense, was important for tactical, operational, and strategic success. This integration focused attention not only on resources, but also on command skills, training, and the ability to learn and adapt.[57] In February 1943, Admiral Sir Dudley Pound, the First British Sea Lord, noted,

> At the moment we are doing all we can to produce super long-range aircraft, so that we can cover the whole of the Atlantic from one side to the other, as there is no question but that if you can put aircraft over the U-boats during the day, it prevents them getting into position for their night attacks. I am hoping very much that we shall be able to blast them out of their operational bases in the Bay of Biscay [by air attack].[58]

The naval dimension, alongside that of the air and often, through carriers, closely linked with it, played a key role in securing Allied victory. The naval dimension was crucial to the strategic axes of Allied power, and both naval and air were central to the delivery of power. The Axis transport systems were repeatedly hit hard by Allied attack while also suffering from the deficiencies of the naval forces and strategy of the Axis powers. Allied attacks both lessened the mobility of Axis forces and crippled their war economy. Alongside greater Allied production, America and Britain had effective maintenance and training programs.[59]

At the same time, alongside the ease with which a clear narrative and analysis can be advanced, there are problems with both. In particular, there is the extent to which the nature of naval tasks during the Cold War affected the subsequent reading of the Second World War. In particular, the postwar significance of carriers in the American and British navies encouraged a reading back to the Second World War, with a downplaying of the role of battleships. Between 1946 and 1951, the Royal Navy produced studies of the Battles of the Coral Sea and Midway, battles in which it had not taken part, in order to provide learning tools.[60]

So also with the discussion of submarines. Because the Cold War at sea with the Soviet Union was to be dominated by the Soviet submarine threat, so the emphasis for the Second World War was on the U-boat challenge, which indeed was very real, rather than that from German surface shipping. In contrast, it is instructive that the war games at the American Naval War College in 1945–46 assumed the combination of fast carriers and fast battleships.[61] Indeed, in the late 1940s and early 1950s, the Soviet Union had an ambitious naval expansion program that included several battle cruisers and fifty *Sverdlov* light cruisers designed to interfere with Atlantic sea routes in the event of war. This program made keeping some Western battleships in commission and more in reserve appear reasonable.

It is also necessary to remember the wider political context. For example, some of the forced labor used to make armaments and batteries for the over one thousand U-boats built was taken from concentration camps. Many workers died, in part as a result of exposure to toxic metals. Unsuccessful efforts were made to stop a German television documentary on these matters, *The Silence of the Quandts*, being broadcast in 2007. The Quandt family business made these products. Moreover, the continuing tendency to treat the German submarine service, which in fact had a high rate of Nazi members, as heroes, able to keep fighting (and killing merchant sailors) despite heavy cumulative losses, which was the presentation in German war propaganda, needs to be countered by a reminder of their fanaticism and of the deadly nature of their long-term goals.[62] It is also important to be reminded of the suffering of those sunk. In 1942, a British naval officer on another warship commented on the sinking of the aircraft carrier *Eagle* in the Mediterranean: "It was a terrible sight to see such a big ship go down so quickly. The great patch of oil and debris was full of heads, there were hundreds swimming and choking in the water."[63]

Chapter Seven

Cold War: The Age of American Dominance, 1946–67

At the close of Ian Fleming's James Bond novel *Dr. No* (1958), the British Empire is presented as still dynamic and potent, and this presentation is linked to the Royal Navy, as indeed is James Bond. In order to establish control of Dr. No's base at Crab Key, an island off Jamaica, the commander of the Jamaican-based Caribbean Defense Force provides a platoon to be embarked on HMS *Narvik*. This is a warship whose name recalled a Second World War naval success in the 1940 Norway campaign at a stage in the conflict before America entered the war. While such an account pleased British readers and their assumptions in 1958, at a moment when Britain still had the largest empire in the world, it was no longer British naval power, however, that was crucial.

The era of the Cold War, 1946–89, was very much one of naval confrontation rather than conflict. Despite the relative lack of conflict between navies, naval power was a key element in the era. The focus was specifically on the rivalry between the United States and the Soviet Union. Nevertheless, other powers took a role in the Cold War, notably Britain and Canada on the American side. Moreover, the confrontation came to play a part around the world, and, indeed, naval considerations, including basing, helped to spread this confrontation. The use of naval power in the Korean and Vietnam Wars was an important part of the Cold War.

Aside from the Cold War, there were a series of conflicts in this period that involved naval hostilities. Some of these conflicts were directly linked to the Cold War, while others were more tangential. There were conflicts of imperial power, for example the "Suez crisis," the Anglo-French attack on Egypt in 1956, and also the Anglo-Argentinian Falklands War of 1982, as well as wars between non-Western powers, for example India-Pakistan, Is-

161

rael-Egypt, and the Nigerian Civil War (or Biafran War) of 1967–70. In this period, changes in technology, capability, doctrine, and procurement were all linked, especially with the demise of the battleship and the rise of nuclear-powered submarines, as well as missile-firing submarines, helicopters, and surface ships. The nuclear-powered submarine made the submarine a truly submerged warship, while the helicopter gave the capability of the surface units in the antisubmarine role a quantum leap forward.

It would be possible to present the Cold War as a unit, but that would be to run together a lengthy period in which, alongside common themes, there were also major shifts. Two in particular command attention: the move to submarines firing intercontinental ballistic missiles and the rise of Soviet naval power and the accompanying change in the naval confrontation between the United States and the Soviet Union. These factors lead to a division in this book of the lengthy Cold War era between chapters 7 and 8, albeit a division without the chronological and thematic precision of the close of the Second World War in 1945.

THE LATE 1940s

The Second World War was followed by large-scale demobilization, especially by the Western powers as the "peace dividend" was taken. This was readily the case with the largest navy, the American. Moreover, the destruction of the Axis navies during the war was followed by their abolition as both Germany and Japan were occupied. The Americans occupied Japan, while most German naval facilities were in the British occupation zone. Despite tensions, notably on the part of the American navy, for example over the exchange of intelligence,[1] America remained allied with Britain, which now had the second-biggest navy, and that alliance further secured America's naval dominance, which was more pronounced than that of America or Britain after the First World War.

However, there was no comparison with Britain's naval position after the Napoleonic Wars ended in 1815 because of the new significance of air power. The Second World War had ended in Europe with the capture of Berlin by the Soviet army and that in Asia as a result of the American dropping of the atomic bombs and the devastation created by those two bombs. The impression would have been different had there been an American amphibious invasion to end Japanese opposition, although such an invasion would have involved many casualties, which might have encouraged war weariness.

Without any obvious opponent at sea, the American fleet was extensively demobilized. This was necessary as the end of the war was followed by the return of most conscripts to civil society. In addition, there were force-structure issues, many of which were bound up with the question of how to understand and respond to a rapidly changing international situation and the attendant tensions for strategy, doctrine, organization, and procurement.[2] The navy's bold plans for an expansion of its carrier force were not implemented. Instead, there was large-scale contraction. For example, the number of amphibious ships in the American navy fell from 610 in 1945 to 81 in 1950.

America was not alone. Most of the Canadian navy was laid up. British plans in the second half of the war for continuing naval expansion, notably the building of major new surface units, were not pursued. Instead, the Royal Navy was faced with aging warships and manpower problems, and by a serious contraction that was more marked than those of the other two services. Dismayed, two successive First Lords of the Admiralty retired in the late 1940s, in 1946 and 1948. Indeed, the navy was seen as the Cinderella of the fighting services.

CHINESE CIVIL WAR, 1946–49

Navies played a major role in many of the conflicts of the late 1940s. They were especially significant in the restoration of European imperial authority in the lands conquered by Japan, for example by the British in Hong Kong and Singapore, the latter an amphibious operation, Zipper, that was prepared during the war. Moreover, warships were employed in counterinsurgency operations, as by the French in Vietnam where they faced an insurgency in 1946–54, and by the royalists in the Greek Civil War.

However, there was less naval activity in the major war of the period, the Chinese Civil War (1946–49). The Chinese communists did not effectively solve their problem of naval inferiority during the war, but that did not matter greatly. Most of the key battles during the war took place on land far enough from the coast that naval power was irrelevant. Even during the important Liao-Shen campaign, in which a key battle (Tashan) was within range of the guns of the cruiser *Chongqing*, the cruiser was too far offshore for the naval artillery fire to make much difference. Indeed, accuracy at that range was pretty low.

Earlier, in the crucial first year of the civil war, in Manchuria, the Soviet Union greatly helped the communists by denying the Nationalists the ability to use their naval advantage. The Nationalists, not the communists, controlled Chinese naval power, which, however, was small scale.[3] Subsequently, the Nationalists could employ their navy to land troops in Manchuria and to withdraw them from there, but not for much more. And landing troops at a port, for example Qinhuangdao, was of scant value if the troops could not fight their way to Jinzhou where they were needed: the communists were blocking them at Tashan. American intervention would not have changed this had it only taken the form of warships.

In turn, the naval limitations of the communists came into play when they had achieved victory on the mainland in 1949 and had to try to deal with Nationalist forces on offshore islands. The communists failed badly when they tried to attack the small offshore Quemoy archipelago in October 1949, which helped lead to the postponement of a planned invasion of Taiwan.[4] When, in contrast, they came to attack the Nationalists on Hainan Island in March 1950, the communists were better prepared, thanks in part to Soviet advisors, and the Fourth Field Army was successful in what was an important amphibious operation, one that deserves to attract more attention.[5] In 1950, China's communist army, the People's Liberation Army (PLA), was working to overcome its naval inferiority. It had acquired some warships and personnel from surrendered Nationalist units. The PLA was also building up naval and air strength with the advice and assistance of the Soviet Union, in preparation for attacking Taiwan and other offshore islands still under Nationalist control.[6] The wider context was crucial throughout: Soviet assistance was central, from the sea denial in the Manchurian theater, to the Hainan Island campaign, to the preparations to attack Taiwan. This assistance very much indicated that it was not necessary to be a leading naval power in order to achieve sea-power goals. This achievement was not primarily a matter of warships at this stage. At the same time, the range of these Chinese communist goals was very limited, essentially to close-shore operations.

In turn, communist success in the Chinese Civil War (1946–49) and the North Korean invasion of South Korea in 1950, led to a marked increase in international tension and to pressure in the United States for rearmament. The United States became committed to the independence of Taiwan, with the powerful Seventh Fleet moving into the Taiwan Strait in June 1950 and thus blocking a communist invasion of Taiwan.

For its part, the Soviet Union encouraged North Korean action in what became the Korean War and was a key regional player. For example, the Soviets were reluctant to return to China the major warm-water Manchurian ports of Port Arthur and Dalian, which they had taken from Japan in 1945. Despite Mao Zedong, the Chinese dictator, wanting the ports returned, the Soviet Union did not do so while Stalin remained in power, which he did until his death in 1953; they were returned in 1955 in accordance with an agreement of the previous year. This stance represented an important continuation from pre-communist Russian interest in Manchuria: Port Arthur had been used as a naval base then and was the site of an important battle in the Russo-Japanese War (1904–5). Such continuation represented evidence for those who, dubious of Soviet discussion of their goals, sought a geopolitical explanation for Soviet policy. This was notably so with issues of maritime access, encouraging interest in containment as the means to thwart Soviet expansionism.

KOREAN WAR

The Korean War (1950–53) escalated in late 1950 when China entered on the North Korean side. Although the fighting was on land and in the air, the naval dimension was an important element in the conflict throughout. The Americans were able to deploy and apply a formidable amount of naval strength. The firepower of naval ordnance from Task Force 95 and from the carrier aircraft of Task Force 77 was of considerable operational and tactical value. This was especially so for ground support. Carrier air power provided about one-third of the total United Nations air effort.

Despite threats to do so in 1953, atomic ordnance was not used in the Korean War. However, carriers took an active role in the war, although far less so than in the Pacific War of 1941–45 as both sides had nearby land air bases. The communist powers lacked carriers, but, thanks to the Second World War, the United States and its allies had them aplenty. However, initial propeller aircraft, such as the Hawker Sea Fury, F-4 Corsair, and P-51 Mustang, had to be upgraded once more modern Soviet land-based aircraft were deployed. In addition to air combat, naval jets attacked ground targets, such as bridges across the River Yalu between China and North Korea, and Chinese troops massing to attack.[7] The Americans dominated the scene, although the British Fleet Air Arm flew close to twenty-three thousand operational sorties, while one British light carrier was on station at any time during the Korean War, and two in 1952–53. Australia had commissioned its first carrier, *Sydney*, formerly the British *Terrible*, in 1948, and it saw service off Korea. France also deployed a carrier there, as well as using carriers off Vietnam against the Viet Minh. The scale of American naval air power was indicated by the number of F9F-2 to F9F-5 jets manufactured for the navy and the Marine Corps up to January 1953: 1,382 in total, with another 600 by February 1960. By late 1954, the American navy had sixteen carrier air groups.[8]

Naval power was crucial to amphibious operations, notably Operation Chromite on September 15, 1950. This was a daring and unrehearsed landing in very difficult tidal conditions on the Korean west coast at Inchon. This landing applied American force at a decisive point. Carried out far behind the front line, and with very limited information about the conditions, physical and military, that they would encounter, about eighty-three thousand troops were successfully landed. They pressed on to capture nearby Seoul. In contrast, the landing on the east coast at Wonsan, delayed until October 25 by the extensive mining of the harbor, was superfluous as, advancing north, the South Koreans had already seized the port. Naval command was also important to the evacuation by sea of units cut off by the Chinese advance south in the winter of 1950–51, especially the American First Marine Division from Hungnam, thus limiting the losses. In total, 105,000 troops, 91,000 civilians, 17,500 vehicles, and 350,000 tons of supplies were withdrawn from Hungnam.[9]

The strategic dimensions of naval power were fundamental throughout the conflict. In particular, naval control permitted easy resupply from the American bases in Japan. Concerned to limit the war, the Soviet Union did not attack the American naval supply routes, not that they would have been able to do so successfully, and the small North Korean and Chinese navies were in no position to do so. Equally, there was no American or United Nations blockade of China, let alone amphibious attack, and the Chinese forces deployed in coastal regions that appeared threatened with an American invasion, for example near Tianjin, were not tested in battle. Any such attack would have greatly affected the American naval resources available for the war in Korea.

The Korean War, therefore, represented the varied nature of naval power and the complexity of its impact. In essence, America faced the problems of working out how to wage effective limited war, the classic dilemma of an oceanic power, that of a power-projection capability that ensured a role in continental struggles but that could not determine an outcome. At the same time, naval factors need to be placed in context. The absence of communist naval power to match that of Russia in 1904–5 during the Russo-Japanese War was not the sole reason that there was no naval dimension to the Korean War comparable to that in the earlier struggle. As a result, the Americans could not win a naval victory in order to convey an impression of success. Conversely, naval power projection created opportunities and flexibility for American intervention, but also ensured a differing range of challenges over capability and effectiveness. To a degree, there was a recurrence of some of the problems faced by the Americans when planning to invade Japan in 1945, but, despite earlier hopes, there was no "magic bullet" offered by the availability or use of nuclear weaponry. The Soviet development of an atomic weapon capability, a capability revealed in 1949, greatly restricted American options.

FORCE STRUCTURES

Combined with concern about Soviet expansionism in Europe, especially after the communist takeover of Czechoslovakia in 1948, a takeover that directly threatened the American occupation zone in Germany, the Korean War led to a major rise in Western military expenditure. What was correctly discerned as a large military-industrial complex came to play a much greater role in the American economy and governmental structure and sought to influence policy. Moreover, the navy was seen in the United States as taking a role in the policy of the global containment of communism, a policy that was clearly enunciated, for example in the National Security Council's NSC-68 document of April 1950. There were parallels in the case of America's allies, but there were also separate requirements, notably of colonial defense for the European powers: Britain, France, Portugal, and the Netherlands were all colonial powers that were part of the North Atlantic Treaty Organization (NATO), which was established in 1949 in order to resist Soviet expansion.

The membership of America and Canada ensured that the North Atlantic was the key alignment, one that reflected a sense of strategic interdependence on the part of Europe and of North American concern about the fate of Western Europe. This legacy of the two world wars dominated defense planning on both sides of the Atlantic, and naval power was regarded as a core component and expression of priorities. On the other hand, this legacy varied. Whereas there had been battleship and carrier battles in the Pacific, there had been no battles between carrier fleets or fleets of battleships in Atlantic or European waters. Alongside the configuration of the Soviet navy, this affected the surface-to-surface capability in NATO navies.

On the communist side, there were also developments. In particular, the Soviet Union supported the establishment of naval forces on the part of its allies. These were largely coastal-defense forces. This choice reflected Soviet priorities and the key role of the army in the Soviet Union, the minor and largely unsuccessful role of the Soviet navy in the Second World War, the lack of maritime and naval traditions and strength among the Soviet client states in Eastern Europe, and the awareness of NATO naval strength and geopolitical advantages. The failure of the communists to win the Greek Civil War, combined with the rift between the Soviet Union and Yugoslavia, proved particularly important, as the Soviets thereby lacked a Mediterranean base or one on the Adriatic. In 1950, the Soviet Naval Advisory Mission to China was established: Soviet training, supplies, and ship designs, as well as continentally oriented naval doctrine, were important in the development of the Chinese navy. However, in 1954, the Soviet Union refused to sell submarines to China. Tensions between the two powers increased from 1956.[10]

At the same time, naval planning in the 1950s was increasingly in the shadow of the threat of atomic warfare. In the late 1940s, this led in the United States, in the aftermath of the successful use of nuclear bombs against Japan in 1945, to a focus on the air force and its air-dropped atomic bombs. These provided a rapid and potent force, and, as the Soviets developed an atomic capability, the American air force, now the USAF, an independent body separate from the army, also offered a means to intercept Soviet bombers. The fear of a Pearl Harbor–style surprise attack focused on Soviet nuclear bombers. There were no similar concerns about Soviet warships. The American navy developed subsonic surface-to-air missiles, the T series of the Tartar (range eight nautical miles), Terrier (range seventeen), and Talos (range seventy), designed to hit Soviet bombers. However, these missiles were not capable of engaging fast, agile aircraft or missiles. In Britain, the threat of Soviet nuclear attack led to consideration of the impact of such an attack on naval bases, especially Portsmouth. Both Britain and France became atomic powers, each devoting considerable resources to this goal.

About 45 percent of annual American military spending from 1952 to 1960 went to the air force, in large part due to the emphasis on nuclear strength in the "New Look" strategy and its stress on the asymmetric containment of the Soviet Union. Alongside a fall in the number of divisions in the army from eighteen in June 1956 to fourteen by that December, the number of naval vessels fell from 973 to 812. The decline in conventional capability, which was resisted in the military, further ensured a reliance in planning on nuclear weaponry. These included nuclear-armed surface-to-air missiles such as the navy's Talos. This decline affected the United States during the Vietnam War, challenging America's ability to respond to attacks in Europe, the Mediterranean, and South Korea and creating military, strategic, and geopolitical opportunities for the Soviet Union.

Although under pressure from the commitment of the British government to air-dropped nuclear bombs, the Royal Navy had been skeptical from the outset about the extent to which the atom bomb had altered the parameters of naval power. The limited availability of atom bombs encouraged initial caution on this head. This caution was followed by equations of deterrence, which sustained the view that the navy had an important conventional role to play, whether alongside or instead of a nuclear conflict. Interest in sea control remained central to naval planners.[11] This control centered on submarine and long-range bomber threats. Moreover, the volatility of the Middle East increased concern about sea routes from the Persian Gulf which were crucial to British oil supplies. These routes lengthened with the closure of the Suez Canal owing to Egyptian-Israeli hostilities in 1967 and with the growing size of oil tankers. Irrespective of the politics of the Middle East, this size obliged more tankers to use the route round the Cape of Good Hope. These supertankers offered peacetime economies of scale but were very big targets.

While long-distance maritime routes remained of importance to Britain, the age of the British battleship was brought to a close in 1960 when the 44,500-ton *Vanguard* was scrapped. Laid down in 1941 and commissioned in 1946, she was the largest battleship built for a European navy, as well as the sole European battleship commissioned after the Second World War, other than the French *Jean Bart*, which, although active (and unfinished) in 1940, was only commissioned in 1955 and decommissioned in 1968. The Soviet Union had canceled most of its construction of battle cruisers and light cruisers in the mid-1950s, and this led the NATO powers to allow their battleships to pass out of commission. The Soviets developed missile boats which very much fitted in with their doctrine and their shipbuilding capability. Their experience with dedicated antiship missiles, which at first had a very limited range, led to the development of more capable missiles, which became much more capable and dangerous. The first Styx-armed missile boat appeared around 1958, and the missiles had an effective range of sixteen nautical miles.

There were no NATO equivalents, although the Swedes used air-to-ship missiles from 1958. Ship-based missiles were developed from the late 1960s. Development of the American Harpoon started in 1968, and it was employed in the late 1970s. The French developed the Exocet as a ship-based missile with a range of about thirty nautical miles, while the Israelis developed the Gabriel weapon.

In a marked contrast to the fate of *Vanguard*, *Devonshire*, the first British dedicated guided missile destroyer, was launched in 1960. Surface shipping also changed with the introduction of a new propulsion system, the gas turbine, which meant a major shift from coaling and oil. For example, in the Royal Navy, combined steam and gas turbines were introduced in frigates in the 1960s and were followed in the 1970s by gas turbines, and, subsequently, the new system was introduced more generally.

NAVAL AIR POWER

Naval air power was very much on display at the royal review of the British fleet on June 15, 1953, by the newly crowned Queen Elizabeth II. Five fleet carriers, the *Eagle*, *Illustrious*, *Implacable*, *Indefatigable*, and *Indomitable*, were accompanied by two light carriers, as well as an Australian carrier and a Canadian one. At sea, indeed, the experience of the Second World War was taken forward in the strategic context of the Cold War. Initially, the carriers available reflected the situation in the closing years of the Second World War. Japan no longer had a fleet, and Germany's planned carriers had not been launched; but Britain and, far more, the United States benefited greatly from the building programs during the conflict. The war ended as the *Midway*, the first of a new generation of three 45,000-ton American aircraft carriers, was completed. It was considerably larger than earlier carriers and had both increased aircraft capacity (144 aircraft) and an armored flight deck. The impact of air warfare was also shown by its carrying over 110 antiaircraft guns. The gunners contributed, with the air group, to a complement of 4,100 men. The *Midway*'s sister ship, the *Roosevelt* (known as the "Swanky Frankie"), was sent to the eastern Mediterranean in 1946 to bolster Western interests in the face of acute Soviet pressure on Greece and Turkey; the battleship *Missouri* had also been sent. From late 1947, there was at least one American carrier in the Mediterranean. This was a part of Europe where it was easy and less politically problematic for America to deploy power than in Western Europe (outside the occupation zones in Austria and Germany) prior to a more intense commitment to the defense of the latter from 1949.

However, notably in competition with the other services, carriers initially struggled to define a strategic role. In 1949, the construction program of the American navy was rejected, and its major project, the supercarrier *United States*, was canceled, in favor of the USAF plans for strategic bombing. New issues and opportunities, nevertheless, arose as a consequence of the introduction of jet aircraft and nuclear bombs. The first successful carrier landing of a jet aircraft took place on the British carrier *Ocean* in December 1945, while the Royal Navy operated Sea Vampires, its first jet, from 1947 and responded to the increased weight of aircraft by introducing steam catapults (first used in 1951) and angled decks (experiments began in 1952). The mirror landing system was first employed in 1953. All three were swiftly emulated by American carriers. Angled decks greatly increased carrier capacity. The first launch of a nuclear-armed aircraft from a carrier took place from the American *Coral Sea* in 1950. As with the *Midway*, the naming of carriers after naval victories was significant, not least in reiterating narratives and establishing norms.

Ground-based air power appeared more potent as a consequence of the development of aerial refueling. However, although the USAF remained dominant, the apparent need for as wide ranging a delivery of atomic bombs as possible ensured that the carriers were assigned strategic bombing duties, not least the use of a nuclear strike capability. The three ships of the *Midway* class accordingly had their flight decks strengthened. Interest in what the American navy could contribute to atomic warfare initially focused on carriers. The A-2 Savage two-propeller naval bomber introduced in September 1949 was designed to carry atomic bombs of the 1945 type. It was deployed on pre-*Forrestal* carriers. Moreover, institutional politics were important in the move from battleships, especially the rise of carrier admirals to prominence in the American navy and the related reading of the Second World War's War in the Pacific in terms of the crucial part of carrier warfare.

The Americans built four "supercarriers" in 1954–58. Authorized in 1951 when Congress expressed concern that the navy should maintain a cutting-edge capability, and launched in late 1954, the *Forrestal* was the first American carrier to have an angled deck, which permitted two jets on two catapults to take off simultaneously. It was also the first American carrier to have steam catapults. The largest carrier hitherto in the American navy, described as a "supercarrier," the *Forrestal* was designed to accommodate large jets like the Douglas A-3 Skywarrior, a two-seat, two–jet engine bomber carrying atomic bombs. The smaller A-4E Skyhawk, a single-seater introduced in 1956 and only retired, other than in a training role, in 1992, was also intended to carry nuclear bombs. As aircraft carrying nuclear bombs required more fuel for their greater range and were therefore heavier, the catapults launching them also had to be heavier. The Soviet introduction of aircraft designed to attack American carriers was stepped up from 1954 when Soviet intelligence confirmed the presence on these carriers of nuclear weapons (bombs and Regulus missiles), as well as aircraft able to deliver them. This represented a major extension in the range of American nuclear attack and the potency of naval power.

Naval air power was used by the British and French in attacking Egypt in the 1956 Suez crisis. The denial to Britain of the use of air bases in Libya, Jordan, and Iraq, hitherto friendly states, encouraged a reliance on naval power, as did the facts that carriers could be moved closer to Egypt than British bases in the colonies of Cyprus and (more distant) Malta and that their aircraft could therefore replace their fuel and load weapons more rapidly. Alongside ground-based aircraft from Cyprus, aircraft from three British and two French carriers destroyed the Egyptian Air Force (EAF). This destruction prepared the way for an airborne assault that included the first helicopter-borne assault landing from the sea: 415 marines and twenty-three tons of supplies landed by twenty-two helicopters from the British light carriers *Ocean* and *Theseus*. The after-action reports argued that the use of helicopters had been proven effective,[12] but that it would be extremely hazardous to enter a hot landing zone,[13] a conclusion that was to be disputed by the Americans.

Despite Suez, the value of naval air power was increasingly doubted in Britain, where the 1957 Defence White Paper was issued only after a successful struggle by the Admiralty to save the carriers in the face of a minister of defense who regarded them as expensive and outmoded. The chiefs of staff reported that it was crucial to retain the Fleet Air Arm, as it offered a way to deploy air power in regions where ground-based aircraft could not be used, and concerns about adequate airfields, overflight rights, and maintenance all played a role in this discussion. Each of these issues was eased by carriers.[14] In 1958, Earl Mountbatten, the First Lord of the Admiralty, observed, "There certainly isn't going to be enough money for a very large independent deterrent which can inflict unacceptable damage on Russia as well as having the 88 [ship] Navy and the all-Regular Army with adequate equipment."[15] Three of the light carriers were transferred to reserve before being broken up in 1961–62, while a fourth became a maintenance ship.

Prefiguring developments in ground-based air power, there was an increasing contrast in developments of sea-based air power, namely a marked differentiation between the policy and capability of the powers. While the United States retained and developed its carrier groups, the British were the only other power to place a heavy focus on the distant-strike capability brought by fleet carriers. Seeking to increase the ability of the fleet to operate without the support of bases, the Admiralty planned in the 1958–59 naval estimates for the continuous maintenance of a battle group centered on a carrier east of Suez. This was more necessary because the Suez crisis had led Sri Lanka (Ceylon) to withdraw the basing facilities at Trincomalee that it had agreed to when it had been granted independence in 1948. In 1960, the large fleet carrier *Victorious* joined the Far Eastern station, carrying nuclear bombs and Buccaneer aircraft able to drop them at very low levels. Subsequent British war planning called for the use of a carrier able to mount nuclear strikes on southern China and for a second carrier to be deployed in 1964. These carriers were to complement RAF aircraft based in Singapore. The Indian Ocean was one in which, despite America's overall position, Britain remained the leading naval power.

At the same time, there were significant changes in naval air power and in naval power as a whole. Both on land and at sea, guided missiles, the progenitor of cruise missiles, offered an ability to hit targets faster, and at less cost, than with manned flight. The Soviet Union was to show particular interest in them. For surface ships that were not carriers, missiles, rather than apparently anachronistic guns, increasingly appeared to be the future, and, unlike aircraft, missiles did not require large ships.

Canada, which, at the end of the Second World War, had had the third-largest fleet in the world, ended its carrier presence in 1970. It had had one carrier operating consecutively from 1946: *Warrior* (1946–48), *Magnificent* (1948–57), and *Bonaventure* (1957–70). The *Bonaventure*, which had been *Powerful* in the British navy, had an angled flight deck and operated Banshee jets. The Canadian navy also established a number of operational and training fixed-wing and helicopter squadrons between 1946 and 1970. These carriers were not involved in any wars, other than training, as a key NATO unit, for a potential conflict with the Soviet Union, notably in the North Atlantic. In addition, the *Magnificent* transported Canadian troops and equipment to Egypt in 1956 when the peacekeeping United Nations Emergency Force (UNEF) was established.

Until taken out of service in 1968 and sold to Argentina, the Dutch carrier, the former British *Venerable*, contributed to the NATO defense of the main sea lines across the Atlantic from the threat of Soviet submarines, served as a key symbol of the importance and pride of the Dutch navy, and, in 1962, was sent to Netherlands (western) New Guinea, when military troubles with Indonesia were expected. However, when the Dutch bought the vessel, they did so because they envisaged the creation of no fewer than four carrier groups. In the end, they could not afford even one such group. After Netherlands New Guinea was lost to Indonesia in 1962, the carrier, a symbol of imperial grandeur, was quietly discarded and sold to Argentina, playing a minor role in the Falklands War of 1982. For smaller states, carriers offered emblematic as well as practical value, with the former proving of particular significance. In 1961, India commissioned the *Vikrant*, originally intended to be the British *Hercules*, and in 1987 the *Viraat*, formerly the British *Hermes*.[16]

NUCLEAR SUBMARINES

The first nuclear submarine, the USS *Nautilus*, was launched in 1954. Hyman Rickover oversaw a program that, within five years, created a nuclear reactor with no size restriction and then one that fitted into a submarine. This was a formidable piece of engineering, management, and political maneuvering. The Soviet launch in 1957 of a land-based missile that carried Sputnik I, the first satellite, into orbit, increased the volatility of cutting-edge military capability and encouraged the army reductions that the Soviet Union had been pursuing since 1955. On January 15, 1960, Nikita Khrushchev, the Soviet leader, told the Supreme Soviet that rockets meant that the Soviet air force and navy had lost their former importance and that, in the navy, the focus was now on submarines.[17]

The strategic possibilities offered by nuclear-tipped long-range ballistic missiles made investment in them appear crucial. How best to use them, however, was debated. The nature of the delivery system, or systems, proved particularly contentious, not least because of the competing views of the different branches of the military. In the United States, notions of graduated nuclear retaliation were complemented by a policy of developing an effective intercontinental, retaliatory, second-strike capability in order to make it dangerous to mount an attack on the United States. This attempt to give force to the notion of massive nuclear retaliation entailed replacing vulnerable manned bombers with less vulnerable submarines equipped with Polaris missiles and also with land-based missiles located in reinforced concrete silos. The smaller, limited-range, submarine-launched missiles, designed to hit "soft targets" (i.e., cities), complemented but did not replace land-based rockets, which carried a heavier payload and could be fired further.

The Americans had successfully launched a V-1 from a surfaced submarine in 1945. Two years later, a LOON, an American-built and modified V-1, was fired from USS *Cusk*, the first launch of a guided missile from a submarine. It was planned to load nuclear warheads, but the nuclear LOON program was canceled in 1948. The first submarine launch of a nuclear Regulus 1 cruise missile was in 1953 by the Americans, while the first surface submarine ballistic-missile launch was from the Soviet *B-67* in September 1956.

The capability of these missiles rapidly increased. The Americans made their first surfaced launch of a ballistic missile in 1959, and on July 20, 1960, off Cape Canaveral (later Cape Kennedy), the *George Washington* was responsible for the first successful underwater firing of a Polaris missile. That November, the *George Washington* set off on an operational patrol with sixteen Polaris missiles. The following year, the Americans commissioned the *Ethan Allen*, the first true fleet missile-firing submarine.

A valuable demonstration of American technological proficiency, submarines had much to offer in practical terms. They could be based near the coast of target states and were highly mobile and hard to detect, all factors that still pertain. Partly as a result, the deployment of Polaris represented a major shift in force structure toward the navy, which argued that its invulnerable submarines could launch carefully controlled strikes, permitting a more sophisticated management of deterrence and retaliation. From 1964, ballistic-missile submarines went on patrol on a regular basis. In 1965, Robert McNamara, the secretary of defense, felt able to state that the United States could rely on the threat of "assured destruction" of about one-third of the Soviet population to deter a Soviet assault. Submarine-launched missiles provided the Americans with a secure second strike, as submarines were far harder to detect than land-based missile sites and were both less vulnerable than aircraft and believed to be so.

In turn, like their land-based counterparts, submarine-launched nuclear missiles became more powerful. Whereas the Polaris A-1 missile had a range of 1,400 miles, the Polaris A-3 (first test-fired in 1962 and deployed from 1964) had a range of up to 2,880 miles thanks to newer synthetic materials, more powerful rocket engines, and greater size. The A-3 missile became operational on September 28, 1964, when the American submarine *Daniel Webster* began its initial operational patrol. The deployment of A-3s, especially in the Mediterranean, posed a serious threat to the Soviet Union as it could be hit from there. Moreover, the Americans developed large missile-firing submarines (the *Los Angeles* class of the early 1970s and the *Ohio* class of the mid-1970s) capable of firing large numbers of missiles, which gave each submarine a greater operational and strategic capability. As a result, B-52 aircraft apparently became obsolete as nuclear-delivery systems. The American government and naval leadership saw the navy primarily as a nuclear deterrence and delivery tool, with everything dedicated to the protection of the delivery platforms, the carriers and submarines. Other "missions" were secondary. This was a military version of the "core competence" concept, with the core competence being the delivery of nuclear weapons.

The American navy was the largest and most developed in the world. This was seen in a number of respects. For example, the capability of submarines had been enhanced by the development of nuclear power plants as a means of propulsion. By enabling submarines to remain submerged for far longer, this increased their range and lessened their vulnerability. In particular, there was concern that Soviet submarines could remain under the polar icecap of the North Pole, coming near the surface only to fire. Initially, the limited load of submarines, nuclear or otherwise, ensured that they offered little by way of second-strike capability. This was true of the *Nautilus* and of the Regulus-armed submarines (which were not nuclear powered), which were deployed from 1953. They carried only two Regulus missiles, and only these submarines were in service until the *George Washington* was commissioned in 1959. It contributed to an assured second-strike capability. [18]

Other states followed. In December 1962, in what became known as the Nassau Agreement, the Americans agreed to provide Polaris for a class of four large British nuclear-powered submarines that were to be built. The first British Polaris test missile was fired from a submarine, *Resolution*, in 1968. The French commissioned their first ballistic-missile submarine in 1969. In contrast, South Africa and Israel did not develop a submarine-based ballistic capability, while China only deployed one from the start of the 1980s. Submarine capabilities led to interest in imperial territorial fragments because communications with submarines prior to the availability of extensive satellite coverage were dependent on extremely low-frequency transmitters and transponder stations. Indeed, in 1958, the Soviet Union sought a radio station based in China to permit regular communication with its submarines in the Pacific, only for Mao to refuse in retaliation for the Soviet refusal to provide submarines four years earlier and in response to rising tensions between the two powers.

CUBAN MISSILE CRISIS

The significance of both missiles and naval force was pushed to the fore in 1962 with the Cuban missile crisis. This followed the unsuccessful attempt to overthrow the Castro regime in April 1961 by means of an invasion by CIA-trained anticommunist exiles. Two of their ships were destroyed by unexpected Cuban air attacks.

Believing, in part due to American naval exercises, reports that an American invasion of Cuba, a Soviet ally, was imminent in 1962 (and indeed it is possible that some such action was intended, in part in order to produce a show of force before the American midterm elections), Khrushchev decided to send nuclear missiles to Cuba, as well as other weapons and delivery systems. The Soviet Union was initially planning to base a third of its nuclear-armed missile submarines in a permanent navy base in Cuba at Mariel and also to develop a base for a sizeable surface fleet. [19] Through the threat posed by intermediate-range missiles, he also wanted to achieve a parity with the United States that the Soviet Union lacked in more expensive intercontinental ballistic missiles. Secrecy was of the essence, but it was lost due to American aerial surveillance. Nevertheless, despite American warnings, the

Soviets persisted. Khrushchev ignored his own assurance not to send offensive or nuclear weapons to Cuba.

In response, President John F. Kennedy decided on a blockade designed to stop the shipment of missiles. Ironically, that January, Vice Admiral Bernard Austin, president of the Naval War College in Newport, had declared,

> Your initial reaction to the word *blockade* may be to suspect that I am bringing out an ancient elephant from a defunct circus, interesting only as an historical relic. If so, I hope to convince you that while it may be dusty from lack of recent use, it is far from dead. In my opinion, it is not unlikely that before too long blockade may again become a live issue.[20]

In an address to the American people, Kennedy used the argument that the 1930s' appeasement of Hitler's Germany must not be repeated. Instead, preparations were made to attack Cuba if the blockade proved unsuccessful. Naval power was therefore regarded as a key way to avoid the failings of the past. On October 25, the blockade took effect in a major and conspicuous display of naval strength. Naval blockade allowed time for a political settlement. Instead of pressing on, as originally instructed, the Soviet ships carrying such material to Cuba stopped. Having decided not to escalate the crisis, Khrushchev successfully sought to settle the matter so as to protect Cuba from invasion and also to lessen the threat to the Soviet Union from American missiles based in Turkey.

Submarines played a role in the crisis, as Khrushchev sought to deploy to Cuba four diesel-electric submarines, each equipped with a single nuclear torpedo with a yield similar to that of the bomb dropped on Hiroshima. To force Soviet submarines to the surface during the crisis, American antisubmarine forces dropped warning depth charges, which led to the risk that their captains would fire their torpedoes. The nuclear weapons in the submarines and in Cuba were under the command of the local commander, which could have led to a rapid escalation as the Americans were unaware of this.

The crisis also involved America's allies. For example, the carrier *Bonaventure* joined the Canadian air force in patrolling waters off Newfoundland and Nova Scotia for Soviet submarines that were located and traced. During the crisis, the problems of maintaining communications with submarines proved serious, and were, more generally, a problem in the 1960s.

VIETNAM WAR

The American navy was prominently involved in 1964 when American intervention in the Vietnam struggle escalated greatly. An attack on the destroyer *Maddox* by the North Vietnamese in the Gulf of Tonkin off Vietnam on August 2, 1964, was followed by an alleged attack on August 4. These attacks were provoked by American support for South Vietnamese comman-do raids on the coast of North Vietnam, but the reporting of the situation was doctored by the American administration. The attacks, which resulted in American carrier strikes on August 5, led Congress, on August 7, to pass overwhelmingly a resolution, the so-called Tonkin Gulf Resolution, permit-ting President Lyndon B. Johnson "to take all necessary measures to repel any armed attack against the forces of the United States and to prevent further aggression," in short to wage war without proclaiming it.

The major naval effort subsequently devoted to supporting the American presence in South Vietnam and the air war against North Vietnam focused in particular on carriers. The carriers were able to provide a nearby safe base for American air operations over both North and South Vietnam. Improvements in supply methods during and since the Second World War, including resup-ply from other ships, ensured that the carriers were able to stay at sea for longer than hitherto. During most of 1972, no fewer than six American carriers were on station, and that summer, an average of four thousand sorties were flown monthly. However, the absence of hostile submarine attacks on the American ships provided a mistaken impression of the general invulner-ability of carriers;[21] now shore-to-ship missiles are the key threat. Although the carrier-based aircraft lacked the payload of the large land-based aircraft, especially the B-52s, they provided significant firepower, both in support of ground operations in South Vietnam and in attacking North Vietnam. Thus, the carriers, which could be deployed close to the Vietnamese coast and readily supplied there from logistics ships, offered tactical, operational, and strategic capability.

Moreover, when, in April 1969, President Nixon decided that the Viet-nam commitment precluded the bombing of North Korea after an American electronic reconnaissance aircraft was shot down, he nevertheless resorted to a show of strength with a carrier task force. The previous year, the *Pueblo*, an American spy ship off North Korea, was attacked and captured by North Korean forces and its crew tortured.

In the Vietnam War, there was also a considerable use of coastal bom-bardment from warships, while the naval riverine campaign was important, especially in the Mekong Delta. Nevertheless, there were many restrictions on the use of naval power. For example, the idea of mining the port of Haiphong through which the Soviet Union was supplying North Vietnam, including with antiaircraft missiles, was not brought to fruition until 1972. More seriously, there was no "northern" landing, similar to Inchon in 1950, around the port of Vinh in North Vietnam in order to advance west into the entrances to the Ho Chi Minh Trail.

TENSION IN THE MEDITERRANEAN

As was also the case for the other services, the heavy naval commitment to the Vietnam War affected the American presence elsewhere. There had been a significant use of naval power in the late 1950s and early 1960s. In 1958, the United States sent fourteen thousand marines to Beirut to protect the Lebanese government from what it claimed was the threat of international communism, but what in practice was the threat of populist pan-Arabist Nasserism. Closer to home, the Americans, again successfully, sent nearly twenty-three thousand troops in 1965–66 to secure the continuation of a favorable government in the Dominican Republic and thus lessen the real and apparent Cuban challenge in the Caribbean. The British made comparable deployments to that of the Americans: notably to Jordan in 1958 and to Kuwait in 1961. In Kuwait, Royal Marine Commandos were landed from the carrier *Victorious* and from *Bulwark*, a "commando carrier," in order to dissuade Iraq from invading, a successful operation that reflected the need for rapid deployment.

However, the Americans found themselves under challenge in the Mediterranean, one of the two flank areas of NATO that posed political as well as military challenges for the United States and its allies.[22] In the early 1960s, the Soviet Union, leapfrogging the American containment ring, pursued plans for a naval base in Egypt, which was increasingly turning to the Soviet Union. Meanwhile, under Colonel Nasser, the Egyptian dictator, tension between Israel and Egypt increased in the 1960s. In intelligence supplied to the Egyptians that was possibly motivated by a wish to secure a naval base in Egypt, the Soviet Union helped stir up Nasser against Israel.[23]

Maritime access played a role in the crisis. As part of the settlement of the previous conflict, that of 1956, Israel's right for passage, via the Strait of Tiran between the Sinai and Saudi Arabia, into the Red Sea was guaranteed. Nasser had already ignored the undertaking that Egypt agree to let Israeli ships go through the Suez Canal, and on May 23, 1967, he closed the straits to all Israeli shipping.

The closure was regarded by the Israeli government as an act of war. Keen to avoid a fresh international crisis, notably while they were committed to the Vietnam War, the Americans unsuccessfully pressed the Soviet Union to get Nasser to reopen the straits. Failure to obtain a solution led to an Israeli attack on Egypt on June 5, 1967, with the war expanded to Jordan and, eventually, Syria. With its allies Egypt and Syria being defeated, the Soviet Union made preparations to intervene against Israel. To preempt the possibility, the American Sixth Fleet was sent into the war zone.

With the sinking of the Israeli *Eliat* by four Soviet Styx missiles fired from Egyptian missile boats, the age of the missile changed naval warfare. Before that, the surface-launched missile was a more obscure threat. The

Americans had no missile similar to the Soviet systems. Instead, they relied on carrier aircraft as their primary weapon against surface units. The Americans indeed regarded Soviet long-range aircraft as their main threat, and their weapons systems were designed to counter this threat: until the late 1970s, the Americans lacked an effective weapons system to oppose surface missiles. After the sinking of the *Eliat*, the Americans began development of the close-in weapon system Vulcan, a 20 mm radar-controlled Gatling gun, which could counter these threats. In contrast, the Soviet Union had begun development of a similar weapon system, the AK-230, in 1959, at nearly the same time as the missiles became operational that they should have shot down. The American Harpoon missile did not become operational on surface ships until 1977.

The rapid buildup of the Soviet navy in the late 1960s challenged the American position in the Mediterranean. The 1960s ended with American naval dominance less clear cut, there and elsewhere, than had been the case in the late 1940s, 1950s, and early 1960s. A traditional sphere of British naval activity, the Mediterranean became an area of American-Soviet confrontation. In a symbolic act, the Queen's Colour of the Mediterranean Fleet was laid up in 1967.

The reduction in the British naval presence in the Indian Ocean became an issue as the American role there was relatively minor. Britain encouraged an American naval buildup in the ocean and made the island of Diego Garcia available to the United States as a naval base. In late 1974, an American carrier entered the Persian Gulf, the first such deployment since 1948, a replacement to the British naval presence.[24]

CONFLICT ELSEWHERE

There was also considerable use of naval forces elsewhere. Again, as in the pre-1914 and interwar periods, there was a range of usage, albeit one that reflected political and technological changes since the 1930s, particularly the decline of European colonial empires and the rise of air power. The protection of empires and imperial interests nevertheless remained a significant factor. Naval power served both for power projection and for its protection. There was also the use of naval units to bombard opposition, launch air attacks, and mount amphibious operations. This was especially significant when the area in question was an island chain, as in the Dutch East Indies (Indonesia) in the late 1940s, or had a lengthy coastline or important coastal or littoral region, as with Egypt in 1956.

Thus, the Netherlands, Britain, France, and Portugal all deployed naval power in support of counterinsurgency operations. For example, confronting opposition in its colony of Aden (now the southern portion of Yemen),

Britain used aircraft from a carrier to conduct raids against dissident tribes in the Upper Aulaqi region in 1960. This was as part of Operation Damon, which was purportedly a pacification campaign. Warships were also involved in the colony's evacuation in 1967. The colony's significance in large part reflected the importance of maritime links, notably due to its being on the southern approaches to the Suez Canal. The evacuation, in turn, affected the geopolitics of the Indian Ocean.

Naval power was also significant for different aspects of colonial display and policing. In 1948, the cruiser *Nigeria* was dispatched to Antarctic waters in order to demonstrate British interest in the face of Argentinian claims. In the Caribbean, the Royal Navy was employed to help maintain control of British Guiana (now Guyana), a colony until 1966. This involved the movement of troops and a carrier as soon as possible to its capital, Georgetown, in 1953 in order to counter unrest and to police a state of emergency. Warships were also occasionally sent to the small islands when serious labor disputes broke out. In 1951, *Devonshire* was dispatched to Grenada after the declaration of a state of emergency in response to the general strike organized by Eric Gairy.[25] Warships were also deployed against piracy, which became more of a problem as imperial authority declined.[26]

Naval air power developed in part in a counterinsurgency direction. British carrier-based Hellcats were used against nationalist targets, and thus in support of the Dutch, in Java in late 1945. The British navy's first operational helicopter squadron was formed in 1952 in order to help antiguerrilla operations in Britain's colony of Malaya. Carrier-based air support played a role for Britain in battling the EOKA insurrection in Cyprus in 1956–59. In 1960, *Bulwark*, formerly a light fleet carrier, was, after conversion, commissioned as a "commando carrier," able to carry a Royal Marine Commando unit along with their arms, stores, and vehicles; the necessary assault craft; and a squadron of helicopters. In 1964, the British sent *Victorious* to Tanzania in order to help the government in the recently independent former colony against a military coup: low-level flights by strike aircraft combined with the use of helicopter-borne marines proved crucial in restoring order. Conversely, in Uganda and Kenya, two other former British colonies in East Africa, where loyal troops held the airfields, it was possible to fly in British troops to help their threatened governments.

In 1963–66, during the "Confrontation," British and Australian carriers provided supporting air and helicopter strikes to help Malaysian and British army units against Indonesian pressure in Borneo. The Royal Navy, which deployed eighty warships, also played a defensive role by blocking Indonesian invasions of Malaya and was important to the force projection and logistics necessary to sustain a presence in the Malaysian part of Borneo.

There was also a "brown water" component in counterinsurgency naval power. This was notably so for the Portuguese in Africa, but also for the Americans in South Vietnam, especially in the Mekong Delta.[27]

Newly independent states that wished to assert and maintain their power, such as Indonesia, also employed naval force. Thus, in 1962, Indonesian pressure on the Dutch over western New Guinea involved both states in the use of naval power. A Dutch frigate defeated an Indonesian attempt to insert troops in Dutch New Guinea, sinking a torpedo boat. The key element, however, was the lack of international support for the Dutch position.

In 1965, warships played their role in the short war between India and Pakistan. Four years earlier, the Indian seizure of Goa from Portugal in 1961 involved an unequal fight between a Portuguese sloop and two Indian frigates at Mormugão harbor in which the sloop was shot up and beached. In contrast, there were no naval hostilities in the even shorter war between China and India in 1962, a conflict restricted to the Himalayas. The Indians asked for American air support, and Kennedy offered to send a carrier battle group to the Bay of Bengal, but the conflict ended first. How effective American carrier-based aircraft would have been in these circumstances is unclear.

There was a more general use of navies, as part of the force of the state, in order to suppress rebellions or to overawe disaffection. Thus, in the Biafran War in 1967–70, the Nigerian navy blockaded Biafra, as part of a policy of limiting weapons supplies to Biafra and bringing on famine there, and also mounted amphibious attacks and protected and supported the resulting positions, notably Port Harcourt. There was no effective counter to this power, and it played a crucial role in the conflict. At a much smaller scale, Mao Zedong sent naval gunboats to Wuhan in 1967 in order to help his protégés gain power there during the Cultural Revolution.

Newly independent states neither invested in the old technology of battleships nor in its replacement, carriers, each of which was highly expensive. Nevertheless, these states showed that it was possible to enjoy naval power at a comparatively modest price. This process was eased by the surplus Second World War warships that were available for sale. This availability was an aspect of the influence of the major naval powers. For example, in 1955, Britain agreed to transfer the Simonstown naval base to South African control. Under the agreement, however, Britain retained important naval advantages, including South African agreement to make the base available to Britain in war, even if South Africa itself was neutral, as well as South African responsibility for the maintenance of the base, orders for *Leander*-class frigates from British yards, and acceptance of British views on the development of the South African navy. The agreement was ended in 1975.[28] Until the late 1960s, the Indian navy was equipped with surplus British warships, and links between the two navies were close.

Both South Africa and India were important second-rank naval powers on the route from Europe and the Atlantic to the Far East. So also with the warships provided to Iran, which, in 1955, joined the Baghdad Pact, part of the Anglo-American international architecture of containment directed against the Soviet Union. Britain sought to retain these states as allies as part of the structure of global power that gave its empire coherence and that provided it with key strength and purpose. Thus, warships were deployed to blockade the port of Beira in the Portuguese colony of Mozambique in order to put pressure on the British colony of Southern Rhodesia (now Zimbabwe), which had unilaterally declared independence. In the long term, Britain's imperial naval policy was not to work, but it provided an important aspect of the naval power politics and geopolitical planning of the period and was significant to the strategic context of the Cold War and to the means of containment.

CONCLUSIONS

The role of naval power in this period focused on the interests and capability of the foremost naval power, the United States. American naval strength and intentions were significant in strategic, operational, and tactical respects. There was no effective challenge, either in terms of the attempt by rival powers to develop a relevant strength or capability or, prior to the deployment of effective missile ships, in terms of improvements in anti-warship weaponry or doctrine. As far as the latter was concerned, the most effective capability was provided by shore-based aircraft, and these remained important. Moreover, an increase in aircraft range and payload was matched by the development of missiles that could be launched from them.

However, as the Korean and Vietnam Wars, as well as the Suez crisis, showed, it was difficult for most powers to oppose or limit naval power in this fashion. It was also as yet difficult for Soviet and, even more, Chinese exponents of naval power to do much to redress the stress on army and air strength. In 1954–55, the Chinese navy relied on asymmetry in the shape of ambush tactics when using torpedo boats to attack Taiwanese warships. Leaving aside the limitations of Soviet and Chinese responses, the American commitment to naval strength, and to being at the cutting edge of naval power, remained strong.

At the same time, the geopolitics of naval power increasingly focused on the Cold War, in part due to the decline of European colonial empires and the related changes in their naval power. From 1949, in response to British overstretch, the Australian navy became largely responsible for the defense of sea communications in the ANZAM (Australia, New Zealand, and Malaya) region, and in 1951 the Radford-Collins agreement underlined cooperation between the American and Australian navies. American naval power was amplified because it was not challenged by most of the other naval powers: Britain, France, and Canada were the other leading members of NATO. There were tensions within NATO, notably at the time of the Suez crisis in 1956, and France left NATO's military command structure in 1966. Nevertheless, there was an essential affinity, and this in part compensated for the development of Soviet naval capability. Western powers focused on the containment of the Soviet Union, with naval power being a key component of this containment.

At the same time, this alliance capability created major issues for peacetime planning, procurement, and interoperability that had not been present in earlier peacetime periods, with the exception of attempts within the British Empire to ensure effective cooperation between Britain and the Dominions. Cold War tasks were of growing significance. Even before the first RE-FORGER exercise in 1967, convoys to Europe were an essential part of the planning for resistance to any Soviet invasion of Western Europe. By the close of the period, the Americans faced growing issues in force structure and weaponry, and this led to an awareness of the need for change. Writing in September 1970, Admiral Elmo Zumwalt, the chief of naval operations from 1970 to 1974, noted the proposal to develop "an interim surface-to-surface missile. . . . This weapons capability will give our ships a reach comparable to that of the Soviets and cut their advantage in that respect. With the carrier force level reduced, our ships cannot always count on air support, and this action will increase our flexibility in the employment of all our forces."[29] There was no suggestion of an unchanging scenario of power.

Chapter Eight

Cold War: America under Greater Challenge, 1967–89

SOVIET BUILDUP

In 1971, the Soviet Union supplanted Britain as the world's number-two naval power, reflecting what became the very different naval situation in the second half of the Cold War. This was important to the more general direction of geopolitical developments in the 1970s and 1980s. The Soviet ability to operate at a distance was enhanced by greater naval strength than hitherto. The Soviet navy challenged the traditional Western dominance of the oceans and its apparent ability to restrict communism to the Eurasian "heartland," which had been the theme of much geopolitical discussion. The conventional doctrine of Soviet naval power, looking back to the formative and influential reign of Peter the Great (1689–1725), had emphasized the support of Russian land forces in the Baltic and Black Seas, key areas of expansion, and the quest for naval superiority in these areas. However, Soviet forces based in these seas could only gain access to the oceans through straits, the Bosporus, Dardanelles, and Kattegat, and shallow waters, such as much of the Baltic, where they were vulnerable.

A similar problem affected the Soviet Far East naval base of Vladivostok. The waters of the Sea of Japan were shallow. Japan's contribution to American naval strategy was that of providing submarine support against Soviet ships trying to reach the Pacific, as well as antisubmarine capability. Japan also wanted to protect its own sea lines of communication, in part drawing on the lessons of the Second World War.[1] Japanese submariners became very skilled at shadowing submarines leaving Soviet bases. So also with Swedish submariners who faced repeated Soviet submarine incursions into their territorial waters.

As a result of this problem of access to the oceans, the Soviet navy developed their Northern Fleet based at Murmansk and nearby Severomorsk. Indeed, the rise of Soviet naval capability was intricately linked with the foundation of submarine bases that gave the Soviets access to the Atlantic without having to face passages through the Baltic, the Black Sea, or the Sea of Japan. As a result, by 1980, the Kola Peninsula, in which Murmansk is located, contained the greatest concentration of naval power in the world. This concentration owed much to the Gulf Stream, which ensured that the water off the peninsula remained relatively warm and did not freeze. The Northern Fleet became the largest Soviet fleet, with a particularly important submarine component. The supply effort required to keep these facilities in operation was immense, including multiple railway tracks and large amounts of rolling stock able to move oil. Over three-quarters of Soviet naval expenditure was on the submarine force. Aside from being designed to launch nuclear-armed missiles, Soviet submarines were intended to attack NATO carriers and submarines so as to stop them from operating close to the Soviet Union, as well as to attack the reinforcement convoys for NATO forces.

As a result of the emphasis on maritime dominance and a balanced fleet, as well as the focus of the Soviet state on military expenditure and its control of the economy, the Soviet Union also built up an important surface fleet, especially, from the 1960s, a fleet that included missile cruisers firing sea-to-sea missiles. The cruiser/surface groups were designed to attack the carrier heart of a NATO task force; attacks on merchant shipping came second. In both his policy and his publications, which received international attention, Admiral Sergei Gorshkov, the dynamic head of the navy, pressed the case for sea power.[2] However, although the Soviet Union supplanted Britain as the world's number-two naval power, the geographical range of its navy was less than that of Britain had been. In particular, in contrast to the American emphasis on carriers, the Soviet Union relied on land-based long-range bombers and reconnaissance aircraft, in both of which it was well provided, and had only one big carrier, the *Admiral Kuznetsov*, launched in 1985, but only commissioned on December 25, 1990, and equipped with aircraft in 1993.

In 1967 and 1973, the Soviet navy was able to make substantial deployments in the eastern Mediterranean in order to advance Soviet views during Middle Eastern crises and to threaten Israel, thus putting considerable pressure on the United States, which was unable to overawe this challenge to sea control. In 1973, there was a standoff between the American Sixth Fleet and the Soviet Fifth Eskadra. The Soviets had a "Battle of the First Salvo" doctrine focused on the destruction of American carriers in which missiles were launched in a first strike, with escort vessels being ignored. The Soviets considered themselves kamikazes, believing that even if they were to sink the carrier, they would be annihilated by the escort ships. Thanks to unrivaled

American air superiority in the region, first strike was given special importance in the 1973 Soviet exercises. Meanwhile, it became apparent to the Americans that, due to overconcentration on the war in Vietnam, with its close air support mission for naval air power, there was a lack of American antiship and antisubmarine capabilities.[3] During the 1970 Jordanian crisis, the Soviet navy became aware that the American naval presence and their available reserve were thin in the Mediterranean. Similarly, at the present time, the American fixation on the "War on Terror" may lead to the navy being surprised by a Chinese attack.

Indicating the geopolitical impact of conflicts and political changes, the Soviets, in the 1970s, developed naval bases in Vietnam (Danang), Somalia (Berbera), and Syria (Latakia and Tartus) to add to the facilities they already had in Cuba.[4] The bases were linked to Gorshkov's forward strategy, notably in the Mediterranean and the Indian Ocean. Naval bases added and offered significant power projection, and the visits of Soviet warships were also intended to demonstrate the effectiveness of Soviet technology. The possibility that this base structure would be far more greatly expanded was voiced by commentators and was an aspect of a highly volatile geopolitics, although the perception of Soviet expansionism belied the degree to which the West had a considerable global advantage in forward basing. There was discussion in the early 1970s of the possibility of NATO's presence in Malta being replaced by the Soviet Union, China, or Libya, where the pro-Western monarchy had been overthrown by an anti-Western regime in a coup in 1969. Malta had provided Britain with a base for tracking Soviet submarines in the Mediterranean.

It would be conventional to move from this prospective of Soviet advance in order further to probe the military dimension, not least NATO countermeasures. These were indeed key parts of the story, but they were only part of it. Instead, an important aspect, separate in causation but highly significant for the strategic consequences, was provided by the American-Chinese reconciliation in the early 1970s and the way in which it greatly affected the Soviet military position by providing the threat of a two-front war. Cooperation between America and China was seen in 1985 when it was planned that the United States would sell China torpedoes and helicopters, a sale later embargoed. In the same period, France sold China naval artillery, surface-to-air missiles, and helicopters. However, in 1990, the Chinese navy, which had been held back by the purges during the Cultural Revolution, was at the technological level of the Soviet navy of the late 1950s to early 1960s. Indeed, in the late 1980s, China developed a surface-launch cruise-missile submarine which would have been the equivalent of the 1950s Soviet *Romeo*-class submarine with added antiship cruise missiles. One of these was built. In 1990, the Chinese navy was beginning to employ more modern and

Western technology, such as a reverse-engineered copy of the 1970s French Crotale missile system.

CARRIER WARFARE

For new naval powers, missiles, rather than aircraft, were the key. Aside from submarines, the Soviets focused on missile cruisers. The Soviets also supplied Styx missiles, which employed radar homing, to their allies, and the Egyptians and Indians successfully used them against Israel and Pakistan, respectively. Nevertheless, in late 1970, as an important enhancement of their naval capability and aspect of power projection, the Soviets began to construct the carrier *Kiev*. This was referred to by the Soviets as a cruiser, as the Montreux Convention forbade the passage of carriers between the Black Sea and the Aegean. Coming into service, the *Kiev* was essentially a very large antisubmarine platform, with two-engine Yak-35 Forger V/STOL (vertical/short takeoff and landing aircraft) local air-defense fighters. Indeed, the *Kiev* was essentially a larger version of the *Invincible* the British had laid down in 1973 with a much better conventional weapons load. Not as effective as the British Harrier, the Yak-35 went out of service in the 1980s, which left the three carriers of the *Kiev* class without a core weapon system. Against American submarines, the Soviets deployed the smaller *Moskva* class of helicopter carriers equipped with dipping sonars and nuclear-tipped antisubmarine missiles. In some respects, these ships were more cruisers with a large helicopter air group. The *Kiev*, the *Moskva* class, the *Invincible* class, and the Italian *Vittorio Vento* could have been the heart of hunter/killer antisubmarine task forces.

In part in response to Soviet naval activity but also as a result of American prompting, the Japanese revived their naval air power in the shape of the aviation component of the Maritime Self-Defense Force. This focused on antisubmarine warfare as an auxiliary force to the American navy. There was investment accordingly in helicopters operated from destroyers (often similar to small helicopter carriers) and in land-based patrol aircraft to chase Soviet submarines.

The British meanwhile had abandoned their attempt to emulate the Americans by building a class of three large strike aircraft carriers. The first, the planned 53,000-ton CVA-01, which would have been the first carrier to be built in Britain since the Second World War, was canceled in February 1966 as part of Britain's retreat from "East of Suez,"[5] a measure that led to the reduction of British naval presence in the Indian Ocean to one of frigates.[6] This cancellation was the product of a bitter controversy within Britain about the future for naval air power, notably as compared with its land-based equivalent. The RAF proved better at lobbying.

It was then envisaged that, after the existing carriers, with their distant-strike capability, came to an end of their service, which was projected to be in the 1970s, British naval air power would amount essentially to carrier-borne helicopters and short-range aircraft designed to act against Soviet submarines in the North Atlantic, which was the core naval role for Britain. The V/STOL aircraft, which for Britain meant the Sea Harriers, did not require fleet carriers,[7] and an ability to support amphibious operations with carriers no longer appeared necessary. *Victorious* was sold in 1969, and *Eagle* went into reserve in 1972 and was broken up in 1978, leaving only *Ark Royal*. The light fleet carrier *Hermes* was converted to a helicopter carrier in 1971–73. The first British carrier designed for antisubmarine duty and equipped for operating V/STOL aircraft, the 16,000-ton *Invincible*, was laid down in 1973. These carriers could be relatively small. American equivalents were similarly designed as a response to Soviet submarines and reflected the view that a large number of small carriers was required against these submarines and to protect convoys.

With a big-deck carrier, the *Ark Royal*, and large amphibious platforms, the British had advantages over the Soviet Union as a naval power, but they were outmatched in overall tonnage, manpower, and nuclear submarines. France maintained a large carrier presence, commissioning the 32,780-ton *Foch* in 1963. Similarly to Britain, and again under NATO, Canada developed the antisubmarine capability its navy had been expanded to provide during the Second World War. In contrast, judging it unaffordable, Canada withdrew its last carrier from service in 1970, a major practical and symbolic blow to Canadian naval power. The emphasis in naval air power was now increasingly focused on the United States, while there was speculation about Soviet naval intentions.

NATO RESPONSES

The threat from Soviet submarines obliged NATO powers to develop patrol areas for their submarines and underwater listening devices near Soviet bases, and also to establish a similar capability in the Denmark Strait between Iceland and Greenland and in the waters between Iceland and Britain through which Soviet submarines would have to travel en route to the Atlantic. To the anger of the Americans, the Canadians encountered problems in detecting Soviet submarines sailing from under the Arctic polar ice pack into the Davis Strait dividing Greenland from Baffin Island and Labrador, and from there into the North Atlantic where they could maintain a station off the eastern coast of the United States.[8] Fishing boats were also used for keeping tabs on Soviet submarine movements, while Soviet trawlers were also looking actively for NATO submarines.

There was a focus on antisubmarine warships, such that the British Type 22 *Broadsword*-class frigates of the 1980s lacked a main gun armament, as this was seen as irrelevant for their antisubmarine duties. The *Leahy*-class cruisers introduced by the Americans in 1962 were designed to defend carriers against air threats from up to forty nautical miles. They lacked guns until an intervention from President Kennedy led them to receive two 76 mm guns that were already obsolete. These cruisers had no antiship weapon and no serious antisubmarine weapons. As a result of such steps, including the emphasis on missiles, the visual impression and impact of warships and of naval power changed greatly. The public image switched from "stupid" cannon to "smart" missiles. The exception was the recommissioning of American battleships during the Reagan administration. This owed something to Reagan being raised during the age of mighty battleships. Officially, they were commissioned to counter the *Kirov*-class battle cruisers which the Soviet Union deployed in the early 1980s.

The significance of submarine warfare resulted in a major expansion in financial support for marine sciences. The NATO framework included a science committee. Oceanography as a subject and institutional structure grew significantly from the 1960s, although some influential Western oceanographers, such as George Deacon and Henry Stommel, were troubled about the consequences of military links.[9]

Soviet naval development led the Americans, from 1969, to focus on planning for naval conflict with the Soviets—rather than, as hitherto, on attacking the Soviet Union itself—for example on amphibious operations, such as acting against coastal positions in East Asia. Standing Naval Force Atlantic was established as a standing NATO force in 1967. The emphasis was on being able to destroy Soviet naval power in battle and in its home waters before Soviet warships, and notably submarines, could depart for the oceans and, more particularly, the Atlantic.[10] This emphasis became stronger after the Vietnam War (and the resulting focus on land tactics) ended for the United States in 1973. It was not assumed that the North Soviet Surface Fleet would attack NATO warships and merchantmen in the Atlantic in what was assumed would be a short war. Instead, the Soviet focus, it was believed, would be on submarines.[11]

Antisubmarine weaponry was developed accordingly, particularly the Harpoon guided missile, which was intended to attack any surface target up to about sixty-five nautical miles, including surfaced submarines: Soviet submarines needed to surface to communicate, notably for reconnaissance purposes, and often to fire.[12] NATO's CONMAROPS (Concept of Maritime Operations) proposed a forward attack on Soviet submarines near their bases in order to secure the North Atlantic sea lines of communication for the supply and resupply of NATO forces in Europe. This stress led to an American focus on big aircraft carriers and large submarines, both intended to attack the Soviet fleet, whether surface or submarine, and the carriers intended to intercept Soviet bombers. The NATO force deployed many effective nuclear-tipped antisubmarine weapons, such as the SUBROC missile torpedo. In turn, the Soviets deployed nuclear-armed missiles and torpedoes on their submarines in order to attack American carriers.

In 1982, in the "Northern Wedding" naval exercise, an American carrier battle group approached close enough to the Kola Peninsula to be able to launch aircraft carrying a full load to attack the Severomorsk naval base and then return to the carrier. This worried the Soviet leadership, which at the time was greatly concerned about American intentions. The danger of accidental war was high in 1982–83.

At the same time, the American navy was going through a profound period of change. Important as that was, it was not so much a case of the replacement of conscription by volunteer service, a change already seen in Britain, but rather a reflection of the cultural transformation of the 1960s. To some extent, the developments in the American navy were, indeed, a consequence of the greater individualism of the 1960s and the spread of rights-based views. However, there was also an attempt, notably by Admiral Elmo Zumwalt, the chief of naval operations from 1970 to 1974, to end abusive personnel policies in order to increase accountable leadership and management capacity, and to make it easier to attract recruits.[13] Separately, the Marine Corps had to recover its amphibious mission after Vietnam.

Very much focused on America and the Soviet Union, the naval arms race of the 1980s was impressive. Six *Typhoon*-class ballistic-missile submarines entered Soviet service from 1980, as did their most impressive surface warships. The *Typhoon* class competed against the American *Ohio* class, as the submarine evolved into an underwater capital ship as large as First World War *Dreadnought*-class battleships, and with a destructive capacity never seen before (or since) in any other type of warship. The USS *Ohio* and its sister submarines were 170.7 meters long with an 18,700-ton submerged displacement. The Soviet *Typhoon* class was 171.5 meters long with a 25,000-ton submerged displacement. In each case, the submerged displacement was somewhat greater than the surfaced displacement. By comparison, the British battleship *Dreadnought* of 1906 was 161 meters long and displaced 18,420 tons. Super-dreadnoughts from 1911 on were twenty to thirty-three meters longer and eight thousand to ten thousand tons larger. These submarines were in a completely different league than the German U-boats of the Second World War. There were also important developments in ballistic-missile technology.[14]

Since the *Typhoons* carried newer, long-range missiles, they could remain under the sanctuary of the Arctic ice cap and then surface just at the edge of it, fire their missiles, and then retreat under the ice cap, or they could lie in their home base and move out. The *Typhoons* looked monstrous because they were triple hulled, possibly because the Soviets did not trust the quality of their welding of the second hull. The titanium used for the pressure hull required more sophisticated welding than regular welding; the welding temperature is much higher and must be done in a vacuum. The Soviets were aware of the shortcomings, or feared that they had shortcomings, in their ability to construct minutely calibrated, pure microenvironments for difficult product fabrication, whether it be computer chips or titanium parts. More generally, as was ascertained from the 1990s, Soviet-era surface warships and submarines were poor, certainly compared to American and British models, and especially in terms of workmanship. Nevertheless, although their safety record was poor, the *Typhoons* were formidable.

The fiscal crisis of the early 1970s ensured that American naval construction declined and that more of the American navy approached obsolescence, which led to a degree of pessimism over the role of the navy. Under Jimmy Carter, president from 1977 to 1981, there was eventually an arms buildup in response both to Soviet expansionism, notably in sub-Saharan Africa and Afghanistan, and to the instability linked to the Islamic Revolution in Iran in 1978–79. Carter planned the cancellation of the nuclear *Nimitz*-class carrier but started developing the Aegis *Ticonderoga*-class cruiser. This buildup was carried forward under Ronald Reagan, president from 1981 to 1989, who both believed that the Soviet Union should be vigorously resisted and did not want to risk nuclear war. As a consequence, other capabilities were developed.

The American blue-water reorientation in 1986, part of the major arms buildup during the Reagan period, saw calls for a maritime strategy and, to give effect to it, a six-hundred-ship navy with fifteen carrier groups. A bold view of what the navy could achieve was increasingly offered from the early 1980s, in part due to the idea of "sea strike" and also thanks to the establishment in 1981 of a Strategic Studies Group based at the U.S. Naval War College in Newport. The *U.S. Maritime Strategy* published in 1986 pressed for a forward, attacking deployment of warships in northeast Atlantic and northwest Pacific waters in order to protect allies and communications, threaten Soviet nuclear missile submarines and bases, and force battle on the Soviet navy. This was seen as a way to offset Soviet strength on land in Europe.[15] As there were no dramatic improvements in warship hulls or propulsion during the second half of the Cold War, there was no need to replace existing warships.

The American navy was also active elsewhere. In September 1983, the American Sixth Fleet bombarded Druze militia positions on the hills near Beirut in support of the Lebanese army. However, the fire support in Lebanon could have been provided much better by carrier aircraft. Aside from that, the military effect of the four recommissioned *Iowa*-class battleships, the *Iowa*, *New Jersey*, *Wisconsin*, and *Missouri*, was highly doubtful. They lacked any serious air defense. Although officially designed to counter the new *Kirov*-class battle cruiser, the battleship was a problematic platform. The sixteen-inch guns were of dubious value given their age and the lack of skilled personnel to man them. Whereas a Spruance destroyer required a crew of 350 sailors, a battleship required over 1,800, which put a burden on the navy personnel roster. Only the United States kept battleships in its fleet, enhancing them so as to be able to fire cruise missiles. They received these upgrades in the early 1980s and carried both Tomahawk cruise and Harpoon missiles in box launchers. Yet they were equipped with thirty-two cruise missiles each, compared to sixty-one on twenty-four of the *Spruance*-class destroyers. The six-hundred-ship navy was not necessarily a six-hundred-good-ship navy.

THE FALKLANDS WAR, 1982

Short of resources, ambition, and confidence, Britain very much drew in its military roles in the late 1960s and 1970s in order to focus on the British Isles, Western Europe, and the North Atlantic. Despite concerns on the part of allies, notably Singapore, British forces were withdrawn from Aden, the Persian Gulf, Singapore, and Malta, and there was no pretense that Hong Kong, where one warship was based, could be defended if China attacked. That Britain was to fight a final imperial war in 1982 with a major naval component was totally unexpected. The Falklands had been under British control from 1833 but were claimed, as the Malvinas, by the Argentinians. Their dictatorial ruling military junta was convinced that, because the British government was uncertain of the desirability of holding on to the colony, the British would accept the colony's seizure by the Argentinians. The decision, in 1981, to withdraw the Antarctic patrol ship, *Endurance*, was seen as a sign of British lack of interest in the South Atlantic, and on April 2, 1982, the virtually undefended Falkland Islands were successfully invaded in a surprise attack.

Assured that the Royal Navy could fulfill the task, and determined to act firmly in what was seen as a make-or-break moment for the government, the British prime minister, Margaret Thatcher, decided to respond with Operation Corporate: an expeditionary force, dispatched on April 5, that included most of the Royal Navy: fifty-one warships were to take part in the operation. As another sign of British maritime strength, fifty-four ships were "taken up from trade," chartered, or requisitioned, including the cruise ships *Queen Elizabeth II* and *Canberra*, which were used to transport troops; fourteen tankers; and the container ship *Atlantic Conveyor*, which was sunk by an Exocet missile, taking a large amount of stores to the bottom, including helicopters that would have aided the mobility of the landing force. Sixteen of the ships were fitted with helicopter flight decks, and all had rapidly to be installed with military communications equipment and gear for replenishment at sea. The naval supply line moved over four hundred thousand tonnes of fuel, one hundred thousand tonnes of equipment and supplies, and nine thousand troops within range of the Falklands, 7,500 miles from Britain, in six weeks.[16] Meanwhile, alongside highly helpful American military assistance, including regular satellite intelligence, American mediation attempts that would have left the Argentinians in control of the islands were rejected.

Thanks to the shift from large fleet carriers, not least the cancellation of the CVA-01 project in 1966, the expeditionary force, which was operating beyond the range of its land-based air cover in the NATO area, lacked a large aircraft carrier and therefore airborne early warning of attacks. This was a serious problem. However, Britain had two smaller carriers, *Hermes* and *Invincible*, designed for antisubmarine warfare. Each carried V/STOL Sea Harriers designed as fighters. Furthermore, the Argentinian aircraft carrier, *25 de Mayo*, built in World War II as *Venerable* and sold to the Dutch in 1948 before being taken out of service by them in 1968 and sold to Argentina, had not been refitted to operate the impressive Super Etendard bombers Argentina had bought from France, and as a result the carrier was unable to play a role in the war.

On April 25–26, 1982, the British recaptured the subsidiary territory of South Georgia, and on May 2, large-scale hostilities began when *Conqueror*, a nuclear-powered submarine, sank the Argentine cruiser *General Belgrano* with 321 fatalities. This step was crucial to the struggle for command of the sea, as it led the Argentinian navy to desist from threatening attack and to return to port. At the time of writing, the *Belgrano* was the largest ship so far sunk by naval action since the Second World War, and the first ship to be sunk by a nuclear-powered submarine.

Air-launched Exocet missiles and bombs led to the loss of a number of British ships, showing that modern antiaircraft missile systems were not necessarily a match for manned aircraft and revealing a lack of adequate preparedness on the part of the British navy. The Royal Navy lacked, as did most units of the American navy, an effective close-weapon system against aircraft and missiles. An Exocet was responsible for the loss of the destroyer *Sheffield*, and bombs for that of the destroyer *Coventry*, both of which affected British public opinion. However, many of the bombs did not prove reliable, some of them hitting ships but not exploding, while, despite initial reports that the *Hermes* and not the *Sheffield* had been hit, the Argentinians did not sink the two carriers, which provided vital air support (but not superiority) for both sea and land operations. Designed for antisubmarine warfare in the North Atlantic, the carriers' Harriers and their Sea King helicopters demonstrated their versatility, while the ships served as amphibious assault command ships. Ultimately, the fleet and its air power won the struggle to isolate the Falklands, a struggle helped by the cautious Argentinian response to British naval persistence and fighting determination.

The Argentinians on the Falklands outnumbered the British force, and they also had both aircraft and helicopters, while the British were short of ammunition because they had underestimated requirements. Nevertheless, landing on May 21, British troops advanced on the capital, Port Stanley, fighting some bitter engagements on the nearby hills and forcing the isolated, demoralized, and beaten Argentinians to surrender on June 14. American logistical and intelligence support aided the British, but in the end it was a matter of an effective strategy of indirect approach, bravely executed attacks, the careful integration of infantry with artillery support, the ability to continue without air control, and the resolve of the British officers, soldiers, marines, and sailors.

The gut patriotism released and displayed in 1982 made many commentators uncomfortable, but Thatcher knew how to respond, and war helped give her leadership a dynamic reputation enjoyed by no Conservative leader since Churchill and cemented her already strong relations with party activists. Thatcher's defense of national interests struck a chord across party boundaries, and most of the Labour Party supported the recovery of the Falklands. This patriotism was very much focused on naval resolve, strength, and success and created considerable political capital for the government.

The war led to a reexamination of the policy of naval force structure and procurement that the Conservative government had earlier introduced with the defense review *The Way Forward* (1981), which had implied that the navy was not concentrating on what should be its core mission and instead that there was an anachronistic emphasis on the surface fleet. Indeed, in 1979, *Blake*, the last active cruiser, had been decommissioned, while the commando carrier *Bulwark*, commissioned in 1960, had been laid up in 1981. Laid down in 1973, *Invincible* was about to be sold to Australia in early 1982 when the Falklands War broke out. Had the Argentinians delayed another year, it is highly unlikely that the Royal Navy could have assembled a fleet that was able to achieve what the task force did. The war revealed the importance of the fleet for the tackling of unexpected tasks, and it created a political head of steam that made further naval cuts extremely difficult. This episode underlined the continued significance of political contexts for naval power. As a result, there was the retention of the carrier and amphibious capability, and, in a bout of expenditure, the ordering of new ships. Although *Bulwark* was broken up in 1984 and *Hermes* was sold to India in 1986, a new carrier, *Ark Royal*, entered service that year, while seventeen frigates were laid down in 1982–91. Nevertheless, the most important commitment was to the 16,000-ton *Vanguard*-class submarines armed with Trident missiles, the replacement to Polaris; four were laid down in 1986–93, and the first, *Vanguard*, was commissioned in 1993.

As with the Israeli success in the air against Syria in 1982, the British triumph in the Falklands both influenced American commentators and also affected procurement and doctrine elsewhere, including eventually China, where it led to interest in acquiring a carrier. The logic and context of the new American maritime strategy in 1986 were very different from the Falklands operation and stemmed from the broader strategic requirements of the Cold War, but the American decision for a major naval buildup was affected by the British success, and notably so in the political dimension.

NAVAL ACTIVITY

A focus on the major powers can lead to a failure to devote due attention to others. Instead, the latter were important. The typology of naval activity was not identical with the previous period, as there were not the imperial possessions to defend. Nevertheless, there were still interests for powers to protect. In addition, conflict or confrontation between recently independent states could also involve naval forces. Key instances included Egypt and Israel, especially in 1967, and Pakistan and India in 1965 and 1971. In each case, missile boats played a key role. They were relatively cheap, and their speed gave them tactical and operational value, particularly in approaching and threatening the harbors of opposing powers. Amphibious operations were less significant in these conflicts.

In the 1973 Yom Kippur War, both sides deployed missile boats, the Israelis sinking at least nine Egyptian and Syrian ships and driving their navies back to harbor. This was important to Israel given the pressure it was under from Egypt and Syria in the conflict and the vulnerability of the Israeli coastal cities of Haifa and Tel Aviv to attack. As with carriers, which were not involved (neither side had any), the emphasis was on an accurate first strike. Compared to the Second World War, all ships now depended, at least in part, on the use of electronic countermeasures to block missile attacks. However, these leave a very large electronic signature, which helps detection by opponents.

The 1965 and 1971 India-Pakistan wars focused on land conflict, but there was also naval activity, and in 1971 much more so than in 1965. In preparation for the Indian invasion, Sea Hawks and Alizes from the carrier *Vikrant* (formerly the British *Hercules*) conducted attacks on shore targets in East Pakistan and laid mines in some of the key harbors. The respective emphasis on land and sea reflected in part the extent to which the two powers had land-centric, "continental" legacies, traditions, establishments, and doctrines. In large part, this was a consequence of the military structure and role of British India, which concentrated on providing large land forces. The Royal Indian Navy and Royal Indian Air Force were small even in the

Second World War. Thus, there was very little upon which independent India and Pakistan could build, and this was significant because navies were (and remain) long-term, costly investments. As with most postcolonial countries, the new states inherited military forces that were inherently biased in favor of land power, and this bias has continued as the armies have remained the leading services after independence. This is especially the case in Pakistan, where army generals have ruled the country for more than half its independent existence.

Even had this not been the case, neither state had a substantial maritime tradition, the importance of maritime trade and Indian Navy promotional materials notwithstanding. This was especially the case with Pakistan. Strategically, there is not much for either side to gain from maritime forces, as the key strategic objectives have been more or less accessible to land power only. This was (and is) especially so in the short and limited wars that both sides envisaged. Furthermore, land forces can be used by India and Pakistan to control unruly parts of the population, while navies are much less useful for these tasks. [17]

So, moreover, for Iran, although oil wealth led to a major buildup in the navy in the 1970s. Surface-to-surface missiles were the key arms. Missile boats were purchased from France, which was also a source for Israel. There was a major force of Iranian hovercraft, the largest such military force in the world. By the time of his fall in 1979, the shah had ambitious plans to develop Iran as an Indian Ocean power, and American long-range destroyers and attack submarines were on order. [18]

Navies continued to play a role in counterinsurgency operations. An Iranian naval task force assisted Oman against Dhofar rebels in the mid-1970s, not least by providing backing for a commando attack against rebel bases in South Yemen in 1975. The Omani navy, a skeleton force in 1970, was strengthened with seven patrol boats that were used to cut sea communications between the rebels and South Yemen. [19] In the Aceh region of Sumatra, the Indonesian army employed amphibious landings as one of its techniques against the Gam separatist movement.

With the continued rise in the number of independent powers, there were more states, for example Angola and Mozambique from 1975, that had to consider how best to respond to new naval opportunities and problems. As with the previous period, there was the acquisition of warships by such states from stronger powers, by purchase, by gift, or by a mixture of both. There was also the provision of weaponry and training, as well as the borrowing of doctrine and tactics, or of aspects of them. As before, warships were used for policing, against disaffection within states, and in the pursuit of international disputes. Nevertheless, many of the latter disputes did not directly involve naval conflict.

The Iran-Iraq War of 1980–88 was the longest-lasting naval conflict of the period. It involved Iranian attempts to interfere with Iraqi oil shipments and Iraqi attempts to maintain passage through the Persian Gulf. This conflict brought in outside powers, especially the United States. Already concerned about the anti-American development of the Islamic Revolution in Iran, which had overthrown the shah in 1978–79, the United States intervened to prevent Iranian interference with oil shipments but also as a geopolitical restraint on Iran's regional ambitions and presence. This intervention led to escorting reflagged Kuwaiti oil tankers in 1987–88. The large-scale injection of American naval power into the Gulf in 1987 was followed by the destruction of the Iranian navy in Operation Praying Mantis in the spring of 1988 following the near sinking of the USS *Samuel B. Roberts* by an Iranian mine. The Americans destroyed Iranian destroyers and patrol ships in the most significant naval engagement involving American warships since the Second World War. That the key issue was fighting capability, as opposed to the actual number of units, emerged clearly. The American intervention reflected America's replacement of Britain's role in the Persian Gulf. This replacement also acted to limit the need for the buildup by America's major regional ally, Saudi Arabia, of major naval forces in order to oppose Iran.

CONCLUSIONS

The range of naval powers is an important feature of the naval history of the period. However, the key element throughout remained that of the Cold War. This struggle was more global in its range from the late 1960s than it had been earlier. This global character, which changed the nature of the Cold War, underlined the significance of naval planning and force structure, as well as the difficulties of assessing effectiveness and evaluating necessary capabilities. These issues became more significant with the rise of independent powers and their development of naval strength.

Chapter Nine

After the Cold War, since 1990

ASSESSING CAPABILITY

Naval capability in the new millennium is very different from that on land because fewer states wield naval than land power, and even fewer wield much naval power. Moreover, the power of nonstate organizations is very limited at sea. As a consequence, it is easier to think in terms of a hierarchy of strength at sea than on land, and of a measure of strength in terms of numbers of warships. However, as in earlier periods, issues of force structure, operational effectiveness, and political combination in practice ensure that this hierarchy is more than a matter of counting warships. Moreover, asymmetrical capabilities, and land- and air-based antiship weaponry, add complications, as does the ability to handle and respond to the mass of data necessary for network-centric warfare.[1] The development of the idea of an operational level of war at sea (a level between the strategic and tactical levels), which for the United States was first introduced as doctrine in 1994,[2] makes analysis more crowded and complex, as well as introducing a useful analytical concept.

AMERICAN DOMINANCE

The last decade of the twentieth century was to witness the rapid decline of the Russian navy after the collapse of the Soviet Union in 1991, and to leave the United States, as a result, an even more prominent leading naval power. Indeed, in 2016, the United States had eleven operational carriers, a number that could rise to twelve as a result of drawing on the *Kitty Hawk* in the reserve fleet, the largest reserve fleet in the world and the only one to include a battleship. The other carriers in the reserve fleet are no longer in a state that would allow them to be recommissioned. Of the eleven active, the fifty-five-year-old *Enterprise* is of doubtful status as the reactor design is completely different from the other active carriers: it is a much more complex design that makes maintenance and refueling a problem. Each carrier strike force is a key element of power projection. The United States also had ten carrier wings in 2008. There was talk of reducing the numbers to ten carriers and eight wings, and, indeed, there was a reduction. However, the American carrier capability remained robust and a reminder of the continuing and prominent close relationship between American power and naval strength.

The launch, in 2009, of the *George H. W. Bush*, the last of the nuclear-powered *Nimitz*-class carriers (which displaced seventy-eight thousand tons), was a testimony to the American defense economy. The ship, built at Newport News in Virginia, is being followed by a new class of four carriers, of which the *Gerald R. Ford* is the first. This class was designed to have a more effective form of propulsion and increased automation to limit the crew, while the aircraft are to be launched by electromagnetic power. This class also employs manning-reduction technology, as well as a superstructure island located more aft than in the *Nimitz* class in order to afford better flight-deck visibility. In 2009, it was estimated that each of these carriers would cost $11.2 billion to build, but by 2015 the figure had risen to about $13 billion, with another $5 to $6 billion for the air wing.

The relative strength of the United States in the 1990s and early 2000s repeated that of the United States after 1945 prior to the Soviet naval buildup, and indeed of Britain after 1815. In each case, there were questions as to whether such dominance was a normal characteristic of naval power and how far traditional naval strategies remained appropriate, both for the leading navy and for others. However, American dominance was unprecedented as technology gave their fleet a strength and capability the Royal Navy had lacked at the height of its power.

This outcome of unmatched American naval power had been less clear in the early 1970s, but even then the Americans were helped in comparison with the Soviet navy, not only by greater naval resources and superior infrastructure, but also by more operational experience and by better, more varied training. This experience was a matter not only of the combat experience of the Korean and Vietnam Wars, but also of peacetime training and a very good safety record. American operational experience was maintained by a range of commitments, which included amphibious (and naval air) interventions, as at Beirut in 1982 and in Grenada in 1983, the Persian Gulf in 1987–88, Panama in 1989, and Somalia in 1992. In each case, air power was also crucial, but naval dominance was the key background to these interventions and was central to their course.[3] Ship-launched cruise missiles were important, as was the sea-basing of command systems. However, the American capability to strike from the sea had limitations: the navy could not control large dissident urban populations. Thus, the *Abraham Lincoln*, its air wing, the marines, and navy seals could not control Mogadishu in Somalia in 1993.

RUSSIA IN THE 1990s

Although the Soviet Union had become the second-largest naval power, its navy became increasingly obsolescent in the 1980s and 1990s as it proved impossible, first for the Soviet Union and then for Russia, to sustain the cost of new units. Under Mikhail Gorbachev, the general secretary of the Communist Party from 1985 to 1991, military expenditure was reduced, while Boris Yeltsin, the Russian president from 1990 to 2000, cut budgets even more sharply. There was a bitter struggle for money between the army, navy, and air force. Moreover, the war Yeltsin launched in 1994 in inland Chechnya understandably focused on the army, which encouraged expenditure on itself.

In the 1990s, the Russian navy failed to sustain the operational effectiveness of both warships and bases. Although major efforts were made to retain some kind of nuclear submarine capability, much of the Russian surface navy literally rusted away. The disastrous loss of the Russian submarine *Kursk* and all its crew in an accident in 2000 suggested that Russia lacked the capacity to maintain its ships and their equipment effectively and drew attention to the poor safety culture. Indeed, radioactive waste from rotting nuclear submarines is a major challenge in the Murmansk region. The Russians decommissioned all their carriers bar the *Admiral Kuzetsov* during the 1990s, and its flight operations were limited.

The navy was also gravely affected by the breakup of the Soviet Union. This breakup was especially important in the case of the Black Sea naval base of Sevastopol, which came under the authority of Ukraine, although it was leased to Russia in return for an annual write-off of debt by $97 million. The Baltic Fleet base of Liepaja came under Latvia, and many of the ethnic Russians who had settled there returned to Russia. Most of the Soviet Baltic coastline went to Estonia, Latvia, or Lithuania. The loss of most of the Black Sea coastline and most of the Baltic Sea coastline influenced the subliminal attitudes toward the character of the Russian navy. However, St. Petersburg, Murmansk, and Vladivostok remained in Russia. Economic, financial, and political problems also hit the navies of Russia's former allies, for example, Bulgaria. The delivery in 1990 of three Soviet corvettes was the last addition to Bulgaria's navy for fifteen years.[4]

The decline in Russian naval strength affected the concerns of other powers. In particular, Russia appeared to pose less of a threat to the Atlantic alignment of NATO. As a consequence, in the early 2000s, Iceland, Greenland, and the Azores were removed from the list of areas seen as vital from the perspective of American continental defense. In 2004, the American navy's P-3 Orion reconnaissance aircraft were withdrawn from Iceland.[5] In turn, the resumption of aerial reconnaissance from the Keflavik air base in order to find Russian submarines was announced in 2016.

THE POLITICS OF AMERICAN NAVAL POWER

American naval policy, like that of other naval powers, reflects not simply an "objective" assessment of interests and threats, but also "culturally-situated images of world politics . . . and of the military objectives of war."[6] The "cultural situation" is a matter of a number of spheres. Aside from the more general views of society as a whole, there are the overlapping suppositions of government and political elites, and the specific views of naval staffs and their supporters.

The domestic basis of modern American naval power does not match that of British naval power in the imperial heyday because the Royal Navy was then far more central to British concerns and self-image, not least the sense of a living history. Moreover, a later alternative, air power (some of which was to be provided by warships), was not a factor in the nineteenth century and was only a relatively minor one in the early twentieth century. The United States succeeded Britain as the strongest naval power after the Second World War, but it was also the leading air power, and air-mindedness was important to the American psyche. Moreover, both army and marines had important roles in American public culture, and thus in perceptions of military identity. In addition, the navy did not come first either in terms of the number of veterans or in related social indices of political commitment. As an instance of the possible significance of political culture, the defeat, in the presidential election of 2008 of John McCain, a former naval pilot who was promilitary, by Barack Obama, a member of a community and political nexus with neither positive views about nor commitment to military power, was significant as far as the issues and nuances of military power politics were concerned. In 2004, John Kerry, a naval veteran, lost to George W. Bush, who had (slight) air force links. Donald Trump, the Republican candidate in 2016, lacks military links and was critical of McCain's war service.

Nor did the navy come first with reference to the combat delivery of American power. The lack of naval conflict played a role in this relative lack of centrality, as America's opponents, having no real naval power, essentially fought on land, a long-standing situation since the defeat of the Japanese navy in 1944. American troops and supplies were delivered in large part by sea, as with interventions between 1982 and 2003 in Beirut, Grenada, Panama, Iraq, Somalia, Haiti, and the Balkans. The same was true of the commitment to Afghanistan from 2001. Initially, this was by air. Subsequently, most of the supplies for allied forces were shipped to Karachi in Pakistan and then trucked on, which underlined the significance of access to Pakistan by sea.

However, the dependence of these military operations on naval power did not engage public attention. Indeed, the navy appeared to lose its function or value as a fighting service. Service rivalry was significant, notably a very effective USAF offensive against the carrier carried out in places like the *Armed Forces Journal*. There were inaccurate charges that naval aviation had performed poorly against Iraq in 1991. The strategic role of the submarine force as an invulnerable second-strike nuclear option, for the United States and Britain, was downplayed in public estimation, especially in the 1990s, and to many appeared of questionable value after the end of the Cold War.[7] More seriously, the impact of "jointness" after the Goldwater-Nichols Defense Reorganization Act of 1986 left the navy vulnerable to the army and unable to exert due influence on its own size, composition, and missions.[8]

Apparent redundancy, certainly in comparison with the "shock and awe" of air power, whether the mighty B-52s of the Vietnam War or the American (and allied) air assaults on Iraq, Serbia, and Afghanistan in 1991–2003, led to an attempt by navies, both American and others, to assert a role that would enjoy government support and command public attention. The expeditionary mode of American foreign policy in the 1990s and 2000s appeared to offer the navy, and also allied navies, such a role, as a seaborne rapid-response force and in the shape of littoral action. As a result, navies devoted much attention to trying to build up relevant warships. "Littoral fighting ships" became a key component of an amphibious warfare capability that sought to mount deep-penetration invasions in which airlifted troops did not have to pass a "killing zone" on the beaches. Doctrine and training were devised accordingly.[9] The Americans converted four *Ohio*-class nuclear submarines into submarines used to support special operations and, subsequently, in order to carry cruise missiles.

Amphibious capability was challenged by air power. Indeed, airborne assault forces had earlier played key parts in the American interventions in Grenada and, more successfully, Panama in 1983 and 1989, respectively. The ability to insert forces by air both provided possibilities for the American navy, as its carriers were an obvious means for launching such attacks, and yet also challenged the navy, as air operations could be based on land. Indeed, the stress, in the 1990s and 2000s, on coalition warfare ensured that such bases were available. Thus, Saudi Arabia provided the crucial base for the 1991 Gulf War, although most of the allied equipment and supplies came by sea to Saudi Arabia, which underlined the importance of secure sea routes. Alongside carriers, Italy provided key air bases for NATO operations against Serbia in 1995 and 1999 and against Libya in 2011. An improvement in aerial refueling stemmed from an increase in the available tanker fleet.

Carriers, however, played a major role in mounting and supporting American attacks. This reflected their mobility and availability. In 1990, in response to the Iraqi invasion of Kuwait and the subsequent threat to Saudi Arabia, two American carrier groups were ordered toward the region, a key display, as well as means, of support. In 1996, America demonstrated its dominant position at sea when two carrier battle groups were deployed in the Taiwan Straits in order to thwart Chinese coercive diplomacy. The Chinese climbdown accentuated a sense of vulnerability [10] and led to their determination to develop antiship capabilities.

The French *Foch* and British *Invincible* both supported the NATO air assault on Serbia in the 1999 Kosovo crisis. In 2001, in the air assault on the Taliban regime in Afghanistan, the American *Carl Vinson* was the first coalition asset to conduct combat operations. In 2010, the *George Washington*'s involvement in large joint naval exercises with South Korea in the Yellow Sea demonstrated an American military commitment against North Korea. In 2014, the *George H. W. Bush* from the Persian Gulf and the *Carl Vinson* from the Red Sea played the key role in airstrikes against ISIS (so-called Islamic State) targets in Iraq and Syria. In March 2016, the *John C. Stennis* and four other American warships were sent into the South China Sea in order to show, according to Pentagon officials, that the United States was the dominant military power in the region. [11]

To focus on prudential considerations and rational analysis of capability in the discussion of carriers, however, is not all that helpful, as impressions of capability and effectiveness rested (and rest) on more diffuse factors and on sometimes irrational assumptions. In particular, the extent to which the sea was seen primarily as another basis for air operations greatly affected the public traction of the American navy and its political placing and encouraged a tendency to turn the navy into providing support units for carriers.

An economic historian might also suggest that the declining role of heavy industry in the American economy, in particular, of steel and shipbuilding, hit the naval interest domestically, with the same process also occurring in Britain, each development reversing the change at the close of the nineteenth century. This explanation can also be related to the rise of different regional constituencies. The Charleston Navy Yard was one of the city's biggest employers, but it was closed down in 1995. There were also naval facilities in Georgia and Florida, shipbuilding on the Gulf of Mexico, in Mississippi, and the large naval air station at Pensacola in west Florida. Nevertheless, much of the South, particularly the areas removed from the coast, had only limited commitment to the navy, and the role of the navy in southern history and traditions is modest. Instead, the army was the major focus in the South, a legacy that owed much to roots during the Confederacy, to southern notions of masculinity, and to the role of engineering skills in the navy. This focus was important as the South became far more important not only to American politics but also to its public culture from the late 1960s and, even more, 1970s, in part as a result of the repositioning of the Republican Party.

Indeed, the clear move of America's center of gravity and power from the northeast can be seen as a move away from the navy, not least because Philadelphia and Norfolk/Newport News, Virginia, were established naval centers with significant shipbuilding capacity, while New London in Connecticut had become the major submarine base. The geography of naval (and air) power had already been changed during the Second World War with the rise of manufacturing activity and military bases on the West Coast, such as San Diego, as the Pacific became more significant. These interests remained influential thereafter for the navy, but, from an overall perspective, the West Coast, and notably California, was more significant in providing a key regional component to the prominence of air power.

The loss of skilled workforces cannot be as readily recovered as that of the shipyards. This might have drastic effects in the future when the United States no longer has the skills to build certain things that can be more cheaply built in China. The Liberty ship output of Second World War America is no longer possible, not least given the increased complexity of modern ships, which often have parts that are mostly no longer produced in the United States.

The role of regional interests can also be probed in Russia where the navy's headquarters were moved from Moscow to St. Petersburg in 2008, and in Britain where the coastal naval interest, and associated shipbuilding, were of declining political and economic significance. This decline in Britain interacted with falling interest in imperial links and was seen in the rise of Scottish separatism. In turn, this separatism had naval implications, with the Trident submarine base on the Clyde and with Rosyth as the sole manufacturing naval yard. In France, the navy suffered because it was not located at the center of power.

Economic changes, regional interests and images, and service rivalries combined to affect the public view of the American navy, which in turn contributed greatly to the more general situation of naval power because the United States had the strongest navy. As this navy did not dominate the public's military imagination in the United States, so it was not surprising that there was a knock-on effect elsewhere. Moreover, American influence in other countries, for example in training, was more a matter of the army than the navy, as in South America. Nevertheless, there was also an important American influence in naval training, alongside a continued role for Britain. Germany proved more successful in building warships for many states, not least because the modern *MEKO*-class ships were relatively cheap. Israel acquired two German-made submarines in 2007. Similarly with Spain's ability to build ships, for example, two LHD (landing helicopter dock) ships for Australia.

CONTESTING THE ROLE OF SEA POWER

In many states, for example China, Russia, India, and Germany, the national navy's role had for long been secondary, and it had scant public impact in the 1990s. Moreover, newly independent colonies that acquired the naval bases of empire frequently made only limited use of the facilities. Thus, Aden was not to be the basis of a strong South Yemeni navy, although there were interesting changes in function there, with a church built for the British military in 1863 requisitioned in 1970 as a naval store and gymnasium. In Islamic states, the emphasis was very much on the army and the air force, not on the navy. Islamic states developed navies, but they remained relatively minor. For example, in wealthy Qatar, the navy is almost never mentioned. Including its marine police force and coastal-defense artillery, it contains 1,800 men, four patrol boats, and seven fast-attack craft armed with missiles and light guns. There is a plan to have corvettes. In practice, Qatar, however, relies on the American Fifth Fleet, which is based in Bahrain, and the navy is largely an antismuggling and antipiracy force. This may change if Iran acquires warships from Russia.

Writing about the recent, current, and likely future situation is difficult because the views of naval staffs and their supporters tend to dominate discussion. Indeed, advocacy plays an important role in analysis. There are major differences among such commentators over force structure, strategy, and doctrine, but it is rare to find a writer on naval matters arguing that navies are anything other than fundamental to military capability and vital for national, indeed international, interests and security. It would be instructive to read naval studies that were not written from this perspective. Indeed, there is a somewhat arid quality to some of the service-based discussion of military affairs. These arguments, always of crucial consequence, became more pronounced from the 1990s.[12] In part, this rise in advocacy reflected the end of the Cold War, because, although that confrontation was a dynamic situation with changing strategic landscapes interacting with the competing interests of particular services, the Cold War was more fixed than what was to follow.

First, the end of the Cold War led to pressure for a "peace dividend" in the shape of lower military expenditure. This pressure greatly sharpened service competition, including in the United States and Britain.[13] Secondly, and as a related factor, the strategic landscape appeared unclear in the 1990s. Thirdly, the "War on Terror" that took center stage from 2001, notably in the United States, gave added point and focus to this service competition and hit the navy hard. Fourthly, the relationship between this War on Terror and the commitment stemming from the revival of great-power confrontation from the mid-2000s became a matter of governmental, military, and public contention that was directly linked to competing priorities in procurement, strategy, and deployment.

Naval staffs played a central role in each of these developments, and the sense of opportunity and concern for the service was readily communicated both by them and by other commentators on the navy. The latter included historians. It would be reckless to imagine that value-free historical (and current) analysis is possible, but, attending conferences and reading publications, it is noteworthy that naval historians frequently do not engage adequately with other branches of the military and do not generally query the value of naval power nor of building more warships, a remark that may guarantee hostile reviews for this book.[14]

POWER PROJECTION

In the case of the 1990s, 2000s, and 2010s, admirals, maritime academic institutions, senior service colleges, and commentators responded to the challenges facing naval power by emphasizing the inherent value of naval power,[15] by arguing the importance of littoral power projection,[16] and by seeing this projection as a key role that also provided the intellectual case for maintaining naval strength. Thus, joint structures, operations, and plans owed much to naval advocates, for example in the American Department of the Navy's *A Cooperative Strategy for 21st Century Seapower: Forward, Engaged, Ready*, initially published in 2007 with a 2015 revision, and the British Navy Board's strategic vision *Future Navy*.[17] The 1998 British Strategic Defence Review focused on an expeditionary, and thus by definition naval, capability. Indeed, in Operation Desert Storm in 1991, the expulsion of Iraqi forces from Kuwait, Britain committed three destroyers, four frigates, three mine hunters, and two submarines, and navy helicopters destroyed fifteen Iraqi vessels. However, many of the merchantmen chartered to take British troops and material, both in the Persian Gulf and subsequently during peacekeeping intervention in conflicts in the former Yugoslavia, were foreign. This reflected the maritime decline of Britain.

Enhanced naval capability, and notably American capability, played a valuable role in a series of crises in this period, and an expeditionary posture was now very different from that in the nineteenth century. Cruise missiles and helicopter-borne assault forces provided opportunities to deliver ordnance into the interior, as well as troops from the sea, without having to fight their way across a defended beach. In 1998, for example, the United States fired seventy-nine sea-launched cruise missiles at terrorist targets in Afghanistan and Sudan, reaching targets that were far inland, for example Khartoum in Sudan. This impressive bombardment, however, was a futile display of force which did not stop the terrorists. Indeed, in Afghanistan, Osama bin

Laden was able to raise funds by selling missiles that did not detonate to the Chinese, who were interested in cutting-edge American military technology.

Cruise missiles were also employed against Serbia in 1999 as part of a combined NATO air and missile assault designed to ensure that Serb forces withdrew from Kosovo. In 1998, the submarine *Splendid* achieved Britain's first firing of a cruise missile, which had been bought from the United States. The following year, *Splendid* fired these missiles at Serb targets in Kosovo as part of NATO operations there. Britain also deployed the 22,000-ton helicopter carrier *Ocean*, completed in 1998, and the assault ship *Fearless* to provide the capability for a maritime assault, although, in the event, such an assault was not launched, as the Serbs withdrew their forces from Kosovo. During the attack in 2001 on the Taliban regime in Afghanistan (like Serbia an inland state), cruise missiles were fired from American and British warships in the Arabian Sea.

In turn, missiles were a challenge to naval power and therefore a constraint on the operations of warships. The capability of land defenses increased. In 2006, the Israeli corvette *Hanit* was hit by a radar-guided C-802 missile fired by Hezbollah from southern Lebanon. Three years later, Hamas fired missiles at Israeli warships that were bombarding Hamas positions in the Gaza Strip. The Israeli navy has a superior capability to that of Israel's neighbors, which is necessary given Israel's situation, but the focus of Israeli public and governmental attention is on the army and air force, which are more frequently involved in combat and deterrence.

Power projection was not simply a matter of delivering ordnance. There was also a greater emphasis, seen most obviously with the American and British navies, on the provision of capacity to move and land troops and supplies. Thus, the American fleet acquired nineteen aircraft-carrier-sized, Large Medium-Speed Roll-On/Roll-Off ships,[18] while the Japanese built the *Kunisaki*, a landing-platform ship.

Power projection, littoral action, the end of the Cold War, and the War on Terror combined to encourage changes in force structure, doctrine, and organization, including the rise in joint command and training structures, and indeed an interest by historians in amphibious operations.[19] In 1999, *British Maritime Doctrine*, the second edition of what had been published in 1995 as *The Fundamentals of British Maritime Doctrine*, declared,

> The maritime environment is inherently *joint*. . . . Naval forces themselves exist to influence events ashore; they have never operated strategically in an exclusively naval environment . . . the sea is a pre-eminent medium because, above all, it provides access at a time and place of political choice. . . . Ultimately maritime forces can only realise their considerable potential when integrated fully into a joint force.[20]

The last point is also true in most scenarios for both army and air force. The British *Naval Strategic Plan* of 2006 stated, "The development of new maritime Equipment Capability will provide the Future Navy with the expeditionary and versatile capabilities essential for success in the future Joint environment."[21] Similar issues and arguments appeared in the German White Book (equivalent to the Strategic Defense Review) of 2006, in the 2011 Defense Policy Guidelines, and in the 2013 concept for the *Bundeswehr* that was designed to explain how the guidelines were to be implemented.

The need to update existing warships was relatively low compared to the situation in the nineteenth century. Most updates in the 1990s and 2000s were able to include the existing platform, and were related instead to major updates in "electronic warfare suites" and improvements in missile systems. Nevertheless, the commitment to power projection led in the 2000s to a clear strand in procurement. For example, by the late 2000s, Denmark had created a projection navy reliant on *Absalon*-class uniform-model ships, commissioned in 2005, that could be adapted to different tasks, Spain was building a strategic projection vessel, and the Americans were developing littoral combatant ships. The United States was deploying twelve amphibious dock transport ships (landing-platform docks), Britain had two (and one landing-platform helicopter), and the Dutch, who were putting a focus on all-water operations (i.e., including littorals, rivers, and lakes) had two. Japan acquired helicopter-equipped destroyers (in effect helicopter carriers) in order to support power projection, while Sweden had fast-attack craft capable of moving troops to the shore, as well as three hovercraft. Having long neglected amphibious capability, Australia built it up in the 2000s. Africa's largest navy, that of South Africa, centered on new ships, including the largest, a support ship for amphibious operations, as well as three German-built frigates and four German-built submarines. This investment, which is due to be continued with landing craft, is more impressive in the context of the cuts in overall South African military expenditure.[22]

The recession that began in 2008 affected the implementation of such plans, in some cases greatly so, but there were already serious and varied problems with resources. Trained manpower was one. In 2008, Australia only had sufficient manpower for three of its six submarines, and Britain also faced serious problems with manpower.

Power projection against the land took a variety of forms. In 2008, there were suggestions that, if Israel attacked Iranian nuclear facilities, they might use missiles fired from recently acquired German-built submarines rather than air attack. The latter posed problems of long range, refueling, and overflight permission, let alone antiaircraft fire. Israel had developed a submarine-based conventionally armed cruise missile, which offered a limited nuclear second-strike capability.

TRADE PROTECTION

The fundamentals of maritime power and concern for many states were not those of confrontation between naval powers, nor attacks on rogue states, nor other aspects of amphibious intervention, but, rather, the extent to which trade continued to be dominated by ships. Indeed, in the mid-2000s, it was estimated that there were about forty thousand merchant ships and that more than 90 percent of global trade was carried by sea. This approach, however, ignored measurement by value, for which the percentage was closer to sixty-five. The emphasis on maritime trade also underrated the importance of land transport to freight movements within states, notably the United States, China, Russia, India, and Brazil, each of which is very large, while most trade within the European Union was carried by land. Moreover, land routes are being developed to link regions, for example German railways have long been seeking to create routes into the Balkans. In contrast, there is no progress on linking North and South America by road: the gap in the Pan-American Highway in eastern Panama is still significant.

The construction of long-distance oil and gas pipelines can be seen as an aspect of the significance of land routes, as with the movement of Russian natural gas to European markets. However, some pipelines go underwater, while others move supplies to ports for subsequent shipping, as with pipelines planned, constructed, or completed for the movement of Central Asian oil to Pakistan, Georgia, or Turkey. Underwater data (fiber-optic) cables are also very significant, carrying most international telecommunications, and led to concern, notably in the United States in the mid-2010s, about Russian plans to tap or sever them and the development of Russian capabilities accordingly.

Alongside the qualifications above, maritime trade is also important for domestic as well as international trade (although less so), and overall maritime trade rose considerably in the 1990s and 2000s, increasing at a faster rate than the growth in world GDP. By 2015, according to the insurer Allianz, modern container ships could easily have an insurance value of over $1 billion. In 2005, two-thirds of the world's hydrocarbon energy flows moved by sea, with 20 percent of the oil supply moving through the Strait of Hormuz. These trade flows across the "global commons" of the "high seas," however, were vulnerable to military action, and notably so for seas and oceans to which access was gained through choke points, such as the Indian Ocean and the Mediterranean, Baltic, and Black Seas. The key choke points were the Strait of Malacca, the Strait of Gibraltar and the Suez Canal, the Skagerrak, and the Dardanelles and the Sea of Marmora. In contrast, such choke points were absent in the Atlantic and Pacific Oceans. Key economic elements that are highly vulnerable include not only these choke points but the undersea fiber-optic cables (and their landing stations) as well as offshore energy platforms producing and pumping for both oil and gas. There is a very limited fleet of ships to maintain and lay cables. Whereas current threats to these are readily apparent, it is less clear what their future counterpart will be. However, this element affects current planning and expenditure for defense. More generally, maritime security became a more prominent issue, theme, and language after the Cold War. This concern encompassed issues of maritime control such as immigration control, drug and other smuggling, piracy, and pollution.[23]

A more traditional resource, fish, also proved a source of confrontation and indeed conflict, notably with the Turbot War between Canada and Spain in 1995, and with Japan and Korea staging a standoff over rocks that would provide fishing rights in the Sea of Japan the following year. By the mid-2010s, the Argentine navy was focused mainly not on preparing, as in the past, for conflict with Britain and Chile, but on patrolling to control fishing in the South Atlantic. In 2016, an Argentine coastguard vessel shot at and sank a Chinese trawler fishing illegally in its exclusive economic zone after the trawler tried to ram the patrol boat. At the same time, this was the first time in fifteen years that the Argentine coastguard had sunk a vessel fishing illegally in its waters, although in 2012 it shot at two Chinese trawlers caught poaching squid. By lessening the chances for local fishermen, overfishing also contributes to piracy, especially in the Indian Ocean and off Southeast Asia.[24]

Trade is a fundamental indication of the globalization that became a more important theme in political discussion from the early 1990s, and this discussion affected strategic thought, not least when terrorism was presented in terms of a challenge to this globalization. The two together led to pressure for distinctive, if not new, ideas in thinking about navies, notably a challenge to the basic concept of discussing procurement, doctrine, and strategy in terms of the traditional practices and uses of competing navies. In particular, in consultation with many other navies, the American navy developed the concept of a maritime strategy based around a "Global Maritime Partnership," a coalition navy netted together, indeed a one-thousand-ship coalition navy, an idea advocated in 2005 by Admiral Michael Mullen, chief of naval operations from 2005 to 2007 and chairman of the Joint Chiefs of Staff from 2007 to 2011. In 2007, the Americans issued *A Cooperative Strategy for 21st Century Seapower: Forward, Engaged, Ready*, a document revised in 2015.[25] The American experience of working with allied navies from the 1940s on, both in the Second World War and in the Cold War, had demonstrated its value in the two Gulf Wars and in other activities. Many states had acquired naval experience in coalition operations and continued to do so. Thus, the Argentine navy participated in UN missions including the First Gulf War and the Haiti peace mission, and also operated off El Salvador in 1990–92 as part of a UN peace mission. This naval operation was designed to interdict the transit, weapons smuggling, military logistics, and medical support of the insurgents. Foreign-policy goals were served by such missions, while interoperability with other navies was secured.[26]

The protection of trade routes was an important aspect of the Japanese view of sea power as a key constituent of national strategy. The navy was also seen as a visual statement of political purpose, with Japan sending minesweepers to the Persian Gulf in 1991 and destroyers to the Indian Ocean from 2001 on. Moreover, in 2008, Tarō Asō, the prime minister, instructed the Defense Ministry to find a way to deploy warships against pirates off Somalia. Similar elements could all be seen with China, but, as discussed in the next chapter, there are also clear and strong Chinese ambitions for offensive capability. The Indian navy, by 2016, was the only Indian service with a comprehensive and comprehensible doctrine and strategy in the public domain.

While piracy, terrorism, and other antinormative behavior offered prospects for international naval cooperation,[27] the sharp revival of great-power competition from the late 2000 challenged the viability of the thousand-ship navy. Moreover, this competition suggested that any naval coalition might, or would, be another version of that very competition, or could be regarded as such. Piracy and operations against it offer the possibility of promoting informal means to make the trade routes used by competitors more difficult. In 2008, President Sarkozy of France highlighted the challenge from piracy, especially based in Somalia. However, by then, the possibility of cooperation spanning the United States, Britain, France, and also Russia, China, and Iran had greatly receded. Indeed, in the winter of 2008–9, Iran sent two destroyers to the Gulf of Aden on the pretext of fighting piracy, destroyers that were suspected, with reason, of taking part in the movement of arms from Iran to the Hamas government in Gaza. At the same time, the American naval task force deployed against the pirates was instructed to track such shipments.

International cooperation would ease action against pirate bases in Somalia and elsewhere, action that is necessary if effective steps are to be taken against pirates. This was a lesson clearly shown by British operations against pirates and slavers in the nineteenth and early twentieth centuries, including in Somalia in 1904. The rise, or perceived rise, of piracy is another sign that naval history, no matter how obscure it now may appear, is a necessary part in the education of potential political leaders and in the military.

DEBATING PROCUREMENT

Differing prospects for naval activity accentuated debates over force structures, and the age-old interaction of proposed capabilities with projected tasks recurred. In the absence of networks of imperial bases and of what would have been a partial replacement—that is, adequate overflight rights for airborne forces—the concepts of carrier battle groups and amphibious battle groups seemed sensible as a means of ensuring or threatening intervention. At the same time, surface ships are highly vulnerable not only to jet-ski-driving terrorists but also still to modern submarines carrying modern torpedoes: the Russians are allegedly employing a kind of missile torpedo that has a speed of two hundred knots. To a degree, this threat appears countered by the concept of a balanced fleet, with its protective hunter-killer submarines designed to keep the threat from hostile submarines suppressed and out of range. However, whether or not in a coalition context, the equations of adequate balance will only be discovered as a result of conflict, and that discovery will be too late. On the other hand, the same point can be made about all modern military systems.

By the 2010s, the emphasis was on smart mines as well as on the threat posed by submarines. Britain is investing in *Astute*-class attack submarines. In 2016, China had five nuclear-powered and fifty-three diesel-powered submarines, along with four *Jin*-class nuclear-powered ballistic-missile submarines. Operational but not yet deployed, the last are built to carry JL-2 missiles with a range of 4,500 miles (7,200 km). China is also developing a next-generation ballistic-missile submarine with an improved missile, the JL-3. Moreover, the impact on land operations of drones encouraged interest in their likely or possible counterparts at sea, as well as a sense of a more general volatility. These factors affected both official and public discussion about procurement and strategy. Thus, in Britain in 2015–16, Labour opponents of the proposal to replace the nuclear submarines that fired Trident missiles with nuclear warheads referred to such drones and argued that submarine vulnerability was increasing.

Similar arguments were employed by critics of the reliance on carriers. Linked to this criticism came the argument that there was an excessive reliance on dated legacy systems, essentially reengineered weapons that had been developed prior to 1950, for example manned submarines, carriers, manned aircraft, and nuclear weaponry, and that there was a need to move beyond this experience and legacy. In response, investment in such systems had many defenders, and indeed they had been greatly developed. Moreover, hunting for pirates is an example of the revival of apparently redundant practices, as (differently) is minesweeping.

The issue of adequate balance in fighting terms very much interacts with that of procurement. Thus, investment in two large *Queen Elizabeth*-class carriers for the British navy, an investment in ships, aircraft, crew, and bases, threatens the number (both existing and to be commissioned) of frigates and destroyers. For long, it looked as though one carrier would be sold or placed in reserve because of the cost of running two. However, in 2014, Britain announced that it was planned that both would become operational. Looked at differently, the specifications for frigates and destroyers are excessive and thus lead to high overall costs, which helps ensure that the number of ships in the Royal Navy cannot be maintained. *Daring*, the first of six Type 45 warships, berthed in Portsmouth, her home port, for the first time in 2009. Designed to replace the Type 42, what was described as the world's most advanced destroyer had a greater range and was armed with a new air-defense missile system called Sea Viper, which can track hundreds of targets up to 250 miles away, but the cost of the 7,350-tonne ship was £650 million.

Similar problems exist elsewhere. For the American navy, the new *Zum-walt*-class destroyer, the first of which departed for its acceptance trials in April 2016, proved so expensive that despite its immense capabilities and state-of-the-art stealth design and weaponry, the procurement will be limited to just the initial three warships. There is speculation that the number will be further cut to two, down from the initial plan for thirty-two ships of the class. The *Zumwalt* class has long-range 150 mm guns able to hit targets up to ninety-six miles away, but by 2016 each destroyer cost about $4.4 billion, making it the most expensive ever built. Instead of the more capable *Zum-walts*, the decision has been made to build more of the less expensive *Arleigh Burke*–class warships.

Indeed, the high cost of new warships, not least of their complex electron-ics and of the weapons (aircraft and intercontinental and cruise missiles) they carry and launch, will ensure a pronounced level of volatility in procurement as economies expand or hit difficulties. Thus, the trajectory of growth, de-cline, and revival seen with Soviet/Russian naval power from the 1970s to today may well be repeated for other navies, not least, but not only, in response to the recession of the late 2000s and to forthcoming recessions. It is unclear, for example, whether British naval plans are sustainable. The Ministry of Defence's Planning Round 09 saw major struggles over expendi-ture on new warships, and these continued with subsequent strategic reviews. The number of Royal Navy ships fell from seventy-one in April 2010 to sixty-five in April 2014. This issue may be even more acute for states with small navies, as they appear more discretionary to state activity, more not-ably so if the state is not an island and does not have a strong naval tradition. On the other hand, to run down navies to an extent where there is no navy or no seaworthy warships is generally unacceptable. Procurement is made more complex by the involvement of hidden subsidies.

The issue is differently present for large states as it is a case of maintain-ing a range of capabilities. So, for example, with Russian plans. In 2008, Putin announced that Russia would build five carriers, each to be the basis of a carrier group, and the number was subsequently raised to six by 2020. In 2011, Russia declared a 30 percent increase in military funding by 2015, increasing to 70 percent by 2020, in order to provide modernization. Howev-er, there is a lack of clarity over what Russia will be able to afford, not least due to the marked fall in the price of oil in the mid-2010s, as well as questions about the availability of sea bases and concerning the politics of the issue. There are legacy Russian programs from the Cold War, notably the 24,000-ton *Borei*-class nuclear-powered ballistic-missile submarines, named after the Greek god of the north wind, that were planned first in 1982 and laid down in 1996, only for there to be serious problems with the missiles they were designed to carry. In 2012, the first of the *Yasen* class of nuclear-powered attack submarines entered service, carrying cruise missiles and torpedoes, with four more under construction. Submarines are very much the Russian focus. The Mediterranean was a key area of Russian naval interest, with Tartus in Syria the sole naval base outside the former Soviet Union. The deployment of Russian Yakhont antiship cruise missiles in Syria suggests a replication of Chinese anti-access and area-denial (A2/AD) policies by Russia's proxy, Syria,[28] and an Israeli submarine-launched cruise-missile strike destroyed a store of these missiles in Syria.

The varied nature of naval power was demonstrated in 2011–12 when Iran threatened to close the Strait of Hormuz to international trade at the entrance to the Persian Gulf. The threat proved redundant in January 2012 when the American carrier *Abraham Lincoln*, supported by five other warships, sailed through in order to underline the right of passage under international law. This encouraged an Iranian focus on asymmetric capability. The key weapon is the guided missile based on a number of platforms, on land, at sea, and in the air. These include the *Zolfaqar* speedboat, which is able to launch Nasr antiship cruise missiles. *Ghadir* midget submarines, domestically produced and based on a North Korean type, as well as mines, contribute to the Iranian capability and to the volume of deployment designed to give effect to "swarming tactics." More generally, mines are an issue for American naval power projection.[29]

NAVAL AIR POWER

Several major states (although not Germany or Canada) sought to maintain or develop carrier capacity after the Cold War. "An aircraft carrier is a symbol of the country's overall national strength as well as the competitiveness of the country's force." This 2008 declaration by Colonel Huang Xueping of the Chinese Defense Ministry[30] reflected the extent to which military power was a matter of image as much as lethality. Yet there were also particular strategic needs. The deployment of American carrier battle groups to protect Taiwan from Chinese threats, notably in 1996, underlined China's determination to develop its naval air power as well as its anti-access missiles. The sea trials in 2011 of *Liaoning*, China's first carrier, a Soviet-era 65,000-ton *Kuznetsov*-class carrier originally launched in 1988 and bought from Ukraine, intensified speculation about strategic rivalry with the United States. So also did the carrier's first launch and recovery of J-15 fighters in 2012 and the tensions when it was deployed in the East China Sea in 2013. China plans to increase the size of its carrier fleet.

For medium-sized powers, carriers imply great-power status. Their procurement is heavily based on considerations of status and image. In 2014, Britain announced that it was planned that both carriers would become operational. This decision can be regarded as political and institutional, in the shape of meeting assumptions about great-power status, rather than reflecting a sensible response to the vulnerabilities of carriers, notably to swarm missile attacks. In this respect, they become too valuable to hazard and thus uneconomic. Moreover, expenditure on carriers threatens to leave little money for other new warships. On the other hand, carriers were designed to play multiple roles: fighting naval battles, launching ground strikes, and mounting amphibious missions.

Other countries have also maintained or increased their carrier force, and resources will continue to be a key issue. The announcement by Vladimir Putin in 2008 that Russia would build five carriers, each to be the basis of a carrier group, lacked credibility, not least due to a lack of shipyards. Moreover, the frequent repairs required by the *Admiral Kuznetsov*, the sole Russian carrier, indicated the problems of maintaining capability. When, in 2007, the carrier was sent into the Atlantic and then the Mediterranean as part of the first deployment of major Russian warships since 1995, it was escorted by two tugs in case of need. The dramatic fall in the price of oil in 2014–15 affected Russia's ability to sustain its naval plans, including claims that by 2020 it would have six carrier groups, eight hundred new aircraft, and 1,400 new helicopters. However, Russian defense expenditure is steadily rising, as is its determination to have hegemonic power over its neighbors.

In 2016, India had only one carrier—the rebuild of the Soviet *Moskva*-class *Admiral Gorshkov*, commissioned in 2013—on active service, as the former British *Hermes* has been decommissioned. The Indians stripped the *Admiral Gorshkov* of all conventional weapons systems and turned the ship into a carrier with an air group consisting of Russian jets and French and British helicopters. An Israeli surface-to-air missile (SAM) system, American radar, and an Italian power generator were all part of the package. A nuclear-powered carrier, a new *Vikrant*, has been launched but is not due to be commissioned by India until 2018, and another is planned. India is experiencing problems with the Russian parts. Italy had two carriers in 2014, and Brazil, France, Russia, Spain, and Thailand each had one; Brazil's is the former French *Foch*. In 2010, France sent a carrier strike group led by the nuclear-powered 41,000-ton carrier *Charles de Gaulle* to the Indian Ocean. This provided an air presence in Afghanistan and the Indian Ocean and paid a port visit to Abu Dhabi as a key element of a new French strategic engagement with the region. In 2011, that carrier played a successful role in NATO operations over Libya, and in 2015–16 in operations against ISIS in Iraq. Although it is small by comparison with American nuclear-powered carriers, the *Charles de Gaulle* is still an impressive vessel. Its air group includes twelve Rafale fighters, two Hawkeye early-warning aircraft, light and medium helicopters, and nine Super Etendard strike aircraft. However, its replacement is proving politically difficult due to the cost, and it is likely that France will not build another nuclear-powered carrier.

The use of carriers addressed some of the issues posed by the deployment of fast jets to ground bases, notably the support and security of the host nation, overflight permission, and logistical capability. For example, in the 2003 crisis with Iraq, the deployment of British aircraft to the region was affected by the reluctance of states, especially Jordan, to provide overflight permission and refueling facilities. As a result, the attitude of Turkey proved important in the Syrian crisis of the 2010s. Carriers provide a piece of floating sovereign territory. It is not necessary to ask permission to use them, in contrast to bases in even the most closely allied state.

A classic instance of the problems of insufficient mass and problematic resilience, problems more generally facing the slimmed-down military of the early twenty-first century, one carrier is not enough to maintain round-the-clock capability. This is especially so if the carrier is under repair, which was an issue for the *Charles de Gaulle* as it had persistent serious difficulties. Ordered in 1986 and laid down in 1989, the carrier was launched in 1994 but not commissioned until 2001. There were problems with propellers and the rudder, while the nuclear power plant was refueled between September 2007 and December 2008. In 2014, the United States (which needs carriers on station) had three on operations and one more en route to a patrol area, with the others of the eleven commissioned carriers on training missions or being maintained or refurbished. Britain requires two carriers in order to keep one ready for action. There has been talk about Anglo-French cooperation to address the problem. In 2003, Britain had joined with France, Italy, and Spain in agreeing to collaborate over maintaining the readiness of their carriers in order to ensure that one was on station at all times.

The apparent significance of carriers rose in 2013–16 as tension over Chinese expansionism in the East and South China Seas increased. At the same time, these interlinked crises, especially that between China and Japan over the East China Sea, indicated the extent to which conventional naval air power was supplemented by other forms and factors, particularly the role of missiles, whether land or sea based. Not all states that could afford it pursued a carrier capacity. Thus, the Australian Defense White Paper of 2009 sought a capability for land-attack cruise missiles deployed in guided missile destroyers, while twenty-four new helicopters were to fly off two new amphibious landing ships.[31] Indeed, carriers bind resources that can be used for a fleet of non-carrier ships. An in-between stage is offered by the American use of converted container ships as "afloat forward staging bases," with a landing deck able to operate helicopters and V/STOL fighters. Such ships can rapidly change roles, for example from antisubmarine to special operations.

CHINA

In East and South Asia, with the exception of Japan, there was little recent history of naval power for the regional states. Moreover, the relevant Japanese history was complicated by the legacy of the Second World War and the provisions of the subsequent peace treaty. The situation was transformed from the 2000s. In China, there was an emphasis on past naval activity, notably the early fifteenth-century voyages of Zheng He into the Indian Ocean. Indeed, the *Zheng He* was the name of the Chinese officer-training ship. Inaccurately linked to these voyages, the *China Daily* claimed in July 2004 that the Chinese circumnavigated the globe in 1421, well before Columbus and Magellan. The voyages of Zheng He were highlighted in the 2008 Beijing Olympics. There was also a more general Chinese presentation of naval strength as a product of government initiative, an aspect of great-power status, and a sign of modernity, all of which were regarded as political goods.

Both elements were seen in the treatment of history in China. In particular, *Da Guo Jue Qi* (*The Rise of Great Powers*), a Chinese government study finished in 2006, attempted to determine the reasons why Portugal, Spain, the Netherlands, Britain, France, Germany, Japan, Russia, and the United States became great powers. This study was apparently inspired by a directive from Hu Jintao, the Chinese president, to determine which factors enabled great powers to grow most rapidly. The study drew together government, academic methods (as many scholars were consulted, some reportedly briefing the governing Politburo), and popular interest. A twelve-part program was twice broadcast on the state-owned television channel in 2006, and an eight-volume book series was produced and sold rapidly. The president of the television channel made the utilitarian purpose of the series clear. The book project argued the value of naval power, but also the need for a dynamic economy with international trade linking the two, a factor seen as suggesting a lesson about the value of international cooperation.

Chinese naval strategy, however, focuses not on the history and interests of other states, but on that of China. The traditional land-based focus on "interior strategies"—the development of expanding rings of security around a state's territory—has been applied to the maritime domain. In part, this is in response to a reading of Chinese history in which it is argued that, from the

1830s, with the British in the First Opium War, the ability of foreign powers to apply pressure from the sea has greatly compromised and harmed Chinese interests and integrity. "Near China" has therefore been extended as a concept to cover the nearby seas. This provides both an enhancement of security and a sense of historical validity, one that gives purpose to the Communist Party. China argued the case for extending what was presented as the strategic depth necessary for security, stressed asymmetric Chinese capabilities in opposition to the United States, and employed arguments from both Chinese and non-Chinese history. A new cohort of naval leaders has come to the fore.[32]

However, the definition and implementation of the relevant attitudes and policies ensure both considerable problems and mission creep. This is because the security of what may seem to be the Chinese near seas apparently requires regional hegemony and an ability to repel any potential oceanic-based power, the latter a task with a bold geopolitical span. This interpretation of Chinese interests can be advanced to explain the past threats from Britain and Japan, but, at present, this power is seen as the United States. The Chinese desire may be motivated by security, in terms of rings of control, and also psychological well-being. Nevertheless, this desire greatly challenges the security of all others and, crucially, does not adopt, or advance, a definition of security that is readily amenable to compromise or, indeed, negotiation. In part, this is a reflection of the Chinese focus on "hard power," a power that is very much presented by naval strength as a support for nonmilitarized coercion in the shape of maritime law enforcement. The Chinese navy, in practice, offers force to support the application of psychological and political pressure on other states.

The long-term maritime strategy outlined by Admiral Liu Huaqing in 1987 has been adjusted from one of peacetime building to one of war preparations. The 1999 air attacks on Serbia during the Kosovo crisis encouraged Chinese interest in an advanced military capability as part of providing defense against such a strike on China mounted from oceanic directions.[33] The launching of major surface warships by China in the 2000s was at more than twice the rate of that in the 1990s. Alongside a theory of "active defense,"[34] a coastal navy has developed into one capable of true blue-water policies.[35] There is also an expansion in China's overseas naval support system.[36] These steps combined to increase tension.

Guides to fleet profiles make a marked improvement in the Chinese navy between 1990 and 2013 readily apparent, and this is more relevant when compared to the Japanese and South Korean navies. However, to judge and describe a navy solely by its inventory of hardware is highly misleading. This is a tendency that is popular with number-crunching experts who often have a problem in accepting and quantifying factors such as experience and tradition. At the beginning of the 2000s, the Chinese navy had a certain amount of

1970s and 1980s technology. In particular, it obtained four Russian ships, *Sovremennyy*-class destroyers which had first been introduced in the Soviet navy in the 1980s.

In contrast, by 2016, the Chinese navy appeared to be superior to the Russians in some aspects of naval technology. The Chinese lack the antisubmarine capabilities of the Russians but are closing the gap. Moreover, the Chinese were replacing "one-mission" ships with "multimission" ships. This made the ships more capable, but also more difficult to handle, on tactical and operational levels. Chinese naval personnel have not been able to follow suit in the technological leap. Moreover, many Chinese ships appear to be having a certain share of wishful thinking in their published overall capability, and the latter can serve as a scare factor in the area of possible power projection. For example, according to a March 2016 American congressional report, the allegedly planned Type 55 cruiser has a hodgepodge of weapon systems and a very diverse mission capability, including a "planned" anti–ballistic missile and anti-satellite capability. This ship, or rather the advertised specifications, sounds like a wish list for a ship that can do everything.

In submarines, especially nuclear-powered ones, the Chinese lag behind much further than with surface ships. The operation of these ships requires experience which cannot be copied or stolen. A similar lack of experience is also seen in the development of a possible Chinese nuclear-powered carrier equipped with a catapult and arrester wires. This requires a need for capabilities and experience that are not readily available. Naval development by means of technological leapfrogging, in particular by copying and stealing technology wholesale, is a major problem due to a lack of quality control; a lack of experience with the technology they are building, employing, and using; and therefore a lack of ability to modify the technology they are acquiring. This means of acquisition shows a serious lack of Chinese naval construction and building capacity. Copying is a keen means. A good example of similarity is between the Chinese Type 712 amphibious transport dock and the American *San Antonio*–class LPD (landing-platform dock) ships.

The Chinese navy simply has not had the time to develop any kind of naval tradition, formal or informal. It has no combat experience, and the infant navy was hit hard by the turmoil of the Cultural Revolution of the late 1960s. Conscription did not provide the necessary talent base, and the alternative posts in the commercial sector are more attractive for those with expertise. The willingness to accept a high level of casualties is a problem from an operational point of view because it is difficult to replace trained crew. The Americans have a highly significant and long-standing advantage in training, experience, and command culture.[37] Moreover, if the internal situation in China deteriorated, its navy would become less of an issue.

GREAT-POWER TENSIONS AND DISPUTES

The utility of naval power in the early twenty-first century in part reflected the extent to which the "end of history" that had been signposted in 1989 with the close of the Cold War proved a premature sighting. Instead, there was a recurrence in international tension focused on traditional interests. Territorial waters proved a particular source of dispute, not least when linked to hopes over oil and other resources.

Indeed, by 2014, there were key disputes over competing claims in the East and South China Seas, disputes that drove a major regional naval race, particularly between China and Japan, as well as the confrontation between China and the United States. The asymmetric nature of the America-China situation ensures that this is not an arms race comparable to those prior to 1914. These disputes were characterized by aggressive Chinese steps, as in 2012 when China took over the Scarborough Shoal west of the Philippines.[38]

Moreover, control over the naval base of Sevastopol and over maritime and drilling rights in the Black Sea were important in the crisis over Crimea and, more generally, Ukraine in early 2014. Natural gas in the Black Sea is at issue. Once the Russians gained control of Sevastopol, they announced an expansion and modernization of their Black Sea Fleet, with new warships and submarines. This was seen as a threat to the NATO position in the Mediterranean. Natural gas is also an issue in the eastern Mediterranean, with Israel seeking to protect exploration in waters between it and Cyprus. In the western Mediterranean, Russian warships refueled in Ceuta. Russian moves were also at issue in the Baltic, notably with pressure on Estonia, Latvia, and Lithuania and with threats to Finland, Poland, and Sweden. This was a challenge to NATO. Aggressive flights over NATO warships in international waters included a simulated attack on the American destroyer *Donald Crook* in April 2016.[39] Concern about coastal waters encouraged a drive to ensure the necessary naval power. The disputes over the East and South China Seas and the Black Sea, and the prospect of their becoming more serious, or of other disputes following, led to a determination, on the part of regional powers, to step up naval strength and preparedness, although this was less the case in Europe. In particular, Germany's expenditure on its navy remained low.

In Asia, the situation was different. In the case of Japan, there was a major strategic shift in focus, from the defense of Hokkaido, the northernmost island, to concern about the southwest part of the archipelago, in particular the offshore islands in the East China Sea. This shift, from confrontation with Russia to confrontation with China, led to a greater emphasis on the navy and a more mobile, flexible, and versatile power profile. Moreover, Japanese military exercises were increasingly geared to maritime concerns and naval power.

North Korea added further volatility to the region. In 2010, a North Korean submarine attack led to the sinking of the South Korean frigate *Cheonan*, but the response was muted, in part because North Korea denied responsibility. North Korea's prime threats are those posed by its army and its missiles. South Korea is improving its navy, with its eye both on North Korea and on maritime and territorial disputes with China and Japan.

Regional disputes also directed attention to the situation as far as other powers, principally the United States, were concerned. These powers were concerned both about these regions and about the possibility that disputes over sovereignty would become more serious in other regions, for example the Arctic. Partly as a result, the nature and effectiveness of naval power became a more prominent topic in the mid-2010s. So also did the extent to which governments and societies identified with this power. American "rebalancing" toward the Asia-Pacific, however difficult, proved especially important for the American navy, which undertook to locate 60 percent of its forces in that theater as it sought to justify its role.[40] The American presence was designed to counter the Chinese argument that China was a geographical fact in the region and America only took an episodic role. For the American navy, confrontation with China demonstrated its role and contrasted with its being overshadowed by the other services in the Afghanistan and Iraq conflicts.

A willingness to resort to force, or to appear to do so, creates for others a key element of uncertainty. In 2016, it was revealed that China had placed surface-to-air-missiles on Woody Island in the South China Sea and an advanced high-frequency radar system on Cuarteron Reef in the Spratly Islands, with radar also being installed on three other outposts in that chain. Such policies provided "A2/AD" (anti-access/area-denial capability) and challenged both American support for the principle of freedom of navigation and American security guarantees. American containment capabilities are threatened. Investment in more conventional naval platforms also served Chinese regional goals, as with the new Type 052D destroyer.

The Chinese emphasis on naval strength as a key aspect of national destiny, and the rapid buildup of the Chinese navy, helped drive the pace for other states, leading Japan and India, in particular, to put greater emphasis on a naval buildup, while also ensuring that the United States focuses more of its attention on the region.

Carriers are banned under the Japanese constitution because they exceed the requirements of self-defense and provide the ability to attack other countries. However, delivered in 2015, the *Izumo* was a "helicopter-carrying destroyer" according to the government and did not have the hangers or engineering facilities necessary to service fixed-wing aircraft, nor the catapults needed to launch them. Nevertheless, the *Izumo* was as big as the Second World War carriers; could take the V-22 Osprey, which Japan intends to acquire; and could be modified to launch V/STOLs, notably the F-35B. After the Cold War, it was argued in Japan that the navy focused too much on antisubmarine warfare and that a more balanced force was required. By the 2010s, however, in response to the rapid increase in the size and quality of the Chinese submarine force, the emphasis on an antisubmarine naval aviation capability had been reaffirmed.

Submarines are an important aspect of regional procurement, with Vietnam, for example, turning to Russia to obtain them. Whereas in 1990, about twelve countries had effective submarines, now the number is about forty.[41] Indonesia also increased its military budget. In 1999, South Korea launched the *Incheon*, the first submarine it had built. As Malaysia and Singapore could no longer rely on Britain for naval assistance, they were encouraged to press on with their own navies. In 2014, Australia considered turning to Japan in order to provide a new generation of submarines that was clearly designed against China; French and German submarines were also considered. Australian strategists are willing to engage in the public sphere. In a white paper published on February 25, 2016, Australia committed itself to replace its existing submarine fleet of six diesel submarines with twelve new "regionally superior submarines" with a "high degree of interoperability" with the United States. Nine new frigates were designated for introduction into service from the late 2020s, while three new destroyers and twelve new offshore patrol vessels were also to be added to the navy. The air force was also to be expanded. The white paper expressed serious concerns about China's rapid militarization of the South China Sea islands and called for a halt. In April 2016, the twelve new long-endurance submarines were ordered, by an administration with different priorities than that in 2014, from France, with the building to be in Australia.

On February 23, 2016, the United States had asked Australia to begin patrols near these islands. The islands provide an opportunity for bases for antisubmarine aircraft and helicopters, thus lessening America's advantages in submarine capability. These issues were accentuated by America's failure to replace the *Los Angeles*–class nuclear-powered attack submarines with sufficient numbers in the *Virginia* class, and by a failure to develop antiship ballistic missiles, which only China has, or to prioritize antiship cruise missiles. Depending on the success of the American LRSAM missile, next-generation American missiles to match Chinese counterparts have not been deployed.

Talk in 2014 that conflict over the East China Sea might lead to a broader international struggle, with the United States backing Japan, underlined the significance of maritime issues and power. The previous October, the United States agreed to base surveillance drones and reconnaissance aircraft in Japan so as to patrol waters in the region. Meanwhile, America's alignment with India encouraged China to step forward with its arming of Pakistan, which, from 2011, introduced F-22P frigates into its navy, while fast-attack craft equipped with Chinese-made antiship cruise missiles were also provided.[42] In 2015, Pakistan agreed to buy eight diesel-powered submarines from China that could carry nuclear-armed cruise missiles with a range of 450 miles. In turn, in 2016, *Arihant*, India's first nuclear-armed submarine, a 6,000-tonne vessel, is due to enter service as the first of five Indian-built submarines set to be added to the navy.

The development of antiship missiles by China able to challenge American carriers, notably the DF-21F intermediate-range (1,500 kilometers) ballistic missile fitted with a maneuvering reentry head containing an antiship seeker, which was revealed at a military parade in 2015, and the YJ-83 antiship cruise missile that can travel at nine times the speed of sound, poses a major problem. As a result, the carriers may have to operate well to the east of Taiwan, in other words beyond the range of the American navy's existing F-18 E-F Super Hornet, the standard fighter/bomber, which has an effective range of 390 nautical miles, or the F-35 aircraft (about 600 miles). A 2016 report by the Center for a New American Security, a Washington think tank, emphasized the vulnerability of American carriers. In 2016, China demonstrated the submarine-launched CM-708 antiship guided missile.

The Chinese missiles are not under the command of the navy but under the Rocket Forces Command. However, the real capability of the missiles is unclear. These are new technologies, and Chinese talk about hitting a carrier as if it were a fixed land target in the Gobi Desert is unproven. The alleged capacity to kill a carrier with a direct hit is also problematic. To a degree, this missile alarm is reminiscent of the alleged "missile gap" of the 1950s. Any capability to hit a ship with a ballistic missile would require a targeting network that would be vulnerable to American weapon systems, notably the Aegis ships.

In 2011, significantly, Taiwan claimed that its missile capability would counter any hostile activities by the carrier China was making operational. Military concerns about the viability of carriers, both American and Chinese,[43] were not matched in the public sphere where, in both countries, there was a widespread continued conviction of their significance. This contrast between concerns and confidence was not so much one of "hard" versus "soft" power, although that was an element, but rather one of an understanding of the different uses and capabilities of naval strength. Alongside Chinese strengths, notably in antiship missiles, there are important weaknesses, including of amphibious lift. Moreover, it is unclear that China has the capacity to produce an effective combined-arms expeditionary fleet.

China's developing capabilities led from 2011–12 to greater American interest in the concept of the AirSea Battle in order to overcome China's "anti-access/area-denial" philosophy.[44] The United States has recast AirSea Battle into the "Joint Concept for Access and Maneuver in the Global Commons." Furthermore, as an aspect of the degree to which interest in the past is in part shaped by present concerns, literature on the subject has developed, particularly in the United States, where access and forward presence are seen as crucial to securing national goals and are thus challenged by the capabilities of adversaries and by changes in the nature of war.[45] "All-domain" access was an aspect of *A Cooperative Strategy for 21st Century Seapower: Forward, Engaged, Ready*, the American policy document published in 2007 and revised in 2015.

The ready willingness of Chinese Internet users to identify with these issues reflected their salience in terms of national identity and interests. Moreover, this willingness suggested a pattern that would also be adopted in other conflicts over maritime rights. Issues of maritime interest and naval power proved readily graspable. To a degree, the Chinese government is struggling to ride the tiger of popular xenophobia, a xenophobia that it at times has helped to stir up. In China, as earlier with Tirpitz and the *Flottenverein* in Germany, popular support for naval expansion has proved easier to arouse than to calm, but there is also considerable governmental and popular pride in the new Chinese carrier, which was launched by the president in 2012.[46]

Thus, the utility of naval power was symbolic, ideological, and cultural, as much as it was based on "realist" criteria of military, political, and economic parity. It has been ever thus, but it became more so in an age of democratization when ideas of national interest and identity had to be reconceptualized for domestic and international publics and in a media world markedly different from that of the 1980s. The ability to deploy and demonstrate power was important in this equation, and navies proved particularly well suited to this ability. This was not least because navies lacked the ambiguous record widely (but far from universally) associated by the public with armies and air forces after the interventionist wars of the 2000s and as a consequence of the role of some armies in civil control.

THE RANGE OF POWERS

As in previous periods, a focus on the leading naval powers can lead to a failure to engage with the bulk of states with navies. In part, however, the latter context is automatically underrated because so many of these states neither seek, nor plan for, warfare at sea, which is not surprising given the cost of major warships. Instead, their navies, focused on coastal defense and constabulary functions, are far more aspects, and means, of policing goals, tasks, and methods, and there is scant sign that this situation will alter. The increasing importance of coast guards is a recent trend in maritime security. Many small states, especially island states, are finding a seagoing police force more appropriate than attempting to form a navy. This is an idea supported by Australia with its "Pacific patrol boat" initiative.

Small navies are variously defined. They are more than big navies in miniature, but they also frequently have very different goals and roles. At the same time, there are common functions and pressures, as well as an impact on the practice of cooperation among navies. Coastal constabulary functions could extend to intervening in nearby states as in the 1990s when Nigeria intervened in the Liberian civil war.

At the same time, goals and roles change. For example, in the mid-2010s, the Irish navy received three *Samuel Beckett*–class ships to replace old existing ones. The primary role is the established one of patrolling the Irish maritime economic zone, but there had also been a humanitarian mission to help with migrants in distress on Malta in the Mediterranean. There is talk of building a larger warship designed for overseas missions and featuring a flight deck, which the *Beckett* class lacks. While that will cost more, and it remains to be seen whether the Irish navy will be able to push that through, the idea reflects the navy's growing ambition. In inland Switzerland, in contrast, a small navy of gunboats on Lakes Constance and Geneva was abandoned as Swiss force structure and strategy changed in 1994 after the Cold War, from an area defense protecting the whole territory from the borders (which included these lakes) to a modular army able to multitask. [47]

For most states, the prospect of disorder is more significant than the risk of war. Looked at differently, these are particular aspects of what has been referred to as "wars among the people." Moreover, the risks of war, or at least of hostile naval steps, are automatically lessened by the real and possible strength of the major naval powers and their capacity accordingly for deterrence. As such, the situation is not too different from that of the late nineteenth century.

CONCLUSIONS

Such trajectories reflect not only economic and fiscal strength, but also the competing constituencies of interest within the overlapping worlds of military, government, and society. The high costs of a large-scale, cutting-edge naval capability is underlined by the fact that, unlike a millennium or even half a millennium ago, there is no overlap between this cutting-edge capability and a direct benefit in the shape of selling naval protection, taking part in privateering, or engaging in trade, although discussion of the threat from piracy emphasizes this relationship. At any rate, and certainly with new weaponry, navies risk following air forces, at least at the cutting edge, in pricing themselves out of the business for most powers. This situation may accentuate the asymmetry in capability that is such a readily apparent feature of modern warfare. Conversely, however expensive, cutting-edge capability may well be the best way to deal with asymmetrical threats.

The relationship between this asymmetry at sea and asymmetry in air power is worthy of consideration, and notably if exposure to sea and air power are included in the asymmetrical relationships. The problems America and its allies encountered in suppressing violent opposition and insurrections in Iraq and Afghanistan in the mid-2000s led to greater emphasis on the difficulties that major states faced in asymmetrical warfare. These difficulties ensured that the value of investment in weapons systems, such as cruise missiles and carrier-borne aircraft, that project power but often can only produce limited results on the ground, was debated. So also was the issue of the significant tension between output, in the shape of military activity, and outcome, in that of an acceptable settlement, although the two questions are not identical.

Navies argue for the particular value of the sea as a sphere in which power has to be maintained, and also as a basis for power projection. Each argument is of great value, but in order for capability to be understood in terms of effectiveness, these arguments will need to be considered alongside the limitations and qualifications of this power.

Chapter Ten

Into the Future

The future is very much with us in the shape of planning, doctrine, procurement, and training, and especially so in a period of high volatility both in geopolitics and in technology. This is the situation at present, and also very much so since the late 1980s, which helps account for the degree of overlap between chapters 9 and 10. At a time of high volatility, it may appear foolish to look to the past. However, although the historical context is not the only one to discuss when assessing naval strength today and into the future, it is a context that offers an ability to assess long-term significance. This context can be approached in a number of ways, not least those of the rise and fall of maritime powers, the impact of new technology and asymmetric capabilities, and their analytical value when considering China and the United States.

The linkages of geopolitics, technology, and power are also key elements. It is now over a century since the meeting in London of the Royal Geographical Society on January 25, 1904, heard Halford Mackinder, director of the London School of Economics, propose his new geopolitics of world power. Basing his argument explicitly on the transformative consequences of railways, Mackinder, both influential geographer and soon-to-be politician of empire, argued that what he termed the capabilities of land power had been greatly enhanced and claimed that the always-threatening Eurasian "Heartland" would be able to redefine power relations in a way that challenged the leading naval power, Britain. At that time, the "Heartland" was dominated by Russia, the power of which reached from the Baltic to the Pacific. A young questioner at the meeting, the future would-be statesman of the British Empire, Leo Amery, however, proposed instead at the meeting a different geopolitics based on a much newer technology, that of air power. [1]

In light of this particular grasping of the future, naval power, the basis of British imperial and military strength, might appear weak if not redundant.

However, in the 1900s, far more commentators looked to the future in the shape of dreadnoughts, while some considered torpedo boats and submarines. From the 1900s and, far more, 1920s, some of those looking to the future placed weight on the new and different in the shape of what air power would apparently be able to do in an undated and unverifiable future, rather than the more limited amount that it could actually do in the present. In this minority perspective, navies did not meet the bill unless as adjuncts of air power in the shape of carriers. Later, missile-firing submarines entered the equation, and in the American case, very much as adjuncts of land-based missiles, for the latter could deliver more ordnance.

And so those looking to the future have continued to focus on air power. From the 1940s and, far more, 1950s, in addition, the world was literally reconceptualized as new map projections and perspectives, for example centered on the North Pole, focused on the potential and exigencies of the aerial dimension, first with aircraft and then, even more dramatically, with intercontinental missiles, and this process has continued. In contrast, the map projections and perspectives, and linked assumptions, associated with the great age of naval power in the late nineteenth and early twentieth centuries came to appear as redundant as the global transoceanic empires that power had sustained and displayed.

To survive, navies apparently had to adapt. This was an argument, also applied to other branches of the military, and indeed to everything, that was to be pursued over the last century, first with an emphasis on carriers and, subsequently, with submarine-based missile launchers, while antiaircraft and antimissile defenses were also emphasized. Moreover, as a further erosion of naval distinctiveness, "jointness" came to the fore in the late twentieth century, as both doctrine and, less successfully, practice. This, again, captured the emphasis on synergy, an emphasis that was both pragmatic and reflective of a quasi-holistic cultural norm.

Irrespective of the challenges posed, or supposedly posed, by adaptability and jointness, the idea of aerial self-sufficiency was taken forward further in the 1990s and early 2000s as a key aspect of what was termed, by its American originators and advocates, the Revolution in Military Affairs (RMA). Air power appeared best to provide the speed and responsiveness that would give force to what was proclaimed to be a revolution in information technology. With specific reference to navies, mid-air refueling, which became more common, apparently provided a power projection for aircraft that made carriers, however dramatic a display of naval power, less relevant. There was much talk not only of *the* RMA but also of "transformation," and past, present, and future were understood in that light.[2] This approach was flawed both empirically and conceptually. In the former case, the vulnerability of information systems to jamming and of air tankers to attack were factors, but such elements did not discourage bold talk.

From a very different direction, the sea also appeared more marginal. Unprecedented and continuing population growth across much of the world, combined with the breakdown of preexisting patterns of social and political deference, greatly increased the complexity of government. This contributed to what was termed, from the 1990s, "wars among the people."[3] These wars, or at least serious unrest, led, both in conflict and in planning and procurement for conflict, to a focus either on major urban centers or on marginal regions that were also difficult to control. Again, this focus scarcely corresponded to an emphasis on the sea. "Wars among the people" was very much a doctrine that suited armies, which propounded it, and left navies apparently redundant, their ships as one with the heavy tanks now deemed superfluous. Instead, air power and rapidly deployed ground troops appeared to provide the speed, precision, and force required, and the politics of military power was propounded accordingly.

Moreover, this shift appeared demonstrated in the 1990s by a series of developments. These included the continued decline of the once great naval power, Britain, as well as the extent to which the United States and Russia, the leading naval powers of the 1980s, no longer focused on this branch of their military and the Russian navy rapidly declined. There was a major rundown in the American navy, both numerically and in terms of particular capacities, such as antisubmarine warfare and mine clearing. The bold plans and impressive achievements of the Reagan naval buildup were abandoned, while the existing navy was run down. More especially, under President Clinton (1993–2001), there was an emphasis on a "peace dividend" that combined a degree of interventionism, notably in Bosnia in 1995, with a lack of commitment to maintaining American capability against other major powers. This was, indeed, "cheap hawkery," but such capability no longer appeared necessary. Russia's navy was not maintained. Furthermore, the degree to which, in the 1990s, the navy and the oceans were not the prime commitment, military, political, and cultural, of the rising economic powers, China and India, appeared striking. Thus, the 1999 clash between India and Pakistan, "the Kargil War," was very much on land.

These indications, however, were and are misleading. Indeed, trends in the late 2000s, and even more 2010s, have pointed in other directions, and there is no reason to believe that this suggestion will change. The perspective from the South and East China Seas is particularly instructive. In practice, naval power remains both very important and with highly significant potential for the future. In addition, a reading of the recent past and of the present that minimizes the role of this power both neglects the place of naval power in power projection and risks extrapolating a misleading impression into the future.

GEOGRAPHY

Geography, as ever, is a key element. Here there is both change and continuity. The main element in change at present is the impact of global warming in the Arctic. As a result, sea routes are opening up and improving via the Arctic, notably from the Pacific to the Atlantic. This has encouraged Russia to devote particular attention to its naval forces in the Arctic and to naval power projection there. In response, there has been greater American interest in the Arctic, while Canada, whose navy is a shadow of its former self, has taken steps to improve its naval strength.

The prime geographical factor is the location of population growth and the related economic activities of production and consumption. Most of this growth has occurred in coastal and littoral regions, and, more generally, within 150 miles of the coast. There was been significant inland expansion of the area of settlement in some countries, notably Brazil, as well as population growth in already heavily settled inland areas of the world, particularly in northern India. Nevertheless, the growth of coastal and littoral regions is more notable. In part, this growth has been linked to the move from the land that has been so conspicuous as petrol-powered machinery became more common in agriculture from the mid-twentieth century. As a result, rural areas lost people: in the United States (notably the Great Plains) and Western Europe from mid-century, and in Eastern Europe and China from the 1990s. The process is incomplete, especially in India and, to a lesser degree, Japan, but it is an aspect of the greater significance of cities. Most of these are situated on navigable waterways, principally the coast or relevant estuaries. Shanghai is the center of Chinese economic activity, and Mumbai and Tokyo its Indian and Japanese counterparts. Inland capitals, such as Beijing, Brasilia, Canberra, Delhi, Madrid, Ottawa, Pretoria, and Washington, often lack the economic dynamism of coastal cities, although each case is different. The development of inland cities in many states requires that of competent road and/or rail systems from the coast, but such an outcome is not a prospect in numerous countries.

ECONOMIC TRENDS

The economic growth of coastal cities is linked to their position in the global trading system. This system is one where maritime trade remains foremost. The geopolitical, and therefore military, implications of the economic value of seaborne trade require emphasis. In large part, this value is due to the flexibility of this trade and of related transport and storage systems. Containerization from the 1950s proved a key development, as it permitted the ready and rapid movement and transshipment of large quantities of goods without high labor needs or costs, and with a low rate of pilfering and damage. Air transport lacked these characteristics, and the fuel cost implications of bulk transport by air made it economically unviable other than for high-value, perishable products, such as cut flowers. The significance of containerization was enhanced by the ability and willingness of the shipbuilding industry to respond to and shape the new opportunity. Containerization led to a marked increase in cargo capacity.

As a result, the character and infrastructure of global trade by sea has been transformed since the 1950s, a transformation accentuated by the need to invest in expensive new facilities at ports. Moreover, this transformation continues and is readily apparent around the world, as in the current widening of both entrances to the Panama Canal so as to take larger container ships, an increased capacity that, in turn, leads to an enhancement of facilities at the ports these ships will ship to, such as Charleston in the United States. A good example of recent and current maritime transformation is provided by the massed cranes in the new container facilities at Colombo, as well as the new harbor being built at Hambantota with Chinese help further along the Sri Lankan coast, and the numerous container ships off the southern coast of that island.

Politics played key roles in this transformation and, yet again, frames naval developments. This is another version of the significance of the expansion of global maritime trade links, volume, and economic consequences for the role of the Royal Navy and the ambitions of Britain's opponents in the nineteenth century and the run-up to the First World War. Correspondingly, this expansion was linked to that role. So also with the significance of American naval ascendancy for the growth of the global economy in the "Long Boom" from the end of the Second World War to the early 1970s, and again during the "Reagan Boom" of the 1980s. The latter boom put particular strain on the self-confidence of the Soviet elite, and this helped lead to the attempted reforms that ultimately destroyed the coherence of the Soviet Union. Yet fiscal conditions and financial flows, notably the recycling of oil wealth into American funds, and the related ability to borrow and invest, were arguably more significant to American strength in this period than the movement of goods.

The development of the global economy after the end of the Cold War focused on the integration into the Western-dominated financial and maritime trading systems of states that had been, or still were, communist, for example China and Vietnam, or that had adopted a communist (or at least Socialist)-influenced preference for planning, such as India. Moreover, in the 1990s and 2000s, the general trend was toward free-market liberalism and against autarky, protectionism, and barter, or controlled trading systems. This trend remains far from complete, but it encouraged a major growth in trade, notably of Chinese exports to the United States and Western Europe. The American trade deficit with China was $202 billion in 2005.

This trend remained significant in the 2000s and early 2010s, despite political tensions, particularly between the United States and China, as well as the consequences of the serious global economic crisis that began in 2008. Crucially, that crisis did not, or did not yet, lead to a protectionism comparable to what was seen in the 1930s. Both prior to the crisis and during it, the focus on trade between East Asia and the United States ensured that maritime trade expanded greatly. The queues of ships daily waiting to go through the Panama Canal are fully laden when transiting from the Pacific northward and westward to the Caribbean and carry East Asian goods to the United States and Europe. Chinese goods are readily found elsewhere in the world, for example in Latin America and Africa, and concern about maritime commerce raises issues of Chinese vulnerability.[4] Indeed, alongside American-Chinese naval competition comes the economic interdependence that has led to talk of "ChinAmerica." Comparisons, however, are not always helpful, or at least encouraging, because economic links between Britain and Germany were also close in the run-up to the First World War.

Speculation about developing trade from East Asia overland to Western Europe, as geopolitical, economic, and strategic goals and tools,[5] has not yet been brought to fruition at any scale. Only the Trans-Siberian Railway was in a position to provide a link. To that extent, Mackinder's 1904 analysis of the potential of rail proved flawed. The ambitious railway construction plans of China and talk of a "New Silk Route" from China into, and across, Central Asia notwithstanding, there is no sign that this will change. The Chinese railway boom has much to do with high-speed lines to carry passengers and troops. It is driven by politics rather than economics, as in the building of a line to Lhasa in Tibet. Overland trade from the Far East has not prospered for economic as well as political reasons. Railway transport costs remain stubbornly higher than shipping; indeed, containers have widened the gap as they offer efficiencies of scale particularly appropriate at sea. Chinese railways, old and new, provide no links to Europe. Talk in 2016 of a Chinese rail link to the Persian Gulf coast of Iran faced the issue of political instability en route, as did the more concrete Chinese attempt to develop Gwadar on the Pakistani coast as part of the "China–Pakistan Economic Corridor." The port of Gwadar is run by the China Overseas Port Holding Company.[6] Moreover, although the Soviet Far East remained part of Russia when the Soviet Union disintegrated, it very much operates in an autonomous fashion.

The growth in trade after the Second World War, much of it maritime trade, was linked to the enhanced specialization and integration of production and supply networks that was a consequence of economic liberalism, as well as to the economies of scale and the rise of the standard container, and to the attraction of locating particular parts of the networks near raw material sources, transshipment points, or the centers of consumption. This growth was further fueled by the opportunities and needs linked to unprecedented and sustained population increases. The latter helped to ensure that regions hitherto able to produce what they required were obliged now to import goods, not only food and fuel, but also manufactured products. Trade links that would have caused amazement in the nineteenth century, or even the 1950s, such as the export of food from Zambia to the Middle East and from Canada to Japan, or of oil from Equatorial Guinea to China, became significant. The trade between Africa and China gave the latter's navy a key role.

Most, although not all, of the resulting international trade, and notably of the bulk trade, was by sea. According to the *Financial Times* of July 10, 2014, $5,300 billion worth of goods crossed the South China Sea each year, which underlined both its economic, geopolitical, and strategic sensitivity and the relative decline of the Suez Canal route. Nodal points in the maritime trade system that are of great geopolitical importance include those on the routes to and from East Asia, notably the Strait of Hormuz, the Strait of Malacca, the Sunda Strait, and the Panama Canal.

PIRACY AND POLICING

Naval power is the key guarantor of this trade, playing the role of providing the security of what was termed the "global commons," and will continue to do so. This concept and reality present sea power in a far more benign fashion than had been the case when it was seen as an expression of imperial power, notably of Britain and the United States. Instead, there was, is, and will be an emphasis on shared value through, and in, the "global commons." This emphasis was greatly enhanced from the late 2000s in response to a major increase in piracy, notably, although not only, in the Indian Ocean. Although not all attempts to seize ships were successful, the number of attempts by Somali pirates rose to 219 in 2010, 237 in 2011, 263 in 2013, and 245 in 2014. This increase also exposed the broader implications for maritime trade of specific sites of instability. It was not only that, thanks to improved ship motors, pirates from Somalia proved capable of operating at a very considerable distance into the Indian Ocean, but also that their range of operations affected shipping and maritime trade from distant waters. This was not new, but, in the 2000s, the challenge appeared greater, both because piracy had largely been stamped out in the nineteenth century and because the scale of international maritime trade, and the number of states directly involved, are far larger than then. Moreover, as trade is increasingly concentrated on higher-bulk container ships, piracy becomes more profitable and poses a much greater risk, not least by driving up insurance premiums.

The operations against Somali piracy reduced its extent and enabled states such as China and India to display their naval power, train their crew, and provide an international and domestic justification of naval strength. These operations proved a clear demonstration of the importance of naval power and its ability to counter limitations and failure on land. In turn, the potential significance of both piracy and naval power was further demonstrated by the expansion of piracy elsewhere, notably off Nigeria and, in the future, maybe in many settings.[7]

The threat from piracy suggested a multilayered need for naval power. For most of the twentieth century, naval power had been dominated by the major states, while most states instead focused on their armies, not least for internal control and policing. In the early twenty-first century, such control and policing increasingly also encompassed maritime tasks. Control over immigration, especially refugee flows; the maintenance of fishing rights (not least against illegal industrial fishing ships that plunder coastal fishing grounds); and the prevention of drug smuggling all proved prime instances of spheres in which maritime presence and capability were increasingly significant.

As a consequence, naval power became as much a matter of the patrol boat as of the guided missile destroyer. Drug money, for example, is a threat to the stability of Caribbean states which, however, have tiny navies. As a result, it is the navies of major powers that have a Caribbean presence, the United States, Britain, and France, each of which also has colonies there (as do the Dutch) that play a key role, one that is greatly facilitated by aerial surveillance and interception capabilities.

Naval action against pirates, drug smugglers, and people traffickers, the last a major task for the navies of Australia, Greece, Italy, and Spain, but not only for them, is reminiscent of the moral agenda of nineteenth-century naval power. Such action is also an implementation of sovereignty as well as of specific governmental and political agendas.

In the case of the European Union (EU), which is an attempt to create a new type of federal sovereignty at a continental level, the ability to police borders became a major issue due first to concern about terrorism and then about immigration, especially in 2015–16. The focus was on maritime borders as they were the principal points of entry for migrants into the EU. This was true both of the Aegean and of the Mediterranean, the latter a far larger sea to police. The Royal Navy was one of the EU navies that, as part of Operation Sophia, deployed warships accordingly. In 2016, there was talk of planning for the movement of EU warships into Libyan coastal waters in order to intercept arms and people smugglers there and return the would-be migrants to Libya. Arms smugglers supplying ISIS were a particular goal. Also, in 2016, the smuggling of immigrants across the English Channel brought a new naval task.

More generally, maritime policing became a key issue. This will not necessarily be done only from the sea but will in part also involve air support. In addition to aircraft, there has been a development of drones for use in coastal surveillance, for example by Malaysia. Nevertheless, one of the biggest problems of the navy in most countries is its lack of capacity in a pacification/antiterror/civil war role. The internal usage of any deepwater ships is very limited, except in sea border control.

NAVAL CAPABILITIES

Mackinder's lecture, 113 years later, appears not prescient but as an instance of the weakness of theory when confronted by economic, technological, and military realities. China, not Russia, is the key power in Mackinder's "Heartland," but this is a China with global trading interests and oceanic power aspirations, not, as Russia seemed to be, the successor to the interior power controlling some supposed "pivot" centered in western Siberia, albeit a state also with naval aspirations. Whereas Russia was a second-rank naval power in 1904, and one about to be totally defeated at sea by Japan in 1904–5, China in the 2010s, already the world's second-largest economy, is becoming a more serious proposition at sea. This is a matter not only of warship procurement and the development of antiship missiles, but also of bases and alliances. In 2015–16, Chinese submarines docked in Karachi (Pakistan) and Colombo (Sri Lanka), while China continued the building of a port at Gwadar in Pakistan that is probably designed to house Chinese nuclear submarines and developed a base in Djibouti.

The likely future trajectory of Chinese naval ambitions and power is currently a, if not the, foremost question for commentators focused on power politics, and that itself is a clear instance of the continuing relevance of naval strength. It has proved far more successful than either armies or air forces in combining the cutting-edge, apocalyptic lethality of nuclear weaponry with the ability to wield power successfully at the subnuclear level. Moreover, this ability is underlined by the range, scale, and persistence of naval power, all of which provide, alongside tactical and operational advantages, a strategic capability not matched by the other branches. Despite aerial refueling, air power lacks the continuous presence, and thus persistence and durability, that warships can convey. Moreover, warships offer a firepower and visual presence that is more impressive than that of many armies or of aircraft circling at the border.

The significance of coastal regions underlines the value of amphibious power projection. In 2005, the development was begun of the American Joint High-Speed Vessel (JHSV), a joint army/navy vehicle designed for the high-speed deployment of forces, sea basing, and littoral maneuver, with a shallow draft, a range of 1,200 nautical miles, a speed of thirty-five to forty-five knots, and a helicopter deck. Construction on the first hull began in 2009 and became operational for the navy in December 2012. The designation was changed to EPF (Expeditionary Fast Transport) in 2015. In 2014, in an exercise in Hawaii, the American Marine Corps displayed the prototype of the Ultra Heavy-Lift Amphibious Connector, a vehicle designed to cut through the waves in order to carry vehicles to the coast. The tracks are made from captured-air foam blocks that stick out like flippers. The full-size version is designed to be eighty-four feet long and thirty-four feet high and should be able to transport at least four vehicles. In March 2016, Japan's defense budget included an amphibious warfare unit modeled on the U.S. Marine Corps.

Also in 2014, the building by France for Russia of *Mistral*-class helicopter carriers intended to support amphibious operations created a serious issue when an international arms embargo of Russia was introduced as a response to its seizure of Crimea. Such warships were seen as a particular threat in the Black Sea and notably to Georgia and Ukraine. Russian naval capability for combined operations is regarded as a key problem. So also in the Baltic, where Russia's ability to use its navy to mount amphibious attacks on Finland, Estonia, Latvia, and Lithuania; to threaten Sweden and Poland; and to block external intervention by NATO forces aroused considerable concern, alongside fears of action by air and land. France eventually blocked the sale, and the ships will probably end up in the arsenal of the Egyptian navy and will be equipped with KA-52 attack helicopters.

At the same time, the ability of land-based power to challenge navies is much greater than was the case when Mackinder was writing in 1904. Indeed, his view both of the relationship between land and sea and of the capacity of technological change did not really comprehend this challenge. It had begun as soon as cannon significantly enhanced the capacity of coastal defenses to resist naval attack, as well as threatening anchorages. The major improvement in artillery in the nineteenth and twentieth centuries greatly increased this capacity, and the surviving sites of coastal defense against naval attack, for example on Waiheke Island off Auckland against the Japanese, remain formidably impressive.

In the twentieth century, the range and nature of such defense was increased, first by aircraft and then by missiles, and increasingly so in the twenty-first century. Both are now central to the equations of naval power projection, not least in the key choke points, such as the Taiwan Strait, the Strait of Hormuz, and the Suez Canal. For example, in 2016, Russia decided to deploy its *Bal* and *Bastion* missile systems on the Kuriles Islands seized from Japan in 1945 and still claimed by the latter. These systems can fire antiship missiles up to 190 miles. There is no suggestion that vulnerability to such missiles will end, and, based in Kaliningrad, they similarly threaten NATO and Swedish operations in the Baltic. Although longer-range weapons allow ships to project power far inshore (at the same time that they permit coastal defenses to project power far offshore), the smaller number of naval targets, and the greater vulnerability of warships, means that this factor of enhanced range does not balance out limitations to naval capabilities. The recent development by the American navy of an integrated air-defense system is highly necessary. At the same time, ship-based weapons have a valuable flexibility in deployment.

Enhanced antiship weaponry has led to the suggestion that the very nature of naval power has changed, with consequent implications for the ranking of the major naval powers. In particular, whereas air power is dominated by the major powers, notably the United States, the possibility of lesser powers using new technologies to counteract existing advantages is significant. This reflects a long-standing aspiration and practice, for example as seen with the ideas of the French *Jeune École* in the 1880s and of Soviet naval planners in the 1920s. Other powers have also adopted this approach. The extent to which small or unconventional forces may be as effective in their chosen spheres as major navies therefore raises the question whether these spheres can extend in order to deny these navies advantage in large areas or, more plausibly, to make that advantage very costly, not least at a time of rising costs for cutting-edge warships. That is the doctrine that Iran, with its proposed tactic and strategy of asymmetrical swarm attacks, appears to be pursuing. The assertion of naval power in this fashion is frequently linked to territorial claims, and, as with other asymmetrical means, it complicates the established military hierarchy and legacy. Swarm attacks will probably be countered by increasing the artillery capacity of warships so that they can sustain a high rate of fire without their barrels overheating or their ammunition running out.

In most states, navies have far less political clout than armies and play a smaller role in national self-image. This is the case, for example, of Turkey, Iran, India, Israel, Pakistan, and Thailand. Yet issues of military need and power politics complicate such situations, as with Iran. For example, the quest for a regional political role judged commensurate to its population size, economic development, resource concerns, and political pretensions will continue to ensure that India seeks naval security and strength. Indeed, India issued a maritime security document, *Freedom to Use the Seas: Indian Maritime Military Strategy*, in 2007 and followed it in 2015 with *Ensuring Secure Seas: Indian Maritime Security Strategy*.[8]

Warships provide the ability both to act at a distance and closer in, notably in establishing blockades, as with Israel and Sri Lanka, and with international powers blockading North Korea. Israel used its navy to stop the movement of military supplies to the Gaza Strip, and Sri Lanka to prevent supplies from reaching the insurgent Tamil Tigers. Such activity will continue. These blockades include reconnaissance and action by air.

There is, and will continue to be, an important contrast between the extent (and possible future extension) of national jurisdiction over the seas, a jurisdiction that covered more than a third of their extent in 2016, and the fact that many states cannot ensure their own maritime security. This is the case, in particular, for the Pacific, the Caribbean, and Indian Ocean states such as Mauritius, the Maldives, and the Seychelles. These weaknesses encourage the major powers to maintain naval strength and intervene, but they have also led to initiatives for regional solutions, such as that supported by India in the Indian Ocean from 2007.

There are therefore a number of potential levels of naval asymmetry, with Russia and China posing the topmost toward the United States. Moreover, the possibility of making advantages and advances in naval capability, notably but not only those enjoyed by the leading naval powers, too costly for them to employ is enhanced by the extent to which, exacerbated by often poor project management and uncertain tasking,[9] the procurement structure of naval power has driven leading navies toward fewer, more expensive vessels.[10] For example, each of the new British D-class Type 45 destroyers, the first of which was launched in 2006, has more antiaircraft firepower than the combined fleet of eight Type 42 destroyers they replaced, destroyers which came into service from 1975. This is because the missile system of the D class can track and attack multiple incoming aircraft and missiles. However, because there are fewer, the maintenance in service of each such vessel thus becomes more significant, and this enhances their vulnerability, irrespective of the specific weapons characteristics of these vessels and their likely opponents. The availability of fewer, larger, and more expensive warships reduces their individual vulnerability but makes each loss more serious, and thus makes them harder to risk, which is the biggest constraint on the American *Zumwalt*-class destroyer. A similar process has affected aircraft. The antisubmarine and antiship defense of these ships requires improvement.

The financial situation helped drive American military retrenchment in the 2010s. Military spending fell with the end of the American military commitment in Iraq and its run-down in Afghanistan. The size of the accumulated debt and of the annual deficit had an impact, as did the political preference, notably under the Obama administration (2009–17), for welfare expenditure. The defense budget fell sharply from 5.3 percent of GDP in 2009 to 3.6 percent in 2015.[11] The predicted defense budgets, $595 billion in 2015–16 and $607 billion in 2020–21, represented a fall from 3.2 percent of GDP to 2.8 percent. In contrast, that of China was predicted to increase from $191 billion to $260 billion in that period, although all figures for Chinese military expenditure, and notably into the future, are highly problematic. The Stockholm International Peace Research Institute reported in April 2016 that global military spending in 2015 exceeded $11.7 trillion (£1.2 trillion), with the United States cutting its spending by 2.4 percent, although still accounting for over a third of the total. China, Saudi Arabia, Russia, Britain, India, France, Japan, Germany, and South Korea, in order, were the other top spenders.

While the American army and marines were scheduled for significant cuts in the 2010s, there were even more substantial ones in the navy. It is scheduled to be reduced to 280 vessels, of which only about 90 will be at sea at any one time. Given the deficiencies of the LCS (littoral combat ship), which in the fleet are popularly known as "little crappy ships," it is clear that too much was demanded of a single platform, leading to weakness in all combat areas, as with mine clearing. The designation for the modified and enhanced versions has changed to FF (Fast Frigate). The plan, as announced in January 2015, was to take the last twenty LCSs produced (originally there were meant to be fifty-two of them, a number reduced to forty in 2015) and "up-gun" them by adding long-range antiship cruise missiles, enhancing the armor protection, and improving the sensor systems. By going to this version and making it an FF, the warship becomes a different type with better war-at-sea capabilities. It also gets away from the very poor LCS reputation for unreliability, lack of mission capability, and design and manufacturing faults, notably bimetallic corrosion.

Partly as a result of weaknesses, the ability of the United States to inflict a rapid defeat on Iran was called into question in 2013–15 at a time of confrontation over Iran's nuclear plans. Moreover, the reduction in American naval strength created great concern among regional allies worried about Chinese naval plans and expansionism, notably Australia and Japan. On the other hand, the American navy has supported the development of new designs, including the *Virginia*-class nuclear submarine and *Blackwing*, an aerial drone that can be launched underwater from a submarine. Finances and costs are also issues for other states, leading to questions about the viability of bold plans for new warships. This was the case for states hit by falling oil prices including Russia and Saudi Arabia, although China benefits from this fall. The British 2015 *Strategic Defence and Security Review* envisaged the two new carriers, as well as eight new global combat ships and nineteen other frigates and destroyers, but the navy was told it would have to wait until 2021 for its new Type 26 frigates (at over eight thousand tons, a very big frigate) and the mid-2030s for any more "general-purpose frigates."

The net effect is to introduce a volatility to naval power that is greater than the situation during the Cold War, a volatility that challenges maritime security at the level of state power. This volatility is not indicated if the emphasis is on the strength of the leading navy and its new weapon systems, for example the American Aegis BMD (ballistic-missile defense) system intended to engage missiles in flight[12] and the gun, known as a "railgun," being developed to propel a projectile using an electromagnetic effect.

These are examples of weapons systems that are not specific to navies, but for which they provide platforms and that can be very useful for them. Thus, in May 2016, aircraft from the American carrier *Harry S. Truman*, then in the Persian Gulf, launched apparently effective cyberattacks on ISIS targets. So also with drones. In May 2013, an X-47B drone took off and landed on a carrier, the *George H. W. Bush*. Researchers sought to teach drones to follow human gestures so that they would be able to respond to the directions of deck handlers. One of the potential future options for the carrier is as a kind of mother ship for a fleet of unmanned fighters that are controlled by the mother ship close by so as to avoid the risk of the jamming or destruction of control satellites. The use of drones to hunt submarines is attracting attention.

Developing technologies, such as electromagnetic discharge defenses and electric drive will require a new class of naval vessel.[13] There will probably be a greater emphasis for the American navy on surface ships and submarines firing missiles rather than on carriers. The navy's Aegis system is central to the global missile defense capability announced by the United States in 2009. Under this, American warships equipped with this system were deployed from 2011, first the *Monterey* to the Mediterranean. As an instance of the range of what naval power and warfare might entail, China is discussing the construction of floating nuclear power plants in order to supply electric power to its new positions in the South China Sea. These reactor ships become a support for territorial presence but also pose a threat of ecological disaster through conflict or accident.

Naval power is broad ranging and multipurpose. This range will be enhanced by competition over resources, as many of these untapped resources are offshore and linked to rival territorial claims. At sea, therefore, we are moving rapidly from the apparent unipolarity of the 1990s, the supposed "end of history," to a situation in which the capacity to display, use, and contest strength is significant to a large number of powers and to their rivals. That spread of capacity does not automatically lead to conflict, for the processes of international relations will be employed to seek to lessen tension. However, insecurity, especially in the sense of an absence of confidence that deterrence will be successfully employed, has become more apparent, a process that will continue. Moreover, this insecurity will probably provide more opportunities for nonstate actors, notably smugglers, pirates, and terrorist groups, keen to use the seas in order to pursue particular interests that create another level of insecurity.

The power of the human imagination offers key guides to hopes and fears about the future. In his novel *20,000 Leagues under the Sea* (1870), the French writer Jules Verne introduced the *Nautilus*, a formidable submarine, indeed described as a possible "nuclear"-powered submarine. In the James Bond film *The Spy Who Loved Me* (1977), a film in no way based on the Ian Fleming novel of that name, the villain, Karl Stromberg, proposed to use nuclear missiles fired from captured British and Soviet submarines, "the instruments of Armageddon," in order to cause a world war that would end human life other than in bases under the sea such as his own. It is unclear what the future will bring, but its nature at sea will continue to be a source of speculation and planning.

Chapter Eleven

Conclusions

The continuing significance of naval power and warfare emerges repeatedly in this book and continues to be the case at present. It would be inaccurate and unhelpful to labor these points at the expense of warfare on land and capability in the air. However, that approach is not necessary. In each case, there was both explicit and implicit cooperation, whether strategic, operational, or tactical, between naval and non-naval capabilities. Aside from synergies, there was also a more profound sense that there was not a zero-sum game (growth or advantage only at the expense of others) in terms of capability. The idea of a zero-sum game might be suggested by differences and clashes in procurement; by contrasts, or at least lacunae, in doctrine; and, most clearly, by the explicit adoption of asymmetric goals and means. Nevertheless, it was also possible to pursue comparable and parallel capability enhancement.

At the same time, both to their advantage and to their detriment, navies were affected by a major reworking of the battle space, thanks in particular to the transformation of range through aircraft and missiles and the integration of sensor and firing systems. As warships were units that could serve as the base, as well as the target, for these weapon systems, so there was not the obsolescence that at times seemed apparent to some commentators. Nevertheless, the length of time it takes to bring new naval projects to completion led to a measure of obsolescence. Whereas, in the early twentieth century, battleships could be designed and built within three years, now it can take up to fifteen years. And in that period, technology and anticipated needs and purposes can change. The recent history of British carriers offers a good example. This leads to the question of how best to produce a navy fit for purpose at the point at which such ships with a long gestation come into commission. How to build adaptability to changing circumstances into a fleet is a key issue. More generally, technology is both a driver and a lagging indicator of competition.

The high cost of cutting-edge warships poses a related problem, and one exacerbated by the extent to which current naval planners do not have much investment leverage or operational experience on which to call. This cost was not to the fore for the navies that acted as coastal protection systems or, at least in practice, gestures, but it became more apparent in the 2000s and, even more, 2010s. Ironically, the general expansion of the world economy meant that more resources were available for purchasing warships, as was seen in the East and Southeast Asian naval arms race in the 2000s and 2010s. Nevertheless, the rise in the price of cutting-edge warships was such that the overall cost of naval power and of its maintenance were key factors. The willingness to spend money was also affected by the extent to which it proved difficult for the United States, the leading naval power, to cost properly its ability to match demand for deterrence through credible combat power with what it could reliably and viably supply. This was, and is, a key problem of capability given America's global commitments, but anyway a problem that is difficult to address with concrete policies.

Related to these commitments, the likely future trajectory of Chinese naval ambitions and power is currently an (if not the most) important question for commentators focused on naval power politics, a process encouraged by the Chinese announcement in May 2016 about intended capabilities. That itself is a clear instance of the continuing relevance of naval strength. Navies have proved successful in combining the cutting-edge, apocalyptic lethality of nuclear weaponry with the ability to wield power successfully at the subnuclear level, an ability that, due to the number of weapons systems, entails combined-arms naval operations.[1] Moreover, this ability is underlined by the range, scale, and persistence of naval power, all of which provide, alongside the tactical and operational advantages offered by combination with air or land units, a strategic capability not matched by the other branches. Despite aerial refueling, air power lacks the continuous presence, and thus persistence and durability, that warships can convey. Furthermore, operating against coastal targets, warships offer firepower and an obvious visual presence that is more impressive than that of many armies. More generally, navies, including naval aviation and marines, tend to have an inbuilt flexibility that provides an edge over slower-to-adapt armies and air forces.

There is a tendency with naval history to approach it in terms of "internal factors," relating, more particularly, to the sources generated by admiralties and to specific issues to do with warships and with their operations in war. These elements are clearly crucial, but they can lead to an underplaying of the wider contexts of naval power. These contexts range from geopolitical problems and political needs to ideological commitments and cultural assumptions.[2] When decisions on procurement, doctrine, tasks, and manning are considered in detail, then the influence of these contextual factors can generally be appreciated. Suggestions for this influence do not solely come from navalists. For example, in 1939, General Sir John Dill, the commander of the British Expeditionary Force's First Corps, then based in France, referred to his troops' response to the British naval victory over the German *Graf Spee* in the battle of the River Plate: "They were all very cheered by the naval successes. It is remarkable how Britain reacts to naval news—it is in the blood."[3]

There are, however, several caveats. There is the danger of reifying proposed cultural factors. There are also source issues. The evidence for the impact of these contextual influences is frequently limited, and the influence was often indirect. Moreover, ministers, politicians, and others were not obliged to explain their intentions or reasons at length, or even at all. As a result, the factors affecting them tend to be underplayed, and notably so if they do not involve military affairs. For example, the role, in the 1900s, of alternative commitments in terms of social welfare payments, notably in the shape of old-age pensions, can be underplayed when there is discussion of the purpose and chronology of British naval developments in the decade before the outbreak of the First World War. At the same time, social welfare and other policies were seen as a way to strengthen society and lessen discontent so that Britain was better prepared in the event of conflict: the range of defense preparations was far from simply military, and strategy and policy should be considered accordingly.

Similar factors were to recur in Britain after the Second World War and may be seen, albeit in different forms, in both America and Britain in recent responses to discussion about defense budgets. This bald summary can, and should, be further refined and contextualized. If this can be readily done by scholars and others for states with the same language as they have, it can be far harder for other states. Indeed, there is a tendency in those cases to focus on relatively schematic accounts of policy and causation. Reasons of space further encourage this for synoptic works. However, this process can lead to a simplification of naval history, one in which the contextual account is made unduly easy, and, in particular, there is often an unproblematic account of national interests. The focus can be on the sharp (or fighting) end unduly, and not on how it was conceptualized and understood. It is the latter that deserves more attention, both in research and in teaching.

Whatever the approach, it is important to appreciate the losses involved. Richard Osborne, a boy seaman, described the damage to the bridge of the *Prince of Wales* from a shell from the *Bismarck* in May 1941: "The first thing I saw . . . were just little bits of flesh spattered all around."[4] And that was for a warship that, unlike the *Hood*, survived the encounter only to be sunk that December.[5]

The maritime dimension to global history is not the same as a history of naval warfare. The warfare tends to crowd out the former subject, but, in many respects, it is relevant as an aspect of this maritime dimension. In particular, it is important to understand naval activity in the context of the structures and dynamics of the maritime dimension. This is readily apparent when commerce interdiction and, therefore, protection have been key themes of this activity. Indeed, from that perspective, the essential unity to the period is provided not by the nature of warships, more especially from the ironclads on to the present, but, instead, that of the great expansion of international maritime trade from the mid-nineteenth century to the present. This expansion was not the product of naval factors except insofar as British dominance helped mean that there was no naval conflict able to harm trade. Instead, free trade and industrial development were more significant.

There was an important technological element to the expansion, especially with the steam power and iron construction also seen with warships. In addition, however, there were a range of other factors that do not focus on the particular nature of shipping, a topic that can assume a disproportionate share in naval history. These factors included the economic expansion in the West that led to rising per capita wealth at a time of growing population, the practice of sourcing raw materials from a great distance, the availability of plentiful investment to finance the expansion of merchant fleets (as well as rising taxation to finance warships), the integration of trade with railways and port facilities, the major growth of port cities, and the relative spread of free trade, especially in, and as a result of, the British Empire. The extent and pace of globalization were unprecedented.[6]

The massive expansion of trade was particularly important to the British Empire but was also significant for all major economies, and notably if they had far-flung imperial possessions, as well as for societies under pressure from globalization. Moreover, the nature of vitalist ideas and the positive intellectual values attached to free trade were such that, aside from its crucial role as an enabler of economic activity, trade, and especially international trade, was very much seen in a positive light. There was a major expansion in overland trade, notably as long-distance railways were opened and as the railway net became more widespread. However, this process was far from comprehensive. It was particularly seen in North America, northern Asia and parts of Europe, Russia, India, Japan, Australasia, and Argentina but was much less widespread in Africa, Southwest and Southeast Asia, and tropical South America. Furthermore, much of this trade was within countries.

In contrast, maritime trade was more comprehensive as far as oceans and seas were concerned. This comprehensiveness increased as a result of technological, organizational, and intellectual developments, notably the greater ease of working ships inshore thanks to steam power, the systematic charting of waters, and the dissemination of the resulting material. Furthermore, these elements extended to major rivers, thus further expanding maritime trade. People also moved long distances primarily by sea.

Technological changes subsequently complicated the situation, notably the rapid improvement in the specifications of motor vehicles and the possibilities of air travel. Yet neither had as transformative an impact for maritime trade as had been suggested. Air freight only proved viable for high-value goods, while containerization improved the economics of maritime freight, as well as of rail, the two frequently being linked in integrated transport systems.

These changes had, and continue to have, implications for the use of maritime force. This is true both of unofficial force, in the shape of piracy and smuggling, and also of official force. Again, the focus for the latter tends to be on large warships and major navies. However, in practice, much of the trade protection is against criminal activity and is carried out by maritime policing agencies, notably coast guards and customs, and by navies, naval units, and supporting aircraft that can be seen principally as coast guards, however they are designated. There is scant sign that this will change or that, in related matters, the maritime dimension to global history will alter. Much of the world's population and power will continue to reside in, and focus on, coastal and littoral regions, not least because much of the flat and fertile land is in such regions. Conversely, the extent and distribution of population growth are such that much of this growth is occurring and will occur in areas that are distant from the sea. Their population may depend economically on maritime links, but there is no necessary understanding of this element.

The public-order implications of unprecedented population growth focus on land forces, both regular and paramilitary, and COIN (counterinsurgency) issues, both doctrine and training, have all assumed great significance since the Cold War ended. With the exception of piracy, this focus has led to an underplaying of the maritime dimension. Nevertheless, in practice, naval air power and marines have both been conspicuously and persistently present in most American and British counterinsurgency operations. Moreover, blockade, commercial interdiction, and their prevention are aspects of COIN and will become more so as food availability is regarded as a pressing issue. Yet, for large-scale disturbances linked to control over fresh water or land distribution, the maritime sphere will be less directly relevant.

That trade control and protection, hydrographic knowledge,[7] and naval power politics can be close is very clear in the case of those linked to the East and South China Seas and to the Persian Gulf. That approach to these issues underlines the extent to which naval tasking is far from uniform or symmetrical, indeed far from either. Again, this will remain the case in the future and will provide a particular strand to political revisionism as far as the naval sphere is concerned. So far, revisionism has been directed against the strongest naval power, first Britain and then the United States. Nevertheless, there is no necessity for this to be the equation, and notably so at the regional level. Thus, China, as a revisionist power, may eventually benefit from being the strongest naval power, not just regionally but even possibly globally. The latter outcome currently may appear unlikely, and foreign commentators are happy to draw attention to deficiencies in Chinese maritime skills.

However, it is unclear how the relationships of economic strength, fiscal solvency, and military priorities will develop in China and elsewhere. As the discussion of maritime trade makes clear, there is a feedback mechanism linked to the value and values derived from trade. The role of values is especially interesting because it matches a particular trend in the literature toward focusing on the values linked not only to naval power but also to particular ship types and naval methods,[8] as well as the more general interest in the cultural dimensions of warfare and of military preparedness.

These cultural dimensions extend to national stereotypes, which can frequently be condescending and misleading, but nevertheless potent. Thus, from a recent novel, "La Ciotat is an old fishing village enlivened by an important French naval shipbuilding yard—if you can use words like important in the same sentence as the French Navy."[9] In naval stereotypes, the Second World War has remained dominant in visual and literary images. Films proved particularly influential at the time. To take American films, submarines were important in *Destination Tokyo* (1943), while *Action in the North Atlantic* (1943) showed a Murmansk-bound convoy, and *The Fighting Seabees* (1944) the marines. These priorities continued thereafter, as in *Run Silent, Run Deep* (1958), an American film about submarine warfare. The focus on surface units can be seen with *Battleship* (2012), which presents the American navy (and the world) as saved by an old *Iowa*-class battleship which was made ready and crewed by retired sailors visiting the museum ship. The film shows a good working cooperation between the American and Japanese navies against an alien enemy described as North Korean or Chinese.

The value and values derived from trade overlap as well as contrast with the emphasis on control to, over, and from the water, as essential, and essentially, aspects of military strategy in struggles between states. This emphasis on control remains central to naval history, but possibly without due consideration to the range of issues in, and means of, contention, and again the extent to which decisive battle is not therefore the key theme in naval history. The absence of such battles since 1944 is readily notable. That, however, does not mean that there has been no naval history of consequence. Instead, as with the period from 1872 to 1913, there is, since 1944, rapid technological change, but no naval conflict between the leading naval powers. Where that will lead is unclear. There is no reason to believe that, because the outcome in 1914 was a major war, the denouement will be the same again.

Notes

1. THE AGE OF THE IRONCLAD, 1860–80

1. Sir Charles Napier to George Villiers, 4th Earl of Clarendon, British foreign secretary, May 26, 1857, NA, FO 5/671, fols. 192–94.

2. Howard Fuller, *Empire, Technology and Seapower: Royal Navy Crisis in the Age of Palmerston* (Abingdon: Routledge, 2014).

3. Andrew Lambert, "Responding to the Nineteenth Century: The Royal Navy and the Introduction of the Screw Propeller," *History of Technology* 21 (1999): 1–28; Charles Iain Hamilton, *Anglo-French Naval Rivalry, 1840–1870* (Oxford: Clarendon Press, 1993).

4. General Sir John Burgoyne, British inspector general of fortifications, memorandum, 1856, BL, Add. 41410, fol. 2.

5. Henry, 3rd Viscount Palmerston, prime minister, to John, Earl Russell, foreign secretary, August 11, 1861, NA, 30/22/21, fol. 527.

6. Alexandre Sheldon-Duplaix, "French Naval Intelligence during the Second Empire: Charles Pigeard Reporting on British and American Shipbuilding (1856–69)," *Mariner's Mirror* 94 (November 2008): 406–19.

7. David Brown, *Before the Ironclad: Ship Design, Propulsion, and Armament in the Royal Navy, 1815–60* (London: Conway Maritime Press, 1990).

8. Andrew Lambert, "'I Will Not Have a War with France': Deterrence, Diplomacy and Mid-Victorian Politics," in *HMS Warrior: 150th Anniversary*, ed. Andrew Baines (Portsmouth: Friends of HMS Warrior, 2011), 19–34.

9. Andrew Lambert, "Politics, Technology and Policy-Making, 1859–1865: Palmerston, Gladstone and the Management of the Ironclad Naval Race," *Northern Mariner* 8 (July 1998): 9–38.

10. Jan Martin Lemnitzer, *Power, Law and the End of Privateering* (Basingstoke: Palgrave, 2014).

11. Dwight Hughes, *A Confederate Biography: The Cruise of the CSS Shenandoah* (Annapolis, MD: Naval Institute Press, 2015).

12. Craig Symonds, *Lincoln and His Admirals: Abraham Lincoln, the U.S. Navy, and the Civil War* (Oxford: Oxford University Press, 2008).

13. Stephen Wise, *Gate of Hell: Campaign for Charleston Harbor, 1863* (Columbia: University of South Carolina Press, 1994).

14. Robert Browning, *Lincoln's Trident: The West Gulf Blockading Squadron during the Civil War* (Tuscaloosa: University of Alabama Press, 2015).

15. Earl Hess, *Civil War in the West: Victory and Defeat from the Appalachians to the Mississippi* (Chapel Hill: University of North Carolina Press, 2012).

16. Howard Fuller, *Clad in Iron: The American Civil War and the Challenge of British Naval Power* (Westport, CT: Praeger, 2008).

17. Niels Eichhorn, "North Atlantic Trade in the Mid-Nineteenth Century: A Case for Peace during the American Civil War," *Civil War History* 61 (2015): 138–72; Marc-William Palen, *The "Conspiracy" of Free Trade: The Anglo-American Struggle over Empire and Economic Globalisation, 1846–1896* (Cambridge: Cambridge University Press, 2016).

18. Up to 1918, Austria throughout refers to the Austro-Hungarian Empire.

19. Lawrence Sondhaus, *The Habsburg Empire and the Sea: Austrian Naval Policy, 1797–1866* (West Lafayette, IN: Purdue University Press, 1989).

20. Lord John Russell to Peter Scarlett, envoy in Greece, September 2, November 12, 1863, NA, 30/22/108, fols. 63, 69.

21. Jonathan Coad, *Support for the Fleet: Architecture and Engineering of the Royal Navy's Bases, 1700–1914* (Swindon: English Heritage, 2013).

22. John Beeler, *British Naval Policy in the Gladstone-Disraeli Era, 1866–1880* (Stanford, CA: Stanford University Press, 1997).

23. Brian Holden Reid, "Power, Sovereignty and the Great Republic: Anglo-American Diplomatic Relations in the Era of the Civil War," *Diplomacy and Statecraft* 14 (2003): 45–72; Jay Sexton, "The Funded Loans and the *Alabama* Claims," *Diplomatic History* 27 (2003): 449–78.

24. Bruce Farcau, *The Ten Cents War: Chile, Peru and Bolivia in the War of the Pacific* (Westport, CT: Praeger, 2000); William Sater, *Andean Tragedy: Fighting the War of the Pacific, 1879–1884* (Lincoln: University of Nebraska Press, 2007).

25. Richard, 2nd Lord Lyons, British envoy in Washington, to John, 1st Earl Russell, January 12, 1864, NA, FO 5/943, fols. 33–34.

26. Thomas Kennedy, *The Arms of Kiangnan: Modernization in the Chinese Ordnance Industry, 1860–1895* (Boulder, CO: Westview Press, 1978); David Pong, *Shen Pao-chen and China's Modernization in the Nineteenth Century* (Cambridge: Cambridge University Press, 1994).

2. NAVAL DREAMS AND RACES, 1880–1913

1. Robin Prior and Trevor Wilson, "Conflict, Technology and the Impact of Industrialisation: The Great War, 1914–18," *Journal of Strategic Studies* 24 (2001): 128–57.

2. Charles Stephenson, *A Box of Sand: The Italo-Ottoman War, 1911–1912* (Ticehurst, East Sussex: Tattered Flag, 2014), 182–83.

3. Katherine Epstein, *Torpedo: Inventing the Military-Industrial Complex in the United States and Great Britain* (Cambridge, MA: Harvard University Press, 2014).

4. Jan Glete, "John Ericsson and the Transformation of Swedish Naval Doctrine," *International Journal of Naval History* 2 (2003): 14.

5. Arne Røksund, *The Jeune École: The Strategy of the Weak* (Leiden: Brill, 2007), 227; Theodore Ropp, *The Development of a Modern Navy: French Naval Policy, 1871–1904* (Annapolis, MD: Naval Institute Press, 1987).

6. Herbert Wilson, *Ironclads in Action: A Sketch of Naval Warfare from 1855 to 1895* (London: Sampson Low, Marston & Co., 1896); William Laird Clowes, *Four Modern Naval Campaigns: Historical, Strategical and Tactical* (London: Unit Library, 1902).

7. Mary Clabaugh Wright, *The Last Stand of Chinese Conservatism: The T'ung-chih Restoration, 1862–1874* (Stanford, CA: Stanford University Press, 1957), 59–66.

8. Terrell Gottschall, *By Order of the Kaiser: Otto von Diedrichs and the Rise of the Imperial German Navy, 1865–1902* (Annapolis, MD: Naval Institute Press, 2003).

9. Patrick Kelly, "Tirpitz and the Origins of the German Torpedo Arm, 1877–1889," in *New Interpretations in Naval History*, ed. Robert Love et al. (Annapolis, MD: Naval Institute Press, 2001), 219–49.

10. C. Martin, "The Complexity of Strategy: 'Jackie' Fisher and the Trouble with Submarines," *Journal of Military History* 75 (2011): 448–49, 469.

11. Shawn Grimes, "Combined Operations and British Strategy, 1900–9," *Historical Research*, doi:10.1111/1468-2281.12136.

12. Robert Seager, *Alfred Thayer Mahan: The Man and His Letters* (Annapolis, MD: Naval Institute Press, 1977); Richard Tuck, *The Ambiguous Relationship: Theodore Roosevelt and Alfred Thayer Mahan* (Westport, CT: Greenwood, 1987); John Kuehn, "What Was Mahan Really Saying? A Re-visitation of the Naval Theorist's Classic Work, *The Influence of Sea Power upon History, 1660–1783*," *US Military History Review* 1, no. 1 (December 2014): 66–80; Thomas Varacalli, "National Interest and Moral Responsibility in the Political Thought of Admiral Alfred Thayer Mahan," *NWCR* 69 (2016): 108–27.

13. Geoffrey Till, "Corbett and the Emergence of a British School?," in *The Development of British Naval Thinking*, ed. Geoffrey Till (Abingdon: Routledge, 2006), 65–88.

14. Suzanne Geissler, *God and Sea Power: The Influence of Religion on Alfred Thayer Mahan* (Annapolis, MD: Naval Institute Press, 2015).

15. Roger Parkinson, *The Late Victorian Navy: The Pre-Dreadnought Era and the Origins of the First World War* (Woodbridge, Suffolk: Boydell and Brewer, 2008); Robert E. Mullins, *The Transformation of British and American Naval Policy in the Pre-Dreadnought Era: Ideas, Culture and Strategy* (Basingstoke: Palgrave Macmillan, 2016). I have benefited greatly from the advice of John Beeler.

16. Norman Friedman, *British Cruisers of the Victorian Era* (Barnsley, South Yorkshire: Seaforth Publishing, 2012).

17. Donald Schurman, *Imperial Defence, 1868–1887*, edited by John Beeler (London: Frank Cass, 2000).

18. Robert Johnson, "The Penjdeh Incident, 1885," *Archives* 24 (April 1999): 28–48, esp. 28, 44; King's College London, Liddell Hart Archive, Hamilton papers, 1/3/3.

19. Arthur Marder, *The Anatomy of British Sea Power: A History of British Naval Policy in the Pre-Dreadnought Era, 1880–1905* (New York: Putnam, 1940), 578–80.

20. Jim Leeke, *Manila and Santiago: The New Steel Navy in the Spanish-American War* (Annapolis, MD: Naval Institute Press, 2009); Derek Granger, "Dewey at Manila Bay: Lessons in Operational Art and Operational Leadership," *NWCR* 64, no. 4 (Autumn 2011): 127–37.

21. Kaveh Farrokh, *Iran at War, 1500–1988* (Oxford: Osprey, 2011), 218–19, 232.

22. Gordon Chang, "Whose 'Barbarism'? Whose 'Treachery'? Race and Civilization in the Unknown United States-Korea War of 1871," *Journal of American History* 89 (2003): 1331–65.

23. Neil Dukas, *A Military History of Sovereign Hawai'i* (Honolulu, HI: Mutual Publishing, 2004), 147–64.

24. Jon Sumida, "The Quest for Reach: The Development of Long-Range Gunnery in the Royal Navy, 1901–12," in *Tooling for War: Military Transformation in the Industrial Age*, ed. Stephen Chiabotti (Chicago: Imprint Publications, 1996), 49–96.

25. Matthew Seligmann, "The Anglo-German Naval Race, 1898–1914," in *Arms Races in International Politics*, ed. Thomas Mahnken, Joseph Maiolo, and David Stevenson (Oxford: Oxford University Press, 2016), 21–40.

26. Matthew Seligmann, ed., *Naval Intelligence from Germany: The Reports of the British Naval Attaché in Berlin, 1906–1914* (London: Navy Records Society, 2007).

27. Crosbie Smith, "*Dreadnought* Science: The Cultural Construction of Efficiency and Effectiveness," in *The "Dreadnought" and the Edwardian Age*, ed. Andrew Lambert, Robert Blyth, and Jan Rüger (Aldershot: Ashgate, 2011), 135–64.

28. Adrian Preston, "Wolseley, the Khartoum Relief Expedition and the Defence of India 1885–1900," *International History Review* 2 (1980): 239–67.

29. Jan Rüger, *The Great Naval Game: Britain and Germany in the Age of Empire* (Cambridge: Cambridge University Press, 2007); Dirk Bönker, *Militarism in a Global Age: Naval Ambitions in Germany and the United States before World War I* (Ithaca, NY: Cornell University Press, 2012); Hazel Bird, "Naval History and Heroes: The Influence of U.S. and British Navalism on Children's Writing, 1895–1914," *International Journal of Naval History* 11, no. 1 (July 2014), http://www.ijnhonline.org.

30. "Precis of the Development of German Maritime Interests in the Last Decade," 1 January 1906, NA, FO 368/22.

31. Matthew Seligmann, Frank Nägel, and Michael Epkenhans, eds., *The Naval Route to the Abyss: The Anglo-German Naval Race 1895–1915* (Farnham: Ashgate for the Navy Records Society, 2015).

32. Matthew Seligmann, "New Weapons for New Targets: Sir John Fisher, the Threat from Germany and the Building of HMS *Dreadnought* and HMS *Invincible*, 1902–1907," *International History Review* 30 (2008): 325, and *The Royal Navy and the German Threat 1901–1914: Admiralty Plans to Protect British Trade in a War against Germany* (Oxford: Oxford University Press, 2012).

33. For different views, see Nicholas Lambert, "Righting the Scholarship: The Battle-Cruiser in History and Historiography," *Historical Journal* 58 (2015): 275–307, and Matthew Seligmann, "Germany's Ocean Greyhounds and the Royal Navy's First Battle Cruisers: An Historiographical Problem," *Diplomacy and Statecraft* 27 (2016): 162–82.

34. Jon Sumida, "A Matter of Timing: The Royal Navy and the Tactics of Decisive Battle, 1912–1916," *Journal of Military History* 67 (2003): 85–136, esp. 131–33.

35. Steve McLaughlin, "Battlelines and Fast Wings: Battlefleet Tactics in the Royal Navy, 1900–1914," *Journal of Strategic Studies* 38, no. 7 (2015): 985–1005.

36. Stephen Cobb, *Preparing for Blockade, 1885–1914: Naval Contingency for Economic Warfare* (Farnham: Ashgate, 2013).

37. David Morgan-Owen, "'Cooked up in the Dinner Hour'? Sir Arthur Wilson's War Plan, Reconsidered," *English Historical Review* 130 (2015): 865–906.

38. Andrew Lambert, "The Tory World View: Sea Power, Strategy and Party Politics, 1815–1914," in *The Tory World: Deep History and the Tory Theme in British Foreign Policy, 1679–2014*, ed. Jeremy Black (Farnham: Ashgate, 2015), 144–48; Rhodri Williams, *Defending the Empire: The Conservative Party and British Defence Policy, 1899–1915* (New Haven, CT: Yale University Press, 1991).

39. Patrick Kelly, *Tirpitz and the Imperial German Navy* (Bloomington: Indiana University Press, 2011); Dirk Bönker, "Global Politics and Germany's Destiny 'from an East Asian Perspective': Alfred Von Tirpitz and the Making of Wilhelmine Navalism," *Central European History* 46 (2013): 61–96.

40. John Maurer, "Averting the Great War? Churchill's Naval Holiday," *NWCR* 67, no. 3 (Summer 2014): 25–42.

41. David Stevens, *In All Respects Ready: Australia's Navy in World War One* (Melbourne: Oxford University Press, 2014); Christopher Bell, "Sentiment vs. Strategy: British Naval Policy, Imperial Defence, and the Development of Dominion Navies, 1911–14," *International History Review* 37 (2015): 262–81; Jesse Tumblin, "'Grey Dawn' in the British Pacific: Race, Security, and Colonial Sovereignty on the Eve of World War I," *Britain and the World* 9 (2016): 32–54.

42. Jon Hendrickson, *Crisis in the Mediterranean: Naval Competition and Great Power Politics, 1904–1914* (Annapolis, MD: Naval Institute Press, 2014).

43. Tony Demchat, "Rebuilding the Russian Fleet: The Duma and Naval Rearmament, 1907–1914," *Journal of Slavic Military Studies* 26 (2013): 25–40.

44. Dirk Bönker, *Militarism in a Global Age: Naval Ambitions in Germany and the United States before World War I* (Ithaca, NY: Cornell University Press, 2012).

45. Mark Shulman, *Navalism and the Emergence of American Sea Power, 1882–1893* (Annapolis, MD: Naval Institute Press, 1995); James Rentfrow, *Home Squadron: The US Navy on the North Atlantic Station* (Annapolis, MD: Naval Institute Press, 2014).

46. Benjamin Cooling, *Gray Steel and Blue Water Navy: The Formative Years of America's Military-Industrial Complex, 1881–1917* (Hamden, CT: Shoe String Press, 1979); Robert E. Mullins, *The Transformation of British and American Naval Policy in the Pre-Dreadnought Era: Ideas, Culture and Strategy* (Basingstoke: Palgrave Macmillan, 2016).

47. Henry J. Hendrix, *Theodore Roosevelt's Naval Diplomacy: The U.S. Navy and the Birth of the American Century* (Annapolis, MD: Naval Institute Press, 2009).

48. William McBride, "Strategic Determinism in Technology Selection: The Electric Battleship and US Naval-Industrial Relations," *Technology and Culture* 33 (1992): 249.

49. Steven Topik, *Trade and Gunboats: The United States and Brazil in the Age of Empire* (Stanford, CA: Stanford University Press, 1996), 145–54.

50. Jason Smith, "'Twixt the Devil and the Deep Blue Sea: Hydrography, Sea Power, and the Marine Environment, 1898–1901," *Journal of Military History* 78 (2014): 602.

51. Katherine Epstein, "No One Can Afford to Say 'Damn the Torpedoes': Battle Tactics and U.S. Naval History before World War I," *Journal of Military History* 77 (2013): 491–520.

52. Stephen Stein, *From Torpedoes to Aviation: Washington Irving Chambers and Techno-logical Innovation in the New Navy, 1876–1913* (Tuscaloosa: University of Alabama Press, 2007); William Trimble, *Hero of the Air: Glenn Curtiss and the Birth of Naval Aviation* (Annapolis, MD: Naval Institute Press, 2010).

53. David Morgan-Owen, "An 'Intermediate Blockade'? British North Sea Strategy, 1912–1914," *War in History* 22 (2015): 478–52.

54. Randolph Churchill, *Winston S. Churchill. II: Young Statesman, 1901–1914* (London: Heinemann, 1967), 690–705.

55. Ibid., 691. For Churchill, see Christopher Bell, *Churchill and Sea Power* (Oxford, Ox-ford University Press, 2013).

56. Nicholas Lambert, "Strategic Command and Control for Maneuver Warfare: Creation of the Royal Navy's 'War Room' System, 1905–1915," *Journal of Military History* 69, no. 2 (April 2005): 361–410; Timothy Wolters, *Information at Sea: Shipboard Command and Con-trol in the U.S. Navy from Mobile Bay to Okinawa* (Baltimore, MD: Johns Hopkins University Press, 2013); Michael Clemmesen, "The Royal Navy North Sea War Plan 1907–1914," *Fra krig og fred* 2 (2014): 59–115.

57. Geoffrey Parker, "The *Dreadnought* Revolution of Tudor England," *Mariner's Mirror* 82 (1990): 301–24. For a more judicious discussion, see David Morgan-Owen, "A Revolution in Naval Affairs? Technology, Strategy and British Naval Policy in the 'Fisher Era,'" *Journal of Strategic Studies* 38 (2015): 944–65.

3. THE FIRST WORLD WAR, 1914–18

1. Jonathan Winkler, *Nexus: Strategic Communications and American Security in World War I* (Cambridge, MA: Harvard University Press, 2008).

2. Annika Mombauer, *Helmuth von Moltke and the Origins of the First World War* (Cam-bridge: Cambridge University Press, 2001).

3. Phillip Pattee, *At War in Distant Waters: British Colonial Defence in the Great War* (Annapolis, MD: Naval Institute Press, 2013); John Reeve, "Maritime Strategy 1914: Some Observations on the Issues," in *Maritime Strategy 1914*, ed. Tom Frame (Canberra: Barton Books, 2015), 138–40.

4. Hervé Coutau-Bégarie, "French Naval Strategy: A Naval Power in a Continental Envi-ronment," in *Naval Power in the Twentieth Century*, ed. Nicholas Rodger (Annapolis, MD: Naval Institute Press, 1996), 59–64.

5. Eric Osborne, *The Battle of Heligoland Bight* (Bloomington: Indiana University Press, 2006).

6. James Goldrick, *Before Jutland: The Naval War in Northern European Waters, August 1914–February 1915* (Annapolis, MD: Naval Institute Press, 2015).

7. Tobias Philbin, *Battle of Dogger Bank: The First Dreadnought Engagement, January 1915* (Bloomington: Indiana University Press, 2014).

8. George Nekrasov, *North of Gallipoli: The Black Sea Fleet at War, 1914–1917* (New York: Columbia University Press, 1992).

9. Alan to Edith Thomson, October 7, 1915, Thomson papers, privately owned.

10. Christopher Bell, *Churchill and Sea Power* (Oxford: Oxford University Press, 2013), 73–74.

11. Keith Neilson, "R. H. Brand, the Empire and Munitions from Canada," *English Histori-cal Review* 126 (2011): 1430–55.

12. Gautam Mukunda, "We Cannot Go On: Disruptive Innovation and the First World War Royal Navy," *Security Studies* 19 (2010): 124–59; Greg Kennedy, ed., *The War They Thought, the War They Fought* (Farnham: Ashgate, 2016).

13. John Brooks, *Dreadnought Gunnery and the Battle of Jutland: The Question of Fire Control* (London and New York: Routledge, 2005); Reinhard Scheer, *Germany's High Seas Fleet in the First World War* (Barnsley, South Yorkshire: Frontline Books, 2014).

14. Richard Guilliatt and Peter Hohnen, *The Wolf: How One German Terrorised the Allies in the Most Epic Voyage of World War One* (New York: Free Press, 2010).

15. BL, Add. 49714, fol. 145.

16. BL, Add. 49715, fol. 210.

17. Justus Doenecke, *Nothing Less than War: A New History of America's Entry into World War I* (Lexington: University Press of Kentucky, 2011).

18. Dwight Messimer, *Find and Destroy: Antisubmarine Warfare in World War I* (Annapolis, MD: Naval Institute Press, 2001); Jan Breemer, *Defeating the U-boat: Inventing Antisubmarine Warfare* (Newport, RI: Naval War College Press, 2010).

19. Peter Jackson, "French Security and a British 'Continental Commitment' after the First World War: A Reassessment," *English Historical Review* 126 (2011): 350.

20. David Redvaldsen, "The Role of Britain in Late Modern Norwegian History: A Longitudinal Study," *Britain and the World* 9 (2016): 16.

21. William Still, *Crisis at Sea: The United States Navy in European Waters in World War I* (Gainesville: University Press of Florida, 2007); Michael Simpson, ed., *Anglo-American Naval Relations, 1917–1919* (Aldershot: Naval Records Society, 1991).

22. Daniel Horn, *The German Naval Mutinies of World War One* (New Brunswick, NJ: Rutgers University Press, 1969).

23. BL, Add. 49714, fol. 28.

24. Robert Feuilloy, Lucien Morareau, et al., *L'Aviation maritime française pendant la Grande Guerre* (Paris: Ardhan, 1999), 277–79.

25. Ibid., 210–19.

26. Richard D. Layman, *Naval Aviation in the First World War: Its Impact and Influence* (Annapolis, MD: Naval Institute Press, 1996).

27. Nicholas Black, *The British Naval Staff in the First World War* (Woodbridge: Boydell, 2009); Mike Farquharson-Roberts, *A History of the Royal Navy: World War I* (London: I. B. Tauris, 2014); Lawrence Sondhaus, *The Great War at Sea: A Naval History of the First World War* (Cambridge: Cambridge University Press, 2014); Norman Friedman, *Fighting the Great War at Sea: Strategy, Tactics and Technology* (Annapolis, MD: Naval Institute Press, 2014).

28. Duncan Redford, *The Submarine: A Cultural History from the Great War to Nuclear Combat* (London: I. B. Tauris, 2010).

29. Jan Glete, "Naval Power and Warfare 1815–2000," in *War in the Modern World since 1815*, ed. Jeremy Black (London: Routledge, 2003), 228.

4. AFTERMATH, 1919–31

1. Evan Mawdsley, *The Russian Revolution and the Baltic Fleet: War and Politics, February 1917–April 1918* (London: Macmillan, 1978), 154; Norman Saul, *Sailors in Revolt: The Russian Baltic Fleet in 1917* (Lawrence: Regents Press of Kansas, 1978), 219.

2. John Ferris, "The Symbol and Substance of Seapower: Britain, the United States and the One-Power Standard, 1919–1921," in *Anglo-American Relations in the 1920s: The Struggle for Supremacy*, ed. Brian McKercher (Edmonton: University of Alberta Press, 1990), 55–80.

3. Christopher Bell, *The Royal Navy, Seapower and Strategy between the Wars* (Stanford, CA: Stanford University Press, 2000).

4. Christopher Bell and John Maurer, eds., *At the Crossroads between Peace and War: The London Naval Conference in 1930* (Annapolis, MD: Naval Institute Press, 2014).

5. Albert Nofi, "An Overlooked Angle on the Naval Arms Limitation Treaties," Combat Information Center, Strategy page, no. 451, http://www.strategypage.com/cic/docs/cic124b.asp (accessed April 28, 2016).

6. NA, CAB 29/117, fol. 78.

7. Thomas Wildenberg, *Billy Mitchell's War: The Army Air Corps and the Challenge to Seapower* (Annapolis, MD: Naval Institute Press, 2013).

8. Robert Workman, *Float Planes and Flying Boats: The U.S. Coast Guard and Early Naval Aviation* (Annapolis, MD: Naval Institute Press, 2012).

9. BL, Add. 49045, fols. 1–2.

10. William Trimble, *Admiral William A. Moffett: Architect of Naval Aviation* (Washington, DC: Smithsonian Institution Press, 1994).

11. *Times*, September 6, 1927.

12. Ian Philpott, *The Royal Air Force . . . the Inter-war Years*, vol. 1, *The Trenchard Years, 1918 to 1929* (Barnsley, South Yorkshire: Pen and Sword, 2005), 194–208.

13. Clark Reynolds, *The Fast Carriers: The Forging of an Air Navy* (New York: McGraw-Hill, 1968); Geoffrey Till, "Adopting the Aircraft Carrier: The British, American, and Japanese Case Studies," in *Military Innovation in the Interwar Period*, ed. Williamson Murray and Alan Millett (Cambridge: Cambridge University Press, 1996), 191–226.

14. Douglas Smith, ed., *One Hundred Years of U.S. Navy Air Power* (Annapolis, MD: Naval Institute Press, 2010).

15. NA, KV 2/871.

16. Thomas Wildenberg, "In Support of the Battle Line: Gunnery's Influence on the Development of Carrier Aviation in the U.S. Navy," *Journal of Military History* 65 (2001): 709.

17. BL, Add. 49045, fols. 1–2.

18. James Goldrick, "Buying Time: British Submarine Capability in the Far East, 1919–1940," *Global War Studies* 11, no. 3 (2014): 33–50.

19. Brian Martin, "The United States Naval Response to the Imperial Japanese Navy during the Interwar Period, 1918–1941" (master's thesis, Hawaii Pacific University, 2009), 14.

20. Louis Morton, *Strategy and Command: The First Two Years* (Washington, DC: Office of the Chief of Military History, U.S. Army, 1962), 27.

21. Edward Miller, *War Plan Orange: The U.S. Strategy to Defeat Japan, 1897–1945* (Annapolis, MD: Naval Institute Press, 1991).

5. PREPARING FOR WAR, 1932–39

1. James Neidpath, *The Singapore Naval Base and the Defence of Britain's Eastern Empire, 1919–1941* (Oxford: Oxford University Press, 1981).

2. Report by the Chiefs of Staff, January 11, 1927, NA, CAB 24/184, fols. 42–43.

3. Edward Miller, *War Plan Orange: The U.S. Strategy to Defeat Japan, 1897–1945* (Annapolis, MD: Naval Institute Press, 1991).

4. Craig Felker, *Testing American Sea Power: US Navy Strategic Exercises, 1923–1940* (College Station: Texas A&M University Press, 2007); Albert Nofi, *To Train the Fleet for War: The US Navy Fleet Problems, 1923–1940* (Newport, RI: Naval War College Press, 2010).

5. Jon Kuehn, "The U.S. Navy General Board and Naval Arms Limitation: 1922–1937," *Journal of Military History* 74 (2010): 1159–60.

6. Garry Weir, *Building American Submarines, 1914–1940* (Washington, DC: Naval Historical Center, 1991).

7. Michael Simpson, ed., *Anglo-American Naval Relations, 1919–1939* (London: Naval Records Society, 2010); Douglas Ford, "A Statement of Hopes? The Effectiveness of US and British Naval War Plans against Japan, 1920–1941," *Mariner's Mirror* 101 (2015): 63–80; William Braisted, *Diplomats in Blue: U.S. Naval Officers in China, 1922–1933* (Gainesville: University Press of Florida, 2009).

8. David Ulbrich, *Preparing for Victory: Thomas Holcomb and the Making of the Modern Marine Corps, 1936–1943* (Annapolis, MD: Naval Institute Press, 2011).

9. Trent Hone, "The Evolution of Fleet Tactical Doctrine in the U.S. Navy, 1922–1941," *Journal of Military History* 67 (2003): 1146.

10. John Kuehn, *Agents of Innovation: The General Board and the Design of the Fleet That Defeated the Japanese Navy* (Annapolis, MD: Naval Institute Press, 2008).

11. Keith Neilson, "The Defence Requirements Sub-Committee, British Strategic Foreign Policy, Neville Chamberlain and the Path to Appeasement," *English Historical Review* 118 (2003): 675.

12. Charles Eade, ed., *Winston Churchill's Secret Session Speeches* (London: Cassell, 1946), 47.

13. David Evans and Mark Peattie, *Kaigun: Strategy, Tactics and Technology in the Imperial Japanese Navy, 1887–1941* (Annapolis, MD: Naval Institute Press, 1997).

14. Geoffrey Till, *Air Power and the Royal Navy, 1914–1945: A Historical Survey* (London: Macdonald and James, 1979).

15. Thomas Hone, Norman Friedman, and Mark Mandeles, *American and British Aircraft Carrier Development, 1919–1941* (Annapolis, MD: Naval Institute Press, 1999); Thomas Wildenberg, *Destined for Glory: Dive Bombing, Midway, and the Evolution of Carrier Airpower* (Annapolis, MD: Naval Institute Press, 1998).

16. Geoffrey Till, "Maritime Airpower in the Interwar Period: The Information Dimension," *Journal of Strategic Studies* 27 (2004): 298–323.

17. Jon Sumida, "'The Best Laid Plans': The Development of British Battle-Fleet Tactics, 1919–1942," *International History Review* 14 (1992): 682–700.

18. Sub-Committee Annual Review, October 12, 1933, NA, CAB 24/244, fol. 136.

19. Gerhard Koop and Klaus-Peter Schmolke, *Battleships of the Bismarck Class* (Annapolis, MD: Naval Institute Press, 1998).

20. Timothy Mulligan, "Ship of the Line or Atlantic Raider? Battleship *Bismarck* between Design Limitations and Naval Strategy," *Journal of Military History* 69 (2005): 1013–44.

21. Joseph Maiolo, *The Royal Navy and Nazi Germany, 1933–39: A Study in Appeasement and the Origins of the Second World War* (Basingstoke, UK: Palgrave Macmillan, 1998).

22. George Franklin, *Britain's Anti-Submarine Capability, 1919–1939* (London: Routledge, 2003).

23. David Massam, *British Maritime Strategy and Amphibious Capability, 1900–40* (Ph.D. diss., Oxford University, 1995).

24. BL, Add. 74806.

25. Lennart Samuelson, "Mikhail Tukhachevsky and War-Economic Planning: Reconsiderations on the Pre-war Soviet Military Build-up," *Journal of Slavic Military Studies* 9 (1996): 804–47.

26. Peter Whitewood, *The Red Army and the Great Terror: Stalin's Purge of the Soviet Military* (Lawrence: University Press of Kansas, 2015).

27. Jürgen Rohwer and Mikhail Monakov, *Stalin's Ocean-going Fleet: Soviet Naval Strategy and Shipbuilding Programmes, 1935–1953* (London: Frank Cass, 2001).

28. Galeazzo Ciaro, *Ciano's Diary 1937–1943: The Complete, Unabridged Diaries of Count Galeazzo Ciano, Italian Minister for Foreign Affairs* (London: Phoenix Press, 2002), 3, 25.

29. Michael Alpert, *La guerra civil Española en el mar* (Madrid: Siglo XXI, 1987).

30. Reynolds Salerno, "The French Navy and the Appeasement of Italy, 1937–9," *English Historical Review* 112 (1997): 73, 76.

31. Michael Morton, *Keepers of the Golden Shore: A History of the United Arab Emirates* (London: Reaktion, 2016), 108, 111.

32. William Garzke and Robert Dulin, *Battleships: United States Battleships, 1935–1992* (Annapolis, MD: Naval Institute Press, 1995).

6. NAVAL ARMAGEDDON, 1939–45

1. James Pritchard, *A Bridge of Ships: Canadian Shipbuilding during the Second World War* (Montreal: McGill-Queen's University Press, 2011).

2. Kalevi Keskinen and Jorma Mäntykoshi, *Suomen Laivasto Sodassa 1939–1945: The Finnish Navy at War in 1939–1945* (Tietotoes: Espoo Finland, 1991).

3. Chiefs of Staff Subcommittee, report, February 9, 1937, NA, CAB 24/268, fol. 104.

4. Patrick Salmon, *Deadlock and Diversion: Scandinavia in British Strategy during the Twilight War, 1939–1940* (Bremerhaven: German Maritime Museum, 2012).

5. Adam Claasen, "Blood and Iron, and 'der Geist des Atlantiks': Assessing Hitler's Decision to Invade Norway," *Journal of Strategic Studies* 20 (1997): 71–96.

6. Adam Claasen, "The German Invasion of Norway, 1940: The Operational Intelligence Dimension," *Journal of Strategic Studies* 27 (2004): 114–35.

7. Geirr Haarr, *The German Invasion of Norway, April 1940* (Annapolis, MD: Naval Institute Press, 2009).

8. NA, PREM 3/328, pp. 23–26.

9. Pound to Admiral Cunningham, May 20, 1940, BL, Add. 52560, fol. 120.

10. Christopher Mann, *British Policy and Strategy towards Norway, 1941–45* (Basingstoke, UK: Palgrave, 2012).

11. Anthony Cumming, *The Royal Navy and the Battle of Britain* (Annapolis, MD: Naval Institute Press, 2010); Garry Campion, *The Battle of Britain, 1945–1965: The Air Ministry and the Few* (Basingstoke, UK: Palgrave, 2015).

12. Philippe Lasterle, "Could Admiral Gensoul Have Averted the Tragedy of Mers-el-Kébir?," *Journal of Modern History* 67 (2003): 835–44.

13. Galeazzo Ciaro, *Ciano's Diary 1937–1943: The Complete, Unabridged Diaries of Count Galeazzo Ciano, Italian Minister for Foreign Affairs* (London: Phoenix Press, 2002), 368–69.

14. James Sadkovich, "Understanding Defeat: Reappraising Italy's Role in World War II," *Journal of Contemporary History* 24 (1989): 38.

15. Ben Jones, ed., *The Fleet Air Arm in the Second World War*, vol. 1, *1939–1941* (Farnham: Ashgate, 2012).

16. Cunningham to Pound, May 28, 1941, BL, Add. 52567, fol. 117.

17. Luke McKernan, ed., *John Turner, Filming History: The Memoirs of John Turner, Newsreel Cameraman* (London: British Universities Film and Video Council, 2001).

18. Blamey to Minister for Army, August 15, 1941, AWM, 3 DRL/6643, 1/2. See, for same, August 2, 1941.

19. Vincent O'Hara, *In Passage Perilous: Malta and the Convoy Battles of June 1942* (Bloomington, IN: Indiana University Press, 2013); James Sadkovich, "Re-evaluating Who Won the Italo-British Naval Conflict, 1940–2," *European History Quarterly* 18 (1988): 455–71.

20. Robert J. Winklareth, *The Battle of the Denmark Strait* (Havertown, PA: Casemate, 2012).

21. Christopher Bell, "Air Power and the Battle of the Atlantic: Very Long Range Aircraft and the Delay in Closing the Atlantic 'Air Gap,'" *Journal of Military History* 79 (2015): 691–719.

22. William Casto, "Advising Presidents: Robert Jackson and the Destroyers-for-Bases Deal," *American Journal of Legal History* 52 (2012): 1–135.

23. Joel Hayward, "A Case Study in Early Joint Warfare: An Analysis of the *Wehrmacht*'s Crimean Campaign of 1942," *Journal of Strategic Studies* 22 (1999): 122–26.

24. Hedley Paul Willmott, *Pearl Harbor* (London: Orion, 2001); Mitsui Fuchida, *For That One Day: The Memoirs of Mitsuo Fuchida, Commander of the Attack on Pearl Harbor* (Kamuela, HI: Experience, 2011); Alan Zimm, *Attack on Pearl Harbor: Strategy, Combat, Myths, Deceptions* (Havertown, PA: Casemate, 2011); "A Strategy Has to Be Able to Work to Be Masterful," *NWCR* 68 (2015): 128–35.

25. Derek Howse, *Radar at Sea: The Royal Navy in World War 2* (Basingstoke, UK: Palgrave, 1993), 123–24.

26. Christopher Bell, "The 'Singapore Strategy' and the Deterrence of Japan: Winston Churchill, the Admiralty and the Dispatch of Force Z," *English Historical Review* 116 (2001): 604–34.

27. Andrew Stewart, *A Very British Experience: Coalition, Defence and Strategy in the Second World War* (Brighton, Sussex: Academic Press, 2012).

28. Edward Harrison, "British Subversion in French East Africa, 1941–42: SOE's Todd Mission," *English Historical Review* 114 (1999): 358–60.

29. Charles Eade, ed., *Winston Churchill's Secret Session Speeches* (London: Cassel, 1946), 47.

30. Milan Vego, "The Port Moresby-Solomons Operation and the Allied Reaction, 27 April–11 May 1942," *NWCR* 65, no. 1 (Winter 2012): 93–151.

31. Mitsuo Fuchida and Masatake Okumiya, *Midway: The Battle That Doomed Japan, the Japanese Navy's Story* (Annapolis, MD: Naval Institute Press, 1992); Thomas Hone, ed., *The Battle of Midway* (Annapolis, MD: Naval Institute Press, 2013).

32. Dallas Isom, *Midway Inquest: Why the Japanese Lost the Battle of Midway* (Bloomington: Indiana University Press, 2007); James Levy, "Was There Something Unique to the Japanese That Lost Them the Battle of Midway?," *NWCR* 67 (2014): 119–24; Carl Hodge, "The Key to Midway: Coral Sea and a Culture of Learning," *NWCR* 68, no. 1 (2015): 119–27.

33. James Smith, "Admiral William Pye's 1943 Evaluation of the Naval Battle of Guadalcanal, November 13–15, 1942," *U.S. Military History Review* 1, no. 1 (2014): 48–51.

34. War Cabinet Minutes, July 29, 1942, NAA, p. 1404.

35. Ian Toll, *The Conquering Tide: War in the Pacific Islands, 1942–1944* (New York: Norton, 2015); Reg Newell, *The Battle for Vella Lavella: The Allied Recapture of Solomon Islands Territory, August 15–September 9, 1943* (Jefferson, NC: McFarland, 2015); Ronnie Day, *New Georgia: The Second Battle for the Solomons* (Bloomington: Indiana University Press, 2016).

36. Carl Boyd and Akihiko Yoshida, *The Japanese Submarine Force and World War II* (Annapolis, MD: Naval Institute Press, 1995).

37. For the valuable individual experience, see Craig McDonald, *The USS Puffer in World War II: A History of the Submarine and Its Wartime Crew* (Jefferson, NC: McFarland, 2008); James Scott, *The War Below: The Story of Three Submarines That Battled Japan* (New York: Simon and Schuster, 2013); and Michael Sturma, *Freemantle's Submarines: How Allied Submarines and Western Australians Helped to Win the War in the Pacific* (Annapolis, MD: Naval Institute Press, 2015).

38. Joel Holwitt, *Execute against Japan: The U.S. Decision to Conduct Unrestricted Submarine Warfare* (College Station: Texas A&M University Press, 2009).

39. David Bercuson and Holger Herwig, *Long Night of the Tankers: Hitler's War against Caribbean Oil* (Calgary: University of Calgary Press, 2014).

40. David Syrett, "The Infrastructure of Communications Intelligence: The Allied D/F Network and the Battle of the Atlantic," *Intelligence and National Security* 17 (2002): 163–72; David Kahn, *Seizing the Enigma: The Race to Break German U-Boat Codes, 1939–1943*, 2nd ed. (Barnsley, South Yorkshire: Frontline Books, 2012).

41. Richard Doherty, *Churchill's Greatest Fear: The Battle of the Atlantic* (Barnsley, South Yorkshire: Pen and Sword, 2015), 176–79.

42. Marcus Jones, "Innovation for Its Own Sake," *NWCR* 67, no. 2 (Spring 2014): 215–17.

43. Michael Dobbs, "Homeland Security Implications from the Battle of the Atlantic," *RUSI Journal* 148, no. 5 (October 2003): 38.

44. Peter Nash, *The Development of Mobile Logistic Support in Anglo-American Naval Policy, 1900–1953* (Gainesville: University Press of Florida, 2009).

45. Mark Peattie, *Sunburst: The Rise of Japanese Naval Air Power, 1909–1941* (Annapolis, MD: Naval Institute Press, 2002).

46. T. C. Hone, "Replacing Battleships with Aircraft Carriers in the Pacific in World War II," *NWCR* 66 (2013): 72–73.

47. Hedley Paul Willmott, *The Battle of Leyte Gulf: The Last Fleet Action* (Bloomington: Indiana University Press, 2005), quote at 57; Anthony Tully, *Battle of Surigao Strait* (Bloomington: Indiana University Press, 2014).

48. Barbara Tomblin, *With Utmost Spirit: Allied Naval Operations in the Mediterranean, 1942–1945* (Lexington: University Press of Kentucky, 2004); Robert Stern, *The US Navy and the War in Europe* (Barnsley, South Yorkshire: Seaforth Publishing, 2012).

49. Simon Ball, *The Bitter Sea: The Struggle for Mastery in the Mediterranean, 1935–1949* (London: Harper Perennial, 2009).

50. Adrian Lewis, "Combined Amphibious Doctrine for the Allied Invasion of Europe: Tactical Surprise vs. Fire Power," in *The Second World War*, vol. 2, *The German War, 1943–1945*, ed. Jeremy Black (Aldershot: Ashgate, 2007), 209.

51. Craig Symonds, *Neptune: The Allied Invasion of Europe and the D-Day Landings* (New York: Oxford University Press, 2014).

52. Howard Grier, *Hitler, Dönitz and the Baltic Sea: The Third Reich's Last Hope, 1944–5* (Annapolis, MD: Naval Institute Press, 2007).

53. William Rawling, "The Challenge of Modernization: The Royal Canadian Navy and Antisubmarine Weapons, 1944–1945," *Journal of Military History* 63 (1999): 377–78.

54. Ismay to Churchill, March 16, 1944, LH, Alanbrooke 6/3/8.

55. Peter Elphick, *Liberty-Ships That Won the War* (Annapolis, MD: Naval Institute Press, 2006), 91; Frederick Lane, *Ships for Victory: A History of Shipbuilding under the U.S. Maritime Commission in World War II* (Baltimore, MD: Johns Hopkins University Press, 1951), 252–59.

56. Richard Mayne, *Betrayed: Scandal, Politics, and Canadian Naval Leadership* (Vancouver: UBC Press, 2007); James Pritchard, *A Bridge of Ships: Canadian Shipbuilding during the Second World War* (Montreal and Kingston: McGill-Queen's University Press).

57. Malcolm Murfett, *Naval Warfare, 1919–1945: An Operational History of the Volatile War at Sea* (New York: Routledge, 2009).

58. Pound to Admiral Layton, February 9, 1943, BL, Add. 74796.

59. Phillips Payson O'Brien, *How the War Was Won: Air-Sea Power and Allied Victory in World War II* (Cambridge: Cambridge University Press, 2015).

60. Jane Harrold, ed., *Turning the Tide: The Battles of Coral Sea and Midway* (Plymouth, Devon: University of Plymouth Press, 2013).

61. Hal Friedman, "Blue versus Orange: The United States Naval War College, Japan, and the Old Enemy in the Pacific, 1945–1946," *Journal of Military History* 78 (2014): 231.

62. Nachman Ben-Yehuda, *Atrocity, Deviance, and Submarine Warfare: Norms and Practices during the World Wars* (Ann Arbor: University of Michigan Press, 2013).

63. Angus Mansfield, *"I Wish I Had Your Wings": A Spitfire Pilot and Operation Pedestal, Malta, 1942* (Stroud: History Press, 2016), 100.

7. COLD WAR: THE AGE OF AMERICAN DOMINANCE, 1946–67

1. Stephen Budiansky, *Code Warriors: NSA's Code Breakers and the Secret Intelligence War against the Soviet Union* (New York: Knopf, 2016), 30–32.

2. Jeffrey Barlow, *From Hot War to Cold: The U.S. Navy and National Security Affairs, 1945–1955* (Stanford, CA: Stanford University Press, 2009).

3. Bruce Elleman, "Soviet Sea Denial in the KMT-CCP Civil War in Manchuria, 1945–1949," in *Naval Coalition Warfare: From the Napoleonic War to Operation Iraqi Freedom*, ed. Bruce Elleman and Sally Paine (Abingdon: Taylor and Francis, 2008), 119–29.

4. Maochun Yu, "The Battle of Quemoy: The Amphibious Assault That Held the Postwar Military Balance in the Taiwan Strait," *NWCR* 69 (2016): 91–107.

5. Odd Westad, *Decisive Encounters: The Chinese Civil War, 1946–1950* (Stanford, CA: Stanford University Press, 2003), 303–4; Li Xiaobing, *A History of the Modern Chinese Army* (Lexington: University Press of Kentucky, 2007), 129–35.

6. He Di, "The Last Campaign to Unify China: The CCP's Unrealised Plan to Liberate Taiwan, 1949–1950," in *Chinese Warfighting: The PLA Experience since 1949*, ed. Mark Ryan, Michael Finkelstein, and Michael McDevitt (Armonk, NY: East Gate Books, 2003).

7. John Condon, "The Marine Air-Ground Team at the Choisin Reservoir," *Joint Force Quarterly* 28 (Spring/Summer 2001): 50.

8. Tommy Thomason, *US Naval Air Superiority: Development of Shipborne Jet Fighters, 1943–1962* (North Branch, MN: Specialty Press, 2007).

9. Donald Chisholm, "A Remarkable Military Feat: The Hungnam Redeployment, December 1950," *NWCR* 65, no. 2 (2012): 105–44.

10. Austin Jersild, *The Sino-Soviet Alliance: An International History* (Chapel Hill: University of North Carolina Press, 2014).

11. Richard Moore, *The Royal Navy and Nuclear Weapons* (London: Routledge, 2001).

12. Employment of Joint Helicopter Unit on Operation Musketeer, January 14, 1957, NA, WO 288/76/JEHU/S.816/G.

13. Helicopters at Port Said, Air Ministry Secret Intelligence Summaries, 1957, NA, AIR 40/2771, vol. 12, no. 5: 12.

14. Stuart Ball, "'Vested Interests and Vanished Dreams': Duncan Sandys, the Chiefs of Staff and the 1957 White Paper," in *Government and the Armed Forces in Britain, 1856–1990*, ed. Paul Smith (London: Hambledon, 1996), 217–34, esp. 232–33.

15. Southampton, University Library, MBI/I149.

16. Norman Polmar, *Aircraft Carriers: A History of Carrier Aviation and Its Influence on World Events*, vol. 2, *1946–2006* (Washington: Potomac Books, 2008).

17. Geoffrey Swain, *Khrushchev* (Basingstoke, UK: Palgrave Macmillan, 2011), 150.

18. Dave Oliver, *Against the Tide: Rickover's Leadership Principles and the Rise of the Nuclear Navy* (Annapolis, MD: Naval Institute Press, 2014).

19. Belfer Center for Science and International Affairs, Harvard University, http://belfercenter.ksg.harvard.edu/files/CMC50/SavranskayaJSSNewsourcesonroleofSovietsubmarinesinCMC.pdf; National Security Archive, George Washington University, http://nsarchive.gwu.edu/NSAEBB/NSAEBB75.

20. Bernard Austin, "Naval Strategy," *Naval War College Review* 14, no. 5 (January–February 1962): 37.

21. John Nichols and Barrett Tillman, *On Yankee Station: The Naval Air War over Vietnam* (Annapolis, MD: Naval Institute Press, 1987).

22. Bernd Lemke, ed., *Periphery or Contact Zone? The NATO Flanks 1961 to 2013* (Freiburg: Rombach Verlag, 2015).

23. Jesse Ferris, "Guns for Cotton? Aid, Trade, and the Soviet Quest for Base Rights in Egypt, 1964–1966," *Journal of Cold War Studies* 13 (2011): 35–37; Guy Laron, "Playing with Fire: The Soviet-Syrian-Israeli Triangle, 1965–1967," *Cold War History* 10 (2010): 163–84.

24. Michael Palmer, *On Course to Desert Storm: The United States Navy and the Persian Gulf* (Washington, DC: Naval Historical Center, 1992), 83–84.

25. Spencer Mawby, *Ordering Independence: The End of Empire in the Anglophone Caribbean, 1947–69* (Basingstoke, UK: Palgrave Macmillan, 2012), 65–66.

26. John Kleinen and Manon Osseweijer, eds., *Pirates, Ports, and Coasts in Asia: Historical and Contemporary Perspectives* (Singapore: ISEAS Press, 2010).

27. John Cann, *Brown Waters of Africa: Portuguese Riverine Warfare, 1961–1974* (Petersburg, FL: Hailer Publishing, 2007).

28. John Young, "The Wilson Government and the Debate over Arms to South Africa in 1964," *Contemporary British History* 12 (1998): 62–86; Ronald Hyam and Peter Henshaw, *The Lion and the Springbok: Britain and South Africa since the Boer War* (Cambridge: Cambridge University Press, 2003), 236–49.

29. Newport Papers, U.S. Naval War College, https://www.usnwc.edu/Publications/Naval-War-College-Press/Newport-Papers/Documents/30-pdf.aspx.

8. COLD WAR: AMERICA UNDER GREATER CHALLENGE, 1967–89

1. Alessio Patalano, *Post-War Japan as a Sea Power: Imperial Legacy, Wartime Experience and the Making of a Navy* (London: Bloomsbury, 2015).

2. Sergei Gorshkov, *Navies in War and Peace* (Annapolis, MD: Naval Institute Press, 1974), and *The Sea Power of the State* (Oxford: Pergamon Press, 1979); Robert Herrick, *Soviet Naval Strategy: Fifty Years of Theory and Practice* (Annapolis, MD: Naval Institute Press, 1968).

3. Lyle Goldstein and Yuri Zhukov, "A Tale of Two Fleets: A Russian Perspective on the 1973 Naval Standoff in the Mediterranean," *NWCR* 57, no. 2 (Spring 2004): 27–63; George Hudson, "Soviet Naval Doctrine and Soviet Politics, 1953–1975," *World Politics* 29 (1976): 90–113; Brian Ranft and Geoffrey Till, *The Sea in Soviet Strategy* (London: Macmillan, 1983).

4. Norman Polmar, "The Soviet Navy's Caribbean Outpost," *Naval History* 26, no. 5 (October 2012): 24–29.

5. Phuong Pham, *Ending "East of Suez": The British Decision to Withdraw from Malaysia and Singapore, 1964–1968* (Oxford: Oxford University Press, 2010).

6. Tae Joon Won, "Britain's Retreat East of Suez and the Conundrum of Korea, 1968–1974," *Britain and the World* 9 (2016): 89.

7. Anthony Gorst, "CVA0–01," in *The Royal Navy, 1930–2000: Innovation and Defence*, ed. Richard Harding (Abingdon: Frank Cass, 2005), 172–92.

8. I owe this point to Peter Brown.

9. Jason Darwin Hamblin, *Oceanographers and the Cold War: Disciples of Marine Science* (Seattle: University of Washington Press, 2005).

10. Paul Nitze et al., *Securing the Seas: The Soviet Naval Challenge and Western Alliance Options* (Boulder, CO: Westview Press, 1979); James Watkins, "The Maritime Strategy," *Proceedings of the U.S. Naval Institute*, January 1986, 2–17; Ed Rhodes, "'. . . From the Sea' and Back Again: Naval Power in the Second American Century," *Naval War College Review* 52, no. 2 (1999): 22–23; David Winkler, *Cold War at Sea: High Seas Confrontation between the United States and the Soviet Union* (Annapolis, MD: Naval Institute Press, 2000).

11. U.S. Central Intelligence Agency, http://www.foia.cia.gov/sites/default/files/document_conversions?89801/DOC_00000261312.pdf, pp. 10–11.

12. Maksim Tokarev, "Kamikazes: The Soviet Legacy," *NWCR* 67, no. 1 (Winter 2014): 61–84.

13. Larry Berman, *The Life and Times of Admiral Elmo Russell "Bud" Zumwalt, Jr.* (New York: HarperCollins, 2012).

14. Graham Spinardi, *From Polaris to Trident: The Development of U.S. Fleet Ballistic Missile Technology* (Cambridge: Cambridge University Press, 1994).

15. "The Maritime Strategy 1986," in *US Maritime Strategy in the 1980s: Selected Documents*, ed. John Hattendorf and Peter Swatz (Newport, RI: U.S. Naval War College, 2008), 203–25; John Hanley, "Creating the 1980s Maritime Strategy and Implications for Today," *NWCR* 67, no. 2 (Spring 2014): 11–29.

16. Kenneth Privratsky, *Logistics in the Falklands War* (Barnsley: Pen and Sword, 2015).

17. The best account overall is Gulab Hiranandani, *Transition to Triumph: History of the Indian Navy, 1965–1975* (New Delhi: Lancer, 2000); the Pakistani version is Pakistan Navy History Section, *Story of the Pakistan Navy, 1947–1972* (Karachi: Elite Publishers, 1991); memoir literature on the Indian side, all by former admirals, include Sardarilal Nanda, *The Man Who Bombed Karachi* (New Delhi: HarperCollins, 2004); Mihir Roy, *War in the Indian Ocean* (New Delhi: Lancer, 1999); and Surendra Nath Kohli, *We Dared* (New Delhi: Lancer, 1989).

18. Steven Ward, *Immortal: A Military History of Iran and Its Armed Forces* (Washington, DC: Georgetown University Press, 2009).

19. Geraint Hughes, "Demythologising Dhofar: British Policy, Military Strategy, and Counter-Insurgency in Oman, 1963–1976," *Journal of Military History* 79 (2015): 440.

9. AFTER THE COLD WAR, SINCE 1990

1. Norman Friedman, *Network-Centric Warfare: How Navies Learned to Fight Smarter through Three World Wars* (Annapolis, MD: Naval Institute Press, 2009).

2. Wayne Hughes, "Naval Operations: A Close Look at the Operational Level of War at Sea," *NWCR* 65, no. 3 (Summer 2012): 23–46.

3. Frederick Hartmann, *Naval Renaissance: The U.S. Navy in the 1980s* (Annapolis, MD: Naval Institute Press, 1990); John Lehman, *Command of the Seas: Building the 600 Ship Navy* (New York: Scribner, 1988).

4. Deborah Sanders, "The Bulgarian Navy after the Cold War: Challenges of Building and Modernizing an Effective Navy," *NWCR* 68, no. 2 (Spring 2015): 71–73.

5. Valur Ingimundarson, "Confronting Strategic Irrelevance: The End of a US-Icelandic 'Security Community'?," *RUSI Journal* 150, no. 6 (December 2005): 69–70.

6. Edward Rhodes, "Constructing Peace and War: An Analysis of the Power of Ideas to Shape American Military Power," *Millennium: Journal of International Studies* 24 (1995): 84; for an earlier example, see Edward Rhodes, "Sea Change: Interest-Based vs. Cultural-Cognitive Accounts of Strategic Choice in the 1890s," *Security Studies* 5, no. 4 (1996): 73–124, esp. 121–22.

7. Peter Hennessy and James Jinks, *The Silent Deep: The Royal Navy Submarine Service since 1945* (London: Allen Lane, 2015).

8. Steven Willis, "The Effect of the Goldwater-Nichols Act of 1986 on Naval Strategy, 1987–1994," *NWCR* 69 (2016): 21–40, at 29. For a more positive account of the value of unified command, see David Jablonsky, *War by Land, Sea, and Air: Dwight Eisenhower and the Concept of Unified Command* (New Haven, CT: Yale University Press, 2011).

9. James Wirtz and Jeffrey Larsen, eds., *Naval Peacekeeping and Humanitarian Operations: Stability from the Sea* (London: Routledge, 2009).

10. Andrew Nathan and Andrew Scobell, *China's Search for Security* (New York: Columbia University Press, 2012).

11. Helene Cooper, "Across Warm Azure Waters, US and China Jockey for Control," *New York Times*, March 31, 2016, A12.

12. Norman Friedman, *Seapower as Strategy: Navies and National Interests* (Annapolis, MD: Naval Institute Press, 2001).

13. I have benefited from discussions with Peter Luff, minister for defence procurement from 2010 to 2013.

14. For similar caveats about air power, see Jeremy Black, *Air Power: A Global History* (Lanham, MD: Rowman & Littlefield, 2016).

15. Colin Gray, *The Leverage of Seapower: The Strategic Advantage of Navies in War* (New York: Free Press, 1992), and *The Navy in the Post-Cold War World: The Uses and Value of Strategic Sea Power* (Philadelphia: Pennsylvania State University Press, 2004).

16. Wayne Hughes, *Fleet Tactics and Coastal Combat*, 2nd ed. (Annapolis, MD: Naval Institute Press, 2000); Eric Grove, *The Royal Navy since 1815* (London: Palgrave Macmillan, 2005), 261.

17. Markus Mäder, *In Pursuit of Conceptual Excellence: The Evolution of British Military Strategic Doctrine in the Post-Cold War Era, 1989–2002* (New York: Peter Lang, 2004).

18. Robert Work, "The Global Era of National Policy and the Pan-Oceanic National Fleet," *Orbis* 52 (2008): 602.

19. Andrew Dorman, Mike Smith, and Matthew Uttley, eds., *The Changing Face of Maritime Power* (Basingstoke, UK: Palgrave Macmillan, 1999).

20. Royal Navy, *BR1806: British Maritime Doctrine*, 2nd ed. (London: HMSO, 1999), 3, 171.

21. U.S. Navy, *Naval Strategic Plan* (Washington, DC: Department of the Navy, 2006), 9.

22. Peter Dean, "Amphibious Operations and the Evolution of Australian Defense Policy," *NWCR* 67 (2014): 30–31; Calvin Manganyi, "Resurrection of the Marine Capability in the South African Navy: The Maritime Reaction Squadron," *Scientia Militaria* 40 (2012): 429–71;

Deane-Peter Baker, "The South African Navy and African Maritime Security," *NWCR* 65, no. 2 (2012): 145–65.

23. Basil Germond, *The Maritime Dimension of European Security: Seapower and the European Union* (Basingstoke, UK: Palgrave Macmillan, 2015); "The Geopolitical Dimension of Maritime Security," *Marine Policy* 54 (April 2015): 137–42; "Ocean Governance and Maritime Security in a Peaceful Environment: The Case of the European Union," *Marine Policy* 66 (April 2016): 124–31.

24. Carolin Liss, *Oceans of Crime: Maritime Piracy and Transnational Security in South East Asia and Bangladesh* (Singapore: ISEAS Press, 2011).

25. Ken Hagan and Michael McMaster, "In Search of a Maritime Strategy: The U.S. Navy, 1981–2008," in *In Peace and War: Interpretations of American Naval History*, ed. Hagan and McMaster, 2nd ed. (Westport, CT: Praeger, 2008), 291–322; Stephanie Hszieh, George Galdorisi, Terry McKearney, and Darren Sutton, "Networking the Global Maritime Partnership," *NWCR* 65, no. 2 (2012): 11–29; Sam Tangredi, ed., *The U.S. Naval Institute on Naval Cooperation* (Annapolis, MD: Naval Institute Press, 2015).

26. Nicholas Tracy, *A Two-Edged Sword: The Navy as an Instrument of Canadian Foreign Policy* (Montreal and Kingston: McGill-Queen's University Press, 2012).

27. Andrew Erickson, *Six Years at Sea . . . and Counting: Gulf of Aden Anti-piracy and China's Maritime Commons Presence* (Washington, DC: Jamestown Foundation, 2015).

28. Jonathan Altman, "Russian A2/AD in the Eastern Mediterranean," *NWCR* 69, no. 1 (Winter 2016): 72–84.

29. Scott Truver, "Taking Mines Seriously: Mine Warfare in China's Near Seas," *NWCR* 65, no. 2 (Spring 2012): 30–66.

30. *Times*, December 27, 2008, 43.

31. For more positive accounts of British naval aviation, see Tim Benbow, ed., *British Naval Aviation: The First 100 Years* (Farnham, Surrey: Ashgate, 2011).

32. Shi Xiaoqin, *Seapower and Sino-U.S. Relations* (Beijing: Academy of Military Science, 2013); Jeffrey Becker, "Who's at the Helm? The Past, Present and Future Leaders of China's Navy," *NWCR* 69, no. 2 (Spring 2016): 66–90.

33. Andrew Erickson, *Chinese Anti-Ship Ballistic Missile (ASBM) Development: Drivers, Trajectories and Strategic Implications* (Washington, DC: Jamestown Foundation, 2013).

34. Kamlesh Agnihotri, "The Chinese Navy's Submarine Arm: Lynchpin of 'Active Defence,'" *Maritime Affairs: Journal of the National Maritime Foundation of India* 8, no. 2 (December 2012): 95–122.

35. Ryan Martinson, "Assessing Chinese Maritime Strategy from Primary Sources," *NWCR* 69, no. 3 (Autumn 2016): 23–44; Toshi Yoshihara and James Holmes, *Red Star over the Pacific: China's Rise and the Challenge to US Maritime Strategy* (Annapolis, MD: Naval Institute Press, 2010).

36. Daniel Kostecka, "Places and Bases: The Chinese Navy's Emerging Support Network in the Indian Ocean," *NWCR* 64, no. 1 (Winter 2011): 59–78.

37. For the significance of these to fleet operations in the late nineteenth century, see James Rentfrow, *Home Squadron: The US Navy on the North Atlantic Squadron* (Annapolis, MD: Naval Institute Press, 2014).

38. Yann-huei Song and Keyuan Zou, *Major Law and Policy Issues in the South China Sea* (Farnham, Surrey: Ashgate, 2014).

39. *Times*, April 14, 2016, 28. Iran has been doing the same to American warships.

40. Carnes Lord and Andrew Erickson, eds., *Rebalancing U.S. Forces: Basing and Forward Presence in the Asia-Pacific* (Annapolis, MD: Naval Institute Press, 2014); Greg Kennedy and Harsh Pant, eds., *Assessing Maritime Power in the Asia-Pacific: The Impact of American Strategic Re-Balance* (Farnham, Surrey: Ashgate, 2015).

41. Andrew Davies, "Up Periscope: The Expansion of Submarine Capabilities in the Asia-Pacific Region," *RUSI Journal* 152, no. 5 (October 2007): 65.

42. Iskander Rehman, "Drowning Stability: The Perils of Naval Nuclearization and Brinkmanship in the Indian Ocean," *NWCR* 65, no. 4 (Autumn 2012): 73.

43. Robert Rubel, "Capital Ships, the Littoral, Command of the Sea, and the World Order," *NWCR* 68, no. 4 (Autumn 2015): 59.

266   *Notes*

44. Aaron Friedberg, *Beyond Air-Sea Battle: The Debate over US Military Strategy in Asia* (Abingdon: Routledge, 2014).

45. Sam Tangredi, *Anti-Access Warfare: Countering A2/AD Strategies* (Annapolis, MD: Naval Institute Press, 2013).

46. Andrew Scobell, Michael McMahon, and Cortez Cooper III, "China's Aircraft Carrier Program: Drivers, Developments, Implications," *NWCR* 68, no. 4 (Autumn 2015): 76.

47. Michael Mulqueen, Deborah Sanders, and Ian Speller, eds., *Small Navies; Strategy and Policy for Small Navies in War and Peace* (Farnham, Surrey: Ashgate, 2014).

10. INTO THE FUTURE

1. Halford John Mackinder, "The Geographical Pivot of History," *Geographical Journal* 23, no. 4 (April 1904): 421–24.

2. Bruce Berkowitz, *The New Face of War: How War Will Be Fought in the 21st Century* (New York: Free Press, 2003); Thomas Mahnken, *Technology and the American Way of War since 1945* (New York: Columbia University Press, 2008).

3. Sir Rupert Smith, *The Utility of Force: The Art of War in the Modern World* (London: Allen Lane, 2005).

4. Andrew Erickson and Lyle Goldstein, "Gunboats for China's New 'Grand Canals'? Probing the Intersection of Beijing's Naval and Oil Security Policies," *NWCR* 62, no. 2 (Spring 2009): 43–76.

5. Wu Zhengyu, "Toward 'Land' or Toward 'Sea'? The High-Speed Railway and China's Grand Strategy," *NWCR* 66, no. 3 (Summer 2013): 53–66.

6. Saeed Shah, "China's Port in Pakistan Is No Safe Harbor," *Wall Street Journal*, April 11, 2016, A8.

7. Mohamed Ingiriis, "The History of Somali Piracy: From Classical Piracy to Contemporary Piracy, c. 1801–2011," *Northern Mariner* 23 (2013); Kamal-Deen Ali, *Maritime Security Cooperation in the Gulf of Guinea: Prospects and Challenges* (Leiden: Brill, 2015).

8. Ajaya Das, "India's Naval Exercises with ASEAN States since 1991: A Time Line," *India Review* 12, no. 3 (2013): 123–29.

9. Ben Lombardi and David Rudd, "The Type 45 *DARING*-Class Destroyer: How Project Management Problems Led to Fewer Ships," *NWCR* 66, no. 3 (Summer 2013): 99–116.

10. Ronald O'Rourke, "Programs vs. Resources: Some Options for the Navy," *NWCR* 63, no. 4 (Autumn 2010): 25–37.

11. NATO, "Defence Expenditures of NATO Countries (2008–2015)," January 28, 2016, table 3.

12. Brad Hicks, George Galdorisi, and Scott Truver, "The Aegis BMD Global Enterprise: A 'High End' Maritime Partnership," *NWCR* 65, no. 3 (Summer 2012): 65–80.

13. Robert Rubel, "The Navy's Changing Force Paradigm," *NWCR* 62, no. 2 (Spring 2009): 18–19, 22.

11. CONCLUSIONS

1. Thomas Hone, "Replacing Battleships with Aircraft Carriers in the Pacific in World War II," *NWCR* 66, no. 1 (Winter 2013): 56–76.

2. Wider cultural assumptions in American society are essentially ignored in Roger Barnett, *Navy Strategic Culture: Why the Navy Thinks Differently* (Annapolis, MD: Naval Institute Press, 2009).

3. Dill to Field Marshal Montgomery-Massingberd, retired chief of the Imperial General Staff, December 23, 1939, KCL, LH, Montgomery-Massingberd papers, 10/14.

4. David Hein, "Vulnerable: HMS *Prince of Wales* in 1941," *Journal of Military History* 77 (2013): 967.

5. More generally on the experience of war, see Glyn Prysor, *Citizen Sailors: The Royal Navy in the Second World War* (London: Penguin, 2011), and Maryam Philpott, *Air and Sea Power in World War I: Combat Experience in the Royal Flying Corps and the Royal Navy* (London: I. B. Tauris, 2013).

6. Jürgen Osterhammel, *The Transformation of the World: A Global History of the Nineteenth Century* (Princeton, NJ: Princeton University Press, 2014).

7. Jason Smith, "'Twixt the Devil and the Deep Blue Sea: Hydrography, Sea Power, and the Marine Environment, 1898–1901," *Journal of Military History* 78 (2014): 575–604.

8. Edward Rhodes, "Sea Change: Interest-Based vs. Cultural-Cognitive Accounts of Strategic Choice in the 1890s," *Security Studies* 5, no. 4 (1996): 73–124, esp. 109, 120–22; Ralph Harrington, "The Mighty *Hood*: Navy, Empire, War at Sea and the British National Imagination, 1920–60," *Journal of Contemporary History* 38, no. 2 (April 2003): 171–85; Duncan Redford, *The Submarine: A Cultural History from the Great War to Nuclear Combat* (London: I. B. Tauris, 2010); on civilians influencing the military, see Brett Holman, *The Next War in the Air: Britain's Fear of the Bomber, 1908–1941* (Farnham, Surrey: Ashgate, 2014).

9. Philip Kerr, *The Lady from Zagreb* (New York: Putnam, 2015), 2. Written in 2011, the novel relates to 1956 at this point.

Selected Further Reading

The quantity of first-rate work published is such that the choice of what follows is necessarily highly selective. Other works can be followed up through the text, notes, and bibliographies of the works cited.

GENERAL WORKS

Bell, Christopher, and Bruce Elleman, eds. *Naval Mutinies of the Twentieth Century: An International Perspective.* Portland, OR: Frank Cass, 2003.

Corbett, Julian. *Some Principles of Maritime Strategy.* London: Longmans, 1911.

Dickinson, Harry. *Educating the Royal Navy: 18th and 19th Century Education for Officers.* Abingdon: Routledge, 2007.

Elleman, Bruce, and Sarah Paine, eds. *Naval Blockades and Seapower: Strategies and Counter- strategies, 1805–2005.* New York: Routledge, 2006.

———, eds. *Naval Coalition Warfare: From the Napoleonic War to Operation Iraqi Freedom.* New York: Routledge, 2008.

———, eds. *Naval Power and Expeditionary Warfare: Peripheral Campaigns and New Theatres of Naval Warfare.* New York: Routledge, 2011.

Evans, David, and Mark Peattie. *Kaigun: Strategy, Tactics and Technology in the Imperial Japanese Navy, 1887–1941.* Annapolis, MD: Naval Institute Press, 1997.

Germond, Basil. *The Maritime Dimension of European Security: Seapower and the European Union.* Basingstoke: Palgrave, 2015.

Goldrick, James, and John Hattendorf, eds. *Mahan Is Not Enough: The Proceedings of a Conference on the Works of Sir Julian Corbett and Admiral Sir Herbert Richmond.* Newport, RI: Naval War College Press, 1993.

Goldrick, James, and Jack McCaffrie. *Navies of South-East Asia: A Comparative Study.* Abingdon: Routledge: 2012.

Harding, Richard, ed. *The Royal Navy, 1930–1990: Innovation and Defence.* New York: Frank Cass, 2005.

Hattendorf, John, ed. *Naval Policy and Strategy in the Mediterranean: Past, Present and Future.* New York: Frank Cass, 2000.

———. *Talking about Naval History: A Collection of Essays.* Newport, RI: Naval War College Press, 2011.

Hobson, Rolf, and Tom Kristiansen, eds. *Navies in Northern Waters, 1721–2000.* London: Frank Cass, 2004.

Kennedy, Greg, ed. *British Naval Strategy East of Suez, 1900–2000: Influences and Actions*. London: Frank Cass, 2005.

———, ed. *The Merchant Marine and International Affairs, 1850–1950*. London: Frank Cass, 2000.

Mahan, Alfred Thayer. *The Influence of Sea Power upon History, 1660–1783*. Boston: Little, Brown, 1890.

Menon, Raja. *Maritime Strategy and Continental Wars*. London: Frank Cass, 1998.

O'Brien, Phillips Payson, ed. *Technology and Naval Combat in the Twentieth Century and Beyond*. London: Frank Cass, 2001.

Redford, Duncan. *The Submarine: A Cultural History from the Great War to Nuclear Combat*. London: I. B. Tauris, 2010.

Redford, Duncan, and Philip Grove. *The Royal Navy: A History since 1900*. London: I. B. Tauris, 2014.

Reeve, John, and David Stevens, eds. *The Face of Naval Battle: The Human Experience of Modern War at Sea*. Sydney: Allen and Unwin, 2003.

Rodger, Nicholas, ed. *Naval Power in the Twentieth Century*. London: Macmillan, 1996.

Rohwer, Jürgen, and Mikhail Monakov. *Stalin's Ocean-Going Fleet: Soviet Naval Strategy and Shipbuilding Programmes, 1935–1953*. London: Frank Cass, 2001.

Scheina, Robert. *Latin Americas: A Naval History, 1810–1987*. Annapolis, MD: Naval Institute Press, 1987.

Speller, Ian, ed. *The Royal Navy and Maritime Power in the Twentieth Century*. Abingdon: Frank Cass, 2005.

Till, Geoffrey, ed. *The Development of British Naval Thinking: Essays in Memory of Bryan Ranft*. Abingdon: Routledge, 2006.

Vego, Milan. *Naval Strategy and Operations in Narrow Seas*. Abingdon: Frank Cass, 1999.

———. *Operational Warfare at Sea Theory and Practice*. Abingdon: Routledge, 2009.

Wirtz, James, and Jeffrey Larsen, eds. *Naval Peacekeeping and Humanitarian Operations Stability from the Sea*. Abingdon: Routledge, 2009.

1860–1913

Fuller, Howard. *Empire, Technology and Seapower: Royal Navy Crisis in the Age of Palmerston*. Abingdon: Routledge, 2014.

Kennedy, Greg, and Keith Neilson, eds. *Far-Flung Lines: Studies in Imperial Defence in Honour of Donald Mackenzie Schurman*. Abingdon: Routledge, 1997.

Moody, Wesley, and Adrienna Sachse, eds. *The Diary of a Civil War Marine: Private Josiah Gregg*. Madison, NJ: Fairleigh Dickinson University Press, 2013.

Olivier, David. *German Naval Strategy, 1856–1888: Forerunners to Tirpitz*. London: Frank Cass, 2004.

Schurman, Donald. *Imperial Defence, 1868–1887*. Edited by John Beeler. London: Frank Cass, 2000.

Sondhaus, Lawrence. *The Habsburg Empire and the Sea: Austrian Naval Policy, 1797–1866*. West Lafayette, IN: Purdue University Press, 1989.

Vego, Milan. *Austro-Hungarian Naval Policy, 1904–1914*. Abingdon: Routledge, 1996.

THE FIRST WORLD WAR

Abbatiello, John. *Anti-Submarine Warfare in World War I: British Naval Aviation and the Defeat of the U-boats*. Abingdon: Routledge, 2006.

Brooks, John. *Dreadnought Gunnery and the Battle of Jutland: The Question of Fire Control*. London and New York: Routledge, 2005.

Fotakis, Zisis. *Greek Naval Strategy and Policy, 1910–1919*. Abingdon: Routledge, 2005.

Frame, Tom, ed. *Maritime Strategy 1914*. Canberra: Barton Books, 2015.

Goldrick, James. *Before Jutland: The Naval War in Northern European Waters, August 1914–February 1915.* Annapolis, MD: Naval Institute Press, 2015.

Gordon, Andrew. *The Rules of the Game: Jutland and British Naval Command.* Annapolis, MD: Naval Institute Press, 1996.

Halpern, Paul. *A Naval History of World War I.* London: UCL Press, 1994.

O'Hara, Vincent, W. David Dickson, and Richard Worth, eds. *To Crown the Waves: The Great Navies of the First World War.* Annapolis, MD: Naval Institute Press, 2013.

Osborne, Eric. *Britain's Economic Blockade of Germany, 1914–1919.* London: Frank Cass, 2004.

1919–38

Aselius, Gunnar. *The Rise and Fall of the Soviet Navy in the Baltic, 1921–1940.* London: Frank Cass, 2006.

Field, Andrew. *Royal Navy Strategy in the Far East, 1919–1939: Planning for a War against Japan.* London: Frank Cass, 2004.

Franklin, George. *Britain's Anti-submarine Capability, 1919–1939.* Abingdon: Frank Cass, 2003.

Mallett, Robert. *The Italian Navy and Fascist Expansionism, 1935–1940.* Abingdon: Frank Cass, 1998.

Marder, Arthur. *Old Friends, New Enemies: The Royal Navy and the Imperial Japanese Navy, Strategic Illusions, 1936–1941.* Oxford: Oxford University Press, 1981.

Moretz, Joseph. *The Royal Navy and the Capital Ship in the Interwar Period: An Operational Perspective.* Abingdon: Routledge, 2002.

Stoker, Donald. *Britain, France and the Naval Arms Trade in the Baltic, 1919–1939: Grand Strategy and Failure.* London: Frank Cass, 2003.

THE SECOND WORLD WAR

Brown, David. *The Road to Oran: Anglo-French Naval Relations, September 1939–July 1940.* London: Taylor and Francis, 2004.

Cumming, Anthony. *The Royal Navy and the Battle of Britain.* Annapolis, MD: Naval Institute Press, 2010.

Hone, Thomas, ed. *The Battle of Midway.* Annapolis, MD: Naval Institute Press, 2013.

Johnson, William Bruce. *The Pacific Campaign in World War II: From Pearl Harbor to Guadalcanal.* Abingdon: Routledge, 2006.

Llewellyn-Jones, Malcolm. *The Royal Navy and Anti-Submarine Warfare, 1944–49.* Abingdon: Routledge, 2006.

Madsen, Chris. *The Royal Navy and German Naval Disarmament 1942–1947.* London: Frank Cass, 1998.

Nitze, Paul, Leonard Sullivan, and the Atlantic Council Working Group on Securing the Seas. *Securing the Seas: The Soviet Naval Challenge and Western Alliance Options.* Boulder, CO: Westview Press, 1979.

O'Brien, Phillips. *How the War Was Won: Air-Sea Power and Allied Victory in World War II.* Cambridge: Cambridge University Press, 2015.

O'Hara, Vincent, W. David Dickson, and Richard Worth, eds. *On Seas Contested: The Seven Great Navies of the Second World War.* Annapolis, MD: Naval Institute Press, 2010.

Ranft, Brian, and Geoffrey Till. *The Sea in Soviet Strategy.* London: Macmillan, 1983.

Redford, Duncan. *A History of the Royal Navy: World War II.* London: I. B. Tauris, 2014.

Simpson, Michael. *A Life of Admiral of the Fleet Andrew Cunningham: A Twentieth-Century Naval Leader.* London: Frank Cass, 2004.

Stevens, David, ed. *The Royal Australian Navy in World War II.* Sydney: Allen and Unwin, 1996.

THE COLD WAR

Gorshkov, S. *Navies in War and Peace*. Annapolis, MD: Naval Institute Press, 1974.

Moore, Richard. *The Royal Navy and Nuclear Weapons*. London: Routledge, 2001.

Tracy, Nicholas. *A Two-Edged Sword: The Navy as an Instrument of Canadian Foreign Policy*. Toronto: McGill-Queens University Press, 2012.

Tunander, Ola. *The Secret War against Sweden: US and British Submarine Deception and Political Control in the 1980s*. London: Frank Cass, 2004.

Winkler, David. *Cold War at Sea: High Seas Confrontation between the United States and the Soviet Union*. Annapolis, MD: Naval Institute Press, 2000.

SINCE 1990

Barnett, Roger. *Navy Strategic Culture: Why the Navy Thinks Differently*. Annapolis, MD: Naval Institute Press, 2009.

Berube, Claude, and Patrick Cullen, eds. *Maritime Private Security Market Responses to Piracy, Terrorism and Waterborne Security Risks in the 21st Century*. Abingdon: Routledge, 2012.

Dutton, Peter, Robert Ross, and Øystein Tunsjø, eds. *Twenty-First Century Seapower: Cooperation and Conflict at Sea*. Abingdon: Routledge, 2012.

Gray, Colin. *The Navy in the Post-Cold War World: The Uses and Value of Strategic Sea Power*. Philadelphia: Pennsylvania State University Press, 2004.

Holmes, James, Andrew Winner, and Toshi Yoshihara. *Indian Naval Strategy in the 21st Century*. Abingdon: Routledge, 2009.

Holmes, James, and Toshi Yoshihara. *Chinese Naval Strategy in the 21st Century: The Turn to Mahan*. Abingdon: Routledge, 2008.

Kane, Thomas. *Chinese Grand Strategy and Maritime Power*. London: Frank Cass, 2002.

Kim, Duk-Ki. *Naval Strategy in Northeast Asia: Geo-strategic Goals, Policies and Prospects*. Abingdon: Frank Cass, 2000.

Milner, Marc. *Canada's Navy: The First Century*. 2nd ed. Toronto: University of Toronto Press, 2010.

Till, Geoffrey. *Asia's Naval Expansion: An Arms Race in the Making?* Abingdon: Routledge, 2012.

———. *Seapower: A Guide for the Twenty-First Century*. 3rd ed. Abingdon: Routledge, 2013.

Till, Geoffrey, and Patrick Bratton, eds. *Sea Power and the Asia-Pacific: The Triumph of Neptune?* Abingdon: Routledge, 2012.

Till, Geoffrey, and Jane Chan, eds. *Naval Modernisation in South-East Asia: Nature, Causes and Consequences*. Abingdon: Routledge, 2014.

Willmott, Hedley Paul. *The Last Century of Sea Power*. Vol. 1, *From Port Arthur to Chanak, 1894–1922*. Bloomington: Indiana University Press, 2009.

Index

warships, 2; antisubmarine type of, 190;
    composite-hulled, 11; cost of, 16; gun
    calibers of, 27; internal order by, 19;
    maneuverability of, 4; *MEKO*-class as,
    205; modern updates for, 209; monitors
    as, 28; radio communication on, 54; of
    Union navy, 10
Washington, 140
Washington Naval Conference, 82
Washington Naval Treaty of 1922, 82, 83
weapons: Aegis BMD, 241; artillery
    techniques of, 72; of battleships, 22–23,
    26–27; deficiencies of, 61; explosives,
    development of, 29; naval strength
    controversies for, 88–89; new systems
    for, 87; nuclear-tipped long-range
    ballistic missile as, 173; Ohka bombs,
    155; railgun as, 241; surface-to-air
    misses of, 168. *See also* missiles
Welles, Gideon, 11
West Indies, 5

Whitehead, Robert, 9
Wilhelm II, 49, 61, 68
Wilkinson, Spenser, 31
Wolseley, Garnet, 45
wooden ships, 7
World War I. *See* First World War
World War II (WWII). *See* Second World
    War

Yamamoto, Isoroku, 132, 137
Yamato "super-battleships," 101
Yangzi river, 113–114
Yeo, Walter, 68
Yokaren system, 103
Yom Kippur War, 196
Young School doctrine, 111
Yugoslav navy, 125

Zheng He, 218
Zumwalt, Elmo, 183, 191
Zumwalt-classy destroyer, 214

About the Author

Jeremy Black graduated from Cambridge University with a Starred First and did graduate work at Oxford University before teaching at the University of Durham and then at the University of Exeter, where he is professor of history. He has held visiting chairs at the United States Military Academy at West Point, Texas Christian University, and Stillman College. Black received the Samuel Eliot Morison Prize from the Society for Military History in 2008. His recent books include *Air Power: A Global History*, *War and Technology*, *Fighting for America: The Struggle for Mastery, 1519–1871*, *Rethinking World War Two: The Conflict and Its Legacy*, and *Insurgency and Counterinsurgency*.